Applied Ecommerce: Analysis and Engineering for Ecommerce Systems

Arthur M. Langer

Wiley Computer Publishing

John Wiley & Sons, Inc.

NEW YORK • CHICHESTER • WEINHEIM • BRISBANE • SINGAPORE • TORONTO

Publisher: Robert Ipsen

Editor: Cary Sullivan

Assistant Editor: Christina Berry

Managing Editor: Penny Linskey

Associate New Media Editor: Brian Snapp

Text Design & Composition: Thomark Design

Designations used by companies to distinguish their products are often claimed as trademarks. In all instances where John Wiley & Sons, Inc., is aware of a claim, the product names appear in initial capital or ALL CAPITAL LETTERS. Readers, however, should contact the appropriate companies for more complete information regarding trademarks and registration.

This book is printed on acid-free paper. ∞

This publication is designed to provide accurate and authoritative information in regard to the subject matter covered. It is sold with the understanding that the publisher is not engaged in professional services. If professional advice or other expert assistance is required, the services of a competent professional person should be sought.

On file with the Library of Congress.

ISBN: 0471-013994

Printed in the United States of America.

10 9 8 7 6 5 4 3 2 1

To my wonderful family, DeDe my wife, and our three beautiful children, Michael, Dina, and Lauren. They have always been my best fans.

University Libraries
Carnegie Mellon University
Pittsburgh, PA 15213-3890

Contents

Acknowledgments

There are many colleagues, students, and clients that provided significant support during the development of this book. My client, Thirteen/WNET, played a major role in providing "real-world" examples of their Web development techniques as well as contributing several sample site designs. I also wish to thank The Corcoran Group for their contributions. My workshop instructors, Greg Vermont and Cynthia Hernandez, provided much of the materials that are available on the Web site that can assist readers on how to actually apply the material presented in the book.

As with all my recent books, I must thank the wonderful students of Columbia University. They continue to be at the core of my inspiration and love for writing, teaching, and scholarly research.

Foreword

"There is no use in trying," said Alice; "one can't believe impossible things?"
"I dare say you haven't had much practice," said the Queen, "When I was
your age, I always did it for half an hour a day. Why, sometimes I believed in
as many as six impossible things before breakfast."

LEWIS CARROLL, *ALICE IN WONDERLAND*

I often recall this quote when thinking about the precipitous rise and fall of the "web economy" over the past seven years. Built upon a strained relationship between conventional business models and the suppositions of tech upstarts, this ecommerce prototype was doomed to fall victim to the impossible expectations of the men and women who managed it. Traditional companies, in their relentless pursuit of automation, failed to investigate the chaotic methodologies of their new tech partners. Armed with financial hype and the promise of new revenue streams, some consultants were often able to broker deals that simply had no proven basis in reality, either in terms of meeting established deadlines or in setting and realizing project goals. As a result, many investors were lead to believe that ecommerce itself was a kind of conceptual fraud, a scam perpetrated by modern-day snakeoil salesman on the unsuspecting hucksters of the brick-and-mortar corporate world.

As Dr. Langer so lucidly reveals in this text, the true obstacle to developing a sturdy electronic business model has seldom been a technical one. Indeed, the talent and infrastructure required to forge ecommerce solutions has long been available to those who have the resources and the initiative to utilize them. The "impossible" belief that trained business managers have held is that the vendors and web consultancies they've engaged to craft their electronic presence can function as independent business entities who, like them, have standardized practices in place that ensure both the quality and the timely delivery of ecommerce projects.

This is, of course, *not* impossible, given the correct framework. The problem is that such ruled frameworks detract from the experimental, creative environment that drives innovation in information systems. Arriving from a business perspective, many project managers, even those with some technical experience, still envision ecommerce as an artifice to be grafted on to more familiar revenue streams, rather than a fully integrated way of conducting business over the Internet. Moreover, their lack of knowledge about how the software that facilitates such enterprise is conceived and developed has crippled their ability to make informed decisions about determining the scope of tech projects.

To avoid incurring the heavy costs of failed web initiatives, IT professionals need to establish a methodology that addresses the obstacles and bottlenecks particular to the software development process. Unlike other work that has been done in this still nascent field of study, Langer's prose has the flavor of an emerging science, offering up a host of guiding principles for solving the complex problem of merging the often contradictory disciplines of technology and marketing. Through his thoughtful analysis of both the creative process of web-based software development and of the organizational structures that enable it, he reveals the kind of general approaches to developing commercial systems that will aid designers and engineers in bridging this gap.

The full integration of electronic communications and the business sector *will* happen. Indeed, it is happening now as ever more modular ecommerce systems are being developed and deployed into the marketplace. How quickly this convergence takes place and who benefits from it, however, will depend highly on the ability of IT professionals to draft a unified approach to development with logical goals that are defined by actual business needs, not sales trends or whims. Web designers, engineers, IT managers and executives—anyone who's ever faced a deadline for an ecommerce project should read on. Possibilities await.

Henry Bar-Levav
President and CEO
Oven, Inc

Introduction

As the Internet has emerged as a significant component of all software development, it has also established false expectations of solving the complexities of application development. Indeed, the recent reduction of Dot.com software developers has proved that software is a complex set of engineering and creative phases that need to be followed to ensure success.

Much of the hoopla over the Dot.com businesses emanated from the idea that ecommerce needed to be separated from the "brick-and-mortar" firms. The term "incubation" became the phrase of the time, and traditional methods of developing software applications were condemned as "out-dated." Furthermore, the industry saw a huge influx of new technology workers with questionable training and credentials. Many of these new workers came from advertising and set out to integrate the functions of software development firms with those of traditional advertising agencies. The process of integrating software and advertising became engulfed in the Internet frenzy. Firms began a process of "globalizing" their businesses by obtaining companies with different cultures, different missions, and in different countries. As a result of this "quick" success approach, many firms created enormous overhead and then needed huge projects to remain solvent. The most problematic aspect was the lack of actual ecommerce software that actually got developed. The result is that most of these ventures have failed or not lived up to the expectations of their investors. The market has become congested with companies still attempting to capture the high-end market—a market that is just beginning to define itself.

Applied Ecommerce: Analysis and Engineering for Ecommerce Systems focuses on the skills and approaches necessary to develop truly successful and maintainable ecommerce systems. It stresses a unique combination of technical and market-oriented capabilities. Understanding how to apply software engineering concepts for web-based ecommerce systems can help developers better integrate their software with the needs of their business. Mastering this nexus will be crucial for the survival of many companies in the wake of the Dot.com era.

The risks involved in performing proper ecommerce analysis and architecture are significant. Indeed, most ecommerce projects are expected to have failure rates in excess of 70 percent. Given the importance that ecommerce will have for businesses to compete in the new millennium, the stakes are more critical than ever. Those software engineers that understand the concepts of analysis and architecture will find greater success in developing ecommerce systems, and thus become more valuable to their organizations and to the industry as a whole.

Overview of the Book and Technology

Applied Ecommerce: Analysis and Engineering for Ecommerce Systems establishes design and technical requirements for the development of integrated ecommerce systems. It offers modeling tools that an ecommerce engineer can use to analyze, design, and develop Web-based delivering systems. The book outlines step-by-step processes from user analysis to the installation and testing of complex transactions for their maximum performance. It also provides new insights into brick-and-mortar IT systems, how to merge them with the Web-paradigm, how to design interfaces to legacy systems, how to design databases and ensure reliability of feature functions required to secure a system's handling of consumer needs.

How This Book Is Organized

This book is organized into two main sections. The first details the process for planning and designing effective ecommerce systems. The second discusses the operationalization of ecommerce, that is, the process of integration and implementation of the system itself. The hybrid approach discussed above essentially creates the "framing" of the analysis and design process. Without effective framing, the quality of engineering tends to suffer as analysts focus on deadlines and specifications. The chapters of this book provide the details of this framing model.

Planning and Design

Chapter 1: What Is Ecommerce?

Chapter 2: Usability: Designing an Ecommerce System for Users, Customers, and Consumers

The first step in developing an ecommerce system is establishing appropriate interfaces with the users of the software. These users include both the internal end-users inside the business and the external users, or customers. This chapter outlines procedures for forming interview approaches, coordinating consumer focus groups, dealing with internal politics, and using Joint Application Development sessions with internal users. The chapter then focuses on the challenges of obtaining the needs of "ecustomers," covering the common web functions required by today's business-to-business electronic operations. Finally, the chapter explores the challenges of determining consumer needs, focusing on the marketing user interface and how it integrates with the process of gathering requirements.

Chapter 3: Developing Application Specifications for Web Programmers

This chapter presents the diagrams and design forms that programmers and web developers need in the development of ecommerce systems. The chapter outlines a step-by-step procedure for designing and developing specifications that reflect the engineering requirements for building ecommerce systems. This portion of the book provides the necessary tools that analysts and designers need to provide program developers with detailed, yet creative technical specifications.

Chapter 4: Designing Databases to Support Web Applications

This chapter covers how the backend database engine is built. The process of logic data modeling to produce Entity Relational Diagrams is covered, as well as methods of transferring data to multiple data storage facilities. Creation of data repositories is also discussed. The chapter also examines the complexities of storing data in multiple environments, covering issues of propagation of data, replication, and data mining technologies.

Chapter 5: Designing Web Page Features, Functions, and Interfaces

This chapter focuses on best practices to building ecommerce websites and describes common features and functions that are expected in competitive ecommerce systems. The material relates to many of the issues developed in Chapter 3, but focuses more closely on the flow of screens, the look and feel and the links to other sites and pages. The focus here is on the design of the web page rather than on the internal programming. Chapter 5 ultimately looks at the complex issue of how analysts participate in determining the most appropriate graphic user interface (GUI) for each user interface.

Chapter 6: Building Interactivity into an Ecommerce System

This chapter focuses on the interactive design aspects of ecommerce systems. Media tools such as Flash are discussed along with voice integration and streaming video design. The chapter focuses on how to do the analysis and design for these types of media. User specified website options are also discussed along with many key technical issues such as sound optimization, streaming video, client art, and grid elements.

Chapter 7: Transaction Processing Design

This chapter focuses on the design of applications for deployment on Transaction Processing systems. Subjects include three-layer architecture design of a transaction process monitor, Processing Communications, Database Recovery, and Replication.

Integration and Implementation

Chapter 8: Integrating Intranet and Internet Web Applications Across Multiple Networks

This chapter depicts the engineering challenges for integrating multiple Internets, Intranets, and Extranets. The design and placement of applications across multiple client/server networks are discussed. Because the installation of the overall network system affects software design, it is important that analysts and designers understand network issues and their impact on the development of ecommerce systems. The chapter also expands its scope across single organizations and discusses the problems of integrating multiple businesses that have different cultures and forms of product fulfillment. The combination and interaction of internally developed proprietary information and externally marketed information is also discussed.

Chapter 9: Legacy Systems and Integration

This chapter outlines the process of interfacing ecommerce systems with brick-and-mortar legacy systems. Issues of product fulfillment, migration of legacy databases and processes, and integration of multiple systems architecture are covered. This chapter combines many of the suggested approaches to user interface and application specifications development that are covered in Chapters 2 and 3, respectively. Furthermore, the chapter also identifies Business Process Reengineering (BPR) as the method of determining how legacy systems need to be changed to interface with new ecommerce technologies.

Chapter 10: XML and Component Middleware: Integrating Data and Processes

This chapter provides a detailed understanding of the engineering of XML systems and its role in integrating data and processes. The chapter also offers a detailed view of how to develop object components that serve as middleware processes. XML is viewed as the vehicle to obtain structured data transfer to sort, select, and manipulate data in documents across the ecommerce environment.

Chapter 11: Securing an Ecommerce Site

This chapter covers the multiple aspects of ecommerce security. These include access security, data security, application security, and functional screen security. Access security focuses on physical access of the data center and corresponding facilities. Data security looks at transaction data and stored data across the ecommerce system, and how to validate and secure it. Functional screen security discusses the process of determining what features and functions are made available to which users. The process and procedures for working with users to develop security specifications are also discussed.

Chapter 12: Database Query, Report, and Transaction Processing

In this chapter the process of engineering web query and reporting options are discussed. The chapter shows alternative data storage methods to enhance reporting performance and covers the recording, storage, and analysis of transactions that occur across ecommerce systems. There is particular focus on decision support systems development, end user query development, and reconciliation of reporting.

Chapter 13: Best Practices for Site Architecture

This chapter covers the topic of content management systems. Content management systems provide automated techniques that allow users to provide changes to content as well as integration of special features such as chat rooms, email interface, and calendaring. The chapter covers the life cycle of content management, establishing the roles and responsibilities of users, analysts/designers, and developers.

Chapter 14: Project Management for Ecommerce Systems

This chapter provides guidance on the alternative web development life cycle methodologies and best practices for project management and change control. Project organization, including roles and responsibilities, is covered along with internal controls. Also discussed are alternative organizational structures that provide maximum efficiency during the life of ecommerce systems.

Who Should Read this Book

This book assumes a reasonable understanding of computer concepts and terminology. The material can be used in a first-level professional course or university program on ecommerce design or development. It may be utilized by practicing Information Systems professionals or executives who are managing transitions to ecommerce systems.

Project managers and first-line managers will also find that this book provides an understanding of the components, procedures, and critical points toward their work in the development of ecommerce. Programmers who are also performing ecommerce design will find in this book a way of developing a useful approach to integrating back-end databases with front-end processing.

Tools You Will Need

While there are no specific tools required for using this book, it is recommended that serious ecommerce analysts obtain Computer Aided Software Engineering (CASE) software that can allow for the development of automated repositories of process and data required to develop complex systems. This book reflects examples using a CASE tool known as System Architect, which is marketed by Popkin Software and Systems (www.popkin.com).

What's on the Web Site

The supporting Web site is designed to provide readers with the materials that are used in my courses at Columbia University. Chapter questions and exercises are included to allow readers to validate their understanding of the concepts presented in the book. Case studies and practical assignments with solutions are included to provide "real-world" practice, allowing analysts to apply the strategies of ecommerce architecture discussed in the chapters. Full instructions are also included for those readers who wish to use Popkin's System Architecture CASE tool. The Web site also has a number of streaming-videos of research interviews with CEOs and CIOs of major corporations, as well as a few on-line training sessions of flow diagramming and database design.

Summary

Many ecommerce books teach business and marketing design concepts yet fail to provide solutions to the pure engineering needs of building the most important component systems for business success. This book breaks important new ground in demonstrating how software engineers and developers can use dynamic methodologies to integrate content management and explore new development cycles. While other books on this subject focus on simple mechanics, *Applied Ecommerce: Analysis and Engineering for Ecommerce Systems* provides the full picture to ecommerce systems step-up activities beyond their simple steps and toward the practical *art* of building successful systems.

CHAPTER 1

What Is Ecommerce?

Ecommerce has been defined in many different ways. Conceptually, it has been understood as an external method of utilizing commerce over the World Wide Web. Schneider and Perry (2000) define ecommerce as "the use of electronic data transmission to implement or enhance any business process." Kalakota and Whinston (1997) offer definitions based on four perspectives:

Communications. Ecommerce is the delivery of information, products and/or services, or payments via telephone lines and computer networks.

Business process. Ecommerce is the application that automates business transactions and workflows.

Service. Ecommerce allows businesses to reduce service costs, while at the same time improving quality and increasing service.

Online. Ecommerce provides the capability to buy and sell goods over the Internet.

This book presents the concept of ecommerce in two major parts. The first part is the *internal, or core, processing* that represents the center of the business. These internal legacy systems need to be linked or integrated with the external portions of the ecommerce system. The second part consists of the *systems* that are designed to interact with outside markets. These markets can vary from limited ones like business-to-business (B2B) to the broad consumer marketplace.

It is important to recognize the interdependency of these two components. No longer is a dot com in and of itself a true answer to creating an ecommerce business. True ecommerce must include the entire enterprise because it entails transforming the enterprise into an integrated technology organization. All parts of the organization must be tailored to serve its most valued component: its customers. Because of this demand, data processing professionals are currently experiencing unprecedented pressure to produce. Now more than ever, businesses depend on data processing to provide crucial competitive advantages.

Research by the Gartner Group has shown that 75 percent of all ecommerce projects fail to be delivered on time and on budget—or at all (Gartner Group, 1999). The difficulty of developing ecommerce systems is apparent in the number of dot coms that fail and the number of systems that do not serve the needs of their businesses.

Many of these failures have occurred because systems are not being built on strong foundations. In particular, there is a lack of understanding of the engineering processes through which ecommerce systems must be built. This book seeks to remedy this problem by focusing on the applied aspects of analysis to create ecommerce systems that meet the needs of their users, consumers, and businesses.

It is important to understand that ecommerce systems, while they do represent a new and unique form of software development, must nevertheless be built with the same basic analysis and design constructs necessary to build any system. As with any computer systems development project, the development of successful ecommerce systems depends on strong analysis, design, and implementation. In my book *The Analysis and Design of Information Systems*, I discuss the "tiers" of software development and how the process of building computer systems resembles the process of designing a building or a bridge. It is very much an architectural or engineering task—a task that must follow a clear set of rules, or risk failure.

However, even though the design of successful ecommerce systems depends on following rules and processes, it is still a highly creative process. Indeed, it is engineering science coupled with creative design, advertising, and marketing concepts that is the distinctive characteristic of the Web. Only the successful integration of creativity with a systematic approach will yield success in ecommerce design. I believe it is possible to integrate the two into a step-by-step approach that can be learned and followed.

The ecommerce analyst/designer encounters many obstacles on the road to delivering a successful system. Many of these obstacles have nothing to do with technical challenges at all—they are problems that come from outside the realm of information technology (IT): politics, budget and time constraints, and marketing pressures. All these can challenge the structured approach to ecommerce design. This book addresses these obstacles and recommends ways to overcome them. As I tell my students, "Follow the Yellow Brick Road." That is, start out on the right path and you will end up in the place you want to be—in spite of all the obstacles you may encounter on the way. I hope this book will provide readers with a Yellow Brick Road that will lead them to successful ecommerce projects.

This book therefore aims to provide the complex set of tools that the ecommerce analyst/designer requires for success: engineering skills, creativity, the ability to understand the market needs of the business. The successful analyst/designer must be able to understand consumer needs; ensure integration with legacy systems; provide user interface requirements; establish standards, security, and network architecture; and finally to provide the necessary project management to ensure implementation.

It is important to note that this book does not adhere to any particular methodology of systems design. Rather, it presents a set of good practices that allow professionals to adjust to the constraints and needs of any business. Strict methodologies tend to depend on the existence of homogeneous conditions in businesses. And what we all must recognize is that every business is different—a fact that methodologies often have difficulty addressing.

Why Do Ecommerce Projects Fail So Often?

I stated above that 75 percent of ecommerce projects are failing. First it is important to understand what is meant by failure. Within the 75 percent, about 22 percent fail because they never get finished; that is, the project is terminated and nothing is ever produced. The remaining 53 percent are late, which is itself considered a form of failure. The average rate of lateness is 100 percent. Therefore, based on these statistics, an ecommerce project with a projected plan of completion in 6 months, has a 22 percent chance of never being completed at all and a 53 percent chance of being completed in a year. These statistics provide us with a picture of a profession that needs a method to improve its performance. The question still remains: Why is this the case? I believe there are some clear reasons for the problem.

The major issue that affects the performance of projects is the lack of governance on standards. Unlike other professions, such as accounting, medicine, and law, the analysis and design profession has no governing body composed of accomplished peers that sets the standards for technology projects. There are no "Generally Accepted Principles" in this field. The computer industry historically has been controlled by companies that have established industry norms through sheer market dominance. In the early days it was IBM creating standards, such as the 3¼-inch diskette. IBM's successor in market software dominance is Microsoft, which through its might and market control has set many industry standards. Yet none of these standards has been chosen for the overall betterment of the profession; they are simply the product of market forces. Some standards groups do exist in the industry, but they have little clout because they have no way to legally license professionals. Without a governing body of professional peers, the software development profession continues to be driven by hearsay and market trends, as opposed to well-thought-out and tested processes. In this book I intend to outline some of the pivotal issues that need to be addressed industrywide.

The other unique aspect of software development lies in the tension between creativity and engineering. These two rely on different values. Engineering uses science and mathematical constructs to arrive at solutions. Within the confines of mathematics, professionals see solutions as the result of algorithms and "universal formulas" that provide architects with the correct answer. To an engineer, the answer must be attainable. Using this approach, estimates of time and expense on a project should be clearly predictable. Even when goals are not met, there are procedures to figure out why. In the arts, however, there are no universal rules or procedures. Beauty is in the eye of the beholder, as they say. Indeed, what answer would an artist provide if asked, "How long does it take to design a great picture?" The creative process cannot be addressed through rigid procedures based on identifiable time frames. So the question becomes: Is software design a creative process or an engineering process? The answer is not clear. We know that the design process, particularly with the advent of the Web, certainly requires creative processes that deal with complex "look-and-feel" issues. Therefore, many Web developers come from creative backgrounds. On the other hand, there are also complex engineering tasks that must be carried out to provide reliable and dependable software. This book seeks a middle ground between the creative and engineering approaches, combining artistry with sound engineering processes. It is this combination that will bring forth the systems that users and consumers need in the ecommerce world.

Real-World Approach

Approaches to providing successful ecommerce solutions must be realistic. While this might sound obvious, I have found that many books on the subject tend to overlook some of the realities of software development. Some of these shortfalls include:

- Limited understanding of how to deal with internal user needs
- Lack of understanding on how to approach developing systems that meet the needs of consumers, who are outside a controlled user group
- Failure to address the political environment
- Inappropriate project organization that people know will fail to deliver on time and on budget
- Lack of organization and management that integrates the creative and engineering process
- Failure to adhere to a methodology that provides planning as opposed to "adjustments as you go"

Although many professionals declare that the above constraints are too complex to be addressed in an IT context, I believe that this attitude is just another way of avoiding the problem. Certainly problems arise that are beyond the direct control of IT professionals—problems with executive management, for example. But IT professionals must be prepared to address such problems, for example, by providing the appropriate education for executives so that they can participate intelligently and with realistic expectations. To manage this kind of challenge, IT professionals need to use a life cycle that blends the traditional step approaches with the more recent spiral cycles. In other words, we need to design a "hybrid" life cycle that integrates creative processes with engineering requirements.

The Traditional Software Life Cycle

The traditional systems development life cycle (SDLC) views projects as a sequential set of steps, typically with each step dependent on the one that preceded it. These cycles are usually depicted as a set of tasks and built in a matrix called a Gantt chart. A Gantt chart shows these tasks against time—so it is a matrix of task versus time as shown in Figure 1.1.

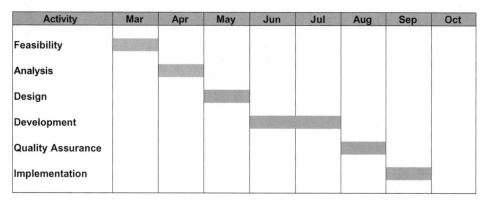

Figure 1.1   Gantt chart showing classic waterfall cycle.

Figure 1.1 shows how the project is designed. Gantt charts always start at the upper left, and work their way down to completion on the lower right of the chart, in a series of steps. Because of this step process, traditional life cycles are often known as the "waterfall approach." The problem with the waterfall approach is that it does not accurately represent what actually occurs during a life cycle. This is particularly obvious when it comes to the assumption that once a given task ends, it is in effect complete. This is typically not the case. Figure 1.2 represents what usually occurs.

One can see that there are often iterations of a task due to rejections or quality problems. These cannot be ignored but rather should be planned for in any project. This is the reason that the object world uses the spiral life-cycle approach.

The Spiral Life Cycle

The spiral approach focuses on each component of the total project. It assumes each component is independent from the rest of the overall system, and as such should have its own life cycle. The cycle is called *spiral* because it continues around, from requirements to testing—it suggests that each component keeps being changed and matured, and that the cycle itself is ongoing as opposed to having a beginning and end as in the

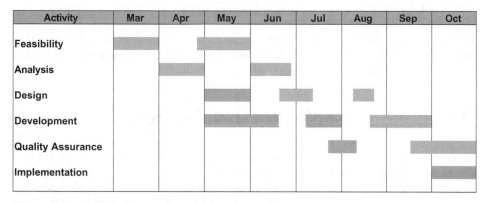

Figure 1.2   Modified Gantt chart depicts the realities.

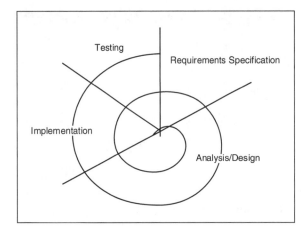

Figure 1.3   Spiral life cycle.

traditional cycle. Each application within a system has its own life cycle, which continues in a spiral, undergoing constant refinement, as shown in Figure 1.3.

The spiral system has been criticized for being confined to the programmer/designer and inhibiting the broadening of the analysis and design to the entire system level. This level in an ecommerce world is distributed, and even component architecture requires interfaces, which in turn suggest tasks that are dependent on others.

So which model is best for ecommerce? The answer is…both. The solution is to create a hybrid model that takes the best from both cycles. In addition, there is a need to create another piece—a piece that embraces the creative side of ecommerce design as well as the engineering requirements. Such a component can help us answer questions like "How do we understand the process of selecting and finalizing pictures and content on the Web site?"

The Hybrid Life Cycle

It is what I call the "hybrid life cycle" that enables the sound development of ecommerce systems. A project will contain many waterfalls, particularly those that encompass the delivery of various components of analysis, development, and implementation. The spiral approach will also be useful, as objects, middleware components, and reusable applications do indeed have their own ongoing cycles. This book provides practical guidance about *how* and *when* each of these cycles should be employed, and what needs to be done to ensure success.

The Six Tiers of Software Development

In *The Analysis and Design of Information Systems*, I described the process of software development using a "tiered" strategy. These tiers provide a road map for how software must be developed. I have modified these tiers for the ecommerce model (see Table 1.1).

Table 1.1   Tiers of Software Development

TIER	ANALYST APPLICATION
6	Ecommerce
5	Network typology
4	Component architecture
3	Content automation
2	Web development tools
1	User and market interface

User and Market Interface

Systems developed without the input of users have little value. Despite the importance of this data, developers tend to guess about how users and consumers are likely to behave on a Web page, when in fact they should be seeking hard information about needs and preferences. The needs of internal users are somewhat easier to identify because they work in a controlled environment. Customer and consumer needs, however, are more difficult to ascertain. Therefore, these interfaces must be carefully planned, usually by working with existing customers and the marketing department. It is also crucial to identify the population that will be using the Web site, because customer and/or consumer profiles and preferences should influence its design.

Web Development Tools

No system can be built without the necessary tools—just as a worker needs a toolbox, so too does an ecommerce analyst/designer. While there are many engineering tools available on the market, few Web analysts and designers know how to develop engineering specifications. Furthermore, the Web also requires tools to establish how a screen should be formatted and structured. Naturally, tools are used for specialized purposes, so it is important to know which is the right tool and when to use it.

Content Automation

Today's complicated Web sites require automated methods that enable changes to be documented and updated without redoing each application. Content management systems are either purchased as a predeveloped third-party product or internally developed to support a particular development methodology (that is, programmed as part of the systems design itself). Content systems vary in feature and/or function and in what they are intended to do. For example, some systems provide chat rooms or automatic response systems that may not be considered by other companies as part of content management. They would, however, require design and maintenance.

Component Architecture

Web sites need to be developed under the auspices of the object paradigm. This means that the analysis and design of ecommerce systems must be decomposed down to reusable object components. This procedure uses the spiral object life cycle and is incorporated into the overall system integration. The concept is to be able to put the pieces together, dynamically load them onto the Web site, and have them work. Too often, this step is left to Web programmers instead of having analysts and designers carefully contemplate how components need to be determined and engineered in the system. Most important is the question of how they need to be documented for maintenance reasons.

Network Topology

Today's networks allow software to operate across multiple computers and systems. The client/server paradigm continues to be a critical part of ecommerce systems. Network design decisions therefore must involve analysts and designers to determine where object components should reside on the network topology. Furthermore, there are interface issues with databases, and movement of middleware products across the network. Active-X, Active Server Page (ASP), JAVA, and CGI are all protocol software issues that need to be well thought out before the development cycle begins rather than during programming, which, unfortunately, happens all too often.

Ecommerce

The final tier, of course, is the aim of the strategy. Ecommerce provides the interfaces of the applications with middleware and back-end databases to form the crucial integrated systems. However, successful development of ecommerce is contingent upon mastering the first five tiers.

Usability: Designing an Ecommerce System for Users, Customers, and Consumers

This chapter focuses on the starting point of all systems: users. Because users establish need, they hold the key to what a system must accomplish. Ecommerce systems have similar as well as unique user requirements as compared to typical computer development projects. For internal Web-based systems, often called *Intranets*, ecommerce users closely resemble those of traditional systems. Because these users are internal, that is, they work within the organization itself, the domain of people who provide requirements is much more controlled, particularly when the proper management participates in the analysis and design of the system. Such is not the case with external systems, which utilize ecommerce activities from the outside market. In this situation, users are either customers or consumers. Customers are business users who interact with your system to do business transactions, or ebusiness (B2B). Understanding customer users requires first understanding the businesses they represent. Consumers, on the other hand, represent a public domain and are the largest and most inconsistent group of users. Because of their wide variety of needs and preferences, they are the most challenging group of users to develop systems for. Customers and consumers, unlike internal users, are not controlled groups, and their preferences are much more difficult to define. Furthermore, customer and consumer groups are often much larger and more diverse simply because they may not be identifiable during the initial design of the system. Even more challenging is understanding their preferences in terms of the way the Web site needs to operate, what is aesthetically pleasing to them, and what is intuitively obvious in terms of its feature and/or function. Finally, customer and consumer populations have much more diverse cultures than internal ones. Specifically, they vary tremendously with respect to interests, behavior, and individual confidence in Web technology.

Depending on the project, ecommerce systems can be internal, external, or both. It is the premise of this book that ecommerce will inevitably encompass both, providing the ultimate client resource management (CRM) that serves internal and external activities. In other words, ecommerce systems will become the tool of integration among all systems within organizations. The following sections will outline the user interface requirements for both internal and external ecommerce systems.

Internal User Interface Techniques

The very first step in internal systems development is analyzing internal user interfaces. To begin, it is important to identify the user typology—in other words, the various types of internal users in the company, the organizational structure, its culture, and its individual computer literacy levels. This section provides a step-by-step approach to gathering requirements from internal users.

Key User Interfaces

The success of analysis activities usually depends on identifying the right user interfaces. It is rare that any single type of interface can provide all of the requirements necessary for the architecture of a new system. Any software system designed to automate the existing activities of a company must serve all of the constituents in the company. The various kinds of user interfaces can be defined as follows:

Executives. These individuals are often referred to as executive sponsors. Their role is twofold. First, they do provide input into the system, specifically from the perspective of productivity, return on investment, and competitive edge. Second, and perhaps more important, is their responsibility to ensure that users are participating in the necessary manner. This area can be problematic because internal users are typically busy doing their jobs and sometimes neglect to provide input or attend project meetings. Furthermore, executive sponsors can help control political agendas that can hurt the success of the project.

Line managers. This interface provides the most information from a business-unit perspective. These individuals are responsible for two aspects of management. First, they are responsible for the day-to-day productivity of their unit, and therefore understand the importance of productive teams and how software can assist this endeavor. Second, they are responsible for their staffs. Thus, line managers need to know how software will affect their operational staffs.

Functional users. These are the individuals in the trenches who understand exactly how processing needs to get done. While they are typically narrow in their perspectives of the benefits of the system, they provide the concrete information that is required to create the feature and/or functions that make the system usable.

These three interfaces provide users with the basis for understanding what must be involved in any analysis and design process. However, the internal user interface for ecommerce systems is even more complex. For ecommerce, it is necessary to understand not only what the interfaces are, but also the flow of business and how each internal user operates within that flow. Figure 2.1 depicts the relationship between user interfaces and ecommerce flow in an organization.

Figure 2.1 depicts a hierarchy of relationships and functions within a business flow. Executive management has responsibilities for overseeing the fulfillment of orders. They need to ensure that economies of scale are met and that the company remains profitable in doing so. Workers need to be paid properly, and line managers need to ensure that productivity, client services, and employee satisfaction are all accomplished successfully. With respect to an ecommerce project, executives must understand how important it is that the organization respond to the needs of those engineering the sys-

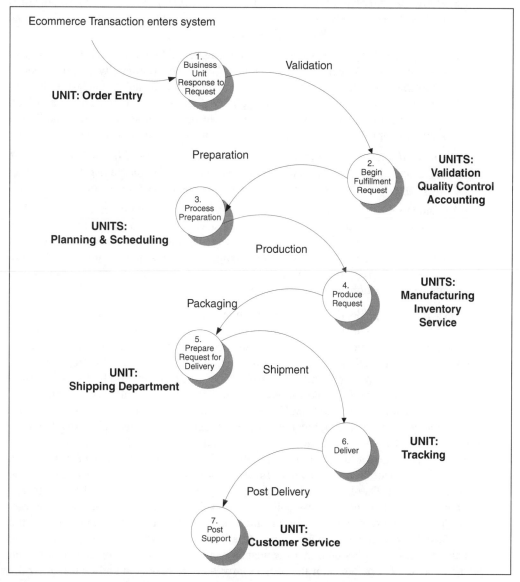

Figure 2.1   Ecommerce flow relationships with internal user interfaces.

tem. This involves the overall coordination of the project, ensuring that political factions do not affect the spirit of the analysis process. This also involves outlining the scope, objectives, constraints, and assumptions of the project to the line managers who will be responsible for carrying out the detail process of interfaces with the ecommerce engineering team. In order to fulfill these requirements, it is important for the ecommerce team to assist executives in the formulation of the scope, objectives, constraints, and assumptions. Do not leave this task to busy executives to do by themselves. This process also provides an opportunity to influence the content and domain of these four important components of ecommerce development.

Scope. This represents the domain of the project itself. The scope often specifies who will use the new business processes, that is, which departments, divisions, and off-site locations (Wood and Silver, 1995).

Objectives. This specifies what is to be accomplished by the project. Project objectives should be quantified, for example, "increase productivity by 20 percent." Quantifiable statements are better because they make it easier to measure the success of the project. While scope is typically a statement, objectives are multifaceted, with a number of bulleted measurable outcomes so that participants will know if the project has been successful—or to what degree it is successful.

Constraints. This describes limitations and delimitations. *Limitations* are most commonly time, budget, and space. *Delimitations* are constraints that are set by the project itself; for example, the product must be ready for the Christmas season.

Assumptions. This involves the setting of things that can be taken for granted. For example, the project will be funded from a special budget, or resources will be provided as necessary. It is important to note that assumptions, which are really general business decisions, can emerge and change during the course of any project life cycle. Therefore, it represents one of the components that may need ongoing executive participation, whereas the other factors tend to be more "carved in stone."

Once the scope, objectives, constraints, and assumptions are formulated and communicated to the line management, it is important to obtain input from the other two levels of internal user interface. It is at this point that ecommerce analysis must follow the business flows as depicted in Figure 2.1. Within each of the ecommerce flow steps shown in Figure 2.1, there is a corresponding internal department or function that is responsible for handling the tasks. The tasks represent the way the business unit must respond to fulfill the needs of the incoming flow. For example, the incoming flow "Transaction" establishes the need to process an incoming order request. The responsible internal business unit is the Order Entry Department. This business unit will likely have a line manager who is responsible for the day-to-day operation of that department. This line manager, in turn, manages operational personnel who are responsible for the actual placement of the order or request. Therefore, the line manager provides the interface for the ecommerce analyst that defines the business unit, its responsibilities, and its organizational structure. The operations users of the Order Entry Department, on the other hand, provide the interface that can define each function in detail. Interviews with these people need to be structured and coordinated under the auspices of the line manager of that department. Of course, the overall goals of the project must still be mandated and regulated by the executive interface, or executive sponsor, as previously mentioned.

The process for determining the user interfaces requires a hierarchical meeting schedule—usually called a *top-down approach*. This means that the first step is usually scheduling an executive meeting, particularly to determine with senior management who would be best in the role of executive sponsor. The executive sponsor must be a demanding and strict person, not necessarily a "nice" executive. To be successful, the executive sponsor cannot worry about being liked, and it may even work well to use an executive who is feared. While this might sound undemocratic, it is necessary for running successful projects for the following reasons:

1. Department personnel cannot always be counted on to voluntarily schedule their time and provide the appropriate attention to the project. Most users tend to consider the project less important than their other job responsibilities.

2. Most organizations are fraught with political problems. Political factions can hurt the probability of success of any project, and they need to be watched carefully. Dealing with political factions is discussed later in this chapter.

3. Individuals are often skeptical about change, and sometimes secretly hope the project will fail. Any change can be frightening, as it may threaten their existing status in the organization, and people often do not understand why the change is necessary at all.

Once the executive sponsor has been selected, a series of meetings must be scheduled in which the line managers can discuss how they would provide the necessary information to meet project objectives. During these sessions, which should be attended by the analysts and designers on the project, it is also important to determine the amount of reengineering (reviewing existing procedures) that should be done during the interviewing phase. That is, the analysis of a new system provides the opportunity to consider changing existing procedures to improve performance and to revisit old procedures that may need to be updated.

The Interview Process

It is important to form an interview approach prior to beginning the internal user sessions (Langer, 2001). This section provides guidance on the process of interviewing for ecommerce projects. The basic goal of interviewing is for the analyst to understand what the user does in the physical world, regardless of whether the existing system is automated or not. Software designing is predicated on understanding the physical world and translating it to the logical realities of software. Software represents the logical equivalent of what users do physically (Langer, 2001).

Planning Interviews

Meeting with users without preparation is not very productive. It is like trying to get lucky—and data processing people never get lucky! Yet in many projects, too little time is devoted to understanding when interviews should take place, who should attend them, the method of the interview (individual or group), and the time requirements for these meetings. This lack of planning and foundation usually results in incomplete meetings, requests for information that never get delivered, and the absence of critical people at the meetings. Poor planning, then, leads to poor projects, which ultimately result in poor products. Because of the complexities of ecommerce, there are more users and processes to cover, and typically existing systems that need interfacing before, during, and after the new systems are in place. The following steps are prepared to provide ecommerce analysts and designers with the proper guidelines for planning interviews.

Step 1: Understand the Organization

Before attempting any interviews, it is important for the ecommerce analyst to understand the organization that supports the processes. He or she should develop an organization matrix that shows the chain of command and the roles and responsibilities that exist in the organization. Certainly having an organization chart will help, but there is a need for more information than is typically shown on an organization chart. Figure 2.2 shows a sample organization matrix and the corresponding information it provides to the ecommerce analyst.

The reasons for capturing this information are multifaceted. First it will teach the analyst something about the management culture of the organization. It will also provide an understanding of how the organization works, and its line of command for authorization. Most important, it allows the analyst to identify the appropriate people to attend the meetings. This point is critical, as many analysts tend to assume that the internal users that have been assigned are the most appropriate. Nothing could be further from the truth—never assume that users know what you need. Thus the organization matrix places the analyst in a position of being proactive, in control, and leading the process, as opposed to reactive, unclear, and dependent on users for guidance.

Organization Hierarchy	Name	Group	Departments	Unit	Reports to	Process Functions
1st Tier						
President	John Smith	Executive	All		CEO	Marketing Operations
2nd Tier						
VP Sales	Harry Masters	Executive	Marketing		President	Market Research Sales
VP Finance	Rhonda Myers	Executive	Finance		President	Purchasing General ledger Office Management
VP Operations	Mary Miles	Executive	Operations		President	Production Warehouse Shipping Receiving
3rd Tier						
Operations Manager	Tom Brand	Operations	Production		VP Operations	Order Processing Fulfillment Scheduling Inventory Control
4th Tier						
Order Processing Mgr	Ralph Harmon	Production	Order Processing	Data Entry Cust Support	Op Manager	Enter Orders Print Orders Order Tracking
5th Tier						
Order Entry Clerk	Sara Marks	Order Processing	Data Entry	Data Entry	Order Proc Mgr	Enter Orders

Figure 2.2   User organization matrix.

Step 2: Focus on Politics

Politics is a powerful independent variable to the success or failure of projects, particularly ecommerce systems, which usually affect everyone in the organization. How does one learn about the politics of an organization? The answer is, ask. Of course there are many ways to do this and some are more appropriate than others, depending on the setting. Let us investigate this approach further. First we must always assume that politics exists—and at every interface level. Therefore, asking about politics depends on the setting and the interface level. When interviewing executives, you might ask, "Can you tell me about conflicts and personality issues that exist within the company that might affect the success of the project?" On the other hand, an analyst can usually be more direct about political factions with line management and operational users. You can never know whether you have received accurate information about all of the political issues—but the more you know, the better. Politics is dangerous, and analysts can be victimized by its impact. Virtually every interview should contain inquiries that relate to knowing about "the way things work" in the organization, department, or business unit. Knowing about politics allows the analyst to develop approaches that can avoid potential pitfalls. It is important to recognize that software developers are not change agents. Their role is to develop what is, not to change what is without the consent of the culture of the organization.

Step 3: Premeetings

Before deciding on a schedule of meetings, it is worthwhile to have short (perhaps 20-minute) meetings with some of the key users. By conducting these meetings, an analyst can get a better perspective on the user. Premeetings should occur at the user's work area. The state of the user's work area can tell you a lot about him or her. Is the user organized or messy? This kind of information can tell an analyst how difficult it may be to get information from a user. An old marketing ploy is to meet in the prospective customer's own office—to see what the customer likes, what he or she is interested in. Pictures on the wall, trophies, and other memorabilia will tell you about the type of person you are dealing with. In addition to offering information about an individual's character and work style, the premeeting will also tell you about this individual's level of interest in the project and his or her level of experience with software and computers in general. Thus, premeetings allow us to "market" to our customers, the internal users of the organization. Being liked also counts, and while I am not suggesting that you should try to be liked at all costs, it does make the job easier. During the life of any project everyone makes mistakes—including analysts and designers. Those who are liked find it easier to get help during times of crisis—or when they need a favor. Remember that.

Step 4: Inventory of User Computer Skill Levels

It is important to know the level of computer experience in the user community. By computer experience, I mean their understanding of the project cycle, knowledge of computer terms, and their actual hands-on experience with software systems. This information can guide you about what technical terms you can use during the interviews, how to ask for information, and, in general, how to orchestrate the interviews overall. This knowledge also allows ecommerce analysts to:

1. Formulate how the interview will be conducted and what information to prepare for the user.

2. Decide how information will be gathered. A questionnaire could be developed for every user skill level, giving everyone an opportunity to understand the process and respond to questions. For example, provide a list of data elements that might be an acceptable approach for experienced users, but not novices. For novices, an analyst might ask for a copy of all forms they use in their processes.

3. Help determine how many sessions are required. The level of user understanding could change the scope of the meeting and determine whether an individual or group meeting with other users is more appropriate.

Skill sets encompass general levels of computer knowledge. While these levels are not part of any empirical research, I have found them to be reliable constructs for planning purposes. There are three general levels: experienced, amateur, and novice.

Experienced users have been through it before. This background counts a lot in terms of understanding the life cycle of software development. Experienced users are vital because they can provide good input that may help avoid the pitfalls that can occur during a project life cycle. While there are many users who have experience with software development projects, few have done so in an ecommerce environment. One potential difficulty when dealing with experienced users is that they may not like your approach.

Amateur users are those who lack professional experience. They are individuals who get enjoyment from working with computers; they are, in effect, hobbyists. Amateurs, while knowledgeable, can be problematic users because they easily lose focus; that is, they become interested in the technology per se rather than the mission of the project. Analysts should be aware of this risk and use written agendas to prevent digressive conversations during interviews.

Novice users are simply ignorant of how technology works. Therefore, they need very specific guidance on what they need to do as it relates to their role in the project. Novice users can be easy to work with because they do not provide alternatives to the approach. However, their lack of knowledge means that they generally offer little input to the process.

Step 5: Determine Internal Order of Process

While the actual detail flowing of the business has not yet been conducted, it is advisable that ecommerce analysts understand the sequential nature of how product fulfillment is accomplished in the business. This can be accomplished at a high level by spending time with the executives to validate what the overall processes are of the business. I call this the Essential Components of the business, which, in effect, answers the question "Why are you in business?" It also defines the phases of the internal processes and can be used to verify where each user resides in the overall scheme of the business. So when the analyst begins to plan the approach to analysis, it makes sense to do the interviewing, mirroring the order of process. The use of process flow diagrams can assist in this process (see Chapter 3).

Interview Methods

There are two ways of holding interviews: individual and group. Both methods have their pros and cons. Individual interviews can show the analyst the details of how tasks are handled by particular people. In organizations where one person handles a specific task or group of tasks, this approach is very productive and can ensure that personal preferences are propagated to the ecommerce system. However, where there are a number of people involved in processing a task, group discussions are generally much more productive, especially since people within a task may disagree about how the system needs to operate. The resolution of different user views can be very time-consuming and plagued with political factionalizing. Group sessions can help prevent this problem. There are two types of group interviews: Joint Application Development (JAD) and group meetings (the latter being a subset of the former). The following sections provide the guidelines for conducting individual and group ecommerce interviews.

Individual Interviews

The previous section on forming an interview approach covers the preparation for an individual session. Of course, it is the actual interview that is most important. I believe in holding the meeting at the user's place of work, although some analysts feel that it can interfere with the interview (interrupting telephone calls, emergencies, etc.). However, I think the benefits outweigh the disadvantages. Having the user in his or her domain provides a context for the meeting—a better understanding of what the user needs to do to get his or her job done. An even more important benefit is the easy access to all of the forms, documentation, and samples in the user's workplace.

During the interviews there are two types of flow methods suggested. They are Process Flow Diagrams (PFD) and Data Flow Diagrams (DFD). The techniques of using these modeling tools are discussed in greater detail in Chapters 3 through 5. These diagrams are used as a method of sequentially walking through the user's process, so it is important to ensure that the user starts the explanation at the starting point of his or her business responsibilities. I sometimes call these points the *process initiators*, or the flows that start things in motion and require responses. Of course, there are other corresponding tools, including data dictionary and process specifications that define the data required and the detailed algorithms, respectively. Ideally, the premeetings should have allowed the analyst to estimate how many meetings and how much time should be necessary with each user. Another important factor is time itself. It is not wise to hold interviews longer than 2 hours; it is difficult for anyone to provide information for that length of time. If possible, a session should cover a specified process from start to finish. In this manner, the analyst and user have a sense of completion.

Analysts should also remember that interviewing is iterative, so that every session will require a follow-up of some sort in which the user will need to validate the contents of the specifications. Therefore, the information from the meeting must be "reviewable," and inevitably will undergo further modification. It is usually sufficient to use simple typing paper to record information in interviews. Lots of paper will be used to record different aspects of the data being captured. Figure 2.3 provides a sample of hand-drawn specifications. It is also necessary to collect documents, which typically include report samples, forms, and receipts. These documents are crucial; as we shall see later, they can often define all the inputs and all the outputs. If an analyst has both of these components, it is a good bet that the ecommerce system is complete.

In terms of the actual interaction, analysts need to lead, yet listen; watch, yet record information; and in many cases look for clues that political issues are behind illogical explanations. It is important not to criticize or challenge the way things are currently done, but it is appropriate to suggest some logical alternatives. Never say, "Would you

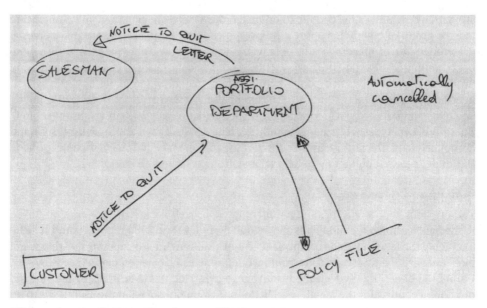

Figure 2.3   Handwritten interview specifications.

like to have this feature or function?" without making sure that the user understands the consequences of what he or she has just agreed to. For example, it is unfair to ask a user if he or she would like to validate the entry of the name of a city unless it is understood that a list of cities will need to be purchased and maintained. On the other hand, the ecommerce analyst has every right to question problems in pure logic, for instance when a user describes a transaction that can have two outputs, yet he or she defines only one of them. For example, when something goes to an entity for approval, logic tells us that two things can occur: It can be approved or rejected. Yet during interviews, the analyst might find that such is not the case. For example, it has never been rejected, so there are no guidelines on how to treat a rejection. In this situation the analyst should press the users to define "what they would do" if in the rare circumstances a rejection did indeed occur. At least then the system will have a way of handling the situation—and we all know that the first day the system is in operation something will be rejected!

Group Interviews: Joint Application Development

There are situations when individual interviews are not feasible or even possible. In these instances it is necessary to consider some form of group sessions that can reduce the number of meetings and the amount of time spent resolving different internal user views. Group interviews are particularly useful when:

- There are too many users to interview individually.

- There is a high probability that there will be differing points of view on require-ments and that reaching agreement among the constituents will be difficult and time-consuming.

- There are a number of locations, and the distance between them is too great to do the interviews individually.

While group sessions can be held in a number of different ways, the most structured is called Joint Application Development (JAD). JAD sessions bring together users and Information Technology (IT) personnel in 3- to 5-day workshops. JADs are held under the auspices of a facilitator who is responsible for the overall management of the meetings. Under the direction of the facilitator, participants define their needs, agree to solutions, and develop the appropriate models that can be used in the engineering of the system. The unique aspect of JAD is that it must be run by the users rather than by IT. The reason for this approach is simple: Getting users to participate in a time-consuming activity like JAD requires management support and buy-in from internal users. JAD is designed to ensure consensus of ideas by allowing all those who have a stake in the system to contribute ideas and to agree to what the system needs to do. Embedded in the process is the assumption that users can be placed in an environment where they can compromise on what they want, and that any political forces should be somewhat neutralized in such an environment.

Therefore, the most critical part of holding an organized JAD session is establishing the correct infrastructure for a structured group exercise. The standard roles used in a JAD are

Executive sponsor. As previously defined, this individual is at an executive level and must be the champion of the project from the company's perspective. The ideal person to take on this role is someone who is clearly in control of allocating resources, is known to be a tough manager who means what he or she says, and is willing to make the necessary decisions to keep the project on time and on budget.

Facilitator. This individual is usually either an IT person or someone from an external organization like a consulting firm. The more independent the facilitator is, the better, since it is this person who is responsible for coordinating the JAD meetings and ensuring that each meeting goes as planned. In the best situations the facilitator should report to the executive sponsor, a structure that gives the facilitator some autonomy and sends a strong message to the rest of the management team. The facilitator is the single most important individual in the JAD. He or she is the equivalent of a project manager. The skill sets required by a productive JAD facilitator overlap with those of the successful analyst/designer. In fact, many ecommerce analyst/designers are ideally qualified to serve as facilitators, and it is my belief that they should be used in this role.

Scribe. This person is similar to a court reporter in that he or she takes the minutes of each JAD session. Minutes can include more than just what transpired; the document has various sections including follow-up items, resolutions, business rules, disagreements, etc. Scribes often come from IT because they need to have a good understanding of logic and the process of analysis. Furthermore, some scribes need to understand how to use modeling tools, such as flow diagrams, and therefore need to know how to use a computer-aided software engineering tool (CASE). While these requirements would seem to point to an IT professional for this role, a scribe must also have excellent listening skills and an advanced command of a computer keyboard—skills that not all IT people have. Scribes, then, are specialists, just like court reporters, and can be obtained from outside consulting firms as a service. Consultant scribes also have the objectivity to take notes without influence from political factions inside the organization.

IT representative. While IT is not managing the JAD per se, there is still an important function for them to play in the JAD process. IT personnel do not attend JADs to provide requirements, rather they are there to answer questions about the existing systems in place at the firm. Without IT resources available to answer these kinds of questions, the JAD's completion could be delayed.

Participants. These individuals are the group of users that have been selected to provide the input for the requirements of the system. The participants are usually at the line-management level described earlier in this chapter and will represent the interests and needs of their respective line business units. The most important quality of these participants, beyond their ability to provide requirements, is their commitment to "agree-to-agree." The philosophy behind "agree-to-agree" is based on the concept that groups need to go through a process of negotiation and conciliation to finalize a computer system that provides value for all interested parties. JAD supporters believe that this process is not a form of "settling for less," but rather the ideal way to establish the best requirements for a new system. The ideal JAD will consist of up to 15 participants, but this rule is often violated. JAD sessions can often exceed 40 participants, which can make sessions difficult to facilitate and focus. JAD session participants are usually selected by the executive management team.

Session leader. There should be at least one session leader for every JAD session. In fact, there are typically many session leaders during the course of any one JAD session. A session leader is responsible for leading the discussion and debate about a particular subject area. A subject area, for example, could be *the processing of electronic purchase orders from business partners*. Session leaders need to be prepared and may require assistance from an IT resource, like a business analyst, who can show them how to gather requirements from their staffs. It is, if you will, the understanding of how to take user requirements and present a summary of their needs to the rest of the organization. IT personnel can also assist the session leader in preparing and presenting information and ideas.

Observer. This person is not allowed to participate actively in a JAD session. Observers are often specialists and participate only when needed—therefore, they wait to be asked to enter the conversation. Observers cannot independently offer information without being prompted by the session leader or the facilitator. In addition, some observers are decision-makers who sit in to see how the session is going or are present to make decisions when groups are in deadlock. Unfortunately, having executives observe sessions may sacrifice the democratic principle on which JAD sessions are based: providing a safe environment for free thought and expression. Finally, some observers are simply attending to understand how system requirements are being gathered.

Understanding the roles and responsibilities of the personnel required in a JAD is only one part of making these sessions successful. Other important considerations include selecting an appropriate room in which to hold the JAD session, managing the process during the meetings, and coordinating the ultimate deliverables from these sessions. Figure 2.4 is a diagram of a good JAD room. The facilitator, who must act as the ultimate manager of the sessions, is at the front of the room (and thus is distinguished in a management role) yet is off to the side so as not to take control of the discussions. The scribe, like the facilitator, is off to the side, yet visible.

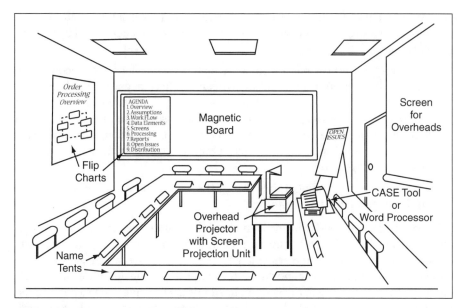

Figure 2.4 JAD room configuration.

JAD sessions can be distinguished from ordinary group meetings because of the number of defined phases that are required to provide the ultimate specifications to develop the ecommerce system. These phases are as follows:

1. Prior to the actual JAD sessions, a session should be held in which the goals, objectives, constraints, and assumptions are defined. A meeting with the executive sponsor should define the history of the project, the time frame of the existing plan, the politics and the current organization, the size and number of the sessions to be held, the role of IT, and the session leaders.

2. After the meeting with the executive sponsor, a meeting should be held with a select group of senior-level managers to assign the participants for the JAD sessions. These participants will come from the pool of line managers representing each business unit. The process of determining who these people should be will vary—it depends on the business, the culture, the number of departments, and the way business is transacted in the company. Ecommerce analysts need to understand that the process will be interactive with the management of the company.

3. Once the line managers who will attend the JADs are selected, there should be a meeting with the participants to discuss and design an overall plan for the sessions. This process marks the transition from an executive focus to a line-management process. The issues that will be discussed, therefore, will be concrete in nature. Typical topics include:

    ■ Analysis of the way the existing systems operate.

    ■ Determination of where and when the JAD sessions will take place.

    ■ Determination of the specific information that needs to be collected prior to each session.

- Assessment of the levels of technical expertise in each JAD so that the sessions are designed to uncover information that can be understood by the participants.

- Gathering of any previous information relating to the needs of the ecommerce system. There is often information in organizations that can provide historical background on the things that have been requested by the user community. Many such requests may never have been addressed or may have been put on hold for a specific reason. In any event, the JAD is a good time to address these past requests so that they can be evaluated for inclusion in the new ecommerce system.

- Determining the amount of time that JAD sessions should last and the format of the agendas to be presented.

4. The fourth phase requires the involvement of IT. As stated earlier, IT offers important insight about the ways the current system uses and stores information. Undoubtedly, all ecommerce systems will need to interface with legacy applications. The IT staff also has important information about the definition and nature of the data that is stored in the system. In addition, IT people need to be included so that they can understand whether the new design will require additional hardware and software, and the extent of support that will be required. IT professionals can also provide background to JAD participants about the usage patterns of people in the organization on the existing systems.

5. The fifth phase requires the actual design of the JAD session. This entails forming an approach to presenting the entire program to the user community. Sometimes premeetings are required, and participants may need offsite meetings to obtain information they need to represent their respective internal organizations. This phase also requires guidelines about how the information that is gathered during the JADs will be formatted and what modeling tools will be used to synthesize the information that has been provided and the agreements that have been reached. During this time, the actual work document should be established, which will outline each session, its intended result, the materials required, who will be in observation, and who will sign off on the information.

6. The sixth phase finalizes the JAD organization structure. This means selecting the personnel who actually conduct the session, deciding what support is necessary, and determining how IT will interface with the team. If there are multiple facilitators, then a JAD project leader should be appointed to be responsible for managing the other JAD facilitators, in particular to ensure there is consistency across the sessions and that outputs are compatible. This phase must also establish how senior management will be kept apprised of progress. Therefore, the facilitator(s) must design a communication system, or status reporting, so that management can understand where the project stands with regard to schedule. The status report can also be used as a vehicle to get help from executives when necessary. It is often suggested that a monthly status meeting be conducted to allow for a regular face-to-face review of the project.

7. Before the JAD workshops are held, it may be necessary to conduct training on the tools to be used during the sessions. This is particularly important if modeling

tools such as data flows, prototypes, decomposition charts, object-oriented techniques, and database diagrams are to be used. Typically a 1-day session is held that teaches what the diagrams mean and reviews the terminology to be used in the sessions. As a result of this training, a document should be produced that summarizes the information covered during the session. This document will then serve as a reference for the participants during the actual sessions.

8. JAD workshops are completed during this phase. Workshops require specific start and stop times and agendas that will typically include the following discussion items:

- **Review of user-created assumptions.** It is important that everyone understand and agree to the assumptions generated during the JAD sessions. Each assumption will be read, and the participants will be given the opportunity to continue with the assumption, to revise it, or to make it an open issue for follow-up. (This is in the case where no consensus can be reached within a reasonable period of time.) User-created assumptions should not be confused with the assumptions established by the executive sponsor, which are not open for discussion or change.

- **Ecommerce business activities.** Discussions should focus on how business processes affect ecommerce activities. In this way, discussions become mapped to the various pieces of the technical specification, which will inevitably be generated for development (see Chapter 3).

- **Database requirements.** This involves the recording of information that must be stored in a database. Data models are used to begin the creation of a data dictionary, which will become the repository of all data to be used in the processing of the ecommerce system.

- **Graphic user screens.** Screens will have two components. The first type of screen is used in internal processing, for which internal users will most likely provide the requirements. The second screen types are those that use browser graphics usually focused more on external B2B and consumer users. However, with the advent and popularity of browser software and Intranet technology, even internal users are becoming much more aware of the benefits of having user-intuitive screens. The focus for the JAD is more on defining the features and functions that need to exist on screens than it is on actually designing the interface itself. This will be accomplished in later sessions where prototypes will be used to provide participants with a visual demonstration of how the system will work.

- **Reports.** Reports continue to be an integral part of user needs. Information that is required for reports also helps define the data requirements. This information normally includes a description of the report, its distribution list, selection criteria, sort options, calculations, and actual field values that need to be displayed.

- **New issues.** These are often annotated as open issues and assigned to certain participants for resolution over a specified period of time. Open issues are simply those that cannot be resolved during the JAD.

9. After the JAD workshops are completed, there must be a concentrated effort to resolve all open issues. Open issues tend to go unresolved unless there is a conscious effort to ensure that answers are received and agreements among the participants are reached. A follow-up list is typically generated by the scribe and distributed to the participants before the JAD sessions are completed.

10. Once the follow-up items are resolved, there is a significant amount of work to create prototypes for subsequent meetings to show the users how the system will actually operate. Sample screens and reports are a big portion of the prototyping phase (to be discussed in Chapter 6) as well as actual architectural design models.

11. After sessions are held, there will be iterations of changes made to the prototype screens and reports, and there will be actual approvals to finalize the specification document. During these sessions it is also important to begin discussing user acceptance procedures, that is, the test plans that will be used to test whether the system is ready for production. Creating user test plans is similar to designing technical specifications in that the test plan is a document that will be used to determine the quality of the system. However, the user acceptance plan is based on what the user says is acceptable, not necessarily on what is absolutely correct. For example, if a user is asked how critical it is if the date of the report is correct, and they reply "not very," it establishes that the report date should not be part of the user acceptance plan. This does not suggest that the report date will not be fixed at some point, just that it is not deemed critical enough by the user to stop the system from going live. Covering this process is critical, and it will be discussed in more depth in Chapter 3.

12. The final phase is the completion of the technical specification document. This document is not complete without adding the steps that are necessary for the customer or consumer component of the ecommerce system. Notwithstanding the addition of the customer and/or consumer components, there should still be a formal document that defines the internal needs of the ecommerce system, which is authorized by those who will use it to fulfill the internal business process needs.

There is also a need for post-JAD meetings, as inevitably certain aspects of the specification document will be unclear, or may even need to change. In many ways, JAD follows a clearly defined linear approach to defining internal requirements. We will see, however, that the customer and consumer interfaces behave differently and thus need other methods.

Customers as Users

This section focuses on customers as users of ecommerce systems. As stated earlier, this type of interface is called *ecustomers* or *B2B*. Ecustomers are external to the organization, but in many ways fall within the domain of what any business defines as its "customers." To that extent, customers' needs are finite and can be a condition of how business is conducted, based on the definitions set forth between the business and its customers. However, there is a certain degree of fragmentation in the ebusiness market with the advent of the alternatives provided by the Web. Customers enjoy a wide variety of ecommerce alternatives, whereas in the past they were limited to geographically convenient options (Windham and Orton, 2000). Therefore, ecustomers need to be understood in terms of their Web consumption behaviors and the specific benefits they derive from the Web. It is also important to determine what constitutes loyalty for these customers, how they feel about privacy, and how the Internet is affecting the way these customers do business. Even more important are their intentions for the future and ensuring that your business will meet their ongoing and developing needs. Designing products for ecustomers depends on understanding the types of interfaces that exist and what value these interfaces offer to customers. With internal users we need only ask, but with ecustomers we must infer need based on skill sets of the people we are dealing with and the nature of their businesses.

Key Customer Interfaces

Online buying is the most important component for the ecustomer, representing about 50 percent of their Web usage. The other preferred functions are outlined in Figure 2.5.

Online buying needs are typically the most difficult to satisfy because of the wide range of products and services that are available and that compete with one another. Research has indicated that the most attractive content for ecustomers is product pricing (61 percent). Therefore, most ecustomers consider the Web a strategic business vehicle. As with internal users, ecustomers can be broken down into three important interface types:

Purchasing professional. This individual is responsible for purchasing products and services for companies or departments. These users rate tracking features on the Web as the most important feature since they are responsible for product availability. Other important features include links to related resources and product documentation.

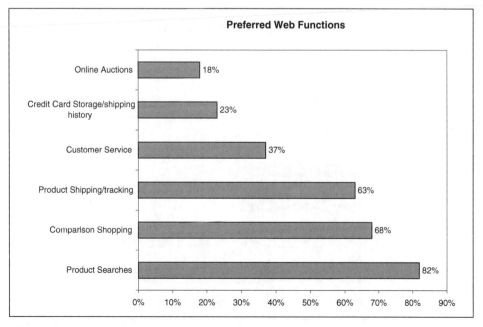

Figure 2.5   Preferred Web functions.

IT professional. This professional spends a significant amount of time on the Web, using the Internet as a daily business tool. There are four primary areas that IT professionals use to satisfy their ebusiness needs:

- Research for products and information
- Order tracking
- Software support
- Tracking competition

IT ecustomers rate downloading software as the most important feature, followed by technical support, product documentation, and marketing information. Therefore, IT professionals are very practical about how they use the Web. If a software company was providing product to IT professionals, this information would drive the feature function of the Web site, as opposed to personalizing the interface, which can be very important to other ecustomer users.

Small business. These individuals tend to adopt many large business needs with those of the consumer market. Small businesses are those with fewer than 20 employees (Windham and Orton, 2000). While many of these users report they use the Internet for their business, there are those who need to use it at home as well. The most popular activities performed by these users are email and product searching as shown in Figure 2.6.

The greatest challenge in serving small business ecustomers is that they have limited time, so interfaces into these systems must be easy to use and allow users to find quickly the information they need. As with internal users, ecustomers have three levels

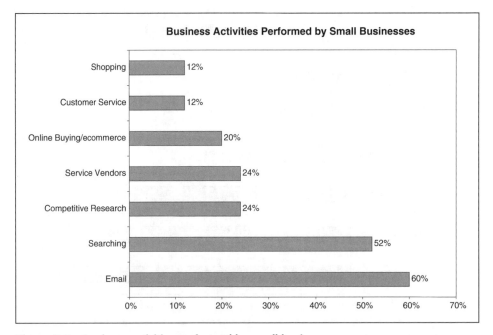

Figure 2.6   Business activities performed by small businesses.

of skill sets that must be considered in the design of ecommerce systems: Online Buyer, Shopper, and Searcher.

Online buyers represent the most experienced ecustomers. They seek the most sophisticated capabilities and understand that Web applications can add to their company's competitiveness. Online buyers view sophisticated Web interfaces as a deciding factor when they select online vendors.

Shoppers are not as sophisticated as online buyers and tend to be more interested in finding sources than in actually placing an order. Thus, it is extremely important to provide these users with the ability to shop through the Web site and see what alternatives can be created with products—such as alternative configurations and option selections. These users often need to print out the results of searches, so providing these users with the necessary report functions is critical.

Searchers, on the other hand, are the least sophisticated of ecustomer users. They search only for information, and are rarely interested in buying anything because they do not have the authority to do so. These individuals are often engaged in product research and need only to find information, print it, and summarize the data that they have found. Web sites for these users need to be very specific, with few options, since the technical sophistication of the user is very limited.

As with internal users, it is necessary to propagate the ecommerce flows with the ecustomer interfaces. The flow diagram in Figure 2.7 shows the relationship between the ecustomers and the actual ecommerce flow within the organization.

Figure 2.7 shows the flow from searcher users to online buyer users and the steps that move the process from one ecustomer function to another. While this may not always be a separate individual, the essence of the steps is consistent among companies. The question, however, is how does an ecommerce analyst obtain the information from this community in order to design the best product? The worst mistake that a company intending to launch an ebusiness can make is to assume that it already knows what its customers want. In such situations, Web sites are not designed to be a critical component of the customer relationship. Ebusiness systems should be treated like any other external product development. Therefore, it is necessary to ensure that analysts will be in contact with customers and prospects so that answers to critical questions can be captured and designed into the system. Within each entity to be targeted, it is important that ecommerce analysts identify the ecustomer profile (IT professional, purchase professional, or small business) and interview the three levels of users within the flow process (online buyer, shopper, and searcher). To cover each of these areas properly, it is necessary to have a life cycle that allows the ecommerce analyst to obtain the information in a structured and creative cycle as follows:

Feasibility and assessment. This step determines whether an ecustomer system makes sense and is within the firm's return-on-investment standards. Feasibility and assessments require a competitive review of what other products exist in the market, customer Web adoption determination, sales strategy and channel assessment, industry best practices, and trade-off analysis.

Develop business flow approach. Create a comprehensive plan complete with a prototype organization of the ecustomer, their business objectives, and interface types and experience levels of their users. The focus of this flow approach is to model the hypothetical business to which you intend to provide services. This should begin with the development of the prototype organization, which is a chart of the business units in the company. Utilizing the ecommerce flow relationships with ecustomer interfaces (see Figure 2.7), the analyst can define the users that will use the ecommerce system. This approach, therefore, allows the analyst to estimate what users will need and, based on their type and skill level, decide how the Web interface should be developed. In many cases, the prototype organization is based on the topology of an existing customer in the hope that its structure will be similar to other companies in a similar business. Notwithstanding this option, the concept behind creating prototypes is to attempt to replicate the controlled user environment that exists with internal users. While the same level of control can never be attained, this procedure does provide a systematic method of defining these users. Another view of this approach is to propagate the hypothetical organization with Figure 2.7, where the flows of the process can be cross-referenced to the business unit responsible for maintaining it. Ultimately the output of this phase is the framework for the design strategy of the ecustomer Web interface (see Figure 2.8).

Develop functional specifications. This phase creates the detailed functions that will be provided by the Web site to your ecustomers. The functional specifications

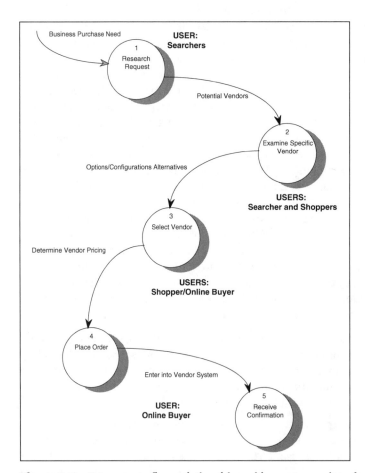

Figure 2.7   Ecommerce flow relationships with ecustomer interfaces.

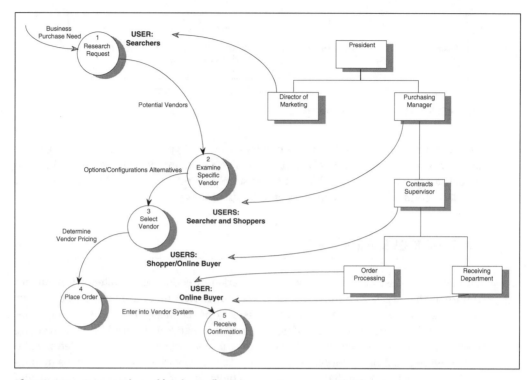

Figure 2.8   Propagation of business flows to ecustomer organization.

will contain a preamble stating its goals, a functional requirements document, a prototype strategy, and a network infrastructure design. The preamble defines the goals and objectives that will become the measurable outcomes for the Web site. This is typically developed by marketing, sales, and product fulfillment. The functional requirements document includes the content that needs to be developed (content is defined as the actual descriptive information to be included as text in the Web site), application design, graphical user interface (GUI), and the software configuration. The prototype strategy defines how ecustomer users will review the prototype designs of these systems. This information is typically captured using marketing research instruments such as focus groups, personal interviews, or surveys. The hardware platform will be designed based on the completion of the software applications design.

Prototyping. A prototype is basically a virtual representation of the system. This means that it appears to be the system, but it does not really function, that is, it has no software programming behind the displayed screens. The purpose of a prototype is to provide users with the "look and feel" of the system once it is completed and to seek their feedback and ultimate approval of the design. Prototypes are usually created by drawing the screens and linking them, using some type of display software such as Microsoft's Powerpoint.

These four phases complete the analyst's responsibilities to confirm with ecustomers how the ecustomer user interface needs to operate. The interface and feature and/or

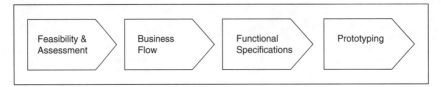

Figure 2.9   The ecustomer life cycle.

functions will be gathered through a combination of a hypothetical organization, or by actually working with the firm's companies. The remaining phases are focused on the actual site building and launching of the system. Figure 2.9 reflects the four phases of the B2B ecommerce system analysis and design process.

Consumers as Users

This section focuses on the vast consumer market of ecommerce systems. Consumers represent the largest and most diverse group of users. Unlike in-house and customer users, consumers are users that a business may never meet or experience feedback from. Satisfying consumers, therefore, depends on many of the traditional marketing methods of understanding the behaviors of a target segment of the population. The wider the segment of the targeted population, the more variation that develops in identifying the preferences of that domain. This is typically known as *target marketing*, and it is assumed that the Web consumer in many ways behaves similarly to the traditional buyer of products and services. However, Web consumers have a distinct variable based on their longevity as Web users. It is believed that consumer segments can be clustered based on how long and how extensively they have been using the Internet (Windham and Orton, 2000). This experience cluster lays the foundation of a new dimension in target marketing that differs from the conventional approach. Consumer clusters form user interface segmentations, which relate to the categories and profiles that we defined for internal users and customer users, respectively. These segments are separated, based on the user's experience and perceived benefits from using ecommerce systems.

Key Consumer Interfaces

According to Windham and Orton (2000), there are six benefit-oriented segments that have emerged in the consumer marketplace:

1. Convenience users

2. Price-sensitive users

3. Comparison users

4. Brand-loyal users

5. Focused users

6. Storefront users

Convenience Users

Convenience shoppers are usually in a hurry and are therefore more concerned with time than money. In many products and services, convenience shoppers are not as interested in making comparisons to benefit from price and service discounts. In a sense, convenience shoppers were the first consumer ecommerce customers because time constraints drew them to the Internet. These users require simplicity and need to enact a transaction as quickly as possible. Ecommerce systems designed for these users must focus on providing information about when and how the product will be delivered and they require little feature function with respect to other merchandise. Certainly comparable pricing messages will have little value. The design of Web page interfaces needs to focus on limited keystrokes and simple graphics so that the order transaction can be completed quickly.

Price-Sensitive Users

Price-sensitive users, unlike convenience shoppers, are concerned with price, and will readily switch sites to save money. Because of their focus on price, these users have little concern about the inconvenience of viewing multiple sites to find the right price. Ecommerce systems that need to attract price-sensitive users should focus on various price-oriented designs. For example, filling out profile information for a free magazine or subscription can attract these shoppers. This is one of the smallest user segments, but is expected to grow with the new wave of ecommerce consumer users.

Comparison Users

These users are related to price-sensitive shoppers in that they want to get the best deal. They differ, however, in what they perceive as a benefit. Price-sensitive shoppers measure benefit based only on price, whereas comparison users look at price, quality, image, etc., as components of value. Comparison shoppers enjoy the act of comparing against others, and embrace the challenge of finding the best buy. Ecommerce systems for these users need to have links to competitors and information that helps the comparison shopper understand the benefit of the product or service being offered to them. Comparison users will quickly dismiss sites that lack competitive analysis.

Brand-Loyal Users

The brand-loyal users tend to continue to buy from the same sites because they trust and/or like the site. These users become loyal to the site and resist changing to another vendor. They are also sensitive to the reputation of a company, as they feel more comfortable with name-recognition as a factor of measuring quality and dependability. The behavior of brand-loyal users can be characterized as lazy, resistant to change, and comfortable with the status quo. Ecommerce systems designed for these users need to continue to tout the image of the business and can easily market related products and services off of its core brand name. That is, businesses that have a strong brand image can leverage more business from their loyal base of users.

Focused Users

A focused shopper is one who is fully intent on obtaining the product or service he or she wants. They find the product, make the selection, and move on to their next task. These users do not respond well to gimmicks, banner ads, email messages, or marketing ploys. In fact, such approaches could alienate these users. The population of focused users is divided between those who hate to shop and those who shop online for convenience. Such consumers also have little concern for price discounts. As a result, ecommerce sites for these shoppers should allow for quick selection of product without the need to go through layers of screen choices.

Storefront Users

Storefront users are those who simply dread the thought of going shopping in the retail marketplace. These users hate crowds and basically hate shopping. Storefront users shop online because they do not want to shop in a retail store. These users are particularly attractive to companies that are extending their products from the retail arena, as well as those companies that are creating dot-com extensions of their businesses. These sites can have an opening to other products offered by the business to tempt their consumers to try them. Ecommerce systems must focus on ease of use and convenience for these users and change often to attract them to try new features placed on the Web.

Consumers can also be grouped into three skill set levels in order to design the user interface: Seasoned, Adventurer, and Anxious.

Seasoned users are very entrenched in their habits and ways they use the Web. These users are very experienced and use the Internet in many aspects of their lives such as reading news, tracking their portfolios, communicating with friends, and, of course, buying products. These users have been using the Internet for a long time, and therefore are very advanced in their use of fancy technology. They expect Web sites to be "state of the art" and to provide a complete solution to their needs. Therefore, ecommerce systems targeting seasoned users must be robust and must allow users to specify their preferences and complete transactions quickly. Seasoned shoppers are also valuable because of their ability to influence the behaviors of many other people, for they are often asked their opinion about what Web sites are best. Most important is that seasoned users do not return to disappointing Web sites, so their first impressions are lasting.

Adventurers are the next skill level below seasoned users. They are building their confidence in using the Web and are beginning to roam through sites and find new things that they can do. Adventurers have become empowered and seek to try new things on the Web. They are not as entrenched habitually as seasoned shoppers; they notice new things on the Web and are focused on the potential benefits of new offerings. Ecommerce systems seeking to support such users can provide new options and banners, as adventurers will be willing to investigate new things. In fact, they expect such challenges, suggesting that ecommerce systems targeting their use should ensure that the software changes in appearance and feature and/or function often. This is an important issue: Many ecommerce systems become old quickly and assume that users find value in the regularity of their sites. Such might not be the case with adventurers.

Anxious users represent the most inexperienced group. They can be considered the newcomers to the world of ecommerce shopping and tend to use the Internet in a safe and conservative fashion. These users lack confidence and worry that they may do

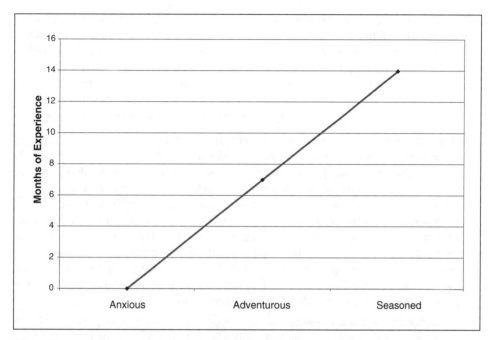

Figure 2.10   Consumer segments and experience level.

something wrong when processing a transaction over the Web. Anxious users are typically targeted by Web portal companies like Earthlink and America Online (AOL). The focus for these companies is to provide their consumers with easy-to-use screens that create a safe environment and are extremely forgiving to a user who makes a mistake. Ecommerce systems that are designed to target new users should be designed with feature functions as described above, or they risk scaring away their audience.

Figure 2.10 summarizes graphically the relationship of experience on the Internet with the consumer segments portrayed above. What is challenging for ecommerce systems designers is to determine who their audience is in terms of the marketplace, and where most of the segment exists relative to the experience levels of their users. In addition, ecommerce developers need to keep track of the migration of their audience to more sophisticated levels of user needs. Figure 2.10 suggests that a certain percentage of anxious shoppers will become more adventurous after 7 months of experience with the Internet, and so on. Therefore, market segments shift, especially with those companies that already have users and need to change along with them.

Implications for Analysts

As stated earlier, the consumer market poses the greatest challenge for ecommerce developers because of its broad base of users with multiple interests and skill levels. Of course, a large component of this complexity is the target market. The broader the intended audience, the greater the challenge to create a successful design for the ecommerce system. Most important is the loss of the concept "one-size-fits-all" as Web developers need to provide multiple views of their company to a diverse audience. The ultimate gamble is to attempt a design that tries to make everyone happy, and what usually happens is that nobody ends up happy. On the other hand, attempting to design multiple products can also be very flawed because of the complexity of keeping multiple versions compatible, and with the overwhelming cost of doing so. Ecommerce systems must be designed to understand users in many dimensions and provide them with a defined way of using the site, knowing in many instances that the developers cannot make everyone happy. The ecommerce analyst must embark on a structured process that will allow him or her to obtain the information to design the system. There are three approaches to doing so:

Interview marketing personnel. The ecommerce analyst will use the company's marketing personnel to represent the consumers. Marketers are traditionally responsible for knowing the preferences of their consumers, and for defining what part of the consumer market they wish to reach. In these cases, ecommerce analysts should follow the same structured approach previously defined for internal users, that is, market personnel are treated as if they were an internal-user organization. This approach has both advantages and disadvantages. On the positive side, marketers are allowed to do their job, and are empowered to represent their target market. The negative aspect is that they do not really understand how consumers will respond to Web sites. It is not easy for marketers to know what consumers want and whether they find the interface satisfying.

Direct feedback from consumers. Here ecommerce analysts must go directly to the market and interview them in a similar fashion to what is done internally. This process will be defined shortly. This alternative also has its good and bad points. On the positive side, dealing with consumer users provides the analysts with an opportunity to speak directly to the user. The analyst can make objective observations rather than relying on potentially distorted information from the marketing organization. Unfortunately, this process can be very time-consuming, costly, and limited in its coverage of the population.

Hybrid market and/or consumer. An alternative is to create a "hybrid" approach, including the advantages of both the internal market and direct consumer alternatives. For example, analysts should begin with internal interviews with the marketing department. In this way, an analyst can get an understanding of the target market as opposed to just meeting consumers directly. The appropriate assumptions and constraints can also be determined prior to talking with consumers. Samplings of consumers are also done so that they can be contacted directly or indirectly. Various research instruments are used to gather their preferences and needs (interviews, surveys, and focus groups). Using this approach, analysts can get both perspectives of the consumer shopper.

Because it offers better coverage, I recommend that the hybrid method be used whenever possible. Marketing personnel should be interviewed either individually or using JAD sessions. In some cases, firms have outside marketing consultants that assist them in formulating market approaches. These consultants should also be invited to participate in the internal interview sessions. Outside interviews are accomplished using three forms of market research.

Interviews. This form of analysis requires that analysts speak to consumers one-on-one. There are two forms of interviewing: face-to-face and telephone. Face-to-face interviews are similar to the individual interviews done with internal users. The difference is that there is limited authority and control over what the consumers will bring with them to the meeting. Location is problematic, so only a limited number of interviews can be done. Ecommerce analysts should use an interview questionnaire to guide their interview with the consumer. A sample interview questionnaire is shown in Figure 2.11. Telephone interviews are obviously less personal and typically shorter in duration. As a result, the amount of information obtained is limited.

Surveys. This is a questionnaire that is mailed directly to the consumer. Surveys are effective research tools to obtain information from a large and geographically distributed population. Questionnaires use both quantitative (answers that are ratings, e.g., select 1 to 5) and qualitative (handwritten comments) questions.

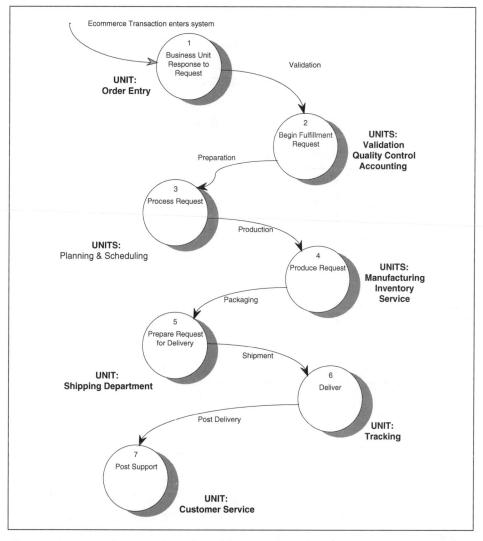

Figure 2.11 Interview questionnaire guide.

Unfortunately, surveys have a low return rate; in some instances it is necessary to provide a gift or other incentive to get consumers to respond. Therefore, it is necessary to mail out many surveys in order to receive a usable number of responses. This process is time-consuming and expensive, but it could render important information about what the Web site should contain. A sample consumer survey is shown in Figure 2.12.

Focus groups. These are meetings with groups of consumers to discuss their collective preferences. It can be compared to a JAD-like session, in which the analyst attempts to generate interactive discussion among the consumers in order to determine their salient needs, and to guide the conversations in such a way as to summarize the central themes of their needs. Focus groups can be used effectively

Consumer Survey

Dept/Project:	Date:
External Consumer Inventory:	Size of Consumer Base:
Analyst:	Consumer Type (see Grid):

Item	Comment
Age Range	
Gender %	
How would you best describe your Consumer buying on the Web	
Reason why you use the Web	
Web Expectations	

Consumer Types:	1. Price Sensitive 2. Quality Oriented	3. Portal Based User 4. Entertainment

Figure 2.12 Ecommerce consumer survey.

after survey results are compiled. The data can then be used to discuss among the members of the focus group. Focus groups are expensive and require months of planning. It is also difficult to get consumers to participate in focus groups without monetary compensation. Unlike JAD, focus groups can rarely last more than 2 hours, so the amount of time to gather the information is very limited.

Summary

This chapter focused on the different types of users that make up the ecommerce community. The most controlled group is internal users. While they are controlled to the extent that they are known and work inside the business, cultural norms and politics can be challenges to the analyst during the interview sessions. Customers represent the users of business-to-business relationships. Although these users are outside the control of the company, their requirements and preferences fall within the domain of customers for the business. As such, users can be identified through the company's existing installed base or their competitors. Consumer preferences, on the other hand, are the least known and most difficult to obtain. Ecommerce analysts must rely on the company's internal marketing group and external market research to obtain a good sample of consumer needs. Each of these three types of users has two attributes that must be investigated and identified in order to design software to suit their technical knowledge and their behavioral preferences and needs.

CHAPTER

3

Developing Application Specifications for Web Programmers

This chapter outlines the procedures and tools needed to create application specifications. Application specifications are the detailed architecture that defines the requirements for the Web developers. These specifications have to define the inputs and outputs of the application. Inputs can originate from inside the system, from a database, user input screen, or from outside the system, such as from a vendor. Outputs can be updates to existing internal databases, generated reports, or flows that leave the system, such as a check being sent to a vendor to pay for services. Specifications also define the business rules of what the program must do, known in computer science as the *algorithms*. This chapter will provide the templates and procedures for developing the structured application specification that will be used as instructions for the developers.

The Realities of Analysis and Design

Before discussing the process of developing application specifications, it is important to understand the scope of these specifications. Whether the application specifications are developed from internal users, customers, or consumers, it is crucial that analysts and designers respect and accept the users' needs rather than try to change them. It is not the role of the analyst or designer to suggest changes to existing procedures. Efforts to reengineer or redesign systems and procedures, unless specifically requested by the users, can easily waste time and damage relationships. It does not matter if your suggested change is a good one; the reality of analysis and design is that you must work within the capabilities of the user community. Analysts and designers often ignore this simple rule.

Let's use an example to illustrate this situation. Assume there is a company that needs to develop a database of information about a sector of its business. Fifty employees are involved with defining the application specifications for connecting to the central IT function. The internal users disagree about the features and functions required in the application, and no one has offered to design the forms and reports that are required. The Executive Sponsor has requested that the system design be completed in 2 months. Hardware and software needs are due immediately.

In this difficult situation, many inexperienced ecommerce analysts might attempt to reach consensus by:

1. Imposing an environment where users were forced to create the requirements before they actually agreed to agree. This will result only in obtaining inaccurate data.

2. Providing hardware and software requirements prior to finishing the applications specifications

3. Ignoring the potential political problems among the staff

4. Designing a project development schedule that is doomed to fail because of all the problems above

This kind of approach can only lead to failure—failure that is long remembered by the user community. Yet this approach is all too often used, especially in those projects that tend to be late in delivering their software. Let us examine an alternative approach to dealing with this application specification dilemma. The objective of analysis is to work within the user environment rather than trying to force it to change. Here is a more realistic way of handling the requirements:

1. Create an environment that takes uncertainty into account. This involves an iterative process of analysis to development. In this case, the initial plan may not be the final one, and some issues may not get resolved until later in the development life cycle.

2. Do not attempt to identify hardware requirements until the application specifications are complete.

3. Use various types of Computer Aided Software Engineering (CASE) tools and prototypes that can assist the users in making joint decisions.

4. Organize various pilot programs to allow users to see certain parts of the system in limited operation. This will provide much-needed confidence in the overall project.

5. Specify a plan for going into production with the new applications that includes a realistic schedule, taking into consideration the realities of the politics and cultural values of the organization.

The goal of this approach is to provide a plan that matches better with the user environment, particularly its politics, culture, constraints, and assumptions. This chapter explores how to provide the most appropriate application specifications to match what users said they needed during the interview process. The less ambiguous the specification, the fewer errors will occur. It is important to mention again the risks of relying on a single methodology to provide a solution: No methodology will fare well when implemented in a company that deviates from the organizational assumptions underlying that methodology. In every case, the best methodology is the one that matches well with the environment.

Defining Development Complexity

We often hear that certain applications are more complex than others. The notion of complexity should be approached with great caution, because it tends to suggest to the development team that the usual procedures do not apply to that particular project. My motto has always been, "The only complex projects are those that people make so." Ecommerce analysts and designers should remember that all software development projects are fundamentally the same: They differ only in the number of people on the project, the time available before delivery, and the cost. These variables can influence the way a particular project is implemented, but they do not change the actual process of analysis and design. Some projects simply need more resources or better hardware and software than others. There are usually two fundamental reasons that ecommerce projects appear to be complex:

1. Personnel are attempting to solve the wrong problem, that is, the identified problem is not, in fact, a problem.

2. The solution to the real problem is probably less difficult than originally thought.

The focus on the complexity of systems rather than on the proper identification of problems is a major factor in the failure rate of software development projects. Ultimately the solution to dealing with complexity is to train analysts and designers to develop application specifications that accurately depict the user needs (internal, customers, and consumers), while at the same time providing unambiguous specifications to the ecommerce development team. Many problems with system development complexity result from simply not understanding the business and technical procedures that must be in place to develop application specifications. Before analysts begin to use specific techniques and tools to create application specifications, they need to recognize *what* these specifications represent. User requirements must be understood and "translated" for the purpose of software development. One tool for this kind of translation is the concept of the logical equivalent (Langer, 2001).

The Concept of the Logical Equivalent

In *The Analysis and Design of Information Systems* (Langer, 2001), I defined the concept of the Logical Equivalent (LE) as "a process that analysts must use to create effective requirements of the needs of a system. The LE can be compared to a schematic of a plan or a diagram of how a technical device works" (Langer, 2001, p. 27). The LE is based on the premise that all software can trace its roots to some physical need in an organization. For example, if Joe, a user, describes his procedure as one that takes a vendor invoice and processes it for payment, then the automated solution must provide the same ultimate output. The procedures that are followed to create a vendor check, however, may be very different from what Joe actually does physically. Indeed, we hope this will be the case, as we depend on automated tools to make processes more efficient. What Joe does physically must be translated into what the application does logically. The logical solution or LE may not match the physical process exactly, and in most cases we hope it does not match.

How does this relate to the design and development of application specifications? Success in creating a concise and accurate application specification depends on the ability of the ecommerce analyst/designer to use interviews with users to create schematics that are unambiguous and that can be used by programmers to develop the LE, the software. The role of the analyst/designer can be compared to that of an architect meeting with a home buyer. The meeting renders two forms of output: a business requirements document or "picture" of the house, and a blueprint, which is an unambiguous technical schematic of how the house needs to be built. This schematic will be the basis for what the builder does. Figures 3.1 and 3.2 show the similarities between the process of designing and building a house and the steps to be followed by an ecommerce analyst/designer.

Figure 3.1 graphically shows how an architect provides a homebuyer with a view of the house that he or she can understand and the builder with the specifications necessary for the house's construction. Figure 3.2 reflects the correlation, where the home-

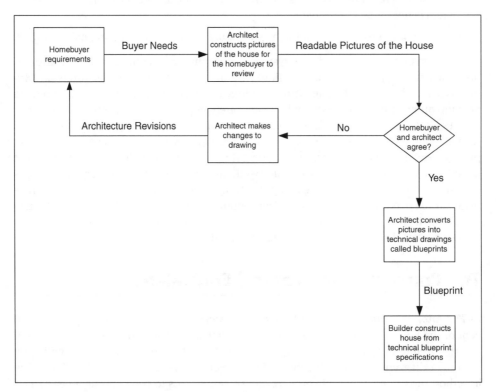

Figure 3.1   The LE of designing and building a house.

Figure 3.2   The LE required to design and build an ecommerce system.

buyer is now a user, and the builder is now a software programmer. The output to the user community is often provided in the form of "business specifications" and prototypes. Business specifications are written communications that reflect, in prose and graphic samples, what the sample will do and how it will appear to the user. Prototypes, on the other hand, are actual screens that provide a more integrated projection of how the system works, without providing the actual programming. That is, a prototype usually involves showing the actual screens of the system and how it moves from one process to another. However, the system does not have the actual programming completed. It is similar to sitting in a demo automobile that has no engine. The output for the programmer must contain schematics that are unambiguous and more focused on the "blueprint" needs of software development, such as defining input flows, file structures, screen manipulations, reports, and the algorithms or business rules to process the data.

The application specification must contain both the user needs and the programming needs to provide the requirements of the ecommerce system. In the same manner, an architect must create documents to ensure that the house meets the preferences of the homebuyer and is also functionally sound from an engineering perspective. This chapter will identify the procedures and tools necessary to accomplish these two outputs.

Creating Application Specifications

Overall, there are only two major components of an application specification: process and data. All application specifications must have a method to address these two components with minimum ambiguity. In the early 1980s Edward Yourdon originally investigated the concept of process and data and established methods for developing structured specifications using various graphic flow tools. We will look at contemporary versions of some of these tools to address the needs of ecommerce software. Yourdon's definition of software was based on process that acted on and changed data. If no change in data results from the process, then there is no real application. Therefore, every process must have input data and output data, and the two must be different.

For example, Figure 3.3 reflects that an incoming invoice from the vendor (input data) is transformed by the process "Vendor Invoice" into an output data flow called "Vendor Check." Thus, the change of data is complete. While there is similar data on both the input and outputs of the process, there are some distinct differences between

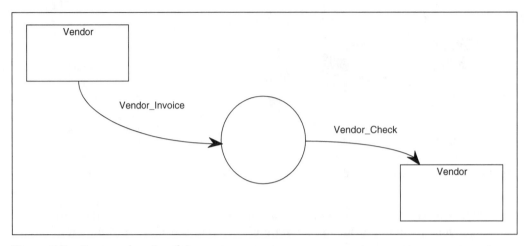

Figure 3.3 Process changing data.

the two. For example, the "Vendor Check" has new data such as "Check Date" and "Check Amount." In accordance with Yourdon, data has indeed changed.

While data and processes are inherently dependent on one another, each has its own distinct identity. These identities have specific reconcilable relations with each other, as we will explore in this chapter. While there are various approaches to defining processes and their corresponding data, this book focuses on defining processes first, and then on determining the related data. Indeed, ecommerce systems are built on the applications that transform data, as in Figure 3.3, from one business unit to another. Processes are discovered through the interview interfaces described in Chapter 2. Most processes relate to the internal component of ecommerce systems, and therefore will be defined via individual interviews or JAD sessions. The overall question then is What do we produce as a result of the internal interviews and group sessions?

Following the strategy of the LE discussed above, the application specification strategy must address both output components of the transformation, that is, both the user business specification and prototype and the programmer's technical schematics. The following sections will describe the tools and outputs of each of these components.

User Specifications

The user specification is composed of high-level flow diagrams, business specifications, and prototypes. High-level flow diagrams depict the sequential steps that take place in a user's process. They therefore paint a picture of the key steps that users take to complete their functions. Business specifications provide an overview of each process and allow users to validate that the analyst has correctly captured the results of the user interviews. Finally, prototypes provide users with an idea of how the new system will operate from an input and output perspective. Input prototypes consist of pictures of the screens and how the navigation within and between screens will operate. Output prototypes consist of sample reports that the user has requested. Each of these deliverables is explained further below.

Interview Data to High-Level Flow Diagrams

The first step in developing user specifications is to understand the flows of the business. Depending on who is being interviewed, these flows reflect what initiates an internal process and what ultimately terminates it. Initiators and terminators will most likely become the links between other processes and events as shown in Figure 3.4.

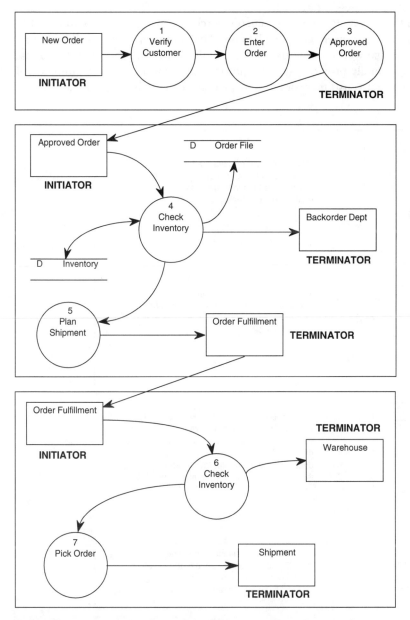

Figure 3.4   Interrelationships of the initiators and terminators.

Figure 3.4 makes use of a diagramming methodology called Process Flow Diagrams (PFD). Process flowing is an excellent first step for the ecommerce analyst to validate the users' processes. Most important is its focus on sequence of steps; users often forget a particular step, and the PFD can prompt them because it requires them to go through each phase of their process in sequence. PFDs were originally derived from flowcharts. Flowcharts, unfortunately, are too clumsy and too detailed to provide an output that can be easily understood by the user community. PFDs have essentially four symbols to work with (see Figure 3.5).

Because of the transactional nature of ecommerce systems, it is critical to use PFDs to validate the steps that users go through to fulfill business requirements. While a PFD is not limited to use with internal users, it certainly is frequently used in this arena. Internal users generally provide the core information about how orders are entered, picked, and shipped to customers or consumers. Users can easily be taught how to read

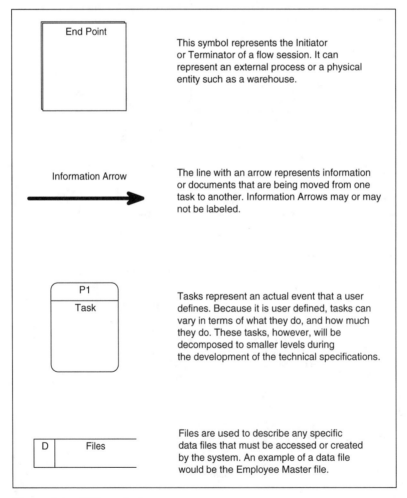

Figure 3.5 PFD symbols.

and understand PFDs, and after PFDs are completed they should always be reviewed and verified by users to ensure their accuracy. PFDs also establish the basis to begin working on the descriptions of the tasks defined in the PFDs, which are called *business specifications*. Business specifications should not be completed until users have verified that the task sequence is accurate. Furthermore, PFDs provide an important approach to working with users at the beginning of both group and individual interviews. Specifically, the PFD is a way of producing an "overview" flow, a template if you will, to create a frame of reference for the rest of the interview. That is, the PFD creates a foundation for organizing the interview process.

Business Specification

The business specification is made up of two levels. First, there should be an overview business specification that correlates to the PFD. This provides an overview of the user's entire domain. For example, a business specification could be titled, "The Order Entry Department." Figure 3.6 represents a sample overview business specification.

The second component is the "functional" business specifications. These specifications refer to each task within the PFD. A functional business specification might be titled, "Entering Orders" or "Checking Inventory." Figure 3.7 represents a sample functional business specification.

Both the overview and functional business specification should be written in prose so that users feel comfortable with the description of their processes and their stated needs—remember, that is the major intent of a business specification. The challenge of creating good and consistent business specifications lies in the formatting. Figures 3.6 and 3.7, while written in prose, use specific format logic. This is accomplished by creating boxes or "frames" that need to be filled in. These frames serve as a kind of questionnaire to ensure that the business specifications will contain the necessary data. The format also simplifies the task of reading the document and finding specific information. Furthermore, the business specification format provides an easy way to track versions and record changes to the original document, as noted in the frame "Supersedes." Finally, the frame method suggests to the analyst the appropriate length of the information. This is important to ensure that business specification documents are neither too sketchy nor too long and to ensure that they present information in a direct and efficient way.

User Prototyping

This component of the deliverable provides sample screens and reports that users have requested. Each functional business specification may have a number of sample screens and report prototypes that can be demonstrated to users for validation purposes. Ecommerce systems pose an interesting challenge for prototyping screens. Some of these screens will be used for internal processing requirements and as a result may need to be designed with greater focus on functionality than graphic design. In fact, some of these "processing" type screens may not be part of the browser design; that is, they are essentially utility screens that operate outside the Web. The screens to be used by customers and consumers, on the other hand, need to be more focused on design. However, it is

Client: XYZ Corporation	Date: 9/2/00
Application: Operations Database	Supersedes:
Subject: Contact Management	Author: A. Langer
Process: Overview - Business Spec	Page: 1 of 2

Overview

The Contact Management Process will allow users to add, modify or delete specific contacts. Contacts will be linked to various tables including Company. A Contact refers to a person who is related to XYZ for business reasons. It can be a Client, a Vendor, a consultant, a person involved in a negotiation, etc.

Contact General Information:

The Database must allow for the centralization of all the contacts handled by all the departments in XYZ. The database and screens will be focused on the following information component groupings:

Basic Information
This is the minimum data requirement and includes such elements as Name, Title, Organization, Phone, Fax, Address, Country, etc.

Contact Profile Information
Further qualification and related elements. Relations include:

    department
    type of client
    nature of client (primary, technical)
    interest of prospect
    importance of client
    memberships (FTUG)
    FT employee

This is a Business Specification which reflects the overall requirements in the Prose format. Its focus is to provide the user who is not technical with a document that they can authorize. This Business Specification should then point to the detailed programming logic that is shown below.

Figure 3.6   Overview business specification.

not the purpose of this prototype phase to create or appraise graphic design. What is much more important is to create functional mock-ups of screens so that the user can agree to the type of screens they need and how these screens should link. Screen design will be covered in more detail in Chapter 6.

User prototyping in this phase of application specifications, however, does provide a path to design development. If the appropriate prototype tool is used, much of the preliminary work can be transformed into the actual models. Various developmental tools also contain screen design components that are so easy to use that they are often used for prototyping as a preliminary to the actual design. Visio, a popular drawing package, is often used to put together quick prototypes for user review. Regardless of the tool used, prototyping usually leads to improvements in the specification of the system (Sommerville, 2001). In a study performed by Gordon and Bieman (1995), 39 different prototype projects were reviewed and the following benefits were found:

Company: XYZ	Date: 9/27/00
Application: Discounting	Supersedes:
Subject: Discounting Plan	Author: A. Langer
Process: Functional Business Spec	Page: 2 of 2

Year-End Reconciliation:

The XYZ discount is guaranteed at the starting discount level. Therefore, should the bookstore not meet last year's order level, the discount cannot be lowered during the year. The only time the discount can be lowered is at the end of the year. At year-end, a process runs, which re-evaluates all the customers based on the current year's and last year's sales. This procedure is only used to create the new level for next year.

> *Although this looks like an overview, it is focused solely on a subprocess called Discounts.*

Screens & Reports:

The order entry screen and all customer inquiry screens need to display the current Book and Bible discount for these customers. The amount used to determine the discount should be available on a customer inquiry screen as well as a report. The current system displays the month-to-date, current quarter, and current year's sales, as well as last year's sales. Total net sales and returns are listed, as well as net sales and returns of the discount items.

Chain Stores:

Another major difference between this plan and others is that for chain stores, all sales for each branch store are added together, and they all receive the discount based on the total net sales for the chain. There can be situations where one of the branches does not qualify to receive the discount, but their sales are still added into the total for the chain.

If two stores become a chain mid-year, their individual annual net sales are added together, and their discount is increased if applicable.

Figure 3.7 Functional business specification.

1. Improved system usability
2. A closer match of the system to end-user needs
3. Improved quality in design
4. Better maintainability of the screens
5. Reduced time to develop

Screen Prototyping

Prototyped screens address navigation, content, and utility (Dalgleish, 2000). There are two basic approaches to showing prototype screens: storyboard and screen painting. Storyboards show users the level of interfacing between functions and screens. They are typically drawn by hand and show a flow of screens that illustrate how the "story" will occur, depending on the options the user selects. Therefore, storyboards provide rough depictions of how the screens can be used to navigate through the system. They represent an easy way to test ideas with the user community before spending a signifi-cant amount of time with polished screen shots that may not have captured what the users were expecting. Figure 3.8 shows an example of a hand-developed storyboard. Storyboards are also called *paper comps* (Powell, 2000).

Screen painting, on the other hand, shows a more functional and polished prototype, but still does not include most of the page graphics. Using screen painting, the ana-lyst/designer creates a digital composite that shows an example of the symbols that will be used on the site. These symbols are usually involved in navigation of the system, con-tent of information, and any utility type functions (link displays, pop-up windows, etc.). Figure 3.9 reflects a screen painting composite.

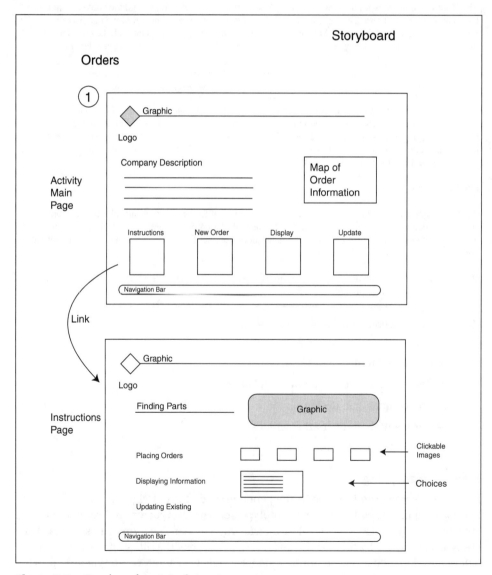

Figure 3.8 Storyboard prototyping.

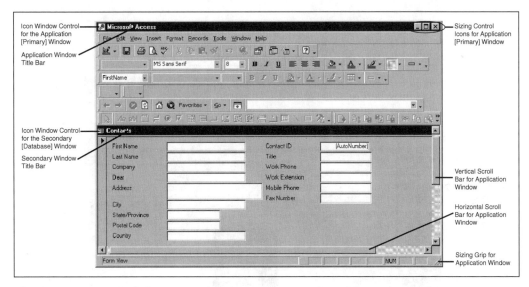

Figure 3.9   Screen painting composite.

Depending on the complexity of the screens, it may be advisable to add to the proto-types some of the data entry and display graphics that are standard in the graphic user interface (GUI). These include check boxes, drop-down menus, and grids. Figure 3.10 shows the various GUI screen features for entering and displaying data.

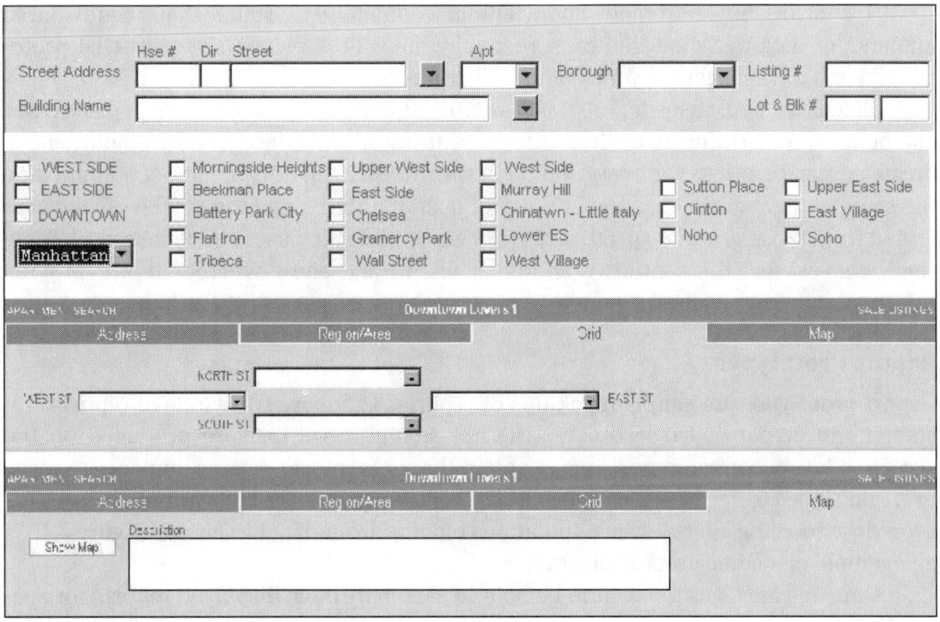

Figure 3.10   GUI component controls.

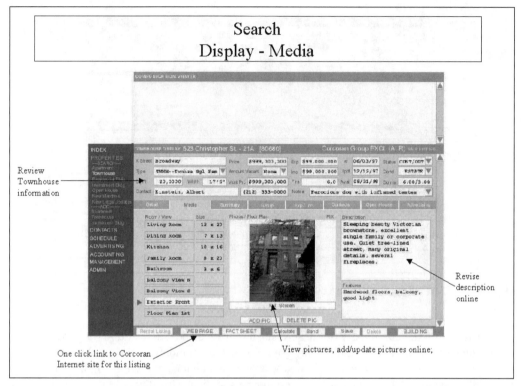

Figure 3.11   Web-GUI control prototype screens.

GUI controls are extremely important in ecommerce systems that require large amounts of data to be entered on screens. Figure 3.11 depicts Web-based GUI prototypes that show navigation, utility, and GUI controls.

As discussed by Dalgleish (2000) in *Customer Effective Web-sites*, screen prototypes can be used to show users critical "slices" of the system. Indeed, it may be difficult to create screen paintings for every screen in the system. The critical slice "could include the search entry screens, customer entry of search criteria, and the search results generated from those criteria" (p. 60). This process would show users how the search function behaves, test their intuitive ability to use it, and show whether it will provide information in the required manner.

Report Prototypes

Report prototypes are simply mock-ups of reports. There are two kinds of reports: on-screen and on-paper. On-screen reports are simply those that are produced on the screen. While on-screen reports may contain the same information as on-paper reports, users may need to see how the report looks on the screen, including various features for browsing, zooming, and view manipulation (moving around in the report). Figure 3.12 is an example of a screen report prototype.

In some instances users want to be able to search through displayed reports for specific information. In these situations, having reports display on screen is more appropriate than on-paper reports. However, paper reports are still more traditional and

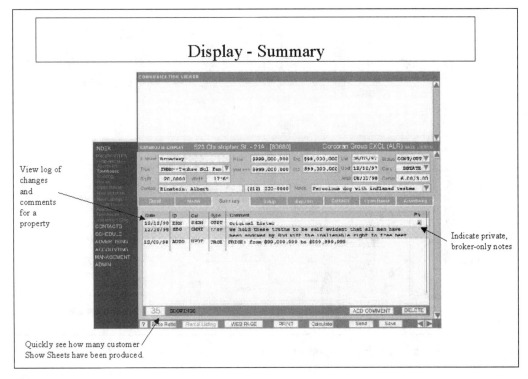

Figure 3.12 Screen report prototype.

require a sample output so that users can concur on columns, subtotals, totals, and summary formats. Figure 3.13 represents a standard report layout.

Summary

This section has provided the user component portion of the application specification. It contained three essential pieces that need to be developed by the ecommerce ana-

Run Date: mm/dd/yyyy Period Covered: mm/dd/yyyy			Report Title: XXXXXXXXXXXXXXXXXXXXXX		Page ___ of _____
Date	ID	Category	Type	Comment	Last Update Date
mm/dd/yyy	xxxxx	99999	xxxxxxxxxxxx	xxxxxxxxxxxxxxxxxxxxxxxxxxxxxxx	mm/dd/yyyy

Key: x: alphanumeric field
9: numeric
mm: month
dd: day
yyyy: year

Figure 3.13 Printed report prototype.

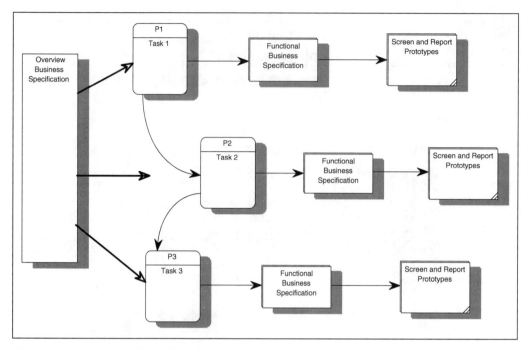

Figure 3.14 User specification component.

lyst/designer as a result of the interview interfaces described in Chapter 2. The first tool is a high-level flow diagram, or PFD, and is used to diagram sequentially each task in the user's business environment or unit. Each PFD has one overview business specification that describes the process. Each task within the PFD maps to a functional business specification that articulates the process of that task. Tasks may contain screen and report prototypes that provide users with a visual depiction of how the screens will appear and how navigation through the system will occur. Prototype reports reflect both screen output options and paper printouts. The user specification components and their interrelationships are shown in Figure 3.14.

Obtaining user acceptance of the user component will most likely be an iterative process. Meetings will result, as changes need to be made to the business specification until the user community can agree to agree on the specification. Upon acceptance of the user specification, ecommerce analysts and designers need to transform the user segment of the specification into the engineering or technical specification. This process is analogous to the process the architect uses to transform the homebuyer's needs into a blueprint for the builder. This next specification component is called the Programmer or Technical Specification.

Programmer Specifications

The programmer specification must contain the technical definitions and algorithms that the ecommerce software programmers need to develop the system. It is the blueprint of the technical requirements that are derived from the business specification.

Programmer specifications must "reconcile" back to the user specifications that were authorized from the user interview sessions. Therefore, the programmer specifications will use the PFD, the business specification, and the prototypes as the basis for developing this blueprint. The method of moving from a higher-level analysis to a more detailed, less ambiguous, technical design is known as *functional decomposition*.

Functional Decomposition and the LE

The most critical step in producing a programmer specification is the understanding of the process of functional decomposition. *Functional decomposition* is the method of systematically obtaining the most basic parts of an ecommerce system, similar to defining all the components of a camera or a television. Once the builder is knowledgeable about each part, then the camera or television can be built. Functional decomposition identifies the parts that make up the whole. A person cannot engineer a camera just by looking at one; it is necessary to take it apart and see how its components fit and work together. Developing ecommerce software is no different. The user specification represents a picture of the camera or television; functional decomposition will provide the detailed components that are required to build it. Thus, the output of functional decomposition is the LE of the system.

The following is an example comparing functional decomposition to a mathematical process. The example shows how functional decomposition is accomplished through the use of tools that can be used as mathematical formulae to derive decomposed components of the original object. In the example, "derive" relates to the use of a mathematical construct called long division—a tool that most of us learned in grammar school to decompose a mathematical problem.

```
      256  remainder 4    } Result or Answer
  5 )1284                 } Problem to solve
     10
     284
     25                   } Formula applied to produce
     34                       result or answer
     30
      4
```

This example reflects what happens when the formula of long division is applied to the problem. The process of long division provides the answer, and if the problem itself is changed, then reapplying the formula of long division will generate a new result. Another interesting aspect of long division is its self-documentation. That is, the steps followed in the formula represent the documentation of how the result was obtained. This means that if someone wanted to understand how the result was achieved, or questioned the result itself, the steps that were followed are self-evident and can be reviewed to see if indeed an error was made. Furthermore, the long division example is a "living" document. If an amount is changed, the problem is changed and the mathematician reapplies the same formula and updates the result. Finally, the answer to the division problem, in many ways, simply provides another view of the same information, and this result is somewhat decomposed.

Following this concept, then, each component of the user specification must undergo functional decomposition, breaking it down mathematically to smaller components and representing these components in an unambiguous blueprint for Web programmers. The decomposition, to be consistent with long division, must be self-documenting, so that errors or modifications to the rules can be clearly demonstrated and reconciled.

Decomposing PFDs

The PFD was defined earlier in this chapter as a sequential flow tool that depicted a user-defined task in a business or unit flow. Each PFD task must now be decomposed down to its processing components or subevents. In order to accomplish functional decomposition of PFDs, another tool called a data flow diagram (DFD) must be used. A DFD is similar in construct to a PFD. Like a PFD, a DFD reflects process, flow, inputs, and outputs. Unlike a PFD, a DFD defines the data to be used and stored; it is not concerned with sequence but rather with the flow and boundary of a particular component of a task. It also is an engineering tool that establishes the data elements that need to be used and stored in the system in order for the task to be successful. In effect, the DFD is a technical modeling tool that begins to build the schematic of the ecommerce system. Figure 3.15 reflects the symbols used for the DFD.

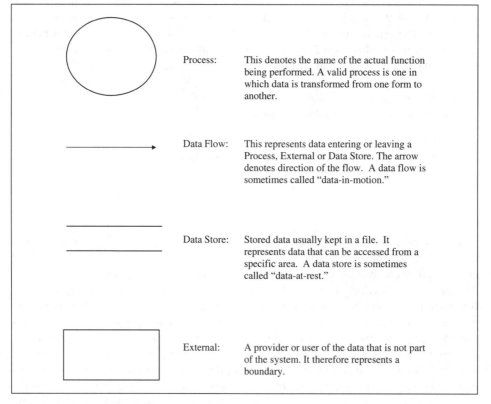

Figure 3.15 DFD symbols.

Therefore, for each task of the PFD, there must be DFDs that depict each event within a task. An event within a task can be determined by creating a DFD that has one input and one output. This is accomplished using the example from Figure 3.4 using the task called Check Inventory. Check Inventory has as input an Approved Order. It has three events defined as follows:

1. Access input order, find inventory part number, locate the part in warehouse, and enter order information into Order File.

2. Check inventory level. If enough quantity, issue Pick-List to Shipping.

3. If inventory level not equal to order, then produce Backorder form and send to backorder department.

The above three events are components of the task with each requiring a separate DFD using the following procedure.

1. Draw the bubble for each event.

2. Determine the input and label the input flow to the event.

3. Determine the output and label the output flow from the event, unless it is to a data store. Data store events remain unlabeled.

4. Determine the "processing" items required to complete the process. These are typically data stores that are utilized to provide or store data during the completion of the event.

Based on the above procedure, Figure 3.16 shows the DFD solution for the Check Inventory task. As in long division, the DFD events cumulatively represent the task Check Inventory. Figure 3.16 therefore is a decomposed view of the task representing its core components. Thus, the DFD is a tool that creates components, or is the vehicle to establish software components that will eventually be used as objects in the ecommerce system. This is what is meant by the term *component architecture*.

DFD 1.0 reflects the processing of the order and has an output data store called "Orders." Orders represents the storing of the order in a database. Note that because it is a data store, no label is placed on the data flow to that store. Event 1.0 also interfaces with the Inventory file, which behaves as a "processing" item, and is therefore not considered an output or an input. DFD 2.0 reflects the creation of the Pick-List for forwarding to the Plan Shipment task, and DFD 3.0 shows the movement of data to the Backorder terminator. The three DFDs are now functionally decomposed components of the task and define more detailed information than the PFD. This technical information needs to be used to develop the detailed information that Web programmers need to develop the software. The DFD establishes the first interaction with data. Every labeled data flow must be defined and decomposed to create a list of data elements needed by each event. This data will be stored in an area called the Data Dictionary, which will become the repository of all data that the ecommerce system needs to have stored in databases.

Creating the Data Dictionary

The data dictionary (DD) contains and defines data. As stated earlier, the application specification must address both components of the ecommerce system: process and data. The DD begins the method of defining the data portion of the application specifi-cation. Data can be many different things in many different forms. For the purposes of this book, data is defined as elements, or fields of information, that represent the small-est addressable information in the system. For example, "Social-Security-Number" is a data element or field of data made up of nine numbers from 1 to 9. Being a data element means that the system can access the nine digits by addressing the data as "Social-Secu-rity-Number," or by whatever name it is stored under in the DD. Eventually, the infor-mation stored in the DD will be used to develop the databases that are discussed in

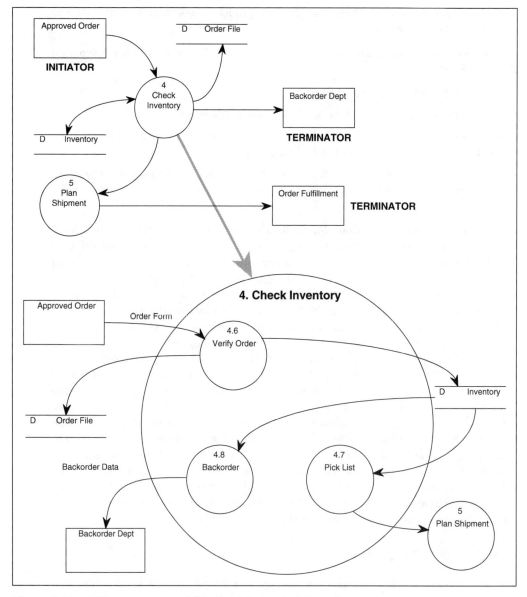

Figure 3.16 DFD components of the Check Inventory PFD task.

Chapter 4. However, it is the process of building the DFDs that initiates the start of the DD, which is the first step in building the ecommerce databases. To better define the creation of data elements in the DD, Figure 3.17 shows a sample order form, which is used by Event 1.0.

Thus, the Order Form flow depicted in DFD Event 1.0 is made up of the data elements shown on the form. These elements must be entered into the DD and defined using SQL definitions. Relational database products that work in conjunction with ecommerce systems define data elements using the construct called Structured Query Language (SQL). SQL was invented by IBM as their standard database query language when they

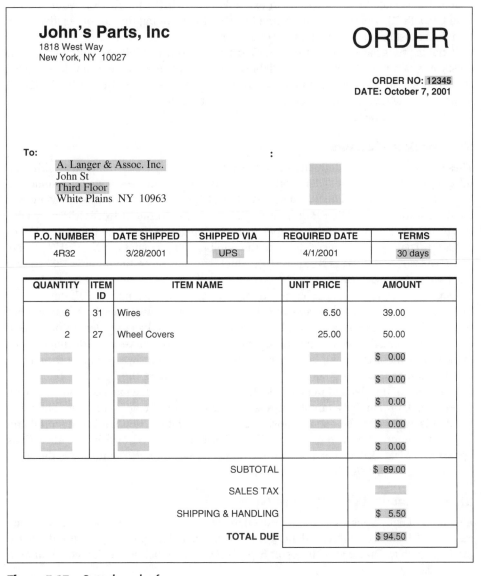

Figure 3.17 Sample order form.

developed the OS/2 operating system. SQL has become the de facto standard in the computer industry; the principal Oracle SQL data types are defined below.

Alphanumeric Data Elements

These data elements are typically either fixed-length or variable-length. They are stored as a string of alphabetic and/or numbers concatenated together. For example, the string "ecommerce" is really nine alphabetic characters stored in succession. Another way of defining a string is to view it as a number of iterations of one character that can either be a number or an alphabetic character, thus the definition "alphanumeric." A fixed-length data type is noted in SQL as CHAR(n), where n is the size of the element. The size is sometimes called the *qualifier*. An example of a CHAR(n) definition would be the field ORDER-ID, which could be defined as CHAR(8), stating that an order identification field must be eight alphanumeric characters.

Variable strings are defined using the VARCHAR2 format. While a VARCHAR format exists, it is rarely used in practice. Variable lengths simply mean a field can store "up to" the string's value, but can also contain fewer characters. Therefore VARCHAR2(40) means that the data element can store up to 40 characters of data, but can also store fewer than 40 characters.

Numeric Data Elements

These data elements are defined as numbers; however, they can be defined as either an integer or as a real number (decimal). Integers, or whole numbers, have no assumed or implied decimal places. The SQL definition for integers can be accomplished using two alternative formats: INTEGER or NUMBER. The integer format is INTEGER(n), where n is the number of digits of the number (e.g., the integer 23 would be defined as INTEGER(2)). The alternate way of defining the number "23" is using the NUMBER clause. The format of NUMBER is NUMBER(n), which will also store the number "23" in two positions or NUMBER(2).

Real numbers contain decimal positions and have two alternative SQL definitions. The first is the NUMBER clause, which is also used for whole numbers. A real number is defined using this format as NUMBER(m,n), where m is the entire length of the real number including the decimal positions, and n is the number of assumed decimal places in the number. For example, a number that contains up to four whole numbers and two decimal numbers would be defined as NUMBER(6,2), where the first digit represents the total size of the element plus two decimal positions, which equal six positions in all. Therefore, n, or *2* in this example, represents the number of places from the total number that is assumed to be decimal positions. The actual decimal point is not stored and does not take up a position in storage. The other notation is NUMERIC. NUMERIC, as opposed to NUMBER, can be used *only* to define a real number. The format is the same except for the word *NUMERIC*.

Other Commonly Used SQL Data Types

A number of data types are commonly used to define special data elements such as time and date. These are powerful data types that are handled internally by the database product, such as Oracle and Microsoft SQL_Server. Listed below are the most common special data types used:

DATE. Defines a valid date. Dates are stored using a four-digit year. The validity of the field value is validated internally by SQL. That is, invalid dates are automatically rejected for the Web developer.

TIME. Defines a valid time using the format hh/mm/ssss, where *hh* is two digits of the hour; *mm* is two digits of the minute; and *ssss* are four digits of the second. This format varies by SQL product.

TIMESTAMP. Defines both the date and the time. This SQL data type stores both the time and day as a string.

FLOAT. Defines the stored value as a floating-point number. The format is FLOAT (n), where *n* represents the size of the field.

The data element list in Table 3.1 reflects the SQL data types and qualifiers from Figure 3.17.

After all of the DFDs have been developed, the application specification will contain a list of all the defined flows and their corresponding data elements. While much of the data has been determined, the data stores contain other elements that need to be fac-

Table 3.1 SQL Data Definitions for Sample Order Form

DATA ELEMENT	SQL FORMAT
Vendor_Invoice_Number	Number (5)
Vendor_Invoice_Date	Date
Vendor_Invoice_Name	Varchar2 (35)
Vendor_Invoice_Address_Line_1	Varchar2 (25)
Vendor_Invoice_Address_Line_2	Varchar2 (25)
Vendor_Invoice_Address_Line_3	Varchar2 (25)
Vendor_State	Char (2)
Vendor_City	Varchar2 (30)
Vendor_Zip	Varchar2 (9)
Vendor_Salesperson	Varchar2 (20)
PO_Number	Char (4)
Vendor_Date_Shipped	Date
Vendor_Shipped_Via	Varchar2 (10)
Vendor_Required_Date	Date
Vendor_Terms	Number (3)
Item_Quantity	Number (5)
Item_Description	Varchar2 (30)

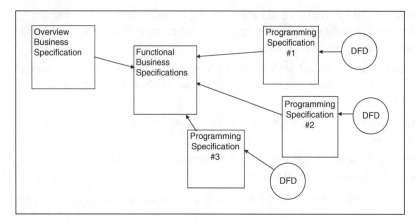

Figure 3.18   Interrelationships of the technical specification.

tored into the design of the specification. The process to complete the DD and create the databases is called Logic Data Modeling, which will be addressed in Chapter 4.

Decomposing Business Specifications

The next component that needs to undergo functional decomposition is the functional business specifications that were created in the user portion of the application specification. These functional business specifications will be decomposed to map to the DFD events. That is, each DFD event must now point to a technical specification that defines the algorithms and business rules that occur inside the DFD process bubble. The interrelationships of the technical specifications with the business specifications, the PFD, and the DFD are shown in Figure 3.18.

Another way to explain the relationship is to view the process as a series of decompositions that lead to component LEs. That is, an overview business specification can have many functional business specifications, which are defined as tasks in the PFD. Each PFD can have many DFDs, although each must have one technical specification defining its functions and algorithms. Technical specifications, like functional business specifications, should be developed using "logic frames" that guide the analyst/designer in terms of the information required. However, in the technical specification, it is important to specify the actual algorithms or business rules that are responsible for the transformation of data. Sometimes, these algorithms can be very detailed as shown in Figure 3.19.

Pseudocode

The sample technical specification reflects the logic of the DFD using a method called *pseudocode* (false code) or structured English. This method is very regimented in that it requires a solid understanding of how to develop written logic code. There are three major rules that govern such written logic:

- Use of Do While with an Enddo to represent logic that is iterative, that is, repeats in a loop format

Client:	Date: 9/15/00
Application: Contact Management	Supersedes: 9/5/00
Subject: Program Specification Detail	Author: A. Langer
Spec-ID FTCM01 - Add/Modify Screen Processing	Page: 1 of 1

Process Flow Description:
The user will input information in the top form. At a minimum, at least the Last Name or Contact ID
will be entered. The system must check a Security indicator prior to allowing a user to modify a
Contact. The Security will be by Department or Everyone. Therefore, if the Modify button is selected
and the user is restricted by a different department, Display:
          "Access Denied, not eligible to modify, Department Restriction"

Do While More Contacts
     If Security authorized, the Add/Modify button will activate the following business rules:

          If Contact-ID (cntid) not blank
                    Find match and replace entered data into record
                    If no match display "Invalid Contact-ID" and refresh cursor

          If Contact-ID (cntid) Blank and Last-Name (cntlname) Blank then
                    Display " Contact-ID or Last-Name must be entered"
                    Place Cursor at Contact-ID (cntid) entry.

          If Contact-ID (cntid) Blank and Last-Name (cntlname) + First-Name (cntfname) is Duplicate
                    Display Window to show matches so that user can determine if contact already in system
                    If user selects the Add Anyway button
                              assume new contact with same name and assign new Contact-ID (cntid)
                    else
                              upon selection bring in existing data and close window.
          Else
                    Create new record with all new information fields and assign Contact-ID (cntid)

          If Company button activated
                    Prompt user for Company-ID (cmpcd) and/or Company-Name (cmpna)
                    If duplicate
                              link foreign-key pointer to matched company
                    else
                              add Company-Name (cntcmpna) to Contact Table only
                              Display "You must use Company Screen to Link, Company Master File Not
                              Updated"
Enddo

ftcm01.doc rev. 8/22/00   Copyright © A. Langer & Assoc., Inc 2001

Figure 3.19 Sample technical specification.

- Use of If-Then-Else to show conditional logic testing
- Use of specific statements that initialize variables, data elements, and other detail
  processing requirements (Move, Print, Save, etc.)

The major advantage of using pseudocode is its completeness and control. The analyst/designer needs to think through the logic in order to develop the code. This can be useful in circumstances where the efficiency and talent of the Web programmers are in question. An example of the use of pseudocode is shown below and represents the technical specification for DFD Event 1.0 from Figure 3.4.

```
Do While more Approved Orders
     Insert new Order to Orders File
     If Order_Part_Number = Inventory_Part_Number then
     If Inventory_Part_Number_Quantity greater than or equal to
Order_Part_Number_Quantity then
             Add Order to Pick_List
             Move "S" to Order Status_Code
             Subtract Order_Part_Number_Quantity from
Inventory_Part_Number_Quantity
             Send to Plan-Shipment Task
     Else
             Move "B" to Order Status_Code
             Send to Backorder Task
     Endif
     Endif
Enddo
End
```

The drawback of pseudocode is that it is very detailed and time-consuming. Furthermore, the analyst must be capable of writing the logic, and it is really not the job of the analyst to be performing this function. In many cases, programmers are insulted because they feel the analyst is doing their job.

Pre-Post Conditions

Pre-Post Conditions is a method that is part of the Use Case methodology under the Unified Modeling Language (UML). This method is much simpler to code than pseudocode. The Pre-Post Conditions have two components: Pre-Conditions and Post-Conditions. Pre-Conditions represent the things that must exist for the logic to work. The Post-Condition defines the required outputs and related calculations that need to take place to provide the correct results. Below is the Pre-Post Condition equivalent to DFD Event 1.0:

```
Pre-Condition 1:
     New Orders Exist
     Plan-Shipment Exists
Post-Condition 1:
     Add Order to Pick-List
     Set Inventory_Part_Number_Quantity less Order_Part_Number_Quantity
     Set Order Status_Code to "S"
     Send to Plan-Shipment Task
Pre-Condition 2:
     New Orders Exist
     Backorder Task Exists
Post-Condition 2:
     Set Order Status_Code to "B"
     Send to Backorder Task
```

As we can see, the Pre-Post Condition specification does not depict how the actual algorithm should be designed or written. It puts more responsibility on the program-

Client: Application: Contact Management Subject: Program Specification Detail Spec-ID FTCM02 - Query	Date 9/15/00 Supersedes: : 9/5/00 Author: A. Langer Page: 1 of 1

Process Flow Description:

Pre-Condition#1

 The user will have the ability to select the Query button after entering information in upper portion of the screen. The Query button will activate a search on the Contact database for matches based on entered information.
 Set Matches

Post-Condition#1

 Display matched records (see screen format) or Display "No Matches Found"

Pre-Condition#2

 Set Matches and User enables Edition buttons
 Select appropriate option for labels or ASCII File creation on matched query records

Post-Condition#2

 User highlights specific match and double-clicks
 Display General and Detail and allow user to activate Modify to make changes

ftcm02.doc rev. 8/22/00   Copyright © A. Langer & Assoc., Inc 2001

Figure 3.20   Pre-Post Condition specification format.

mers to do their job, that is, to design the structure of the program. The benefit of this approach is that the analyst need not be that technical and need not spend significant time in detailing the structure of the program. While the Pre-Post Condition approach is a simpler representation, it is still logical and very organized. It also works nicely within the concept of technical specification frames as shown in Figure 3.20.

Decomposing Screen Prototypes

This section will focus on the design of screen template frames to provide developers and Web page designers with a more detailed understanding of the screen content, structure, navigation, and overall functionality. Using template frames or screen schematics can have multiple benefits. First, it helps Web designers understand the elements on each page so they can appropriately design the pages, understand the ecommerce performance issues, and begin to see the reusable template components that will be used in the entire ecommerce system. These reusable components are typically called *design themes*; they can be pictures, logos, content, or even common functions. While most of this section has concentrated on the internal user, the creation of the template frames begins the process of integrating the needs of the external users of the ecommerce system: customers and consumers. These schematics can be demonstrated to customers before the design is under way and precious time is wasted in the Web design phase. It also allows customers to better see how the system will work for them,

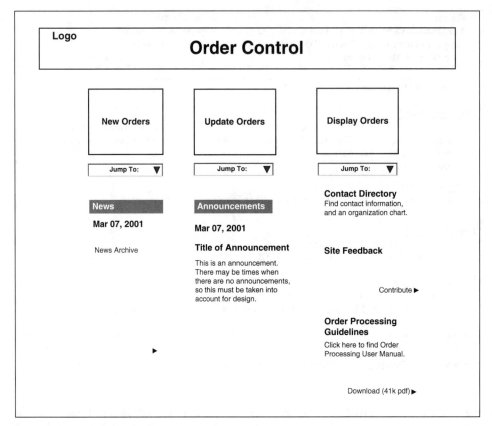

Figure 3.21   Web page template frame schematic.

and add enough vision so they can provide important input. Figure 3.21 is a sample template frame.

Template frames must also reconcile with the data elements that are required for data entry and display purposes. Unlike many commercial Web sites, ecommerce sites often contain the interaction of data that will inevitably enter the internal system for processing. Therefore, part of the template frames should contain an analysis of the data elements that are actually part of the processing of the information. In other words, the Web page serves as the vehicle to capture and display information, which inherently needs to be defined. Figure 3.22 is an example of a Screen Processing Specification that provides information relating to the definitions of several GUI button functions on a Web site.

Furthermore, every data element (now defined in the data dictionary) must be referenced in a specification so that the Web programmer can understand how it will be used in relation to a particular Web page session. Figure 3.23 is an example of a Screen Data Element Definition.

Certain screens will display what is known as "derived" data elements. These are elements that may not be stored in the database because they are results of calculations, solely for the purposes of display or reporting. Figure 3.24 shows an example of a screen

Client:	Date: 2/28/01
Application: Vendor Expense Allocation	Supersedes: 12/28//00
Process: Screen Processing	Author: A. Langer

Description & Source:

This screen allows for the entry of expenses and other pertinent information about vendors. The screen can also be executed in edit mode and allows users to browse sequentially by Vendor. The screen allows for up to three (3) expense allocations. The expense allocation is used to calculate the ELC (see Item-1)

ANALYSIS OF SCREEN FUNCTIONS

Button Function:	Process Definition:
Select Vendor	Locates a particular vendor to add or edit information.
Next Vend	Displays next sequential Vendor stored in the database
Previous Item	Displays previous Vendor in database
Save	Saves contents of screen to database
Clear	Clears screen values (only in Add New Item mode)
Exit	Cancel execution of screen program and display calling screen

Figure 3.22 Screen processing specification.

data element definition for a derived element called Estimated Landing Cost. Note that the actual calculation is defined. It is important not to confuse these definitions with those in the technical business specification. Those algorithms are part of the internal processing within the DFD. The screen specification is simply limited to how the data is entered, displayed, or calculated within the functional DFD.

Thus, every user screen prototype must be translated to another level of detail. Not only does the template frame provide more detail for external users, it also provides the necessary components to start the Web design process, which is the first step to developing the entire site architecture, and then moving into artistic design. This procedure will be covered in Chapter 5.

Client:	Date: 12/28/00
Application: **Vendor Expense Allocation**	Supersedes:

Process:
    Screen Data Element Definition
	Author:
	    A. Langer

Data Element:
    Vendor
	SQL Data Type and Qualifier
	    Varchar18

Description:
This element represents the Vendor Name. Vendors can be created only from Unisys. Therefore, they may be assigned to only for further editing with respect to expenses and other important specific information. The changes do not update the Unisys system.

ANALYSIS OF DATA ELEMENT

Values:
Value is assigned from Advanced Selection button.

Definition:
Search/Select from table. New Vendor may not be added. Entry required.

✓	Data Element Action	Table Action	Name / Value
✓	ADDED	Assign from Vendor table	Vendor_No
	DELETED		
✓	MODIFIED	Assign from Vendor table	Vendor_No

Copyright A. Langer 1994-2000
Form xxxd01

Figure 3.23   Screen data element definition.

Decomposing Report Prototypes

The procedure for creating report specifications is to determine how reports are to be produced. For example, display reports on screens can be delivered using a number of methods. First, database query programs can be written to go directly to the back-end data to produce reports. In these cases, the SQL product will automatically format the output for the analyst. When using query programs, screen manipulation is somewhat tricky, in that the analyst must provide specific instructions on how to scroll and view the reports. The second method relates to report-writer software such as Crystal Reports, which also uses SQL as the basis of selection, but contains many advanced features that allow developers to format their output reports on the screen or on paper. With products like Crystal Reports, scrolling options and format controls are not as critical, since these options are built into the report-writer. The third and most popular Web viewer is Acrobat, which allows reports to be viewed as PDFs (Portable Document

Client:	Date: 12/28/00
Application: **Vendor Expense Allocation**	Supersedes:

Process:
    Screen data element definition
	Author:
	    A. Langer

Data Element:
    ELC Season
	SQL Data Type and Qualifier
	    Number 15,2

Description:
This element represents the calculated Estimated Landing Costs Season-to-Date.

ANALYSIS OF DATA ELEMENT

Values:
Must be calculated from all ELC from Vendor items season to date.

Definition:
Calculated field IMP_ELC_SN. Add all Item ELCs for Vendor for season. See Item-Ent.

✓	Data Element Action	Table Action	Name / Value
	ADDED	Add	
	DELETED	Delete	
	MODIFIED	Modify:	

Copyright A. Langer 1994-01
Form xxxd01

Figure 3.24   Derived screen data element definition.

Files). Products like Adobe Acrobat have extensive "Reader" software that allows users to view, search, and print reports. Formatting of reports, scroll functions, and page breaks become irrelevant in the design of such output. Most important, PDF files do not need separate processes for screen display and paper output.

Reusable Specifications

The concept of reuse relates to the object paradigm. The application specifications discussed in this chapter relate specifically to analysis based on process. We have provided a mechanism and procedure to interview users and depict how they define their processes. The tools, then, have been designed to provide the architecture to replicate the LE of what these users do and want. During the process of functional decomposition, we find that a number of DFD events can be combined to form reusable components. Reusable components are simply features and functions that can be embedded into many different processes because their functionality is replicated in many different places. Think of a reusable component as a part in a car that can be used in other cars. We discover these reusable components during the process of functional decomposition. These components, from a concrete perspective, usually surface as "utility" type functions, like saving a file, or updating account information. However, reusable components have a larger and more important role to play. Components are "cohesive," meaning that they contain all of the information and processes necessary to complete a task or group of tasks. As a result of their cohesiveness, they are more maintainable because they are more self-reliant. Thus, a change to a component typically does not necessitate a change to other components, which has been a long-standing dilemma in data processing. Have you ever heard someone complaining that "the programmers made a change to the system, and now another application appears to be affected"?

Reusable components are designed using a model called Classes. Classes are an abstraction of the concrete model of objects. Thus, classes are what analysts need to design, so that they can be programmed and executed as objects in the system. Classes have two main components: Process and Data. Recall that earlier we have seen that all software is made up of the same two components. Therefore, a class, in effect, is a system within a system. A class can be used in many other systems, even those outside the target ecommerce software. In class design, processes are called *methods*, and data is called *attributes*. Methods represent the DFD events and the attributes are defined as the data that these DFDs need in order to accomplish their tasks. The process of how methods control the data is called *encapsulation*—the way to get to the data or attributes is only accomplished through the method. Therefore, it is the method, not the data, that is the focus of reusability in software. Figure 3.25 is an example of a class structure.

The Order class depicts all of the functions or methods that can be used with orders. Note that the class contains methods that create an order, update an order, read-only or display an order, and delete an order. These four methods control all possible ways to utilize Order information. The four methods spell the word *CRUD* (Create, Read,

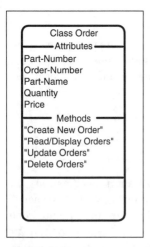

Figure 3.25   Class structure.

Update, and Delete), which is an important concept in object design. Indeed, for a class to be cohesive, the methods must spell CRUD! Based on this approach, DFD event specifications can be joined based on their use of the same data. To put this concept into perspective, an ecommerce analyst would look for all of the event specifications that used the same data, reconcile that its methods can spell CRUD, and then form a reusable class that can be embedded in many different functions, screens, and systems. The attributes are listed based on the cumulative data elements needed by all the methods in the class. The attributes in most object-oriented systems are not stored in the object, but rather linked or mapped to the actual data element, which is stored in the back-end database. Figure 3.26 shows the relationship between DFD events and the formation of an object class.

Note that more than one DFD can be related to a single class. This means that multiple programs can call the same object to provide a specific function. The maintenance of the Order processing should be evident. Should a new attribute be added, or a modification made to a method relating to Orders, only the Order class needs to be modified. Once that has occurred, future executions (called instances) of the Order object will automatically contain the changes. This is a major benefit over older technologies, where changes to the same data or processes would need to be propagated across many programs. In essence, this is the whole benefit of the reuse paradigm. The Web programming team will do much of the ultimate object design; however, class design should be the role of the ecommerce analyst. Thus, one of the parallel outputs of the

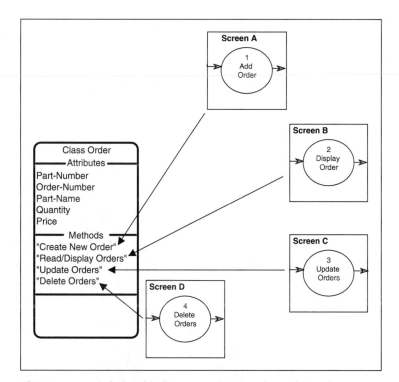

Figure 3.26   Relationship between a DFD and an Object class.

application specification process is Object class identification. I mentioned in Chapter 1 that there are two life-cycle approaches. Until we looked at Object classes in this section, we had been using the waterfall life cycle, which was defined as a step-by-step sequential process. Class definitions and completion are parallel to this process, and their maturity is usually never complete and certainly not limited to the life cycle of the ecommerce system. Rather, it keeps maturing in a spiral, as depicted in Chapter 1.

Designing Databases to Support Web Applications

Chapter 3 focused on application specifications as they relate to process. Using DFDs, I showed how data elements are defined in the DD. However, the process of completing the DD and building complex relational databases has further steps. This chapter focuses on how to design databases for use with ecommerce Web applications. The completion of the DD and the creation of the database schematic, called the *Entity Relational Diagram*, provide developers with the data architecture component of the system. We call the process of creating this architecture *Logic Data Modeling*. The process of logic data modeling not only defines the architecture but it also provides the construct for the actual database, often called the *physical database*. The physical database differs from its logical counterpart in that it is subject to the rules and formats of the database product that will be used to implement the system. This means that if Oracle is used to implement the logical schema, the database must conform to the specific proprietary formats that Oracle requires. Thus, the logical model provides the first step in planning for the physical implementation. First we will examine the process of building the appropriate schematic.

Logic Data Modeling

Logic Data Modeling (LDM) is a method that examines a particular data entity and determines what data elements need to be associated with it. There are a number of procedures, some mathematically based, to determine how and what the analyst needs to do. Therefore, LDM only focuses on the stored data with the intent to design what can be defined as the "engine" of the system. Often this engine is called the *back end*. The design of the engine must be independent from the process and must be based on the rules of data definition theory. Listed below are the eight suggested steps to build the database blueprint. This blueprint is typically called the *schema*, which is defined as a logical view of the database.

1. Identify data entities.
2. Select primary and alternate keys.
3. Determine key business rules.
4. Apply normalization to third-normal form.
5. Combine user views.
6. Integrate with existing data models (e.g., legacy interfaces).
7. Determine domains and triggering operations.
8. De-normalize as appropriate.

Prior to providing concrete examples, it is necessary to define the database terms used in this chapter. Below are the key concepts and definitions.

Entity. An object of interest about which data can be collected. Larson and Larson (2000) define an entity as "a representation of a real-world person, event, or concept." For example, in an ecommerce application, customers, products, and suppliers might be entities. The chapter will provide a method of determining entities from the DFD. An entity can have many data elements associated with it, called *attributes*.

Attribute. Data elements are typically called attributes when they are associated with an entity. These attributes, or cells of an entity, belong to or "depend on" the entity.

Key. A key is an attribute of an entity that uniquely identifies a row. A *row* is defined as a specific record in the database. Therefore, a key is an attribute that has a unique value that no other row or record can have. Typical key attributes are "Social Security Number," "Order Number," etc.

Business rule. This is a rule that is assumed to be true as defined by the business. Business rules govern the way keys and other processes behave within the database.

Normalization. A process that eliminates data redundancy and ensures data integrity in a database.

User view. The definition of the data from the perspective of the user. This means that how a data element is used, what its business rules are, and whether it is a key or not, depends largely on the user's definition. It is important that analysts understand that data definitions are not universal.

Domains. This relates to a set of values or limits of occurrences within a data element or attribute of an entity. An example of a domain would be STATE, where there is a domain of 50 acceptable values (e.g., NY, NJ, CA, etc.).

Triggers. These are stored procedures or programs that are activated or *triggered* as a result of an event at the database level. In other words, an event (insert, delete, update) may require that other elements or records be changed. This change would occur by having a program stored by the database product (such as Oracle) automatically execute and update the data.

Cardinality. This concept defines the relationship between two entities. This relationship is constructed based on the number of occurrences or associations that one entity has with another. For example, one customer record could have many order records. In this example, both customer and orders are separate entities.

Legacy systems. These are existing applications that are in operation. Legacy applications sometimes refer to older and less sophisticated applications that need to be interfaced with newer systems or replaced completely (see Chapter 9).

Entity Relational Diagram (ERD). This is a schematic of all the entities and their relationships using cardinal format. An ERD provides the blueprint of the data, or the diagram of the data engine.

Logic Data Modeling Procedures

The first step in LDM is to select the entities that will be used to start the normalization process. If DFDs have been completed in accordance with the procedures outlined in Chapter 3, then all data stores that represent data files become transformed into data entities. This approach offers the major advantage of modeling process before data. If DFDs or some comparable process tool is not used, then analysts must rely on the information they can obtain from the legacy systems, such as existing data files, screens, and reports. Figures 4.1 and 4.2 depict how a data store from a DFD becomes an entity. The data contained in the data store called "Orders" is represented as an actual form containing many data elements (see Figure 4.1). Thus, this example represents a physical form translated into an LE called a data store, which then is transformed again into an entity (see Figure 4.2).

Key Attributes

The next step in LDM is to select the primary and alternate keys. A *primary key* is defined as an attribute that will be used to identify a record or occurrence in an entity. The primary key, like any key attribute, contains a unique value. Often there is more than one attribute in an entity that contains unique values. We call an attribute that can be a primary key a *candidate* key attribute. This simply means that this attribute can serve in the role of the primary key. If there is only one candidate, then there is no issue: That candidate becomes the primary key. In the event that there is more than one candidate attribute, then one must be selected as the primary key, and the others will be called *alternate* or *secondary* key attributes. These alternate key attributes provide benefit in the physical database only. This means that they can be used to identify records in the database as an *alternative* should the primary key not be known. Take the following example. Suppose that an employee entity has two candidate keys: Social-Security-Num-

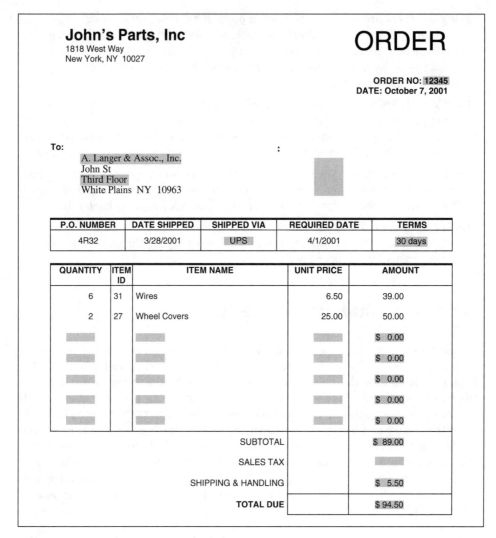

Figure 4.1   Sample customer order form.

ber and Employee-ID. Employee-ID is selected as the primary key, so Social-Security-Number becomes an alternate key. In the logical entity, Social-Security-Number is treated as any other nonkey attribute; however, in the physical database, it can be used (or indexed) to find a record. This could occur when an employee calls to ask someone in Human Resources about accrued vacation time. The Human Resources staff would ask the employee for her Employee-ID. If the employee did not know her Employee-ID, the Human Resources staff could ask for her Social Security Number, and use that information as an alternative way to locate that individual's information. It is important to note that the search on the primary key will be substantially faster, because primary key searches use a method called *direct access*, as opposed to index methods, which are significantly slower. This raises the question: When there are multiple candidate-key attributes, which key attribute should be selected as the primary key? The answer is the

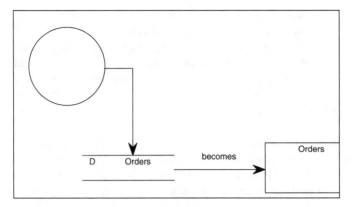

Figure 4.2   Transition of the order data store into an entity.

attribute that will be used most often to find the record. This means that Employee-ID was selected as the primary key attribute because the users determined that it was the field most often used to locate employee information. Therefore, ecommerce analysts must ensure that they ask users this question during the interview process. Figure 4.3 provides a graphic depiction of the employee entity showing Employee-ID as the primary key attribute and Social-Security-Number as a nonkey attribute.

There is another type of key attribute called *foreign* keys. Foreign keys provide a way to link tables and create relationships between them. Since foreign keys are created during the process of Normalization, I will defer discussion about them to the next section on Normalization.

Normalization

Although the next step in LDM is to determine key business rules, it is easier to explain the process of Normalization first. That is, Normalization occurs in practice after Defin-

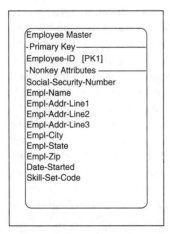

Figure 4.3   Primary key and alternate key attributes.

ing Key Business Rules, but not when introducing the topic for educational purposes. Therefore, Key Business Rules will be discussed after Normalization.

Normalization, without question, is the most important aspect of LDM. As mentioned above, *Normalization* is defined as the elimination of redundancies in an entity and ensures data integrity. It is the latter point that is critical in understanding the value of Normalization in the design of ecommerce database systems. Understanding of the LDM process depends largely on understanding how to implement the Normalization process.

Normalization is constructed in a number of "Normal Forms." While there are five published Normal Forms, Normal Forms 4 and 5 are difficult to implement and most professionals avoid them. Therefore, this book does not discuss Normal Forms 4 and 5. The three Normal Forms of Normalization are listed below. Note that a Normal Form is notated as "NF."

1st NF	No repeating nonkey attributes or group of nonkey attributes
2nd NF	No partial dependencies on a part of a concatenated key attribute
3rd NF	No dependencies of a nonkey attribute on another nonkey attribute

Each Normal Form is dependent on the one before it, that is, the process of completing Normalization is predicated on the sequential satisfaction of the Normal Form preceding it. Normalization can be best explained by providing a detailed example. Using the Order form provided in Figure 4.1, we can start the process of Normalization. Figure 4.4 shows the Logical Equivalent of the Order form in entity format. In this example, the primary key is Order-Number (signified by the "PK" notation), which requires that every order have a unique Order-Number associated with it. It should also be noted that a repeating group made up of five attributes is shown in a separate box. This repeating group of attributes correlates to an area on the Order form, which often is referred to as an order line item. This means that each item associated with the order appears in its own group, namely the item identification, its name, unit price, quantity, and amount. The customer order in Figure 4.1 shows two items associated with the Order-Number 12345.

The process of determining compliance with Normalization is to evaluate whether each normal form or NF has been satisfied. This can be accomplished by testing each NF in turn. Thus, the first question to ask is Are we in 1st NF? The answer is no because of the existence of the repeating attributes: Item-ID, Item-Name, Quantity, Unit-Price, and Amount, or, as specified above, an "order line item." In showing this box, the example exposes the repeating group of items that can be associated with a customer order. Another way of looking at this phenomenon is to see that within the Order, there really is another entity, which has its own key identification. Since there is a repeating group of attributes, there is a 1st NF failure. *Anytime an NF fails or is violated, it results in the creation of another entity.* Whenever there is a 1st NF failure, the new entity will always have as its primary key a concatenated "group" of attributes. This concatenation, or joining of multiple attributes to form a specific value, is composed of the primary key from the original entity (Orders) attached with a new key attribute from the repeating group of elements. The new key must be an attribute that controls the other group of attributes. In this example, the controlling attribute is Item-ID. After the new "key attribute" is determined, it is concatenated with the original key attribute from the

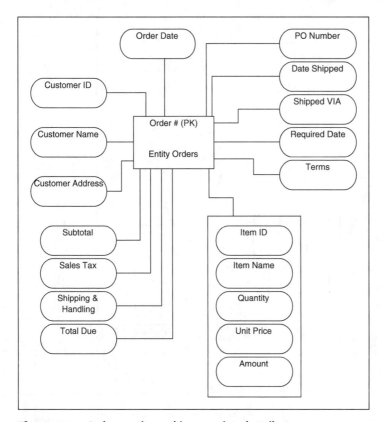

Figure 4.4   Orders entity and its associated attributes.

Orders entity. The remaining nonkey attributes will be removed from the original entity to become nonkey attributes of the new entity. This new entity is shown in Figure 4.5.

The new entity, called Order Items, has a primary key that reflects the concatenation of the original key Order-Number from the entity Orders, combined with Item-ID, which represents the controlling attribute for the repeating group. All of the other repeating attributes have now been transferred to the new entity. The new entity, Order Items, allows the system to store multiple order line items as required. The original entity left without this modification would have limited the number of occurrences of items artificially. For example, if the analyst/designer had defaulted to five groups of order line items, the database would always have five occurrences of the five attributes. If most orders, in reality, had fewer than five items, then significant space would be wasted. More significant is the case where the order has more than five items. In this case, a user would need to split the order into two physical orders so that the extra items could be captured. These two issues are the salient benefits of attaining entities in their 1st NF. Therefore, leaving the entity Order as is would in effect create an integrity problem.

Once the changes to the entity Orders have been completed and the new entity Order Item has been completed, the system is said to be a database in 1st NF. It is important to note that the new primary key of the entity Order Items is the combination of two attributes. While the two attributes maintain their independence as separate fields of data,

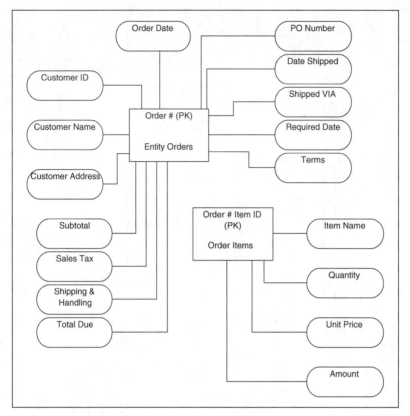

Figure 4.5   Orders in 1st NF.

they are utilized as one combined value for purposes of their role as a key attribute. For example, based on the data in the Order form from Figure 4.1, the entity Order Items would have two records. The first record would have the primary key of 1234531, which would be the concatenation of Order-Number (12345) with Item-ID (31). The second record would be 1234527, which is the same Order-Number, but concatenated with the second Item-ID (27). From an SQL feature perspective, while the key attribute concatenates each attribute into one address, it can be searched as separate fields. So a user could search for all the items associated with Order 12345, simply by searching on Order Items that contain an Order-Number = "12345." This exemplifies the power of versatility in the relational model. Once 1st NF has been reached, the next test must ensue, that is, testing for compliance with 2nd NF.

Second-normal form testing applies *only* to entities that have concatenated keys. Therefore, any entity that is in 1st NF and does not have a concatenated primary key must already be in 2nd NF. In our example, then, the entity "Orders" is already in 2nd NF because it is in 1st NF and does not have a concatenated primary key. The entity Order Items, however, is in a different category. Order Items has a concatenated primary key attribute and must be tested for compliance with 2nd NF. Second NF requires the analyst to ensure that every nonkey attribute in the entity is totally dependent on all components of the primary key, or all of its concatenated attributes. When we apply the test, we find that the attribute "Item-Name" is dependent only on the key attribute "Item-ID." That is, the Order-Number has no effect or control over the name of the item. This condition is considered a 2nd NF failure. Once again, a new entity must be created. The primary key of the new entity is the portion of the concatenated key that controlled the attribute that caused the failure. In other words, Item-ID is the primary key of the new entity, because "Item-Name" was wholly dependent on the attribute "Item-ID." It is worthwhile at this time to further explain the concept of attribute dependency. For one attribute to be dependent on another infers that the controlling attribute's value can change the value of the dependent attribute. Another way of explaining this is to say that the controlling attribute, which must be a key, controls the record. That is, if the Item-ID changes, then we are looking at a different Item Name, because we are looking at a different Item record.

To complete the creation of the new entity, Items, each nonkey attribute in the original entity Order Items must be tested for 2nd NF violation. Note that as a result of this testing, "Quantity" and "Amount" stay in the Order Items entity because they are dependent on both Order-Number and Item-ID. That is, the quantity associated with any given Order Items occurrence is dependent not only on the Item itself, but also the particular order it is associated with. We call this being wholly dependent on the concatenated primary key attribute. Thus, the movement of nonkey attributes is predicated on the testing of each nonkey attribute against the concatenated primary key. The result of this test establishes the three entities shown in Figure 4.6.

The results of implementing 2nd NF reflect that without it, a new Item (or Item-ID) could not have been added to the database without an order. This obviously would have caused major problems. Indeed, the addition of a new Item would have to precede the creation of that Item with a new Order. Therefore, the new entity represents the creation of a separate Item master file.

Figure 4.6 represents Orders in 2nd NF. Once again, we must apply the next test—3rd NF—to complete Normalization. Third NF tests the relationship between two nonkey attributes to ensure that there are no dependencies between them. Indeed, if this dependency were to exist, it would mean that one of the nonkey attributes would, in effect, be a key attribute. Should this occur, the controlling nonkey attribute would become the primary key of the new entity. Testing this against the sample entity reflects that Customer-Name and Customer-Address are dependent on Customer-ID. Customer-Address would normally be composed of three address lines and the existence of City, State, and Zip Code. It has been omitted from this example for simplicity.

Therefore, the entity Orders fails 3rd NF, and a new entity must be created. The primary key of the new entity is the nonkey attribute that controlled the other nonkey attributes; in this case Customer-ID. The new entity is called Customers, and all of the nonkey attributes that depend on Customer-ID are moved to that entity as shown in Figure 4.7.

What is unique about 3rd NF failures is that the new key attribute remains as a nonkey attribute in the original entity (in this case: Orders). The copy of the nonkey attribute Customer-ID is called a foreign key and is created to allow the Order entity and the new Customer entity to have a relationship. A relationship between two entities can exist only if there is at least one common keyed attribute between them. Understanding this concept is crucial to what Normalization is intended to accomplish. Looking at Figure 4.7, one can see that the entity Order and Order Items have a relationship because both

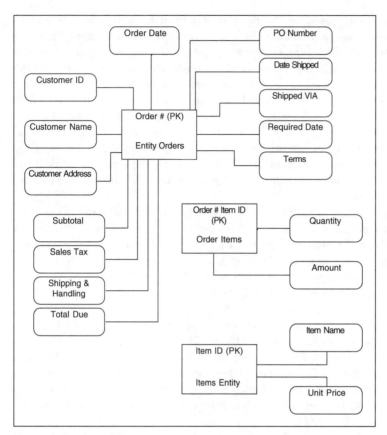

Figure 4.6 Orders in 2nd NF.

entities have a common keyed attribute: Order-ID. The same is true in the creation of the Item entity, which resulted from a 2nd NF failure. The relationship here is between the Order Item entity and the Item entity, where both entities contain the common key attribute Item-ID. Both of these relationships resulted from the *propagation* of a key attribute from the original entity to the newly formed entity during the Normalization process. By propagation, we mean that a pointer, or copy of the key attribute, is placed in the new entity. Propagation is implemented using foreign keys and is a natural result of the process. Note that the "PK" is followed by an "FK," signifying that the keyed attribute is the result of a propagation of the original key attribute. Such is not the case in 3rd NF. If Customer-ID were to be removed from the Orders entity, then the relationship between Orders and Customers would not exist because there would be no common keyed attribute between the two entities. Therefore, in 3rd NF, it is necessary to force the relationship because a natural propagation has not occurred. This is accomplished by creating a pointer from a nonkeyed attribute to the primary keyed copy, in this case Customer-ID. The concept of a pointer is important. Foreign key structures are typically implemented internally in physical databases using indexes. Indexes, or indirect addresses, are a way of maintaining database integrity by ensuring that only one copy of an attribute value is stored. If two copies of Customer-ID were stored, changing one of them could create an integrity problem between Orders and Customers. The

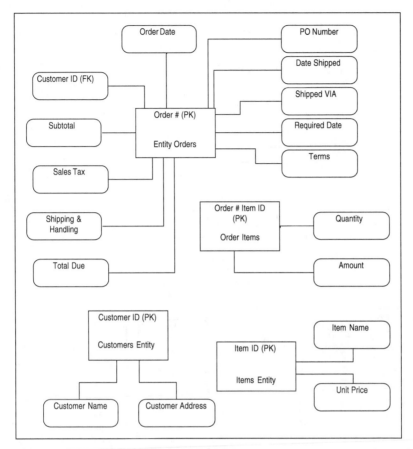

Figure 4.7   Orders in preliminary 3rd NF.

solution is to have the Customer-ID in Orders "point" indirectly to the Customer-ID key attribute in the Customer entity. This ensures that a Customer-ID cannot be added to the Orders entity that does not exist in the Customer master entity.

The question now is whether the entities are in 3rd NF. Upon further review, we see the answer is no! Although it is not intuitively obvious, there are three nonkey attributes that are dependent on other nonkey attributes. This occurs first in the Order Items entity. The nonkey attribute Amount is dependent on the nonkey attribute Quantity. Amount represents the total calculated for each item in the order. It is not only dependent on Quantity, but also dependent on Unit-Price. This occurs frequently in attributes that are calculations. Such attributes are called *derived* elements, and are eliminated from the database. Indeed, if we store Quantity and Unit-Price, Amount can be calculated separately as opposed to being stored as a separate attribute. Storing the calculation would also cause integrity problems. For example, what would happen if the quantity or unit price were to change? The database would have to recalculate the change and update the Amount attribute. While this can be accomplished, and will be discussed later in this chapter, it can be problematic to maintain in the database and can cause performance problems in production ecommerce systems. The Orders entity also contains two derived attributes: Subtotal and Total-Due. Again, both of these attributes

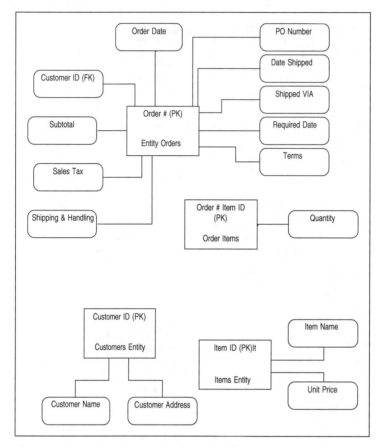

Figure 4.8   Orders in second phase of 3rd NF.

are removed. The issue is whether the removal of derived attributes should be seen as a
3rd NF failure. C. J. Date (2000) views these failures as outside of 3rd NF, but in my view
they represent indirect dependencies on other nonkey attributes and should be
included as part of the 3rd NF test. In any case, we all agree that derived elements should
be removed in the process of LDM. The 3rd NF LDM is modified to reflect the removal of
these three attributes as shown in Figure 4.8.

Once 3rd NF is reached, the analyst should create the Entity Relational Diagram,
which will show the relationships or connections among the entities. The relationship
between entities is established through associations. Associations define the cardinality of the relationship using what is known as the Crow's Foot Method as shown in Figure 4.9.

The Crow's Foot Method is only one of many formats. The method contains three key
symbols:

<   denotes the cardinality of many occurrences

○   denotes zero occurrences

| denotes one occurrence

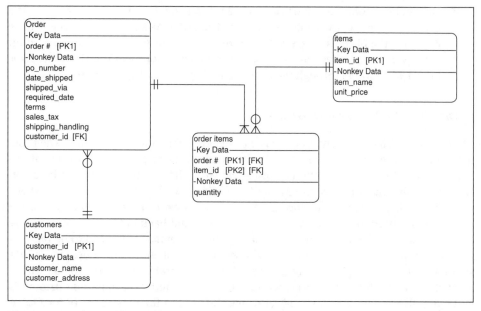

Figure 4.9 The entities in ERD format using Crow's Feet.

Therefore, the ERD in Figure 4.9 depicts the relationships of all the entities as follows:

1. One and only one (signified by the double lines) Order record can have one to many Order Item records. It also shows that any Order in the Order Items entity must exist in the Order entity.

2. One and only one Item record can have zero to many Order Item records. The difference in this relationship and the one established between Orders and Order Items is that Items may not have a relationship with Order Items, signified by the zero in the Crow's Foot. This would often occur when there is a new item that has not yet received any orders.

3. The Order Items entity has a primary key, which is a concatenation of two other primary keys: Order-ID from the Orders entity, and Item-ID from the Items entity. This type of relationship is said to be an "associative" relationship because the entity has been created as a result of a relational problem. This relational problem exists because the Order entity has a "many-to-many" relationship with the Items entity. Thus the 1st NF failure, which created the associative entity Order Items, is really the result of a "many-to-many" situation. A many-to-many relationship violates Normalization because it causes significant problems with SQL coding. Therefore, whenever a many-to-many relationship occurs between two entities, an associative entity is created that will have as its primary key the concatenation of the two primary keys from each entity. Thus, associative entities make many-to-many relationships into two one-to-many relationships so that SQL can work properly during search routines. Associative entities are usually represented with a diamond-shaped box.

4. One and only one Customer can have zero-to-many Orders, also showing that a Customer may exist who has never placed an order. As an example, this would be critical if the business were credit cards, where consumers can obtain a credit card even though they have not made a purchase. Note that the Customer-ID is linked with Orders through the use of a nonkey foreign key attribute.

Limitations of Normalization

Although 3rd NF has been attained, there is a major problem with the model. The problem relates to the attribute Unit-Price in the Items entity. Should the Unit-Price of any Item change, then the calculation of historical Order Item purchases would be incorrect. Remember that the attribute Amount was eliminated because it was a derived element. This might suggest that Normalization does not work properly! Such is not the case. First we need to evaluate whether putting Amount back in the ERD would solve the problem. If the Unit-Price were to change, then Amount would need to be recalculated *before* it was done. While this might seem reasonable, it really does not offer a solution to the problem, just a way around it. The actual problem has little to do with the attribute Amount, but more to do with a missing attribute. The missing attribute is Order-Item-Unit-Price, which would represent the price at the time of the order. Order-Item-Unit-Price is dependent on both the Order and the Item and therefore would become a nonkey attribute in the Order Items entity (i.e., it is wholly dependent on the entire concatenated primary key). The only relationship between Unit-Price and Order-Item-Unit-Price is at the time the order is entered into the system. In this situation, an application program would move the value or amount of the Unit-Price attribute into the Order-Item-Unit-Price attribute. Thereafter, there is no relationship between the two attributes. Because this is a new data element that has been discovered during Normalization, it must be entered into the Data Dictionary. Thus, a limitation of Normalization is that it cannot normalize what it does not have; it can normalize only the attributes that are presented to the formula. However, the limitation of Normalization is also an advantage: The process can help the analyst recognize that a data element is missing. Therefore, Normalization is a data-based tool that the analyst can use to reach the Logical Equivalent. Figure 4.10 shows the final ERD with the addition of Order-Item-Unit-Price.

The Supertype/Subtype Model

A troublesome database issue occurs in the LDM when there are records within an entity that can take on different characteristics or have many "types" of attributes. *Type* means that a portion of the attributes in a specific record can vary depending on the characteristic or identification of the row within that entity. Another way of defining type is to describe it as a group of attributes within a given record that are different from other records of the same entity, depending on the *type* of record it represents. This type is referred to as a "subtype" of the record. A *subtype*, therefore, is the portion of the record that deviates from the standard or "supertype" part of the record. The supertype portion is always the same among all the records in the entity. In other words, the *supertype* represents the global part of the attributes in an entity. The diagram in Figure 4.11 depicts the supertype/subtype relationship.

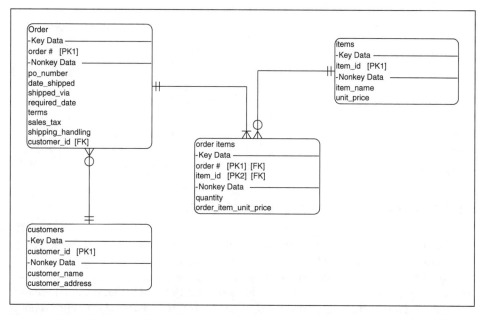

Figure 4.10   Final ERD with Order-Item-Unit-Price.

The difference between a subtype and an ordinary type identifier (using a foreign key) is the occurrence of at least one nonkey attribute that exists only in that subtype record. The major reason to create a supertype/subtype relationship is the occurrence of multiple permutations of these unique attributes that exist in just certain subtype records. Limiting these permutations of attributes within one record format can be problematic. First, it can waste storage, especially if each subtype has significant numbers of unique attributes. Second, it can create significant performance problems particularly with the querying of data. Using Figure 4.11, we can see two ways to store this data. The first (see Figure 4.12) is a basic representation where all the permutations

Rec #	SS #	Last_Name	First_Name	Middle_Init	Type of Educator
1	045-34-2345	Morrison	Ralph	P	High School
2	986-23-7765	Johnson	Janet	L	Professor
3	213-45-3621	Herman	Dan	R	Dean

Rec #	Grade Level	Master's Degree Date	Subject
1	10	5/19/89	History

Rec #	Department	School	PhD Subject
2	Science	Engineering	Chemical Transformation

Rec #	Schools	Total Students	
3	4	5,762	

Figure 4.11   Supertype/subtype relationship.

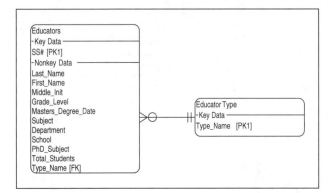

Figure 4.12   Educator ERD using foreign key identifier.

exist in one entity called "Educators." The type of row is identified by using a foreign key pointer to a validation entity called "Educator Type."

Although this representation of the data uses only one entity, it wastes storage space because no one type of record ever needs all of the attributes of the entity. Furthermore, a user must know which attributes need to be entered for a particular type of record. This method of logic data modeling violates the concepts of Normalization, and entrusts the integrity of values of elements in an entity to either an application program's control (stored procedure), or to the memory of the user. Neither of these choices is particularly dependable nor has either choice proven to be a reliable method of data integrity.

On the other hand, Figure 4.13 provides a different solution using the supertype/subtype model.

This model constructs a separate entity for each type of educator, linked via a special notation in the relational model, known as the supertype/subtype relation. The relationship is mutually exclusive, meaning that the supertype entity Educator can have only one of the three subtypes for any given supertype occurrence. Therefore, the relationship of one record in a supertype must be one-to-one with only one subtype. The supertype/subtype model creates a separate subtype entity to carry only the specific attributes unique to its subtype.

There are two major benefits to this entity structure. First, the construct saves storage because it stores only the attributes it needs in each entity. Second, the subtype information can be directly addressed without accessing its related supertype. This is possible because each subtype entity contains the same primary key as its parent. This capability is significant because a user can automatically obtain the unique information from any subtype without having to search first through the supertype entity. This is particularly beneficial when the number of records in each subtype varies significantly. Suppose, for example, there are 6 million educators in the database. The Educator database would therefore contain 6 million rows. Let's say that 5 million of the educators are high school teachers, and as such, the High School subtype entity has 5 million records. There are 800,000 educators who are professors, and the remaining 200,000 educators are deans; therefore, the Professor database and Dean database have 800,000 and 200,000 records, respectively. The supertype/subtype model applications could access each subtype without searching through every record in the database. Furthermore, because access to one subtype does not affect the other, performance is greatly improved.

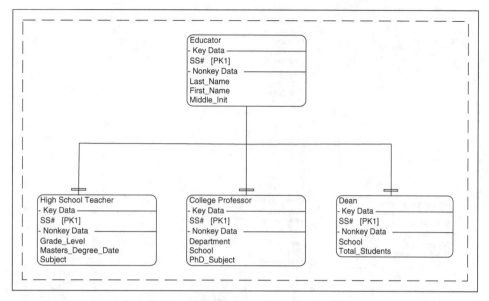

Figure 4.13   Educator entity supertype/subtype model.

It is important to note that the supertype/subtype model is not limited to mutual exclusivity, that is, it can support multiple subtype permutations. For example, suppose an educator was a high school teacher, college professor, and a dean at the same time, or any permutation of the three types. The sample model would then be modified to show separate one-to-one relationships as opposed to the "T" relationship shown in Figure 4.13. The alternative model is represented in Figure 4.14.

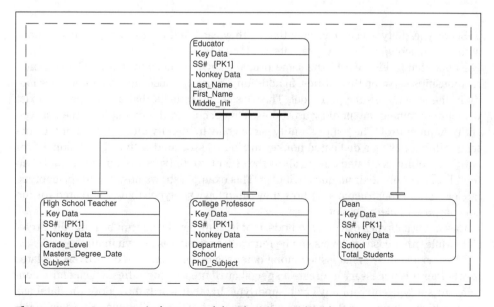

Figure 4.14   Supertype/subtype model without mutual exclusivity.

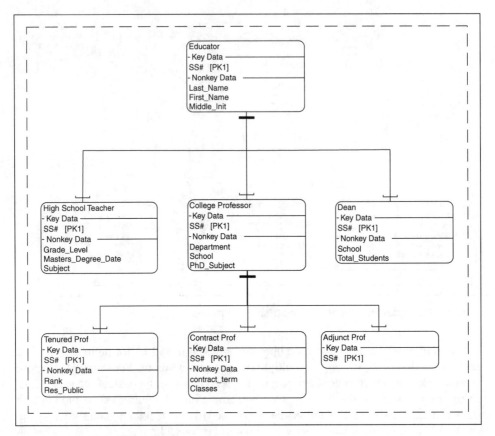

Figure 4.15   Cascading subtypes.

Supertype/subtypes can cascade; that is, they can continue to iterate or decompose within each subtype. This is represented in Figure 4.15.

Notice that in Figure 4.15 the same primary key continues to link the "one-to-one" relationships between the entities. In addition, Figure 4.15 also shows another possibility in the supertype/subtype model. This possibility reflects that a subtype can exist without containing any nonkey attributes. This occurs in the example in the subtype entity Adjunct Prof. The "empty" entity serves only to identify the existence of the subtype, without having a dedicated nonkey attribute associated with it. The Adjunct Prof entity, therefore, is created only to allow the other two subtypes (Tenured Prof and Contract Prof) to store their unique attributes. This example shows how supertype/subtype models can be constructed, and how they often have subtypes that are created for the sole purpose of identification.

Cascading subtypes can mix methods, that is, some levels may not be mutually exclusive, while other cascade levels can be mutually exclusive as shown in Figure 4.16.

There is a controversial issue among database developers. The controversy relates to whether it is necessary to create a special attribute that identifies which entity contains the subtype entry for any given supertype. In other words, how does the database know which subtype has the continuation information? This dilemma is especially rel-

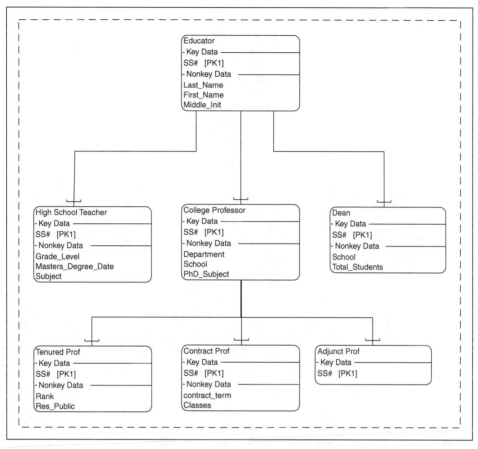

Figure 4.16 Cascading subtypes with alternating exclusivities.

evant when mutually exclusive relationships exist in the supertype/subtype. The question is ultimately whether the supertype/subtype model needs to contain an identifier attribute that knows which subtype holds the continuation record, or is the issue resolved by the physical database product? Fleming and von Halle (1989) addressed this issue in the *Handbook of Database Design*. The Handbook of Relational Database Design, Addison-Wesley, New York. where they suggest that the "attribute is at least partially redundant because its meaning already is conveyed by the existence of category or subtype relationships" (p. 162). Still, the issue of redundancy may vary among physical database products. Therefore, I suggest that the logical model contain a subtype identifier for mutually exclusive supertype/subtype relationships as shown in Figure 4.17. Note that the above example has the subtype identifier Professor Types as a validation entity in 3rd NF.

Supertype/subtypes must also be normalized following the rules of Normalization. For example, the subtype Educator Types contains elements that are not in 3rd NF. Attributes Grade_Level and Subject in the subtype entity High School Teacher can be validated using a look-up table. Department, School, and PhD_Subject can also be validated. The resulting 3rd NF ERD is shown in Figure 4.18.

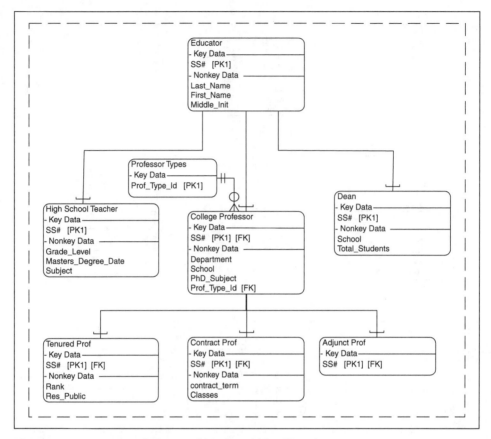

Figure 4.17   Supertype/subtype with subtype identifier element.

Key Business Rules

Key business rules are the rules that govern the behavior between entities when a row is inserted or deleted. These business rules are programmed at the database level using stored procedures and triggers (see the section Logic Data Modeling above). These procedures are typically notated as constraints. *Constraints* enforce the key business rules that will be defined by the analysts and are the basis of what is meant by referential integrity, that is, the integrity based on the relations between tables. The process of insertion and deletion focuses on the relationship between the parent entity and the child entity. A child entity is always the entity that has the Crow's Foot pointing to it. Based on the ERD in Figure 4.10 the parent-child entity relationships are as follows:

- Orders entity is the parent of Order Items entity (child).

- Customer entity is the parent of Orders entity (child).

- Items entity is the parent of Order Items entity (child).

When discussing insertion of a row, it is always from the perspective of the child entity. That is, key business rules governing the insertion of a child record concern what

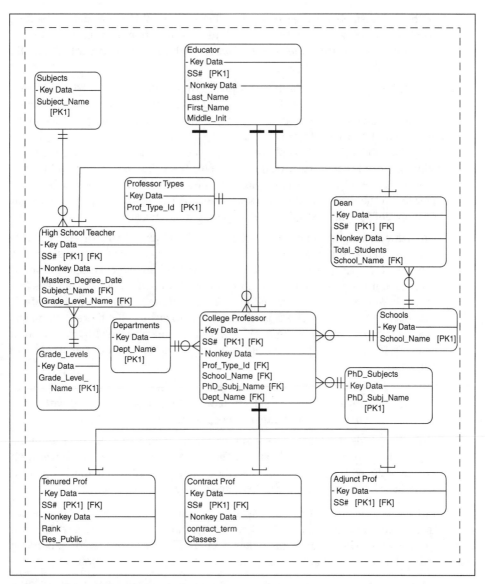

Figure 4.18   Supertype/subtype in 3rd NF.

should be done when attempting to insert a child record that does not have a corresponding parent record. There are six alternatives to the insertion operation:

1. **Not Allowed.** This means that the constraint is to disallow the transaction. For example, in Figure 4.10, a user could not insert an Order Item (child) for an Order-Number that did not exist in the Orders entity (parent). Essentially, the integrity of the reference would be upheld, until the Order-Number in the Orders entity was inserted first.

2. **Add Parent.** This means that if the parent key does not exist, it will be added at the same time. Using Figure 4.10, this would mean that the user would be prompted to

add the Order-Number to the Orders entity before the child Item would be inserted. The difference between Not Allowed and Add Parent is that the user can enter the parent information during the insertion of the child transaction. Using this rule still enforces referential integrity.

3. **Default Value.** The use of a default value allows a "dummy" row to be inserted into the parent. An example of the use of a default occurs when collection agencies receive payments from an unknown person. The parent entity is "Account," and the child entity is "Payments." The Account entity would have a key value called "Unapplied," which would be used whenever an unidentified payment was collected. In this scenario, it is appropriate to have the dummy record because the child transaction is really unknown, but at the same time needs to be recorded in the database. It is also useful because the user can quickly get a list of "unapplied" payments and it upholds referential integrity.

4. **Algorithm.** An algorithm is an "intelligent" default value. Using the same example as (3), suppose the user wanted to track unapplied payments by state. For example, if an unapplied payment were received in New York, the parent (Account entity) would have a record inserted with a value "Unapplied-New York." Therefore, each state would have its own default. There are also default keys that are based on sophisticated algorithms to ensure that there is an understanding to the selection of the parent's key attribute value. Again, this selection ensures referential integrity because a record is inserted at both the parent and child entities.

5. **Null.** Assigning a null means that the parent does not exist. Most database products such as Oracle allow such selection, and while it is maintained within the product, it violates referential integrity because the parent is unknown.

6. **Don't Care.** This essentially says that the user is willing to accept that referential integrity does not exist in the database. The user will tell you that they never wish to balance the records in the child with those in the parent. While this happens, it should be avoided, because it creates a system without integrity.

When discussing deletion of a row, it is always from the perspective of the parent entity. That is, key business rules governing the deletion of a parent record concern what should be done when attempting to delete a parent record that has corresponding child records. There are similarly six alternatives to the deletion operation:

1. **Not Allowed**. This means that the constraint is to disallow the deletion of the parent record. In other words if there are children records, the user cannot delete the parent. For example, in Figure 4.10, a user could not delete an Order (parent) if there were corresponding records in the Order Items entity (child). This action would require the user first to delete all of the Order Items or children records before allowing the parent Order to be deleted.

2. **Delete All.** This is also known as *cascading*, because the system would automatically delete all child associations with the parent entity. Using the same example as (1), the children records in Order Items would automatically be deleted. While this option ensures referential integrity, it can be dangerous because it might delete records that are otherwise important to keep.

3. **Default Value.** The use of a default value is the same as in insertion; that is, it allows a "dummy" row to be inserted into the parent. This means that the original parent is deleted, and the child records are redirected to some default value row in the parent entity. This is sometimes useful when there are many old parent records, such as old part-numbers, that are cluttering up the parent database. If keeping the child records is still important, they can be redirected to a default parent row, such as "Old Part-Number."

4. **Algorithm.** The use of the algorithm is the same as with an insertion. As in the case of (3) above, the default value might be based on the type of product or year it became obsolete.

5. **Null.** As in the case of insertion, the assigning of a null means that the parent does not exist. This creates a situation where the child records become "orphans." Referential integrity is lost.

6. **Don't Care.** This is the same as an insertion. The database allows parent records to be deleted without checking to see if there are corresponding child records in another entity. This also results in losing referential integrity and creates "orphans."

In summary, key business rules are concerned with the behavior of primary keys during insert and delete operations. There are six alternative options within each operation (insert and delete). Four of the options uphold referential integrity, which is defined as the dependability of the relationships between items of data. Data integrity is an issue any time there is change to data, which in ecommerce systems will be frequent. Thus, the ecommerce analyst must ensure that once primary keys have been determined, it is of vital importance that users are interviewed regarding their referential integrity needs. Analysts should not make these decisions in a vacuum and need to present the advantages of referential integrity appropriately to users so that they can make intelligent and well-informed decisions.

This discussion of key business rules was predicated on using examples derived from the discussion on Normalization. As discussed earlier in this section, the application of Normalization occurs after the determination of key business rules, especially since it may indeed affect the design of the ERD, and in the programming of stored procedures. This will be discussed further in the Determining Domains and Triggering Operations section later in this chapter.

Combining User Views

The application of Normalization focused on breaking up or decomposing entities to include the correct placement of data. Each NF failure resulted in creating a new entity; however, there are situations where certain entities may need to be combined. This section is labeled "Combining User Views" because the meaning of data is strongly dependent on how the user defines a data element. Unfortunately, there are circumstances where data elements are called different things and defined differently by different users in different departments. The word *different* is critical to the example. In cases where we think we have two entities, we may, in fact, have only one. Therefore, the process of combining user views typically results in joining two or more entities as

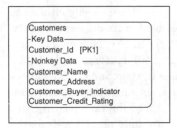

```
Clients
-Key Data ─────────────
Client_Id   [PK1]
-Nonkey Data ──────────
Client_Name
Client_Address
Client_Age
Client_Quality_Indicator
```

Figure 4.19   The Client entity.

opposed to decomposing them as done with Normalization. The best way to understand this concept is to recall the earlier discussion on Logical Equivalents. This interpretation of the Logical Equivalent will focus on the data rather than the process. Suppose there are two entities created from two different departments. The first department defines the elements for an entity called "Clients" as shown in Figure 4.19.

The second department defines an entity called "Customers" as shown in Figure 4.20.

On closer analysis and review of the data element definitions, it becomes apparent that the two departments are looking at the same object. Notwithstanding whether the entity is named Client or Customer, these entities must be combined. The process of combining two or more entities is not as simple as it might sound. In the two examples, there are data elements that are the same with different names, and there are unique data elements in each entity. Each department is unaware of the other's view of the same data, and, by applying logical equivalencies, the following single entity results, as shown in Figure 4.21.

This example uses names that made it easier for an analyst to know they were the same data elements. In reality, such may not be the case, especially when working with legacy systems. In legacy systems, names and definitions of elements can vary significantly among departments and applications. Furthermore, the data definitions can vary significantly. Suppose Client is defined as VARCHAR2(35) and Customer as VARCHAR2(20). The solution is to take the larger definition. In still other scenarios, one element could be defined as alphanumeric, and the other numeric. In these circumstances the decisions become more involved with user conversations. In either situation, it is important that the data elements do get combined and that users agree to agree. In cases where user agreement is difficult, then analysts can take advantage of a data dictionary feature called Alias. An *Alias* is defined as an alternative name for a data element. Multiple Aliases can point to the same data dictionary entry. Therefore, screens

```
Customers
-Key Data───────────────
Customer_Id   [PK1]
-Nonkey Data ──────────
Customer_Name
Customer_Address
Customer_Buyer_Indicator
Customer_Credit_Rating
```

Figure 4.20   The Customer entity.

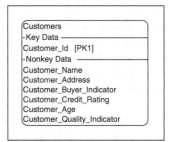

Figure 4.21   Combined Client and Customer entity.

can display names that are Aliases for another element. This alternative can solve many problems when it is necessary to use different names.

Another important issue in combining user views is performance. While analysts should not be overly concerned about performance issues during LDM, it should not be ignored either. Simply put, the fewer entities, the faster the performance; therefore, the least number of entities that can be designed in the ERD the better.

Integration with Existing Data Models

The purpose of this section is to discuss specific analysis and design issues relating to how to integrate with existing database applications. The connectivity with other database systems is difficult. Indeed, many firms approach the situation by phasing each business area over time into a new redeveloped operation. In these circumstances, each phased area needs a "Legacy Link," which allows the "old" applications to work with the new phased-in software. Chapter 9 will focus on the procedures for integration of both the data and application components of ecommerce systems. This section is limited to only those issues that affect the design of entities during LDM.

Linking entities with existing databases may force ecommerce analysts to rethink how to preserve integrity while still maintaining the physical link to other corporate data. This occurrence is a certainty with ecommerce systems given that certain portions of the data are used inside and outside the business. The following example shows how this problem occurs.

The analyst is designing a Web site that utilizes the company's Orders Master database. The Web site needs this information to allow customers to see information about their past orders for items so they can match it to a product database supplied by the ecommerce system. This feature is provided to customers to allow them to understand how items have been utilized to make their products. Unfortunately, the master Order Items database holds only orders for the past year and then stores them offline. There is no desire by the Order department to create a historical tracking system. The ERD in Figure 4.22 shows the relationships with the corporate Order Items database file.

Note that the Order Item Products entity has a one or zero relationship with the Order Item Master entity. This means that there can be an Order Item in the Order Item Product entity that does not exist in the Order Item entity. Not only does this violate Normalization, it also presents a serious integrity problem. For example, if the customer wanted to display information about his or her products and each component Item, all

Items that do not exist in the Order Item entity will display blanks, since there is no corresponding name information in the Order Item file. Obviously this is a flaw in the database design that needs to be corrected. The remedy is to build a subsystem database that will capture all of the Order Items without purging them. This would entail a system that accesses the Order Item database and merges it with the Web version of the file. The merge conversion would compare the two files and update or add new Order items without deleting the old ones. That is, the master Order Items would be searched daily to pick up new Order Items to add to the Web version. Although this is an extra step, it maintains integrity, Normalization, and, most important, the requirement not to modify the original Order Item database. The drawback to this solution is that the Web version may not have up-to-date Order Items information. This will depend on how often records are moved to the Web database. This can be remedied by having a replication feature, where the Web Order Item would be created at the same time as the master version. This will be discussed in greater detail in Chapter 9. The ERD would be reconstructed as shown in Figure 4.23.

In Figure 4.23, the Order Item master and its relation to the Web Order Item entity are shown for informational purposes only. The master Order Item becomes more of an application requirement rather than a permanent part of the ERD. In order to "opera-

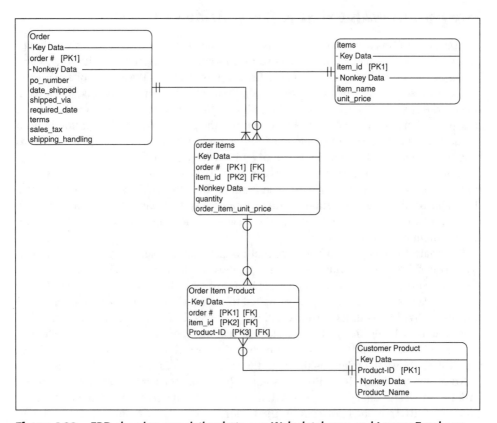

Figure 4.22 ERD showing association between Web databases and Legacy Employee master.

tionalize" this system, the analyst must first reconstruct the history data from the purged files, or simply offer the historical data as of a certain date.

Determining Domains and Triggering Operations

The growth of the relational database model has established processes for storing certain application logic at the database level. We have already defined key business rules as the vehicle to create constraints at the key attribute level. However, there are other constraints and procedures that can occur, depending on the behavior of nonkey attributes. Ultimately, business rules are application logic that is coded in the database language, for example, PL_SQL for Oracle. These nonkey attribute rules could enforce such actions as If CITY is entered, the STATE must also be entered. This type of logic rule used to be enforced at the application level. Unfortunately, using application logic to enforce business rules is inefficient because it requires the code to be replicated in each application program. This process also limits control, in that the relational model allows users to "query" the database directly. Thus, business rules at the database level need to be written only once, and they govern all types of applications, including programs and queries.

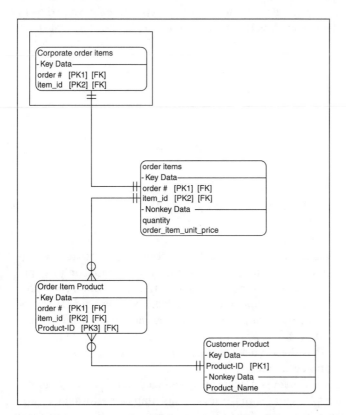

Figure 4.23   ERD reflecting legacy link to the Order Item entity.

As stated earlier, business rules are implemented at the database level via stored procedures. Stored procedures are offered by most database manufacturers, and although they are similar, they are not implemented using the same coding schemes. Therefore, moving stored procedures from one database to another is not trivial. In Chapter 8, the importance of having portable stored procedures and their relationship to partitioning databases across the Internet, Intranets, and wide area networks (WANs) will be discussed further. It is important to note that distributed network systems are being built under the auspices of Client/Server computing and may require communication among many different database vendor systems. If business rules are to be implemented at the database level, the compatibility and transportability of such code become a challenge.

Business rule implementations fall into three categories: Keys, Domains, and Triggers. Key business rules have already been discussed as part of the Normalization process. Domains represent the constraints related to an attribute's range of values. If an attribute (key or nonkey) can have a range of values from 1 to 9, we say that range is the domain value of the attribute. This is very important information to be included and enforced at the database level through a stored procedure for the same reasons as discussed above. The third and most powerful business rule is triggers.

Triggers are defined as stored procedures that when activated "trigger" one or a set of other stored procedures to be executed. Triggers act on other entities, although in many database products, triggers are becoming powerful programming tools to provide significant capabilities at the database level rather than at the application level. Triggers resemble batch type files, which when invoked execute a "script" or set of logical statements as shown below:

```
/* Within D. B.. only authorized users can mark          */
/* ecommerce corporation as confidential                 */

  if user not in ('L','M') then
 :new.corpConfidential :- 'N';
  end if;
end if;
/* Ensure user has right to make a specific users private    */
if exec= 'N' then
  :new.corpexec:= 'N';
end if;
```

This trigger was implemented in a contact management ecommerce system. The trigger is designed to allow corporate information to be marked as confidential only by specific executives. This means that an appointed executive of the corporation can enter information that is private. The second component of the trigger is programmed to automatically ensure that the executive's contacts are stored as private or confidential. These two stored procedures show how application logic executes via Oracle triggers. It is important to remember that these business rules are enforced by the database regardless of how the information is accessed.

Triggers, however, can cause problems. Because triggers can initiate activity among database files, designers must be careful that they do not impair performance. For example, suppose a trigger is written that affects 15 different database files. Should the trigger be initiated during the processing of other critical applications, it could cause significant degradation in processing, and thus affect critical production systems.

The subject of business rules is very broad, yet must be specific to the actual database product to be used. Since analysts may not know which database will ultimately be used, specifications for stored procedures should be developed using the specification formats presented in Chapter 3. This is even more salient in ecommerce systems, given the possibility that different databases can be used across the entire system. This dilemma will be discussed in Chapter 8 as part of the integration issues facing ecommerce analysts and designers.

De-Normalization

Third NF databases can often have difficulty with performance. Specifically, significant numbers of look-up tables, which are actual 3rd NF failures, create too many index links. As a result, while we have reached the integrity needed, performance becomes an unavoidable dilemma. In fact, the more integrity, the less performance. There are a number of ways to deal with the downsides of normalized databases. One is to develop data warehouses and other off-line copies of the database. Data warehousing will be discussed in Chapter 12. Another alternative is to de-normalize. There are many bad ways to de-normalize. Indeed, any de-normalization hurts integrity. But there are two types of de-normalization that can be implemented without significantly hurting the integrity of the data.

The first type of de-normalization is to revisit 3rd NF failures to see if all of the validations are necessary. Third NF failures usually create tables that ensure that entered values are validated against a master list. For example, in Figure 4.10, the Customers entity, created as a result of a 3rd NF failure, provides a validation to all customers associated with an Order. This means that the user cannot assign any customer, but rather only those resident in the Customer entity. The screen to select a Customer would most likely use a "drop-down" menu, which would show all of the valid Customers for selection to the Order. However, there may be look-up tables that are not as critical. For example, zip codes may or may not be validated. Whether zip codes need to be validated depends on the use of zip codes by the users. If they are just used to record a Customer's address, then it may not be necessary or worthwhile to have the zip code validated. If, on the other hand, they are used for certain types of geographic analysis or mailing, then indeed, validation is necessary. This process—the process of reviewing the use and need for a validation table—should occur during the interview process. If this step is left out, then there is a high probability that too many nonkey attributes will contain validation look-up entities that are unnecessary and hurt performance.

The second type of de-normalization is to add back "derived" attributes. While this is not the preferred method, it can be implemented without sacrificing integrity. This can be accomplished by creating triggers that automatically launch a stored procedure to recalculate a derived value when a dependent attribute has been altered. For example, if Amount is calculated based on Quantity * Unit-Price, then two triggers must be developed (one for Quantity and one for Unit-Price), which would recalculate Amount if either Quantity or Unit-Price were changed. While this solves the integrity issue, analysts must be cognizant of the performance conflict should the trigger be initiated during peak processing times. Therefore, there must be a balance between the trigger and when it is allowed to occur.

Summary

This chapter has provided the logical equivalent to the data component of the ecommerce system. The process of decomposing data is accomplished using LDM, which has eight major steps that need to be applied in order to functionally decompose the data. Data Flow Diagrams (DFD) are a powerful tool to use during process analysis because they provide direct input into the LDM method. Specifically, data flows provide data definitions into the data dictionary, which is necessary to complete LDM. Furthermore, data stores in the DFD represent the major entities, which is the first step in LDM. The output of LDM is an ERD, which represents the schematic or blueprint of the database. The ERD shows the relationships among entities and the cardinality of those relationships.

The LDM also makes provisions to develop stored procedures, which are programs developed at the database level. These procedures allow "referential integrity" to be enforced without developing application programs that operate outside the data. Stored procedures can be used to enforce key business rules, domain rules, and triggers. Triggers are batch-oriented programs that automatically execute when a particular condition has occurred at the database level, typically, when an attribute has been altered in some way.

The process of LDM also allows for the de-normalization at the logical design level. This is allowed so that analysts can avoid significant known performance problems before the physical database is completed. De-normalization should occur at the user interface time, as many of the issues will depend on the user's needs.

Designing Web Page Features, Functions, and Interfaces

This chapter builds on the analysis and design of screens that were introduced in Chapter 3. In Chapter 3 we saw that prototypes are part of the process of decomposition. In this chapter we will focus on Web page creative design, another crucial part of the ecommerce system. In addition, this chapter will define the important components of designing effective Web sites—Web sites that represent the mission of their organization. Web design has conventionally been considered an artistic process, outside the traditional analysis and design process. Yet, clearly Web design has a place in the development cycle; the key is to integrate it into the life cycle without destroying its creative identity.

Web designers face significant challenges. Powell (2000) pointed out that many Web sites create visual effects that do nothing more than replicate paper brochures. While these designs rely on sophisticated software, ultimately they do little to establish the brand and identity needed by successful ecommerce systems. Furthermore, attractive design does not necessarily function effectively; to be successful, Web designs must be technically sound. On the other end of the spectrum are Web sites that are too focused on technology and pay little attention to the user experience. The features and functions of these sites tend to be sound, but confusing and complicated to the user. These sites may become so "dressed up" that each function becomes a design in itself. This is sometimes known as "brochureware."

Unlike in more traditional analysis and design projects, users in ecommerce are not designers. Therefore, the job of ecommerce analysts and designers is to translate what users want. Effective Web sites must be useful to their users. Usefulness can be defined as a combination of utility and usability (Grudin, 1992). Utility describes the site's functionality, which ideally meets the user's needs. Usability describes the user's ability to manipulate the site's features in order to accomplish a specific goal.

The Primary Components of Web Design

The essential focus of Web design is *who* will be using the system and *what* features and functions will provide the best experience for the user. There are essentially four component parts to Web design:

1. *Content.* The features that will persuade users on the site
2. *Technology.* Ways to implement the functions of the Web site
3. *Visuals.* Form of the site and its navigation
4. *Purpose.* Economic ramifications for the site's implementation

Figure 5.1 is a graphical depiction of the four components in the form of a pyramid (Powell, 2000). In this picture, content provides the building materials to build the pyramid; the visuals and technology (form and function, respectively) are the foundation of the pyramid, and the economics are the critical factor or purpose for creating the pyramid. For the purposes of this chapter, technology will not be considered part of Web page design, but it will be discussed under the subject of Web integration in Chapter 10. In addition, the economics of Web development are beyond the scope of this book. That is, readers of this book should assume that return-on-investment (ROI) is acceptable for the approval of the project. Therefore, the focus of this chapter will be on two of the four components: Content and Visuals. These two components include the requirements that Web analysts and designers must have in order to create the features, functions, and interfaces of effective ecommerce systems.

Content

Content is a very tricky subject. While content represents the core of the message to be communicated, it must be carefully crafted to accommodate the limitations of user abilities—abilities that become more varied and mysterious outside the controlled internal user base.

Branding

The first component of good content Web design is the process of strategic brand building. Brand building or "branding" has become an important part of how a company shapes the image it projects to a large audience across the Internet. A business's brand can be seen as a set of promises to its customers: for example, Federal Express's "The World on Time," or iSky's "Real Time Customer Care." A brand is also a set of expectations. Successful brands connect to users on an emotional level; Burger King's "Have It Your Way" campaign, for example, seeks to establish emotional connections with their customers. The brand is the cumulative effect of all the interactions a user has with the

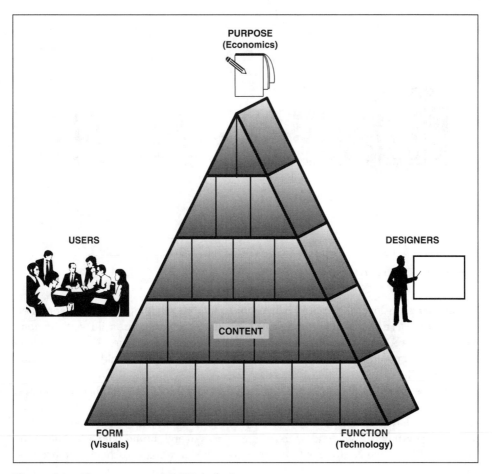

Figure 5.1   The components of Web design.

Source: Web Design (Powell, 2000)

business; it represents a company's personality. Why is branding so important for ecommerce? The answer lies in its ability to reach wide varieties of markets across the Internet. Strong branding is even more important when Internet-based transactions replace personal transactions. What does branding have to do with the analysis and design of ecommerce systems? The answer lies with its contribution to making the ecommerce process attractive to its users. Users may include internal constituents who use the system every day and can receive a strong company brand image from the site. External users—customers and consumers—may be attracted or impressed with the brand image of the business projected on the Web site. Understanding these external users represents a challenge—so the branding exercise becomes a significant part of the Web design process. A well-designed brand on the Web leaves a lasting impression on users, especially customers and consumers. Great Web brands have a consistent look and feel and a high level of design integrity.

Figures 5.2 and 5.3 show two examples of the Web branding created by Thirteen WNET New York. Thirteen is a public television station that recently changed its logo.

Figure 5.2   Old brand logo.

The change in logo gave the Thirteen brand a more contemporary, younger, energetic, and modern feel, while at the same time, upholding the core values of the company and its products. The red three-dimensional sphere dotting the "i" was conceived as an activation point, reminiscent of the Big Apple, and one that could be used to click to the Web site.

Of course, Web branding does not require a firm to rebrand itself or change its image. The Thirteen example serves merely to illustrate that brand elements can exist at many different levels within a firm. A Web site for ecommerce systems should have a brand, which may or may not be identical to the company's overall brand. The branding of the site in relation to the company's brand must be considered during the design process,

Figure 5.3   New brand logo.

Figure 5.4 Thirteen WNET Web site.

and ecommerce analysts and designers need to be part of this process. How do brands affect a Web site? Let's look again at our Thirteen example, but this time at their ecommerce Web site (see Figure 5.4).

Notice that the new logo is visible, but the brand/identity is also used effectively on the site. This is accomplished by using link names such as "explore thirteen," "join thirteen," etc. Thus, in this case, the brand is complemented within the Web site scheme of navigation. This is what we mean by Web site branding.

The Web Branding Process

Too many organizations associate Web branding narrowly with marketing. According to Susan Baston (Vice President and Creative Director at the New York–based Interactive Bureau) "Branding is more the foundation on which to build every experience the customer has with the company." This foundation includes the existing legacy applications or brick-and-mortar parts of the business. Earlier, I stated that ecommerce encompasses *all* of the components of the system. Branding can be broken down to its subcomponents as well. Effective branding for a customer, for instance, may not be the same for internal constituents. It is necessary to operationalize these concepts into a clear, coherent process for analysts/designers to follow.

The User Interface

The first component of the branding process concerns the users. In each interview, certainly in a JAD, ecommerce analysts are encouraged to invite the creative staff to participate, so that they can learn what is important to the user community. Creative staffs may also want to hold their own sessions, but such meetings should be incorporated into the entire project plan and should be attended by analysts. For customers and consumers, market information may be required along with focus group sessions; these sessions must also be integrated with the overall analysis and design process. In sum, the creative work relating to branding really represents the first aspect of Web design, and it must be treated as part of the analysis and design process. In essence, the creative outputs from the user interfaces should be clear graphic branding concepts that

1. Define the user marketplace

2. Define what users want to do on the site

3. Establish the way the Web will provide a method for users to use the firm's products and services

4. Create some excitement and a message for the experience

Care must also be taken that the process does not destroy or dilute the brand recognition that the firm may already have established. It is important that Web brands be allowed to evolve. Evolution is an important concept to relate back to the discussion in Chapter 1 about life cycles. Chapter 1 defined two types of cycles: the waterfall and the spiral. In many ways the user specifications and Web branding match up with both these processes, respectively. For example, the creation of ecommerce user specifications was presented in Chapter 3 as a waterfall type of approach. Each step was clearly laid out sequentially, and in most instances was dependent on its prior step. The Web ecommerce branding, however, more closely resembles the spiral method, which was defined as a never-ending evolving circular process. This process is very similar to evolving identities. The message with Web site design then is simple: The brand must keep redefining itself. This philosophy supports the concept that Web sites need to change or evolve. The design of Web pages should, in some orderly way, constantly change and redefine itself to its users. An example of this approach is The Corcoran Group, a New York City–based real estate firm. Barbara Corcoran, the company's founder and a very visible part of its presence, changes her personal image frequently, and the Web site design changes in concert, as shown in Figures 5.5 and 5.6.

In order to address branding during the interview analysis phase, it is important to ask users what their objectives are for using the ecommerce system. Part of the discussion should focus on the degree to which the user base is concerned with branding versus feature function. Obviously the more "external" the user, the more important branding and image will be in the design of the site. However, internal branding is also important because it makes employees more knowledgeable about the company's image, its mission, and how it wants to be seen by its customers. This all becomes part of the ecommerce design solution.

User Profile Strategy

A user profile strategy is a plan for registering users and collecting information from them that can make their Web experience more personalized (Smith, 2000). Typically this step might be considered part of design and development, but it is arguably more a component of branding because it allows users to define their personal relationship with the company. Care needs to be taken in this evaluation. For example, if your users are leery about supplying personal information, it really means that they are not seeking

Figure 5.5   The Corcoran Group Web site.

Figure 5.6   Updated Corcoran Web site.

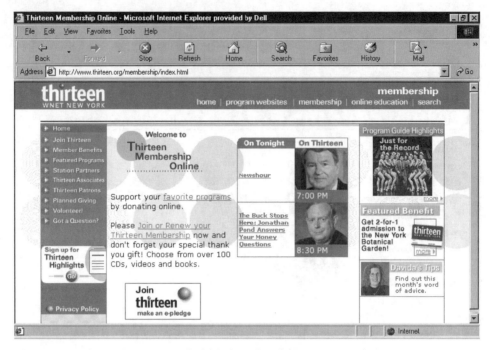

Figure 5.7   Thirteen WNET membership brand Web site.

a personal relationship with the brand. This would not be the case, though, for a business such as Thirteen WNET, which projects its brand and identity to users who may wish to become members. So the "membership branding" is critical to the success of the ecommerce system. Figure 5.7 is an example of the "membership brand" Web page of Thirteen WNET.

Decisions about how brand should affect design should be made during focus groups with external consumers. Therefore, analysts and creative designers need to work together to understand ecommerce Web branding strategies. Profile strategy is another technique that aids the evolution of Web site branding design. Profiles can continually collect information about your user community and can be used to ascertain changes in preference, level of computer sophistication, and the array of preferences and capabilities of the user interfaces that were presented in Chapter 2. Furthermore, profiling substantiates the need to adopt the spiral life cycle, as the process of tracking user brand preferences by using profiles is a constantly evolving process. Given the complexity and sophistication of implementing user profiles, it is wise to start with a simple strategy and build on it. It is easier to go from a simple profile strategy than to undo a complex one that completely misses the mark.

Content Preference

Content and branding seek to make users feel that they see themselves on your Web site. That is, users should feel that they are in the setting that they prefer in interfacing with your business. How can you accomplish this, and how can you deal with users who have alternative preferences? The answer to the first question is to treat branding as part of the analysis phase of the user interface. Customer preferences must drive the

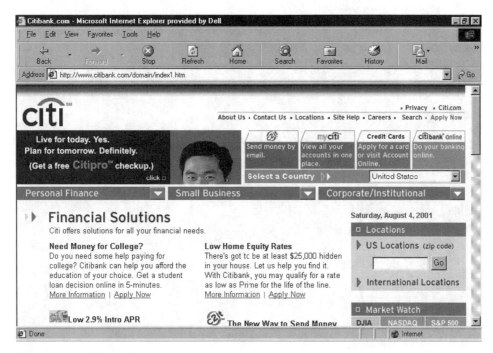

Figure 5.8   Citibank home page.

design decisions made by creative branding professionals. All too often, the brand process is segregated from the application, and the result is a disjointed Web site design. The second question raises another issue: Should a brand attempt to be all things to all users? I believe not, and as a result, it is suggested that your brand be tailored to your most important user base. If the user base is not dominated by any single preference design, then analysts might consider having multiple home pages. This concept was discussed earlier and raises the challenge of maintaining multiple content sites. Another alternative is to pick a type of site that many users can accept, that is, a "middle-of-the-road" style that will alienate no one. Figure 5.8 shows Citibank's home page, designed in an attempt to facilitate many different ecommerce user preferences.

Still another approach is to allow users to modify the site by choosing from a select group of design preferences. Figure 5.9 shows Egomedia's Web site that allows users to customize the site, offering options to change shapes, desktop features, and music.

Web Site Personalization

Personalization is another way to build a brand on the ecommerce system. The goal of personalization is to allow users to feel that they have a special relationship with the business. Personalization adds brand equity because the user feels "valued." An example of personalization is Amazon.com's Web site (see Figure 5.10).

On Amazon's personalized ecommerce site, returning buyers are greeted by name. The site saves a lot of information about the user, such as credit card numbers, shipping address, and prior book preferences. The personalization enables the user's site to cater to their specific preferences and creates a one-to-one relationship between the company and user. This one-on-one can be created through a greeting message and through

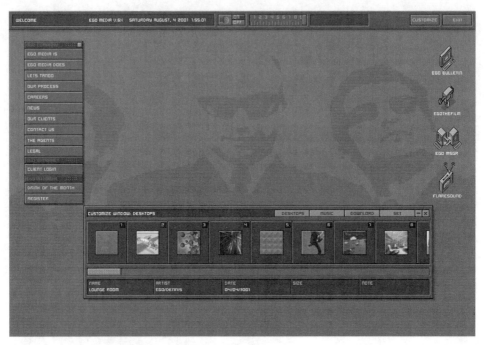

Figure 5.9   Egomedia's Web site customize feature.

Figure 5.10   Amazon.com screen personalization.

suggestions to the user that fit their prior shopping preferences. It also allows the company to "speak" to users in their language, for example, as college kids, as adults, etc. Gender also plays a role in attracting users and branding the Web experience. Once again, analysts should be capturing this information as part of their user requirements documentation, that is, it should appear as a requirement of the system in both the business specifications and technical specifications as presented in Chapter 3.

Furthermore, content "language" is an important factor in creating Web brand. Content language refers to writing style. Writing styles can create comfort for users or insult them. The latter can occur when user content assumes that the customer knows little about the product, or does not recognize users as returning customers. A site that contains too much selling content runs this risk. The process of creating good content requires that skilled copywriters and editors be involved in the analysis and design process. The solution is either to have such personnel attend the interviews (a difficult and time-consuming process) or to have analysts provide writers with information about the style of the content that should be used. In many projects, there is little planning of the written content, and as a result first drafts need to be significantly modified. This type of "hit-and-miss" approach to site content is another reason that ecommerce projects are frequently over budget.

Customer Service

Customer service has always been an important way to develop brand identity. Words associated with customer service are *quality* and *caring*—words that convey an important message to users. Notwithstanding the personalization of the ecommerce system, it is important for ecommerce businesses to convey the same quality and caring to users as brick-and-mortar companies traditionally do. Quality characteristics can be conveyed over the Web by having a dedicated section about how products are made and why they should be considered high quality. Caring can be accomplished by providing customer testimonials and by sending customers messages that (1) thank them for their order, (2) advise them of when they can expect to receive their order, and (3) keep them posted on the status of their order. The easiest way to provide these services is to replicate the procedures in the current business. Unfortunately, this kind of caring is not always easy to transfer from brick-and-mortar situations to ecommerce Web sites. In retail stores, for example, good customer service is often provided by individuals who are especially dedicated to their work. Therefore, it is advisable that reliable ways to provide good customer support be explored during the analysis phase. Some common branding-related customer service options are listed below (Smith, 2000):

- Offer more services for purchasers of higher-margin products
- Provide online support for the most valued customers
- Provide exclusive hot lines
- Offer discounts for customer lifetime value, volume orders, and frequent purchases
- Adjust shipping prices according to volume and frequency of purchase
- Create a special sale area on the site
- Offer advance-purchase opportunities on new products for existing customers

All of the above options create special relationships between the company and its customers. These customers become part of a "preferred" group, and they are treated differently because of their loyalty to the company. The loyalty is an identity that is then presented to the users as a reminder of how important they are to the company.

This section provided a perspective of how Web branding integrates with the process of analysis and design. In a number of cases I stated that the ecommerce analyst should provide or participate with creative personnel during the user interview process. The purpose was to attempt to capture as much about the creative brand vision that users have, as well as the technical feature functions that they need. In order to provide creative staff with this information, it is necessary for analysts to integrate into the business and technical specification sections that are devoted to assisting the creative development of the system. Figure 5.11 summarizes the information that has been discussed above into a sample questionnaire and checklist that can be used during the interview cycles.

Text

What is the role of ecommerce analysts and designers in the creation of text content? Certainly their responsibilities lie outside the actual content itself. Many ecommerce books confuse the issue of who is to create the text content. To clarify this issue is to simply go back to the core definition of analysis and design, which is essentially to create logical equivalents for development. Therefore, ecommerce analysts/designers need to understand how users want the text arranged, categorized, and formatted. There are also architectural issues of how content needs to be maintained. This section sets forth the key components to provide Web developers with what they need to complete the site.

Text Layout

Layout refers to the placement and arrangement of text on the page. This includes text justification (left, center, etc.), columns, and text frames. Layout also has to do with formatting text—for example, bolding, type size, type color, etc.—to highlight important information. Such methods of text contrast work to direct users' interest to the focal point of the page. For example, the center and top part of a page are usually the best places to get a user's attention. Consideration of the focal point also involves repetition—of key design elements and patterns of text. Repetition is important to consider, because users seek to become comfortable with any Web site they use. Consistent layout and formatting can help users begin to feel "at home" on a site.

Text Categorization

Text categorization relates to placement of text. Categorization also focuses on the grouping of text to enable users to find it. Text can be grouped by categories like location, gender, date, time, etc. Such grouping allows users to find relevant information quickly, such as in searching for movie theaters in a specific location. Included in text categorization is the use of search criteria, which allows users to see views of data based on some dynamic sorting of text. One method to determine the proper groups and categorizations is the storyboarding concept. In storyboarding, slides are developed to represent the text that needs to appear on a specific Web page. Having each slide in a

Client:	Date: 2/28/01
Application: Web Branding	Supersedes: 12/28/00
Process: Information Questionnaire	Author: A. Langer

Type of User: Internal _____   Customer: _____   Consumer: _____

User Market: (Briefly Describe)

Expected Length of User Longevity: _____

Number of Users in the Market: _____

What Functions do Users need on this Web Site:

Briefly Describe Why Users will use this Web Site:

What Products and Services do you Plan to Offer:

What Messages, Logos, and Other Information do you want Users to Experience:

How often does the Design and Content need to Change?	**Profile Strategy: Define Information that you plan to obtain from your users**
Daily: _____	Address: _____
Weekly: _____	Age: _____
Monthly: _____	Gender: _____
Quarterly: _____	Computer Experience: _____
Other: _____	Connectivity: _____

Preferences: Describe the audience and the overall goals that you want your users to experience:

Preference Type: Focused: _____   Multiple: _____   General: _____

Personalization Options:
Color: _____
Music: _____
Graphics: _____
Other: _____

Customer Service:

Order Confirmation Message: _____
Messaging: _____
Message Attachment: _____
Selective Email: _____
Order Status: _____

Special Service Offers:
Service Types: _____
Basis of Eligibility: _____
Description:

Figure 5.11   Web branding information questionnaire.

particular order allows analysts, designers, and users to get a better understanding of how the text needs to be viewed and what options need to be available. Storyboarding, which was also utilized in prototyping, can be used during design to determine text placement in relation to graphics. The prototype storyboards that were used in Chapter 3 lack the combination of real text and real graphics, so this step during Web design is really the basis of finalizing the Web page prototypes.

Text Formatting

The formatting of text focuses more on presentation than the other two components. Formatting refers to the methods of screen presentation usually through the use of menus, maps, and frames.

Menus can be defined as single-column lists or multiple-column lists; they can even be designed as tables. Functionally, menus can be used for two purposes: (1) to display information in a hierarchical format, or (2) as a way of linking to other sites from the current Web page. Combinations of the two are also often used, as shown in Figure 5.12 (www.fathom.com). This example shows how a menu of member schools appears when the user places the mouse pointer by the word "Member Institutions." The user can then click on items in the list to go to the sites of the member institution.

While menus are easy to develop, they sometimes can be boring to a user. An alternative format is a map that combines a graphic with text. This is accomplished by placing a cursor over an image. The cursor will eventually display the name of the description in text, which also contains a hyperlink to another Web location. These hyperlink areas are called *hot regions* (Conger and Mason, 1998). Figure 5.13 is an

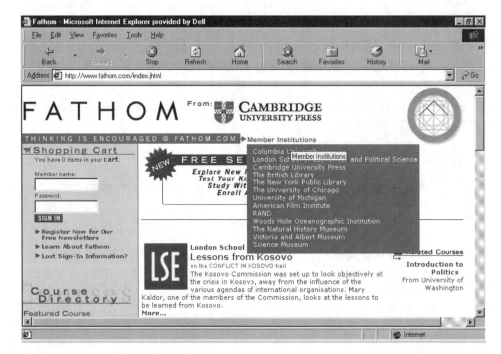

Figure 5.12 Text formatting using menus.

Figure 5.13   Text formatting using maps.

example of how a map is used in the Web site www.cluetrain.com. When the user places the mouse pointer on the book, it displays text that tells the user more about the graphic and allows the user to hyperlink to another Web page.

The problem with maps is that they tend to be very large and can take time to load on the Web page. Because of this dilemma, many Web designers also provide a text-only version on the site, which can add to the complexity of design and incur more development time.

Frames are a way to segregate Web page text into separate windows that can behave independently. These subareas allow certain parts of the Web site to remain visible while the user moves to another screen. Frames are similar to headers or sidebars in printed text. Figure 5.14 shows the site www.alanger.com. The first example shows a screen with a standard header screen and a body section for "Programs at Columbia," which is one of the options in the header menu. The second screen shows the same header frame, with a different body section for "The Firm."

A key benefit of frames is that they can accommodate multiple types of media including graphics and text. They are also easy to display in different browsers and compatible with lower versions of HTML. Another benefit of frames is that they can be used as reusable components. So once the frame has been designed, it can be encapsulated within many screens and even within ecommerce systems. Developers need only employ an engineering tool or program that allows frames to be updated when changes are made. These tools are usually called "content management systems" and will be discussed further in Chapter 13. The disadvantages of frames are that they tend to be small, and they have limited space on each screen. Sometimes the display of a

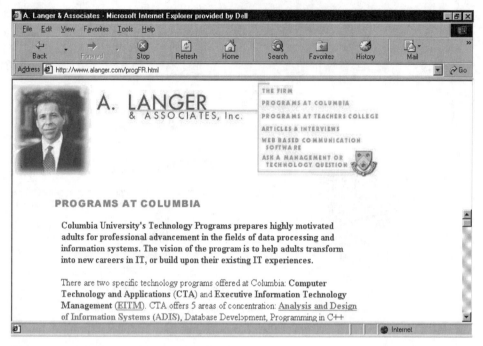

Figure 5.14 Web page formatting using frames.

frame on one Web page may need to be different on another, so formatting frames can be a problem.

Content Templates

I have mentioned briefly that frames can be devised in the form of reusable objects and that there are systems that automate the updating of changes in content. The actual unit of the frame's storage is called a content template. Content templates are objects of text and/or graphics that are stored as separate files, and reused by a Web site. Using content templates reduces the need to reprogram information and graphics that are repeated throughout an ecommerce system. The benefit also relates to maintenance programming. Instead of changing multiple sites, Web developers simply "link" content templates to frames within a Web page. Each time the Web page is loaded, the most current version of the template is loaded. The benefits in maintenance savings must, of course, outweigh the overhead considerations, which affect the load time and storage requirements for the site. The other obstacle in template development recalls the challenge of creating object-oriented systems: the overall effort, scope, and complexity of designing reusable systems. While it sounds easy, it requires the necessary cooperation of skills to develop, especially for ecommerce systems, which have an enormous reach throughout the organization. Finally, an important benefit of content templates relates to good publishing practices; they allow the appropriate personnel to participate in the creation and updating of content, from logos, to text, to graphic images that need consistent presentation for the ecommerce system to be successful. More implementation benefits of content templates will be covered in Chapter 13.

Visuals

A Web site's visual design is often the first thing that users notice (Powell, 2000). Indeed, first impressions are lasting ones, and the impact of visuals will heavily influence a user's perception of a site's value. However, users tend to focus less on visuals as they become more familiar with using a site. There is much written about "take-away value" and "e-loyalty," which are defined as the influences that make users come back to a site. Thus, it is important to focus on the visual effect but also to recognize the site architecture and navigation as important components. Good analysts and designers understand that form is function. Design is not a battle between form and function, but rather the intertwining of them both, as great architects have always known. This section explores the challenge of how to combine great navigation and site architecture with the psychology of visual design.

In order to explore the psychology of design, it is important to agree that for most users, the Web is a visual experience. Because of this reality, there are concepts, moods, and identities that can be portrayed on a Web site through its images. And let us not forget the old saying "You remember 50 percent of what you read, but 100 percent of what you see." However, understanding the visual experience is complex; it includes color, images, and backgrounds. Color must be used properly to convey the appropriate mood and cultural meaning. Images, on the other hand, can be slow to load, a factor that will affect the usability of the Web site. From a usability perspective, background contrast is critical to the way users work with the images and foreground texts. Thus, color, images, and the use of backgrounds all contribute to the success or failure of a Web design.

Color

There are three components that define color:

1. *Hue.* Represents the actual name of the color and refers to the quality itself.
2. *Value.* The degree of the lightness or darkness of the color.
3. *Saturation.* The intensity or purity of the color. The brighter the color, the more saturated it is.

There are also three descriptors of color. First there are chromatic hues, which are all colors other than black, white, and gray. Second are neutral colors, which are black, white, and gray (nonchromatic hues). Third are the monochromatic combinations that represent variations of value and saturation to form a single hue. There are a number of factors relating to how these definitions of color are used in the analysis and design of ecommerce Web sites. The first significant issue is to determine the domain of colors to be supported by your Web site. This decision is directly correlated to the type of browser to be supported. Within a browser is what is known as "safe colors," or colors that are supported by most browsers. This "safe color" also relates to the differences in the hue, saturation, and value that each type of computer and browser might display. What appears as one set of colors on one machine might look different on another computer. Sometimes such variations can affect the mood and experience of the site. In some cases, such as with logo colors, variations can confuse the brand image being presented to the user. From an analysis and design perspective, color selection is a critical step in creating mood. During interviews with users, it is important that they understand the alternatives in selecting colors, especially as they relate to the "safe" domain.

Another important analysis step is defining bit depth. Bit depth controls the number of bits used to display the image on the screen. The number of bits supported by a computer are controlled by its video card and its monitor. Users need to be aware of the type of computers needed to support the color schemes and hues they wish to attain. These issues may result in either changing the color scheme, or in requesting standardized computer interface units. Obviously, if the users are consumers, the probability of knowing this information is limited or based on market research data. In many cases decisions on color support are strategic decisions, that is, an informed decision to force users to bring their computers to a level that allows them to interface with the system. This decision is typically based on whether continuing at a lower or "safer" color level inevitably creates an inferior product. Perhaps the most important decision is to determine the browser-safe limit. The range of colors can vary from 256 or fewer to well over a million. Furthermore, it is important to remember that PCs and Apples have different 256-color match-ups, meaning that one blue may not match the other. In many instances the computer will attempt to "dither" if you go outside the domain of browser-safe colors. *Dithering* is a method that the computer uses to attempt to match the color selected, and it results in speckled or dotted color schemes, not the kind of look that ecommerce systems desire. Ultimately the decision about how to implement the color scheme is up to developers, but analysts should explain to all concerned parties the importance of determining the limit early in the analysis process.

Aside from physical issues and limitations, it is important to understand the meanings that colors convey to users. Colors often have different meanings in different cultures, so analysts need to focus on where the audience is, or how many different audiences will use the ecommerce system. For example, Western cultures associate black with death, but in Japan the color of death is white. On many Web sites, color is used as part of the identity and branding. Table 5.1 lists common themes associated with color.

Furthermore, with advancements in color hand-held devices, issues surrounding color compatibilities are becoming more challenging and provide even more reason to stick within the boundaries of safe colors. However, color alone can be deceiving. The use of contrast, particularly with hand-held devices that support only gray scales, can present another problem when designing Web sites. The more platforms that are supported, the more reason to have separate Web sites to support them. Of course, this means having multiple sites to support one product. Once again, having content templates and reusable components can become very attractive for portable software projects.

Images

Images represent things visually. Effective images convey thoughts, concepts, and identity, with or without supporting text. Meanings can be displayed through images such as a button, a heading, or a graphic caption that helps convey an experience or a message. The difficulty with images is determining which provides the best experience for the user and conveys the message and identity that the company desires. From an architectural perspective, images can be stored in a number of different formats. Some of these formats can affect the file size and compression requirements. File size is a major factor in the time it takes to display an image.

Table 5.1   Common Color Themes

COLOR	THEME
Red	Hot, error, stop, warning, aggression, fire, lushness, daring
Pink	Female, cute, cotton candy
Orange	Warm, autumnal, Halloween
Yellow	Happy, caution, sunny, cheerful, slow down
Brown	Warm, fall, dirty
Green	Envy, pastoral, jealousy, inexperience, fertility, newness
Blue	Peaceful, sadness, water, male
Purple	Royalty, luxury
Black	Evil, death, mourning, ghostly, night, fear
Gray	Overcast, gloom, old age
White	Virginal, clean, innocent, winter, cold

Source: The Complete Web Reference Guide (Powell, 2000)

Analysts also need to determine the image type. There are two basic types of image storage: vector images and bitmapped images. Unless a plug-in is installed on the computer, the Web supports only bitmapped images. Vector images will be discussed in Chapter 6. Bitmapped images are essentially a group of pixels of different colors that combine to form the image. Because of the large number of pixels they contain, bitmaps are usually very large files. There are alternatives to compressing bitmap files, but uncompressing these files wastes more time than is saved by compression. The most popular compression image types are Graphics Interchange Format (GIF) and Joint Photographic Experts Group (JPEG). GIF files are the most widely used on the Web because they work well with large areas of continuous colors. The downside of GIF images is that they support only 8-bit color for a maximum of 256 colors in a given image. Therefore, GIF files may have color loss when displaying true-type images, such as photographs. JPEG, on the other hand, is more suited for working with photographs, particularly those that have many shades of gray. JPEG is not as efficient in compression as GIF and also may display different levels of clarity, depending on the color range on the computer. JPEG also does not provide good quality compression for line drawings or text. Therefore, the basic rule is for analysts to require GIF images for illustrations and JPEG images for photographs.

Backgrounds

The use of backgrounds is a tricky proposition, particularly backgrounds that contain texture. In general, busy backgrounds are not good for Web pages. When a background is desired, it is usually developed with a product like Photoshop, which can generate seamless shapes. The other problem associated with backgrounds is load time. Indeed,

Figure 5.15   Use of background to enhance image.

a background is nothing more than a large image. When using background loads, it is recommended that the software use tiles or sections; this reduces the overall time it takes to display the page.

Effective backgrounds are usually subtle images that convey a message, mood, or identity. For example, Figure 5.15 shows the alanger.com site, which has a background that identifies my association with Columbia University.

Another interesting example of background design is Figure 5.16, which is the site of the Rhode Island School of Design (www.risd.edu). This site shows how background can be integrated with imagery to convey a cultural view of the school.

The other issue with background is contrast with text. One of the problems with the Rhode Island School of Design Web site is the difficulty in seeing the text on the site. The number of images, from this perspective, serves only to clutter the site and make it more difficult for users to get the information they want. This kind of problem leads Web designers back to the original concept of approaching site design: Who are the users?

Web designers will continue to be challenged in handling all of the diverse color, image, and background problems that exist in ecommerce systems. Furthermore, the movement to wireless hand-held devices will create yet another group of difficult decisions that need to be made among users, analysts, and designers. It is important to note that while Web design continues to be an art form, there are very real engineering issues that need to be discussed before the aesthetics of what is delivered to the user's desktop is decided. This is the area in which analysis and design must cooperate with the artistic element.

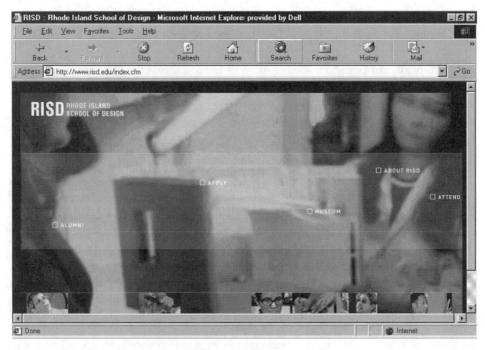

Figure 5.16   Use of background to convey culture.

Web Site Navigation and Architecture

The other important aspect of visual design is the architecture and navigation of the system itself. Indeed, the navigation and use of color, images, and background are inherently related. Navigation can be defined as the science and art of getting people or things from one place to another. While text can be predetermined based on *what* we want to convey to the user community, visuals are strongly influenced by *how* the site is architected. The key components of Web navigation are

- Where am I?
- Where can I go?
- How do I get where I want to go?
- How can I return from where I've gone?

Design of visuals and placement of text will be based on the answers to the above questions. Fleming (1998) offered 10 principles of successful Web navigation:

1. **Be easily learned.** Web navigation must be intuitively obvious to its users.
2. **Remain consistent.** The navigation style should be consistently represented across all Web pages.
3. **Provide feedback.** This involves creating controls that provide information to users to confirm their understanding of an image or option.

4. **Appear in context.** This relates to allowing users to get back to, or to understand where they are on the site, so that the page can direct them to the next possible task that they might want to do.

5. **Offer alternatives.** Provide as many options of things that the user might want to do, without creating a clutter effect.

6. **Require an economy of action and time.** Web designers need to be aware of how long it takes to complete a function or a task.

7. **Provide clear visual messages.** The visual guidance of the site through hierarchies of selections and icons that define functionality.

8. **Use clear and understandable labels.** Common-sense and user-sensitive labels that depict the meaning of a given selection. Terminology must match users.

9. **Be appropriate to the site's purpose.** Create ecommerce systems that meet the goals and objectives of the business. For example, a shopping site will be different from a site created for informational services. Mismatches between a site's purpose and navigational approach can cause user confusion.

10. **Support users' goals and behaviors.** Ensure that the site is what users want it to be, not what you think it should be.

There are no easy solutions to good navigation and site architecture. The real answer lies in the user community, so it is important to explore how ecommerce analysts and designers can formulate the navigation and architecture that will work for users. This challenge, like so many others, must be faced during the user interface phase. One of the best methods of approaching the design of navigation is to categorize the type of site you are planning to deliver. There are six categories of design sites that will assist in the process of determining the style of the navigation and site architecture.

Shopping sites. Focus on serving consumers and deal with issues of trust and security. Areas of concern include the security of financial information, protection of privacy, finding items of interest quickly, assistance for those who are unsure of what they want, preview of products for review, and dealing with problems or returns.

Community sites. These sites need to explore creating shared spaces. Issues of concern are rules of participation, privacy of identity, obtaining feedback, authenticity of information, learning more about users from the community, and getting assistance from the community.

Entertainment sites. Focus on avoiding user distractions and attracting users to immerse themselves in the activities. Issues of concern relate to whether users know where to begin, understanding what will happen, how do they receive help, what practice do users need to have, and how will users know when they are finished.

Identity sites. These sites need to ensure they send the right message to their users, and to create various attractions to get users onto the system. Issues to be addressed relate to knowing about the company, finding out about products, and finding contact information.

Learning sites. Must deal with multiple learning preferences and allow users opportunities to improve their skills. Users of these sites need to know where to begin, what special knowledge they need to have, authenticity of information, obtaining information that is appropriate, and knowing how to experiment.

Information sites. These sites must allow users to find information quickly. Therefore, they employ shortcuts for speed. Issues relating to these users are confirming whether they are on the correct site, finding the specific information they need, helping them look for what they think they want, authenticity and practicality of information, and storing information for later use.

Navigation Placement

A difficult question to answer is Where on a Web site should navigation occur? There are five places to put navigation elements: top, bottom, left, right, and center. As with so many other issues in technology, there are positives and negatives for each placement.

Navigation at the Top

Placing navigation at the top of the screen ensures that users will see it first as a screen loads. Also, as with the Windows paradigm, key navigation menus appear at the top of the screen, so putting navigation capabilities at the top seems consistent and natural to the user. The largest problem with top navigation is that it can disappear off the screen as a user scrolls down. This problem can be addressed by providing navigation links that take users back to the top. A navigation palette can also be used, as in Netscape, which ensures that the palette stays on the screen regardless of which feature is being used. Figure 5.17 depicts the Netscape menu palette on the alanger.com site. Still another option is to provide navigation links at the bottom of the page.

Navigation at the Bottom

In most cases, bottom navigation seems unrealistic since it requires the user to scroll to the bottom first. Not only is this unnatural but it can also be difficult for users to find. Furthermore, it is not in the logical progression of steps to find information. The most significant reason to have bottom navigation is to allow for more important information to be represented at the top of the screen. Not only does this provide more space but it also allows for the company's brand and identity to be more significant than the site's navigation. Bottom navigation can also be effective when the screen is short and scrolling is not an issue. However, it is highly recommended that bottom navigation be avoided for primary tasks.

Navigation at the Left or Right

Left navigation is commonly used and is consistent with the Microsoft Outlook format and has thus become something of a convention for Web designers. When used in conjunction with a frame, left navigation allows users to control the size of the navigation portion and the display portion of the screen. The downside to left navigation is that it does reduce the amount of content that can be displayed between the left and right margins. Furthermore, it precipitates the need to display smaller text and graphics, which can reduce a site's overall attractiveness. Figure 5.18 is an example of left-side navigation design.

Right-side navigation has recently become more popular. Some support it as an easier way for users to see content and then decide on navigation choices. This sequence

Figure 5.17 Use of palette in Netscape browser.

Figure 5.18 Left-side navigation.

conforms somewhat to the Western style of reading from left to right. The other positive aspect of right navigation is that it is close to the right scroll bar, thus limiting mouse distance for the user. As with the other choices, right navigation has its drawbacks. First, it is difficult to know where the right actually occurs because of variances in screen sizes. Second, the benefit with closeness to the mouse can be criticized for not really saving time for users.

Navigation in the Center

Center navigation is usually reserved for home pages, where the page contains "lift-off" navigation links. Center navigation also sets the home page apart from other pages. Figure 5.19 shows the home page of Mercedes-Benz. Note that the center buttons allow the user to select the language they want to use.

Web site pages other than the home page should not have center navigation, especially those that are graphics-heavy; it tends to clutter and confuse the message to the user. Analysts and designers should remember that the center of any Web page is the focal point of the image conveyed to the user community.

Navigation Consistency and Scrolling

Regardless of the position of the navigation, it is important that it be placed consistently across all Web pages. Studies have suggested that consistency is the key to usability. Therefore, elements should reflect stability in position, order, and elements (Powell,

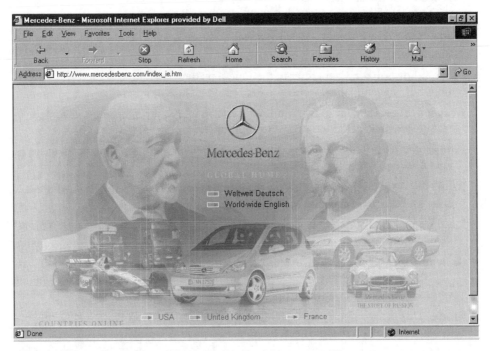

Figure 5.19   Mercedes-Benz center navigation.

2000). Navigation design, then, requires analysts to determine the overall site architecture in order to ensure this consistency before actual design and development occur.

Another debatable issue is whether pages should scroll when navigation elements are involved. Those against scrolling say that the page is more cohesive and better presented to the user. Furthermore, scrolling can be annoying and time-consuming to the user. Proponents suggest that fixed pages limit what can be displayed, and that scrolling is a better alternative than linkage. Whereas scrolling takes time to see, linkage directly inhibits Web performance. Therefore, Web pages with navigation should fit vertically on one screen. This perspective also supports the concept that Web pages are like leaves in a book. Book pages that have folds tend to annoy readers. Finally, scrolling incurs more mouse movement, and there is much being reported about the wear and tear on users who suffer from overextending their wrists and hands during Web site interactions.

Navigation as a Metaphor

Metaphor is a concept that has been used to help people understand things by using symbols, concepts, or words. A metaphor can be an important concept for learning as well as for communication. Technology has for some time used metaphors to provide simpler and more exciting definitions for users: for example, the Internet as the "information highway," or the Web as "cyberspace." Thus, a metaphor allows us to provide our view of the world as we want others to see it—a perfect concept for Web design. The navigation, along with metaphors, can be a significant component of ultimately deciding on the correct strategies and alternatives that have been offered in this chapter. Indeed, metaphors and navigation form the center of creating the kinds of experiences that we want our users to have. According to Dalgleish (2000), site metaphors include:

Lobby. Users are greeted by a virtual representation of a physical lobby they are familiar with.

Personal organizer. Users refer to the functions that a personal organizer performs to use organizational tools on the Web.

Desktop. This is similar to the Windows desktop in that it represents a virtual physical desk with specific tools for different functions.

Folder. A virtual folder is one that keeps data in separate files and allows users to navigate easily through each folder.

Briefcase. The physical act of having a collection of information that is always available. This can be correlated to a collection of information and tools on Web sites.

Shopping cart. The virtual shopping cart collects information as one "shops" through the Web site.

Gallery. Users can browse a virtual space in the same manner as if they were there physically. This is often done with multimedia software to enact a movement within and around a particular space.

Guide. This is a virtual tour through a space, and typically provides advice on particular areas of interest to the user.

Neighborhood. Individuals are collected into a community where they have a role to play or a stake in what occurs.

These metaphors can be classified into three types:

1. Organizational metaphors, which relate to important concepts in the known organization. These metaphors are very useful in the development of internal or Intranet ecommerce systems.
2. Functional metaphors that attempt to match the virtual to the physical functions.
3. Visual metaphors, which virtually leverage from a user's visual recognition of known concepts.

Overall, the concept of metaphor is a fitting conclusion to the section on navigation. Indeed, it is the use of metaphor that allows analysts and designers to relate the physical world to the logical experience. Thus, I again use the concept of the logical equivalence to describe the design of virtual equivalents to what people are accustomed to experiencing. The difference in this case is the aesthetic and creative foundation that is required to provide the same experience, while at the same time creating the brand and image of the business. All this needs to be accomplished through design and navigation and represented in an intuitive, consistent, and organized manner.

Site Architecture

Web navigation needs to be finalized by ultimately developing the site architecture. The site architecture provides the blueprint for the movement from one Web page and site to another. It is the schematic of the Web design. The first purpose of this section is to define the different site organizational models. There are four main logical organizations: *linear*, *grid*, *hierarchy*, and *web*.

Linear

Linear architecture is common because it resembles the way we read a book, that is, it starts and moves forward in a linear fashion. In linear site architecture, users can move from screen to screen without jumping around in some progressive sequence. Linear Web architecture allows for bidirectionality. Figure 5.20 represents the different types of linear models.

Grid

Grid sites use a dual linear structure that provides for both horizontal and vertical relationships between pages. When properly designed, grids provide for orderly movements both vertically and horizontally. While a grid allows for many options in moving around a site, it can be dangerous. Too many vertical and horizontal alternatives can create disjointed Web sites. While grids seem to be appealing, they tend to be too unstructured and often are not useful for good Web navigation designs. Figure 5.21 represents a grid architecture format.

Hierarchy

Hierarchies are one of the most common architecture structures. Indeed, the hierarchy is a visual representation of functional decomposition. In essence, the hierarchical concept is consistent with the way most common Web sites operate. Hierarchical structures are typically called *trees*. The concept of a tree is that as you go down the

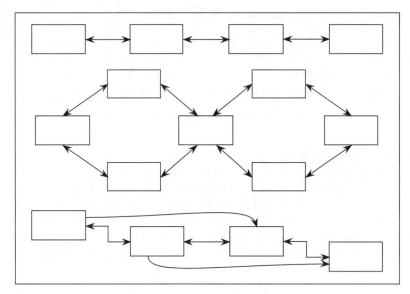

Figure 5.20 Types of linear site organization models.

hierarchy, the number of children or nodes expands, so it becomes wider horizontally. The overall view resembles a physical tree. The other significant feature of a tree is that no node, or child, can have more than one parent. This is an excellent site concept for Web structures because it supports the "only one way back" process. Thus, the movement from a home page to other pages can be very structured and clearly represented; the way back retraces the footsteps without jumping around. Figure 5.22 represents the different types of hierarchy trees that can be designed into the site architecture.

Where there is structure, there can be violations of the pure tree model. This violation is called a "mixed" hierarchy, in which parents can talk directly to grandchildren, thus skipping over a node. Furthermore, nodes or Web pages at the same level, called siblings, can also communicate with each other. While this format is very versatile, it typically leads to similar problems as does the grid. Too much versatility destroys structure, and without structure there can be no order. Figure 5.23 is an example of a mixed or unstructured hierarchy.

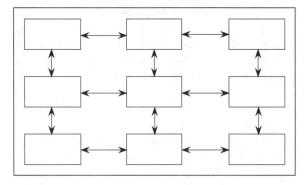

Figure 5.21 Grid site organization model.

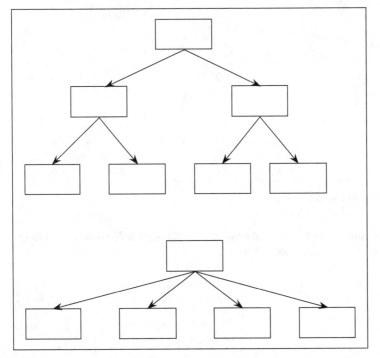

Figure 5.22   Hierarchy site organization model.

Web

Multiple permutations of Web page linkages create an unstructured model. Interestingly enough, an unstructured site is called a web structure. Figure 5.24 represents a web structure and shows the possible confusions that can occur when there are multiple links to the same Web page. While there is a problem with structure, the model lends itself to more expression by allowing dynamic links to be added to the site without concern of a strong mental model.

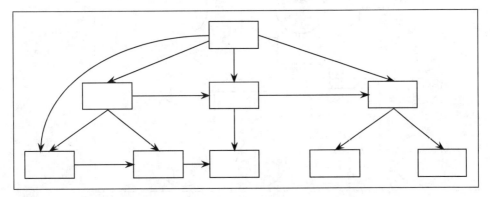

Figure 5.23   Mixed hierarchy site organization model.

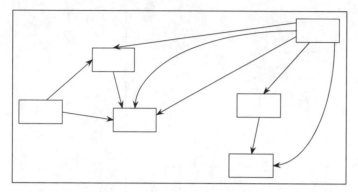

Figure 5.24 Web organization model.

Actual site architecture diagrams can take many forms. Figure 5.25 shows some alternative completed site architecture examples.

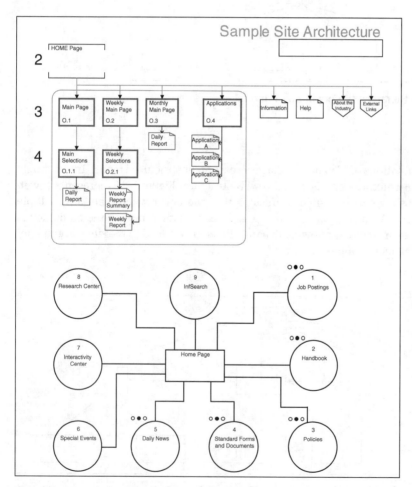

Figure 5.25 Site architecture format examples.

Building Interactivity into an Ecommerce System

Multimedia is defined as a computer-based, interactive experience that incorporates text, graphics, sound, animation, video, and virtual reality (Shuman, 2001). The focus of multimedia is its interactivity, meaning that it allows a user to interact with the application during its execution, also known as operating in real time. The multimedia experience is one in which the user determines what is delivered, when it is delivered, and in what media it is delivered to the Web. This interactivity offers a wide range of experiences that can be provided to a user during the execution of software on the Web. Despite its advantages, though, interactivity comes with a price: The user needs special software and hardware that can support interactive features and functions. Analysts and designers must be aware of these requirements when designing the network infrastructure to support the ecommerce system. Multimedia applications can be implemented in a number of ways and for a number of different reasons. Figure 6.1 shows some sample Web sites demonstrating specific uses of multimedia products.

Text, graphics, sound, animation, video, and virtual reality are high-level concepts in multimedia. To design effective applications, analysts and designers must have a detailed understanding of each of these components. For example, graphics multimedia can consist of either drawings or photos, while animation can be implemented in two-dimensional (2-D) or three-dimensional (3-D) styles. In many instances, careful combining of multimedia components is the most effective way to provide a useful online experience for users. The following sections will investigate each component of the multimedia paradigm.

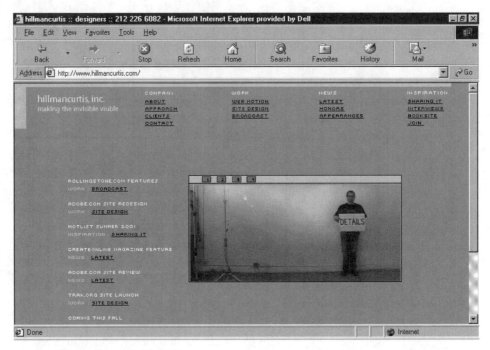

Figure 6.1 Multimedia Web sites.

Text as Media

Text can be considered a component of multimedia, especially when it is combined with imagery and animation. Text is the easiest medium to manipulate. This is particularly important since research has shown that first-time visitors to a Web site spend less than 53 seconds on a Web page. There is not much time to capture a visitor's attention (Shuman, 2001), and text is the fastest medium to present a message to a user.

In working with text, many media designers make use of a template system called Cascading Style Sheets (CSS). CSS ensures that all fonts are displayed consistently across all Web pages and thus creates a consistent "look and feel" for the ecommerce system. More important, CSS allows developers to make changes to a template master and then have the changes propagated to all of the Web screens that use that template. As mentioned in Chapter 5, these template systems can be operationalized with content management software (see Chapter 13). CSS is implemented using two competing standards: OpenType, which is supported by Microsoft and Adobe, and TrueDoc, which is supported by Netscape and Bitstream. These products allow designers to embed fonts in a Web page. The analyst's role is to determine which of these standards will be used. This kind of text display fits a media mode more closely than a standard text mode.

Transforming text into an image allows that text to be displayed the same way regardless of the fonts that are supported on the user's computer. The downside of using this technique is that it takes longer to load this text-as-image than it does to load simple text. Another problem is that graphics text cannot be edited. The alternative to complete text graphics is to communicate messages through graphics with a combination of

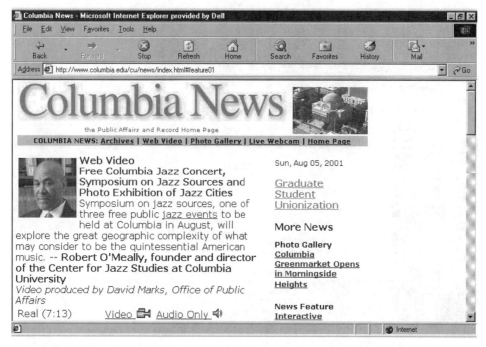

Figure 6.2   Columbia Web site.

text and hyperlinks. The design requires a smaller amount of text, which in turn allows the user to link to another area showing the remaining body of text. Figure 6.2 shows an example of text and hyperlinks on the Columbia University Web site.

The advantage of using this method is not that it saves on actual content, but rather that it allows designers to put more text-oriented topics on a single page, allowing users to get more detail by following the linking to another page. Users get to see more in less time, and those who want more information can get it easily and quickly. Text and graphic animation combinations can also decrease the space and load time of pure text images. This is accomplished by providing small amounts of descriptive text followed by an option to load an animated file. Figure 6.3 is an example of a Web site that features this option.

Graphics in Multimedia Applications

Graphic images are designed to add emphasis, direct attention, illustrate concepts, and provide a background for the content. Graphics, like illustrations and photographs, are an integral component of multimedia applications. There are two types of multimedia titles: DrawType and Bitmap. Bitmap graphics were described in Chapter 5.

Drawtype, or Vector graphics, are geometric shapes made up of straight lines, ovals, and arcs. Using vector graphics has advantages and disadvantages. One of the advantages is that vector design allows images to be resized and rotated without affecting the relative size distribution in the object, so the proper proportions are maintained. Another advan-

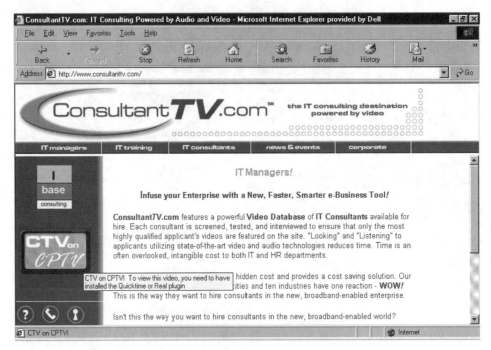

Figure 6.3   Web site that loads animated files.

tage is that vector files are significantly smaller than bitmap files. A disadvantage of vector graphics is that its smaller files can take longer to load into the Web page thus reducing performance. In addition, vector graphics cannot display images in photo quality.

Using Sound

Web sites often use sound to convey a message. Streaming video presentations are becoming more common, and sound will increasingly become a more critical component of ecommerce systems. The most important consideration in using sound is file size. Uncompressed audio files are extremely large and require unacceptably slow playback time. Therefore, audio files must be compressed, using advanced compression formulas. These compressions are automatically accomplished in most audio formats, including RealAudio (Windows-based), Audio Interchange File Format for Macintosh (AITF), WAV, Musical Instrument Digital Interface (MIDI), and Motion Picture Experts Group (MP3). The definition of each of these formats is presented in Table 6.1.

Streaming media is another alternative to audio file compression. Streaming media allows both audio and video to be played on a Web site by downloading portions or streams of the two media in real time. The advantage of streaming media is that it can start playing while the stream of information is still loading on the computer, unlike compressed audio files, which must load fully before executing. The stream occurs between a server and the computer hosting the Web site. Streaming media has two potential disadvantages. First, the host computer must have a resident program that can execute the

Table 6.1   Audio File Formats

AUDIO FILE FORMAT	DESCRIPTION
WAV	Waveform files are the most common sound format used on the Windows platforms. WAV files can also be used with the Apple Macintosh with special software.
MPEG (MP3)	Motion Pictures Experts Group format is the standard format with significant compression capabilities. MPEG level 3 is the most common format used to transport music files on the Web.
RealAudio (.rm)	RealAudio is the major streaming technology used on the Web. It uses proprietary player software, but is commonly available for free on the Web.
MIDI	Musical Instrument Digital Interface format is used to synthesize audio. It is well supported but can only be used with certain applications because of problems with sound quality on a PC.
AU	Sparc-audio, or u-law format is one of the original Internet sound formats. It is available on most platforms.
RMF	Rich Music Format is supported by Beatnik and is a high-quality download-and-play audio format.
AIFF	Audio Interchange File Format is common on the Mac, but not common on the Web.

streaming data. There are currently four software products on the market that can execute streaming data: RealPlayer, Windows Media Player, MP3, and QuickTime. Figure 6.4 shows examples of these video and audio products. Second, streaming media is prone to the real-time problems of connectivity and broadband. The speed and connectivity to the server are always in jeopardy because the activity occurs in real time.

A serious issue with audio is deciding when and how to use it. In most cases sounds are used in relation to other content. Streaming audio is often used when filming a class, speech, or show, where both the video and audio are necessary. Sound can also be used to set the tone or mood of a Web page. However, because of the high overhead associated with this technology, analysts should avoid using sound if there is no compelling reason to use it. If it is possible and appropriate, it is advisable to allow users to control the audio, for example, allowing users to skip an audio session or to avoid hearing introductory music over again. Figure 6.5 is an example where audio is optional and controlled by the user.

Animation

Animation on the Web has many uses, including logos, icons, and demonstrations. There are a variety of animation programs on the market including Flash and Shock-

Figure 6.4 Sample streaming media product.

wave, animated GIFs, and DHTML. Table 6.2 shows the definitions of these different animation tools.

Animation should be used in splash pages or advertising banners. It is often used to grab the attention of customers and consumers. Like other interactive tools on the Web,

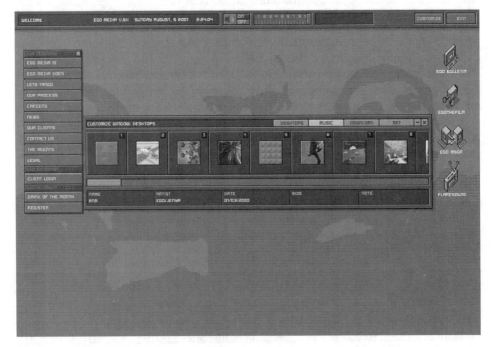

Figure 6.5 EgoMedia's optional audio control option.

Table 6.2 Animation Tools

ANIMATION TECHNOLOGY	DESCRIPTION
Animated GIFs	The simplest form of animation and is supported by most browsers. GIFs cannot handle complex animation.
DHTML	Also known as Javascript. This technology is used to move objects around on the screen. It is considered a simple form of moving objects.
Flash	Macromedia Flash is the leading format for sophisticated Web-based animations. Flash files are compact, but require the product to be installed on the client's computer.
Shockwave	These files are compressed Macromedia director files. The advantage over Flash is that it supports complex scripting. Unfortunately, Shockwave files are much larger than Flash files.
Java	Java can be used for animation, but is not the best tool as it is very complex for creating simple animations.

it should not be overused. Animation can easily overwhelm users and overcrowd a Web page. Designers should avoid competing animations and animations that run in continuous loops. Another issue in using animation is dimensionality. There are two types of dimensions: two-dimensional (2-D) and three-dimensional (3-D).

2-D Animation

Animation dimensions are an illusion. There are two types of 2-D animation: Cel animation and Path animation. Cel animation is based on frames that change, like a cartoon. Therefore, Cel animation creates an illusion of movement. Computer-based Cel animation usually uses programs like TOONZ. Path animation moves an object across the screen in a predetermined path. The path could be a straight or curved line. Because it requires fewer frames, Path animation is easier to create than Cel animation. Analysts should understand what animation products are available before completing the design of the Web site or ecommerce system. 2-D animation software can range from shareware products to sophisticated multimedia authoring programs costing hundreds of dollars. The more powerful 2-D animation programs allow programmers to integrate animation with audio; therefore, it can be used as an alternative to expensive video applications.

3-D Animation

Creating 3-D animation is far more complex than 2-D animation. The purpose of 3-D animation is to create the illusion that users are being brought into the Web as participants rather than merely observers. 3-D animation involves three steps: modeling, animation, and rendering.

Figure 6.6   Corcoran Group virtual reality apartment tour.

Modeling is the process of creating actual models and structures in 3-D objects and scenes. Animation is the procedure for defining the object's motion. This phase requires that other variables be considered, such as light and shadow. Rendering is the process of giving objects such attributes as color, texture, and transparency.

Virtual reality is another tool commonly used in 3-D animations. Virtual reality is used to create "real" experiences for the user, such as the Boeing Corporation's flight simulator programs that look like the cockpit of a real airplane. The user, in this case a pilot in training, can feel as though he or she is inside the cockpit of a plane. Another type of virtual reality is CD-based game software. This software creates images on screen that depict an actual experience, like running down stairs, falling, etc. Virtual reality can also be used to show the interior of a room—as in the Corcoran Group's virtual tour shown in Figure 6.6.

Using Video

The inclusion of digitized video in multimedia titles was a significant achievement in bringing media to the Web. However, video can be extremely expensive and slow to load on Web sites, so analysts must carefully consider its use before any programming begins. Video, like sound, is typically recorded using analog and must be converted to digital. The digitization of the video occurs in five steps as shown in Figure 6.7.

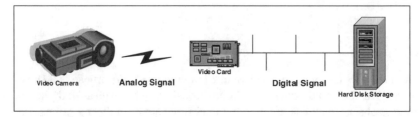

Figure 6.7   Digitization from analog video.

Whereas digitized video has many advantages, the file size dilemma creates many problems for its implementation on Web sites. Therefore, analysts and designers need to determine how to reduce the size of digitized videos. Before deciding what method to use, it is important to forecast the size of the video file. Analysts and designers can assess video file size using the following formula:

Video file size = Frames/second × image size × color depth / 8

Four methods can be used to minimize the size of video files:

Color depth. Reducing the color depth to fewer than 256 colors limits the size but creates a poorer-quality image.

Frame rate. Slowing the rate helps reduce file size; however, if the rate drops below 15 seconds per frame, there is noticeable reduction of quality.

Reduction of video. This entails restricting the use of video to only those images that are moving on the screen. In other words, only the streaming portions of the video are downloaded, not the entire screen.

Display size. Most multimedia programs do not show images in full-screen video. The smaller the window, the faster the video plays.

Another method of video reduction is compression and editing. There are two types of compression: lossless and lossy. *Lossless* ensures that the image is not changed in any way during compression. This results in files that are still large. *Lossy* compression, on the other hand, eliminates some of the data from the image and therefore provides greater reduction. The higher the compression ratio, however, the poorer the quality of the image.

Video editing is the process of incorporating the compressed video into a multimedia application. This process takes a number of steps to complete, including capturing the video image, editing the video, and compressing it. The editing step is comprised of the following activities:

- Superimposing titles

- Applying special effects such as rotation and zooming

- Synchronizing sound with the video

- Implementing filters to reduce noise and control balance of color

Motion Graphics

Motion graphics focuses on communicating visually using various interactive media such as sound and animation. According to Curtis (2000), the idea is to communicate graphically the essentials that must be included in an effective ecommerce experience. The important issues here are defining the role of the ecommerce analyst/designer in the creation of motion graphics and defining its use in the design of the system. Ecommerce analysts are again confronted with a creative Web site component that needs to be incorporated in the software engineering life cycle. The medium of motion graphics itself carries a message; indeed the means in which the message is delivered can often have more meaning than the message itself.

According to Curtis (2000), motion graphics must communicate in the universal language called the Global Visual Language (GVL). GVL is a language comprised of simple symbology and motion that is understandable to all users regardless of the language they speak. Symbology includes elements like the "@" symbol. Symbology should be clear, simple, and quickly understood. Curtis defined a four-stage process to bring the theory of motion graphics from theory to practice:

1. Work toward a global visual language
2. Respect the technical environment
3. Address the multitasking attention deficit
4. Identify the emotional center

Global Visual Language

The Global Visual Language requires that we move away from traditional text-based motion graphics. While this is not always possible, the creation of universal symbology combined with motion is the development of a new language that is much more organic. Analysts need to think about how visual symbols, along with a motion, can deliver a more effective and universal message, notwithstanding the global cultural issues that exist among different user constituents. The more universal the message, the more long-lasting the meaning it conveys. Take, for example, the Coca-Cola Web site in Figure 6.8.

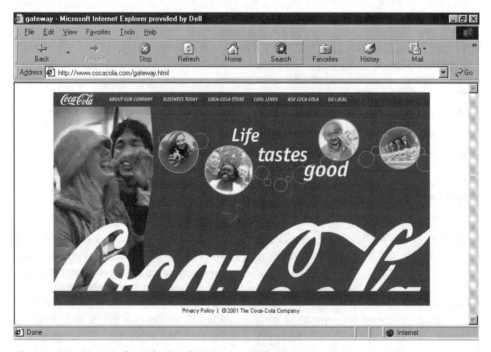

Figure 6.8   Coca-Cola Web site showing symbology.

The site shows how the Coca-Cola symbol or brand, along with a moving banner, represents the international message of the product.

Respecting the Technical Environment

This phase addresses the technical limitations that users may encounter. The trick is to find the limitations and use them to your advantage. Every disadvantage has an advantage. It is therefore important that ecommerce analysts have a clear perspective of what hardware and software exists in the user base. This may not be possible when providing product to consumers. In this case, the ecommerce team may need to decide the minimal configuration of hardware and software that will be supported by the multimedia. There are also methods of providing users with automatic or selective updates to help them install the required software. This was discussed in Chapter 5.

Addressing Multitasking Attention Deficit

The purpose of this phase is to ensure that even busy users who are engaged in multiple online tasks will understand the message and that the message will keep their attention. The goal is to present a message that will not be ignored. The best approach is to be lean and mean; that is, do not communicate a message that takes longer than 5 to 10 seconds. Another aspect is to focus on the user's experience. What does the user want to obtain from the session, and, in minimal time, what can you convey to the user?

Identifying the Emotional Center

Identifying the emotional center is a technique that developers can use to understand what is most important to users and to ensure that the development team stays focused on those areas. When meeting with users, analysts should ask them to describe the ecommerce system they would like, using keywords and phrases, and keep a list of responses. Analysts should then start to distribute the collected words within a three-ring target. The words with the highest emotional impact go in the center of the target, and the ones in the second and third rings support the center. In this way, analysts can define the emotional center of the brand. The process may take some time, but it gives designers important information to work with as they develop symbolic messages to be conveyed on the site. The most important words make their way into the smallest ring—or the center of emotion. Figure 6.9 shows the three-ring emotional center.

The emotional center is about communication, which is the most important part of graphic design. Web designers must create with passion—focusing on the desires that users themselves have conveyed for the ecommerce system. The emotional center is more important than word choice or storyboarding, and it needs to be integrated with motion and rhythm.

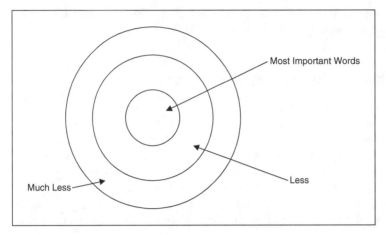

Figure 6.9 Three-ring center of emotion.

Analysis and Design of Multimedia Titles

The previous section provided the technical background to enable ecommerce analysts and designers to understand the capabilities of the technology. This section is devoted to the engineering requirements that multimedia developers need to program the system. That is, this section represents the process for creating the logical equivalent for multimedia. All too often, multimedia developers start programming before the analysis and design phases are properly completed. In contrast, according to Shuman (2001), multimedia development is 80 percent planning and 20 percent production.

The multimedia analysis and design process can be represented in eight steps as follows:

1. Create the idea
2. Specify goals and objectives
3. Identify users
4. Create metaphors
5. Determine emphasis
6. Determine the treatment
7. Create technical specifications
8. Determine storyboarding and navigation

Creating the Idea

Based on interviews as well as some of the processes identified in the Global Visual Language, analysts must identify the emotional center. After completing the key words, analysts should be capable of developing the multimedia vision statement, the synthesis of what the Global Visual Language is trying to say. Good vision statements should point to the center of the three-ring title.

Scope/Vision Statement:

To establish Bank X as a leading technology firm in the banking industry

Objectives:

1. Provide multimedia experience that educates users on the benefits of doing online banking.
2. Create new Web Brand that provides a sense of trust to consumers.
3. Increase Web site hits by 50% over a six-month period.
4. Enroll 25 new online customers each month.
5. Reduce hand-written checks by 20% over the next 12 months.

Figure 6.10 Sample multimedia goals and objectives statement.

Goals and Objectives

Goals simply support the vision; the objectives, when met, accomplish the goal to attain the vision. Figure 6.10 provides a sample vision, goal, and objectives statement.

Identifying Users

This step should occur in accordance with the process outlined in Chapter 2. The one difference for multimedia is in its focus on users as the "audience." Indeed, the multimedia paradigm is more of a strategic marketing show than an operational selection of the applications. Once the user selects the application, there is another level of instructional information provided.

Metaphor

In Chapter 5, I described a Web metaphor as a concept that is used to help people understand things by using symbols and comparisons. A metaphor is used in a multimedia application to create a central theme. For example, a number of multimedia application games provide rewards of various kinds when questions are answered correctly.

Emphasis

The ecommerce analyst needs to balance the desires of the users against the inevitable constraints of time and budget. This balance can be achieved by understanding the relative emphasis that needs to be placed on different aspects of the system in order to develop requirements that meet the original project scope and objectives. Multimedia applications are easily prone to going "beyond" where the emphasis needs to be.

Technical Specifications

The specification of a multimedia title needs to include what will appear on each screen. The information also needs to represent where each element will be placed and describe the functionality of each image and object. The components of each screen should include the following, at a minimum:

Playback system. This should define the operating system and processing speeds.

Media components. This includes many design issues such as recording speed, icons, graphic resolution, object sizes, colors, etc.

Functionality. This includes how the multimedia will respond to actions, such as mouse clicks. For example, does a mouse click play the music, or make the music louder? This also includes help text interface, error messages, and pause options.

Design interface. The general presentation of how multimedia applications will be seen by users and how to make the appearance consistent across applications.

Storyboarding and Navigation

Both of these topics have been discussed in reference to other phases of ecommerce design. With respect to multimedia, storyboarding and navigation have the same role as in other phases of ecommerce systems. In effect, storyboarding tells us what the media will look like, and navigation will show us how it is linked. One important concept in multimedia storyboarding and navigation is that it is nonlinear. That is, users can jump freely from one option to another without going through the more traditional prescribed steps. Indeed there are three scenarios in which storyboarding and navigation can be presented to users:

Sequential scenario. In essence this represents the traditional and step-by-step approach to navigation where users are in a controlled linear scheme. Examples are books, stories, and electronic slide shows (such as Microsoft PowerPoint). With multimedia, users can see and hear various animations and sounds to create the desired visual language.

Topical scenario. This allows users to select from a number of choices, or to search for specific things on the ecommerce system. These include multimedia reference materials, encyclopedias, and information icons. It is important that analysts who use this style ensure that users know where they are in the system and how to navigate where they wish to go.

Exploratory scenario. There is little information or direction given to users, but rather there is a "cafeteria menu" mode of interface, where users select the options they want. This mode is designed more for the "intuitive" user.

Design Concepts

The overall considerations that drive multimedia analysis and design are (1) attracting user attention, (2) keeping user interest, and (3) assisting users to get what they want from the ecommerce system. Because of the variety in user expectations of Web interfaces, it is often desirable to design different experiences for different targeted audiences or different user biases. Thus, these sites provide for methods to change the user experience as shown in Egomedia's Web site (Figure 6.11).

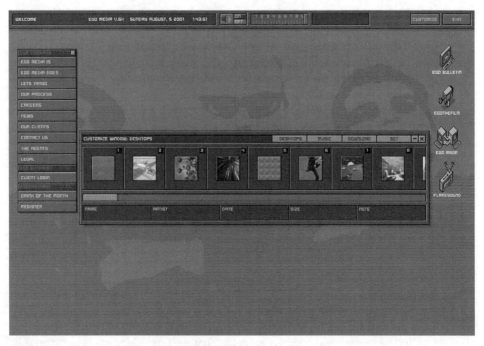

Figure 6.11   Egomedia's user-designed Web site.

Notwithstanding the number of different approaches to addressing user multimedia preferences, there are a number of general rules that most multimedia designers follow:

- Users should be able to display any page within three to five mouse clicks.
- Users should be able to return to the home page in one click.
- Navigation options should appear as buttons or in well-formatted tables.
- Text links should be color-coded.
- A site map should be available to provide users with an understanding of the major themes in the site along with a quick reference.
- General search tools should be available to allow users to quickly get to the information they need.
- Users should have the option to skip any multimedia session.
- Users should be provided with quick downloading images.
- The site should be kept fresh with new ideas and images.
- Get to the point quickly.

There are also general design guidelines that most professionals use in multimedia design, notwithstanding the preferences of users. Multimedia design guidelines ensure that the ecommerce system is consistent and flows well from a media perspective. These considerations should be documented by the ecommerce analyst/designer as outlined below.

Balance. The appropriate distribution of optical weight within the page layout. Optical weight is defined as the ability of an element on the screen, such as an icon, to attract the user's eye. Every element has a degree of optical weight, which is determined by its nature and size. The nature of an element relates to its shape, color, brightness, and type. Balance is ultimately determined by the weight of the elements on the screen and their positioning there. The concept is actually quite simple: If you divide the screen in half, there must be equal total balance on both sides. This does not suggest that each half must have the same number of elements, but rather each must contain equal balance. Balance is measured in two ways: symmetrically or asymmetrically. Symmetric balance is achieved by mirroring elements horizontally and vertically on both sides—so the page achieves balance. Symmetrical design is appropriate for static sites and conveys uniformity and formality. It is often used on the sites of conservative institutions, like banks and insurance companies. Asymmetrical balance is achieved by having nonidentical objects on both sides. Asymmetrical design is appropriate for more dynamic and diverse types of sites. Examples of symmetrical and asymmetrical sites are shown in Figures 6.12 and 6.13, respectively.

Unity. There are two types of site unity: inter-screen and intra-screen. Intra-screen unity focuses on how the elements *within* the screen relate to each other: Are they consistent, and do they match up to create a good color scheme? Inter-screen unity refers to the *consistency* across screens, that is, how elements work together throughout the entire ecommerce system. Unity is typically achieved by maintaining a consistency in shapes, colors, text, brand, and image.

Movement. Relates to how the user's eye moves across a screen, particularly across objects. Specifically, movement measures how well users are drawn to the center of the screen—the position called the optical center. Ultimately, the movement should be controlled by the design, and as a general rule be focused on the following concepts:

- There needs to be a graphic or headline text that controls where the user initially starts on the screen.
- Use lines or objects to help point the user in the direction in which you want him or her to proceed.
- Use color schemes that fluctuate from light to dark.
- Objects or text that need to be emphasized should be highlighted in a different color.

As discussed in Chapter 5, the design of a Web site is based heavily on the type of ecommerce system being developed. This really means that the ecommerce system must be sensitive to its user base or audience. Multimedia, as a subset of the Web design construct, must adhere to the fundamental procedures suggested in Chapter 5. The importance of this issue becomes significant when a media application needs to be interactive. Interactive means that the user will need to interface with the application in such a way that it could dictate the outcomes of the system's execution. There are three components that can affect the design of interactivity.

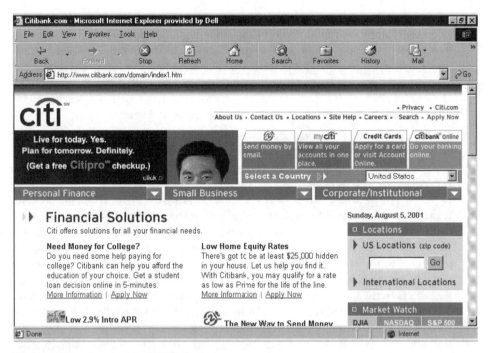

Figure 6.12   Symmetrical Web design.

Figure 6.13   Asymmetrical Web design.

Type of application. Types relate to the functionality of the title or program. If the title is a month-end report for viewing, then little interaction is necessary. Any interaction would be based on providing users with the ability to select an animated option for playing. If the title is for reference, let's say for an encyclopedia, then the user could select a video or animation to support the caption, as used in Microsoft's Encarta. If the title is a game, on the other hand, then the design will be highly interactive and filled with videos, animations, and sounds.

Content. Content in multimedia affects the design of the interactivity. Analysts must be aware of two issues: (1) the amount of content and (2) the nature of the content. The amount of content is important because it affects the length and navigation design of the Web site. Too much content requires that users continually link or jump to other areas, which can become frustrating for them. When the content is large, analysts should consider designing shortcuts that allow users to jump quicker to find exactly what they might want to read. These shortcuts are implemented using "hotwords" (highlighted keywords), pop-up windows that display additional information, scroll bars, or tabs that indicate where the user has been and allow him or her to return quickly to a previous screen. The nature of the content refers to the theme of the interactive design. That is, what concept, brand, or message does it need to reinforce? For example, if the video relates to looking at a college campus virtually, then the mouse pointer might be used to navigate through the site as if the user were actually on site at the college campus. This might also include a zoom function that could emulate what a student could see at a detailed level (see Figure 6.14).

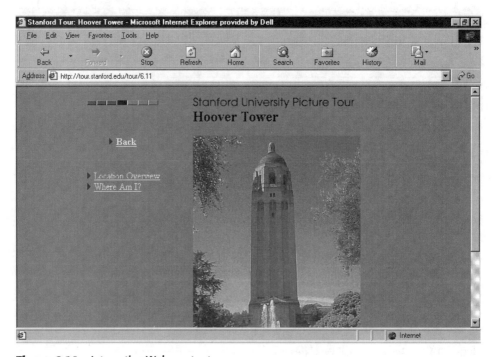

Figure 6.14 Interactive Web content.

Objects used in the application. Objects used in the application refer to the elements that are used in the title. For example, if a video is used in a site, then questions must be answered about how the video will be initiated and by whom. Furthermore, there are issues about how users might wish to replay the video, rewind it, and so forth. All of these options need to be analyzed and included in the final specification. Furthermore, decisions must be made surrounding the design of the video controls.

In addition to guidelines on interactive design, there are five general interactivity navigation guidelines that assist the analyst/designer to create multimedia that is user-friendly and maintainable.

Simplicity. Ultimately, good media design is simple, easy to understand, and, most important, easy to use. A word often used in technology is *robust*, which means that software should be "intuitively" obvious. Users should not need training or a user manual to be able to utilize interactive software. Ultimately, the home page must provide users with what they need to know to navigate through the system. Icons and other graphic symbols must complement one another and be consistent with the entire system's architecture.

Consistency. Interactive media must be consistent. Sites must show a continual reminder that they are within the same session or interaction. From this perspective, Figure 6.15 depicts site navigation and video consistency on the alanger.com site.

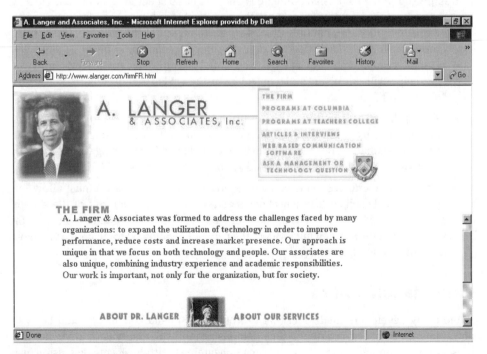

Figure 6.15   Consistent interactive Web design.

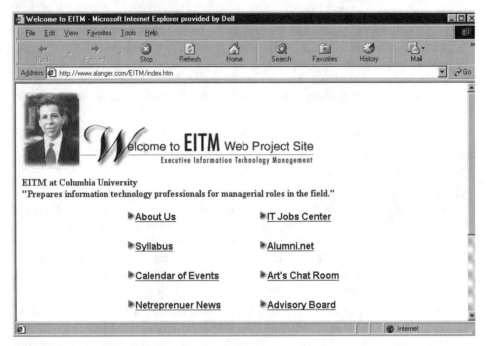

Figure 6.16   Consistent Web template design.

Design templates. A design template is one that has a specific layout that is carried throughout the ecommerce system. Figure 6.16 shows how a specific format adds to effective media communication. Templates offer benefits beyond just format consistency. Their use often shortens the development time because there are reusable components that can be propagated to other screens. Using templates also helps with an object's placement by using grids to limit what is known as "object shift."

Feedback. Interactive multimedia sites provide for two-way communication. This is accomplished by designing the interaction to allow for users to select options that allow for feedback. This concept can be accomplished by selecting various objects that represent options to click responses, or send messages and feedback.

Allow for user choices. This concept is not a new one. Software must allow for users to easily select different choices and/or be able to click out of the screen completely. The easier this is, the more effective the multimedia will be. For instance, if a user is viewing a video, they should be allowed to place the video on hold, or just quit the session.

Presentation Boards

While many developers might feel that prototypes of media activities would be best accomplished by showing actual online demonstrations, the reality is that it is not the most efficient approach. First, it is very time-consuming to produce a media session just for review purposes, which most likely will undergo changes. Second, live demonstrations are prone to technical problems that can occur during the sessions. Third, and perhaps most important, users find it more difficult to grasp the work when it is presented piece by piece, without visually seeing excerpts of the entire Web site.

The remedy for analysts and media designers is to establish equivalent logical specifications to the ones used in other aspects of ecommerce analysis and design. This is accomplished by using print materials as opposed to actual live media demonstrations. This print work should be done using large-format presentation boards. Presentation boards, along with well-organized oral presentations, appear to be the most productive and user-accepted vehicle to obtain media approval (Curtis, 2000). Furthermore, the presentation boards provide the necessary documentation that is consistent and in conformance with functional decomposition methodologies. Finally, having screenshots formatted on presentation boards allows for a better oral discussion and helps designers to control the flow of discussion similar to the way JAD sessions provide organized feedback.

Using this method creates a control that allows for the following:

- Review of how the media representation is consistent with the organization's brand
- Allows users to better understand how the ecommerce site will ultimately communicate with users—users who can see multiple screens at once, as opposed to the sequential nature of online presentations
- To better communicate the vision of the site as well as what will be delivered to the user
- Reduce costly revisions

Workflow Methodologies

Workflow is an important concept in how analysis and design are actually implemented with multimedia projects. The life cycle must be modified to include or integrate the following components:

1. During user interviews (most likely, JAD), the media strategy and site architecture for the multimedia component must be covered. This will be accomplished using high-level interaction diagrams that depict how the media will work with the Web page.
2. The multimedia "look and feel" will include a number of "key" screens that convey the mood and objective of the interactive experience. These prototypes will be integrated with the other nonmedia screens.
3. Presentation boards using (1) and (2) are presented for feedback during subsequent JAD sessions.
4. Media screens are made available on an extranet development site so that users can view the screens that have been modified. Using an extranet allows outside users to view Web sites that are in production. This is especially important when changes from previous feedback are completed and need to be reviewed quickly by the members of the JAD sessions.

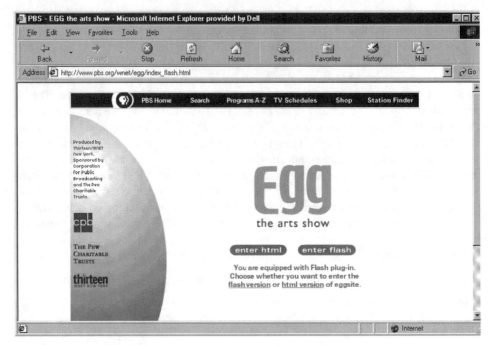

Figure 6.17 EGG home page.

Case Study

The following screens represent a project developed at Thirteen/WNET. The project, named EGG, represents an example of the challenges with integrating media with consumer-based ecommerce systems. Because of the diverse user base that accesses Thirteen's Web site, it was important for the EGG system to support both Flash and HTML. Thus the home page allows users to select their preference as shown above in Figure 6.17.

The flash animation option displays an animated chicken that walks across the Web site (Figure 6.18). The HTML option displays a similar screen, but the chicken is much less animated and does not walk (Figure 6.19).

Both Web sites allow users to preview a show. Figure 6.20 reflects the flash selection option; Figure 6.21 shows the HTML format. The flash and HTML Web site display video clips using RealPlayer (Figure 6.22).

The above case study shows how multimedia must be carefully configured into a complete site that services a broad audience. Many parts of Thirteen's Web site, particularly its membership Web page, do not use a lot of multimedia features because they want to reach as many people as possible, without causing complications with Web access and performance (Figure 6.23). This occurs when a Web site requires a plug-in to view the media, as in the case of RealPlayer. In the Membership Web page, interactive functions are limited to basic Javascript or Common Gateway Interface (CGI) scripts.

Figure 6.18   EGG flash page.

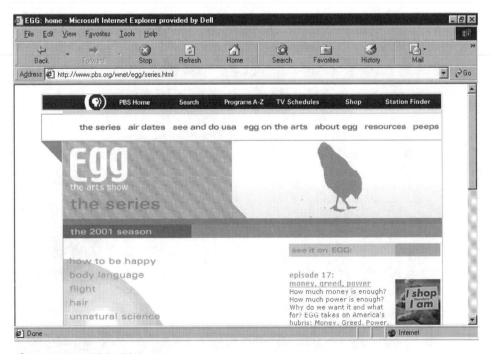

Figure 6.19   EGG HTML page.

Figure 6.20   Flash preview option.

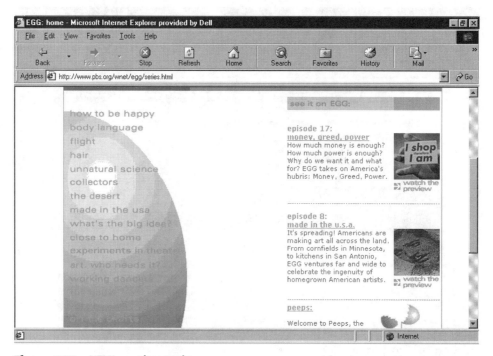

Figure 6.21   HTML preview option.

Figure 6.22   RealPlayer video.

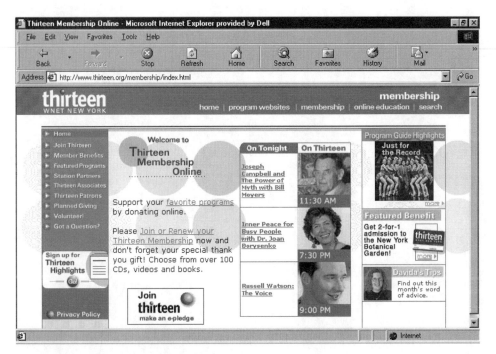

Figure 6.23   Membership home page.

Transaction Processing Design

Transaction processing is a software technology that enables distributed processing to be reliable. Any software that uses the Internet is effectively using the largest distributed processing system in the world. Therefore, ecommerce systems must utilize transaction processing to process and service requests. Processing and servicing requests are by definition the heart of ecommerce activities. This chapter focuses on the application analysis that is required to design products for deployment on transaction processing (TP) ecommerce systems. This analysis encompasses:

- Application development and deployment
- Communications processing
- Database systems
- Operating systems
- Network design

Background of Transaction Processing

This section will cover TP applications and structures, including transaction properties, two-phase commit protocol, TPC standard performance, and decision support design.

Put simply, a *transaction* is an exchange of information or products. Thus any transaction must start with a request and end with a response. A transaction is also a kind of process. Recall from the earlier discussion of data flow diagrams that a process is defined as something that changes data. In the transaction process, then, the request undergoes change and is returned as transformed data. What makes TP more complex than a simple process is the myriad of inter-processes that may occur as part of preparing a response. There are often many subprocesses needed to fulfill one specific request. Examples include the updating of several files, parallel programs that execute, or even batch-related processes that are invoked at a later time. All of these indirect effects of the request must be organized, designed, and configured as part of the application analysis and design. Most transaction programs need to access shared data as part of their assigned activities.

Another important aspect of TP is that it must be designed to be scalable. *Scalability* means that the system can adapt, without redesign, as the number and size of transactions increase. Scalable applications need only to add more hardware, such as disk space, to respond to increases in the number of transactions that occur. Therefore, TP design must define the limit of the scalability. With this in mind, transaction processing applications can be defined as a collection of programs designed to do the functions necessary to automate a given ecommerce activity. Table 7.1 provides a list of typical application transactions.

A TP's main function is to accept a request and independently execute it once and produce permanent results (Bernstein and Newcomer, 1997). Originally, TP systems were designed to operate on large mainframe systems, such as the SABRE airline system, which automated the airline scheduling process. Today there are many TP applications, most of which are focused on reducing the cost of administration and generating revenue as a service to users. The benefits of TP applications, therefore, provide an

Table 7.1 Transaction Processing Applications

APPLICATION	EXAMPLE TRANSACTION PROCESSING
Banking	Deposit or withdraw money from an account
Securities trading	Purchase 100 shares of stock
Insurance	Pay an insurance premium
Inventory control	Record the arrival of a shipment
Manufacturing	Log a step of an assembly process
Retail	Record a sale
Government	Register an automobile
Internet	Place an order using an online catalog
Telecommunications	Connect a telephone call
Military command and control	Fire a missile
Media	Download a video clip

Source: *Principles of Transaction Processing* (Bernstein and Newcomer, 1997)

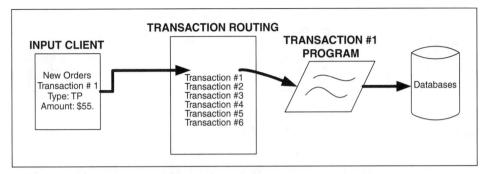

Figure 7.1   Transaction processing components.

ideal fit for ecommerce business, as ecommerce is designed to reduce administration while increasing revenues. However, ecommerce differs from traditional TP applications in its ambitious goals to expand the market. TP systems designed to facilitate Web access are not only reducing costs, but also substantially expanding the existing user base of the business. Scalability thus becomes a crucial concern in ecommerce design.

Figure 7.1 represents a schematic of a TP application that depicts the three components of TP:

1. The first component gathers input to prepare for processing. That is, it represents the user interface over the Web and allows for data input by displaying menus that are designed to capture the request. The input is eventually formatted and converted into a communications message or record.

2. The second component takes the communication message and turns it into a "call" or request to the appropriate transaction program. In order to implement such a system, there is a need for a sophisticated internal routing table that searches for the appropriate program based on the request. This component must be implemented using object-oriented component architecture, which will be discussed later in this chapter.

3. The third component is the TP itself. The TP application executes the request by performing the necessary task for a proper response. This is typically accomplished by reading and writing to a shared database or even calling another application to complete the task. In any event, the TP eventually responds to the calling program or user request.

From a software perspective, a TP system resembles a client/server configuration as shown in Figure 7.2. The client or requestor component is called the *presentation manager*, which is typically implemented using a Web browser like Microsoft's Explorer or Netscape's Navigator. The responsibility of the client is to capture the input or request and transfer it to the server. The server part of the TP is more complicated. It consists of three distinct units:

Workflow control. This program moves the request to the appropriate application program. If more than one application program is needed, the Workflow Control module keeps track of which program is handling the request at any given time.

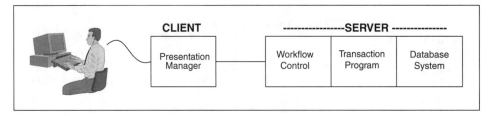

Figure 7.2   Software components of the TP system.

Transaction program. These programs wait until they are called upon by workflow control, and either complete the request or call another TP to continue handling the request. The ecommerce analyst needs to ensure that these transaction programs are designed using object-oriented techniques.

Database system. As mentioned above, most TP systems eventually interface with databases—databases that were designed using the techniques outlined in Chapter 4.

In the example from Chapter 4, the processing of a new order shows how the TP operates. The client allows a customer to place an order using presentation software on a desktop workstation. The server receives the request from the client and initiates the right program to handle the request, which in this case is the program that handles new orders. The order database is eventually updated with the new order. There might be additional programs called into operation. For example, the process may need to update the warehouse inventory. The executing program would eventually confirm the completion of the task back to the workflow control system, which in turn might send a message back to the client, displaying a confirmation that the order was processed. In some instances it might also provide shipping information.

When the number of transactions becomes very large, especially when there are multiple clients and multiple databases, many ecommerce systems use a TP monitor. A TP monitor acts as a router and dispatcher of traffic between multiple clients and multiple servers. It may even be required to interact with different operating systems and thus can be used to optimize the performance of the network. This will be discussed in greater detail in Chapter 8. Figure 7.3 depicts the use of a TP monitor.

Transaction Properties

Analysts must be aware that there are four critical transaction properties: atomic, consistency, isolation, and durability, known by the acronym ACID.

Atomic. The transaction executes completely or not at all. That is, the transactions are binary in nature. The TP system design must guarantee atomicity through database design that tracks the progress of a given transaction. For example, if a deposit transaction of $100 is posted to an account, the TP system must ensure that the cash balance is also updated. This is an example of what we mean by completing the transaction. The TP system ensures integrity by allowing the update only if all parts of the transaction are confirmed as complete. This is handled by the work-

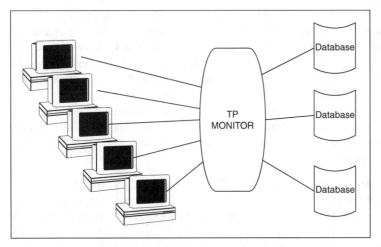

Figure 7.3   TP monitor functions.

flow control component of the server architecture. The successful completion of a transaction is called a *commit*; a failure is called an *abort*. Another component of TP behavior is handling committed transactions that turn out to be in error. For audit trail purposes, a commit cannot be reversed; therefore, as in accounting rules, an adjusting transaction must be presented. An adjusting transaction, in effect, is a negative transaction that reverses the original bad transaction.

Consistency. Transactions must behave consistently with the database structure. A transaction must be formatted to align with the referential integrity rules of the database (see Chapter 4). Unlike the other components of TP properties, the TP system can do little to ensure that a transaction is consistent with referential integrity rules. In this case, the application design must ensure it—so analysts need to develop specifications that ensure integrity. For example, two different transactions cannot have the same Identification Code, if, for instance, the Identification Code is a primary key in the database.

Isolation. Transactions must execute in a vacuum, without concern for what other transactions might be doing in the system. Another definition of isolation is *serialization,* that is, the running of transactions in succession. Take online banking as an example. Suppose two different transactions were attempting to withdraw the last $500 in a given account. If they both were able to request the withdrawal at the same time, then there would be an integrity problem with the database. Because of isolation, each transaction must execute sequentially and completely, and, as a result, the second transaction requesting the withdrawal would be denied. The database integrity assists the TP system by placing locks on records when they are in use, and automatically supports referential integrity constraints. Poor database constructs that do not provide for 3NF design can suffer from serious integrity issues when working with TP systems.

Durability. The transaction's results cannot be lost due to a system failure. This means that once a transaction is completed, its results will be put in the database and stored in a virtual disk, making it separate from TP internal failures. TP failures typically occur on the server hardware. The durability property is usually obtained by using log files that have copies of the transactions that have executed over a specific period. When the TP issues a commit operation, the system ensures that all of the transactions are indeed in the log file before allowing the transaction to be written. If there is a system failure, the TP system can always go to the log file to recreate the transaction. *Log files* are effectively audit trail transactions that ensure that an appropriate backup exists. The log file backups are created during real-time processing so that there is no chance for a transaction to complete that is not mirrored in the system.

Thus, a transaction is a set of operations that transforms data from one state to another and must exhibit the four ACID properties described above. In ecommerce systems, transactions are distributed and can be spread across multiple machines. Each of these machines can be running a particular process that represents one component or part of the total transaction. Therefore, each subprocess needs to coordinate its activity with the others and ensure that it exhibits ACID properties. This is not as easy as it sounds and is handled by a protocol called "two-phase commit."

Two-Phase Commit

A serious problem can occur in TP applications if updates are made to more than one database and if one of the databases is updated, but not the other. This situation can occur when something goes wrong with the TP system while a transaction is attempting to complete. Should such an error occur, the best method to fix it is usually to undo the original transaction and restart the process. Unfortunately, such an algorithm would be difficult to code and implement. TP monitors address this potential nightmare by using a protocol called a *two-phase commit* that acts to coordinate all of the updates that one transaction makes throughout the system. The two-phase commit is implemented by decomposing the process into smaller programs that track or log the progress of the transaction. This process involves two phases: preparation and resolution. The preparation phase sends a message to the TP monitor alerting it that a transaction needs to be processed. The TP resource manager checks its resources and confirms that it can process the transaction only if it is sure that it can commit to completing the process. In this case, a *resource* may be defined as a necessary file or a hardware device. The resource manager will confirm that the file or device is free to use. This procedure also ensures that the TP monitor will not be interrupted or aborted during the processing of that resource request. The second phase is resolution. When all of the specific resource requests have been accepted, the TP manager can commit the entire transaction for processing. Figure 7.4 depicts the flow of the two-commit methodology.

Thus, the two-phase commit protocol is used first to ensure that every resource is available to complete its part. Once all of the resources have confirmed their availability, then the TP monitor executes the transaction. It is important to note that if a transaction requires only one resource, the system should automatically use a one-commit instead of a two-phase commit.

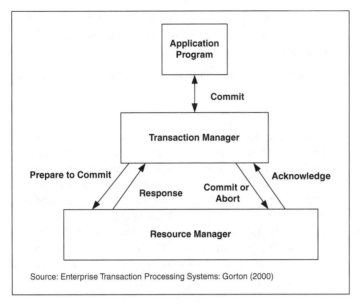

Figure 7.4 Two-phase commit process.

The two-phase commit is required to guarantee the ACID properties of a transaction when there is more than one resource requirement per transaction. But ecommerce analysts need to understand that there is a price to pay for ensuring completion: performance delays. This is why the network design of ecommerce systems must be integrated with the design of applications, particularly TP monitor systems. The architecture of distributed transaction processing systems will be discussed further in Chapter 8.

Authentication

When designing the presentation layer or client, ecommerce analysts must ensure that user security information is authenticated. The process of authentication means that the user's name, password, and device are compared against a master list to validate access permission. The actual authentication usually occurs at the TP server level, meaning that the workflow control has the responsibility to validate the user information. Thus, analysts must design the client application to request user name and password information that will be captured and forwarded to the TP system for authentication. Once the workflow control receives the transaction, it will validate the data against a master file of user names and passwords. The master user table is designed in various ways: Some have built-in facilities in the software that provide security functionality; others require that the analyst actually design the user security table into database schemas. That is, the storing of the security information must be part of the internal database design. In addition, the messages going to and from the client/server must be encrypted to ensure privacy of information over the Internet. Therefore, ecommerce analysts must ensure that specifications that address authentication are included in the requirements document. These technical specifications must include:

- Screen capturing logic that requests the user's name and password
- Logic that specifies how the captured information will be formatted and forwarded to the TP monitor for processing
- The database entities that are to be used to validate the information contained in the message
- The encryption routine to be used to secure the transactions

As a final note, each database entity that is used to validate information requires what is called a *maintenance application*. Maintenance applications are those that allow the appropriate users to insert new records, update their information, and, in some instances, delete themselves from the system. For example, if a new user is added to the system, a designated operator would need to access the maintenance system to add a new record to the User Security Table. The User Security Table is a database that contains every user's security information. The same operator might need to access the system to delete a user that is terminated. The processes of designing authentication and building maintenance tables are shown in Figures 7.5 and 7.6, respectively.

AUTHENTICATION SPECIFICATION

Date:	Module/Program:	Project:

Element	Length	Data Type	Valid Values
User-ID	15	Varchar2	See below
Password	12	Varchar2	See below
Device-Type	35	Numeric	See below
Access Level	1	Number	0,1,2

BUSINESS RULES

User-ID: Must be at least 4 alphanumeric characters. The first character cannot be numeric.

Password: Must be at least 7 characters. The first digit must be alphabetic and the last digit must be an integer. Passwords must be updated every 60 days. When Day=>55, a message is displayed "Password must be changed within the next X days," where X is the number of days before 60. If less than 0, reject request.

Device-Type: Determined by checking device settings. Users cannot override.

Access-Level: This code sets the level of access granted to the user as follows:

0	All
1	Display
2	Query Only

Figure 7.5 Authentication specifications.

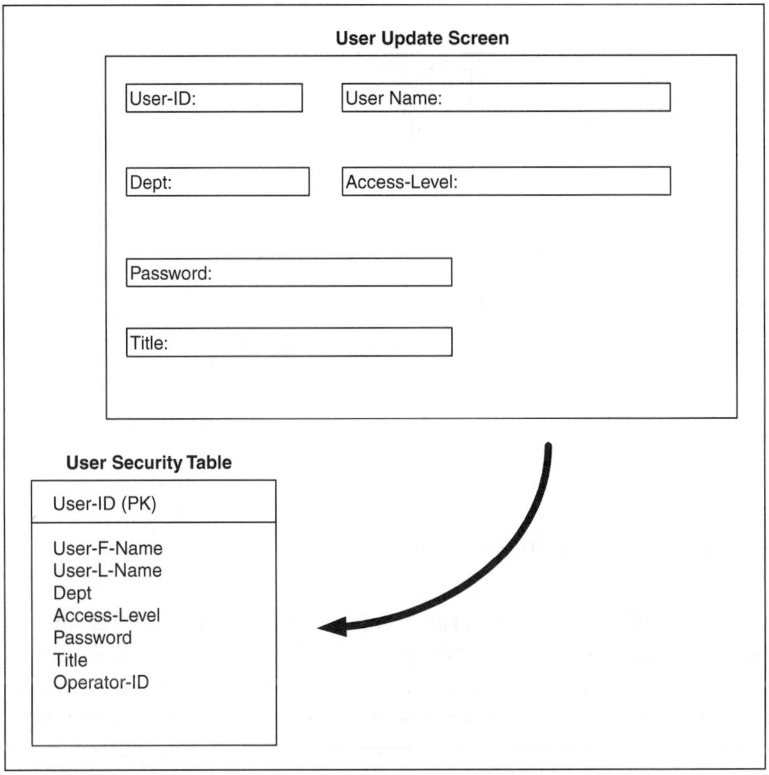

Figure 7.6   Authentication maintenance table design.

Application Design

Developing applications for the TP system requires the implementation of reusable object components. These object components will be designed based on the methodology set forth in Chapter 3. In Chapter 3, reusable components were designed using a model called *classes*. Classes are comprised of data (attributes) and processes (methods) and become the abstraction of reusable objects that can be utilized by many different operations to provide application functionality. Indeed, a program that reads a transaction, authenticates it, and updates a specific database can be required by many different applications across the ecommerce network. Many of these applications will have transactions that need the same object programs at the same time. Furthermore, ecommerce systems may need to integrate many packaged applications and generate them under a single TP monitor system. Figure 7.7 depicts the reuse component architecture of the TP system within an ecommerce environment.

The salient issue is how to design the application components in the TP system. The process starts by defining the "business objects" that relate to all of the functions of the business model. Examples of business objects are customer, account, product, order, and shipment. The functions incorporated into the TP system are the universal business rules that govern the entire ecommerce system. This means that any program in the TP

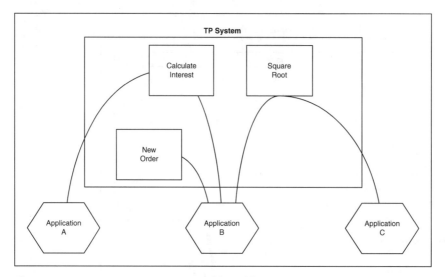

Figure 7.7 TP system reuse component architecture.

system is designed to provide reusable programs that contain global or universal features. For example, a universal business rule for a new order is that it decreases inventory and creates a shipping address for a particular account. Thus, regardless of which application is executing across the ecommerce system, the rules for handling a new order are always the same. Therefore, the logic for handling a new order is placed in the TP system as a separate object program. This object program is then accessed by any application in the ecommerce system that needs to create a new order. So, the TP system acts as the repository for holding these universal object programs and provides the infrastructure to make it available to other programs in the ecommerce system.

The TP monitor architecture of the system is comprised of three tiers:

Tier 1. The presentation server, which defines the Web forms and menus, including data validation operations. Ultimately the presentation server gathers the input and transforms it into a request.

Tier 2. The workflow controller houses the global business rules, which allow the TP monitor to select the appropriate transaction server that contains the back-end data.

Tier 3. The transaction server contains the business objects that actually perform the operations.

Figure 7.8 shows the relationship between the three-tier TP monitor architecture and the corresponding object-oriented application architecture.

The Tier 1 specification represents the client. The specification process for screen development was discussed in Chapter 5. However, in a distributed environment, ecommerce analysts must define whether a TP system will be used to accept requests from each client, as opposed to allowing applications to make SQL calls directly to the back-end database. The latter would no longer represent a transactional designed system. With the assumption that most ecommerce systems require multiple databases to be

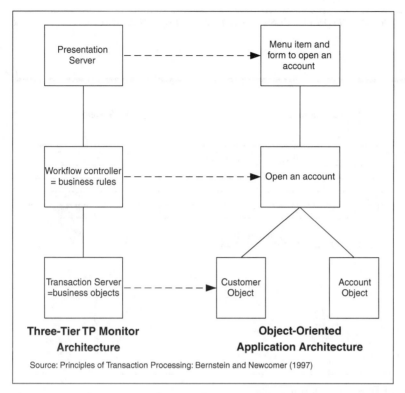

Figure 7.8   Object-oriented versus three-tier TP architecture.

updated simultaneously from one transaction, the Web page specifications need to identify the objects in the TP monitor that will handle any inserts, reads, deletes, or updates. This also means that the analyst must define the middle tier (Tier 2) processes that will be created as reusable object components. Figure 7.9 shows a specification that identifies a TP object call.

The specification must contain a format layout of the request from the client, which contains the name of the user entering the request, the user's device, the type of transaction being requested, and parameters that are being requested. Each of these fields is described below.

User name. The name of the user identifies the individual who is processing the request. It will typically be based on the user's log-in information, which has been captured and stored by the system when the user logged onto the system and/or the application.

Device identifier. This information is usually stored by the network and tells the system the type of client that is making the request. A client could be a dumb terminal, a PC running Windows, or an Apple Macintosh. The TP monitor must know this information so that it can send the proper response format to the requesting client device. If the wrong format is returned, it might not display properly on the screen, or, worse, its response may be misinterpreted.

TRANSACTION PROCESS OBJECT CALL SPECIFICATION		

Date:	Application:	TP System ID:

User Name	Device Identifier	Object Name	Call Parameters

Comments

Figure 7.9   Client TP object call specification.

Request type/name. This identifies which object program in the middle tier needs to respond to the request. The request identifier allows the TP monitor to know which object program needs to be executed.

Parameters. A parameter represents a piece of information or message that needs to be interpreted by the selected object. It might contain a value that tells the object program how many items are associated with the order, thus providing the application with valuable information regarding the number of inserts that will be required.

Based on the above request, the TP's workflow controller will assign the appropriate object program to fulfill the request from the client presentation layer. Tier 2 must therefore have a repository of all reusable object applications. Ecommerce analysts can define the object applications by using the following object-oriented specification format.

Creating Class Diagrams

The definition and functionality of classes were defined in Chapter 3. However, classes, like all other modeling tools, may be decomposed to smaller components. Thus, a TP application may consist of many classes that execute as objects (remember that classes

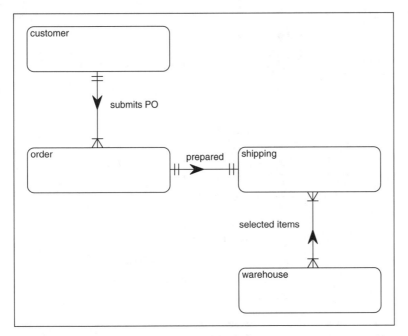

Figure 7.10 A class diagram.

are abstract, and only objects can execute). Figure 7.10 shows a typical class diagram for an order-processing TP activity.

The class diagram in Figure 7.11 shows how a customer class submits a purchase order for items to the order class. The orders are then prepared for shipping from the warehouse. The arrow on the flow between each class signifies the initiator of the transaction. That is, an order class cannot send a purchase order to the customer class. The crow's foot cardinality shows that a customer class must have at least one order to create a relationship with the order class. After an order is processed, it is prepared for shipment. Notice that each order class has one related shipment class; however, multiple warehouse items can be part of one shipment. Each class may also be further decomposed into other primitive classes as shown in Figure 7.11, which decomposes the warehouse class into three more primitive classes. This is consistent with the concept of the logical equivalent and with functional decomposition. The further the decomposition, the more reusable the class across multiple applications.

Identifying Classes

The most difficult challenge in designing classes to be incorporated into the middleware component is understanding what constitutes an object. Objects are based on the object-oriented (OO) concept, which assumes that every function or method must inevitably belong to an object. For the purposes of the TP system, we are interested only in those objects that may be required for multiple applications from the presentation layer (Tier 1). Earlier in this section, I defined the concept of business

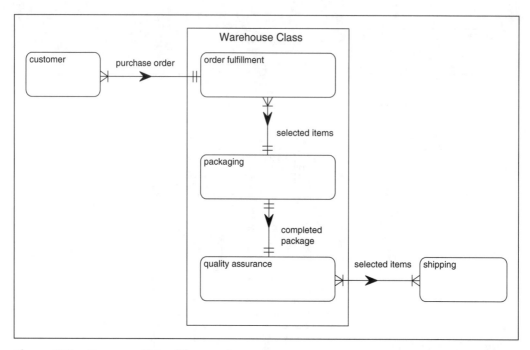

Figure 7.11   Decomposition of the warehouse class.

objects. These business objects are essential components for the processing of transactions. Therefore, the first step in developing the middleware layer is to create all of
the business essential objects. One approach to creating essentials is to ask the question: What is the purpose of the business from the user's perspective? If we were to
use the business depicted in Figure 7.11, we would have created the following four
essentials:

1. Record and place orders

2. Ship orders to customers

3. Track inventory

4. Service customers

Each one of these essentials is then transformed into a class and addressed as a
noun. Thus the resultant four reusable essential components become the customer
class, order class, shipping class, and warehouse class. Each class must then be internally defined with respect to its attributes and methods. A *class* is defined as "all the
common methods and all the common attributes for that class." Based on this definition, the customer class would be composed of "all the common attributes and all the
common methods for all customers." Thus, the customer class is said to be cohesive
because it is self-contained, meaning it can handle any request relating to a customer.
Cohesion is the measurement of how independent a program is with respect to its own
processing. The analyst must ensure that all of the attributes and methods are defined,
or the level of reusability of the object will be limited.

Table 7.2 Methods of Selecting Cohesive Classes

TIER	METHOD	METHOD DESCRIPTION
1	By function	Processes are combined into one object and/or class based on being a component of the same function. For example, Accounts Receivable, Sales, and Goods Returned are all part of the same function. A sale creates a receivable, and goods returned decrease the sale and the receivable.
2	By data	Processes are combined based on their use of the same data and data files. Processes that tend to use the same data are more cohesive.
3	By generic operation	Processes are combined based on their generic performance, for example, "editing" or "printing."
4	By lines of code	Processes are created after an existing process reaches a maximum number of lines in the actual program source code.

In the object paradigm, the attributes cannot be accessed directly without invoking a method. Another way of stating this rule is to say: "The only way to get to the data of an object is through its methods." The concept is simple: Methods are the programs that need certain data to complete their tasks, so the method controls which attributes are stored in a particular class. Because of this rule, ecommerce analysts should first define all of the methods of the class. This is accomplished by mapping each method to a functional primitive dataflow diagram (DFD). Indeed, a functional primitive DFD contains a process specification, which will become one of the methods in a class. The question remains: What functional primitive DFDs belong to a particular class? The way to answer this question is to create a process that incorporates the definition of cohesion. Table 7.2 illustrates how processes can be combined to obtain the best cohesion.

The above tiers are based on best to worst, where the "function" method is the most desirable and the "by lines of code" method is the least desirable. Tier 1 is the preferred method, and thus analysts should look at ways to capture all of the operations that are involved within an essential component. Whenever the analyst is confronted with an environment that he or she is not familiar with, then reliance on matching cohesive methods is difficult. Under these circumstances, ecommerce analysts should depend on Tier 2, "by data." The reason is as follows:

- Similar data is easier to identify in a functional DFD by simply matching processes that use the same data stores.

- Cohesive classes formulated by function always use similar data. While the converse is not always true, it provides a fairly good cohesive schema.

Once the methods have been established, then the analyst can begin the process of including the attributes that are required, thus completing the class design as shown in Figure 7.12. Note that the methods point to the DFDs and the attributes point to the Entity Relational Diagram (ERD).

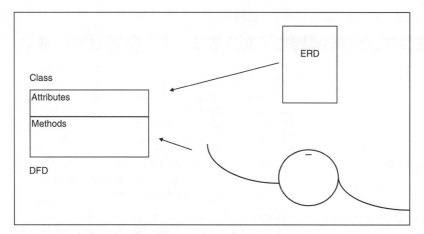

Figure 7.12 The relationship of a class to the DFD and ERD.

Providing Data Access and Integrity

Once the ecommerce analyst has completed the design of the reusable object programs, then the middle tier can be programmed with the logic it requires to do the selection. That is, the workflow control in the TP monitor will handle the request and then determine which object needs to be executed. For each request, there is one object component relationship, meaning that the same object may be executing in two or more simultaneous operations. This situation is known as "multiple instances" of the same object. In Tier 3 the TP servers are now required to enforce integrity by ensuring that two or more instances of the same object do not overlay the data that is being transformed. Figure 7.13 shows the dilemma of multiple instances of the same object program.

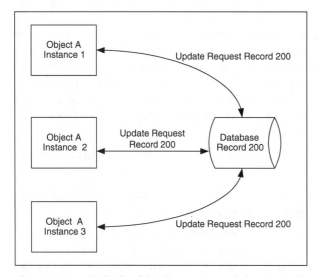

Figure 7.13 Multiple object instances and data integrity.

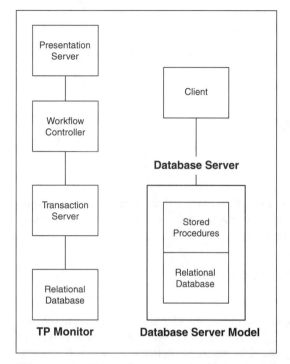

Figure 7.14 TP monitor versus database server tier architectures.

Figure 7.13 reflects the challenge of maintaining data integrity when two or more objects are operating on the same data. Tier 3 processing is also controlled at the database level. In fact, many TP monitor activities can be included within the database server. For example, the multithreaded features in the TP monitor, which provide the integrity of multiple instances of the same object, can also be included as a stored procedure at the database level. Given that integrity focuses on where and what is happening to the stored data, the programming of stored procedures using SQL can provide many of these constraints. When the database server is used to provide the workflow control features of the TP monitor, then the system resembles a two-tier structure rather than a three-tier architecture as shown in Figure 7.14.

The relative advantages and disadvantages of TP monitors versus database servers are complex. Database vendors continue to create new features and functions in an attempt to eliminate the need for TP monitors. However, there are several distinct advantages that database servers cannot offer. The following list provides a comparison of the two systems.

TP MONITOR

Standard programming languages

Better set of debugging tools

Compiled languages

Handles multiple file systems

Better systems management

Scalability

Formatted request messages

DATABASE SERVER

SQL-based

Interpretive run-time

Product-based

Better protocols

While this list provides a quick overview, it is important that ecommerce analysts and designers fully understand the meanings of each of these items so they can make informed decisions about the architecture of the software.

Advantages of TP Monitor Features and Functions

Standard programming languages. TP monitors offer a wide choice of software programming languages such as C, C++, JAVA, and even COBOL. These languages are transportable, meaning they can operate on multiple hardware platforms that use different operating systems. This is particularly important when using work-flow control in a distributed ecommerce system where multiple hardware and software environments exist. While database vendors provide an industry standard relational database format, their implementation of stored procedures is very proprietary. This means that the coding of workflow programs most likely will not work across different database vendor products.

Better set of debugging tools. Given the specialized and proprietary environment of relational databases, these products typically do not supply sophisticated debugging and development tools for programmers. As a result, debugging and maintaining relational database servers can be very detailed and primitive as compared to those provided with TP monitors.

Compiled languages. Languages that are compiled simply run faster, especially when systems need to be scalable. Most database-stored procedures are interpreted, meaning that they are transformed into machine language at execution time. While some database vendors do offer compiled versions of SQL, there is still the problem of compatibility of the generated code across operating systems and hardware platforms.

Handles multiple file systems. A TP monitor covers multiple database system products, unlike stored procedures written for a particular database server. Indeed, relational database systems generally support distributed transactions that access data in that one product (Bernstein and Newcomer, 1997). Further-more, the TP monitor can handle other specialized formats such as record-oriented file systems and queue managers.

Better systems management. TP monitors offer richer systems management environments than those supported by database servers. This is accomplished through geographical entitlement, meaning that the TP monitor knows about the different applications executing on multiple client machines across the ecommerce system. Because the TP monitor knows their disposition, it can prioritize the applications, do application-based load control, perform name resolution, and provide security. All of these are very difficult to do in database servers because they do not differentiate an application from a database. That is, they treat an application execution and a database transaction as the same event.

Scalability. Because of the presence of the third tier, TP monitor–based systems can be easily expanded when necessary. This is accomplished by adding another workflow control server to the middle tier. This is much more difficult to do with database servers. To add another database copy is very problematic because of the intricacies of data integrity. Replication of databases can also be complicated and have a significant impact on performance.

Formatted request messages. Formatted request messages operate better in TP systems because their workflow control uses a multistep process. Request messages are formatted to operate in a step-by-step process, carrying parameters between each step. This capability is not available in database servers.

Advantages of Database Server Features and Functions

SQL-based. SQL allows applications to be written and integrated in the database system. Clients can call stored procedures in the same way that presentation clients invoke transaction server programs. Most important is the similarity of database servers with database systems, their similarity being the support over transactions.

Interpretive run-time. While compiled languages offer efficiency in execution, they do not do so in terms of storage and resource allocation. Interpretive executions only use what they need, and can be modified for special circumstances. Compiled procedures, on the other hand, must provide all of the alternatives that might occur during an execution, and therefore use more code and reserve more resources than are actually needed.

Product-based. This is a two-way predicament. When describing the benefits of TP systems, professionals condemn the use of proprietary code as lacking in ability to be transportable. However, proprietary code is more efficient, executes in its intended native mode of operation, and can be modified to provide a dependable level of portability.

Better protocols. The proprietary nature of database servers allows them to be better tools for supporting database operations. This results in databases that are better tuned and faster in operation. While these protocols can be proprietary, they are more portable than it appears. Many database systems, such as Oracle, support their products across a wide range of hardware platforms, including

Unix, IBM mainframe, and Windows. Supporters of database server architecture are quick to point out that portability across many different brand databases will never exist, regardless of whether a TP object approach is used to offer geographic entitlement.

TP Monitors and Web Access

In ecommerce systems, the client node is implemented using a Web browser. Indeed, it will be the Web browser that will access the TP server. When using a Web browser, menus and forms can be submitted as a Uniform Resource Locator (URL) transaction. In this situation each URL specifies a particular transaction type. The menu, therefore, identifies the transaction to run, and the form contains the parameters of the transaction. The sequence of the interface with the TP monitor is shown in Figure 7.15.

When the user clicks one of the URLs displayed on a HyperText Markup Language (HTML) Web page, the browser forwards the address to the Web server. The Web server finds the URL and returns the HTML page that describes the URL form. The user then enters data into the form (thus creating the parameter). When the form is completed, another URL is sent back to the Web server as input to the transaction server. Thus, the Web server establishes itself as another layer between the client node and the TP system. The Web server has two components: daemon and TP monitor client.

A Web server daemon is really a dispatcher; that is, it takes URL requests from the browser and finds the appropriate Web page for return to the client. However, the browser request could also function as a call for a program script (the script is found at a particular URL). A program script is similar in function to a stored procedure. In this case the Web server acts as a client for the TP system. This part of the Web server is called the TP monitor client and submits the script as a transaction to the TP system. The TP system executes the transaction, and eventually returns the message in HTML to the Web browser via the Web server. Thus, the Web server acts as a gateway between the requesting browser and the TP system whenever the request is a program script. In this case, the TP system is relieved of being involved in satisfying the request. The Web server tier, therefore, acts to reduce traffic to the TP system by functioning as a workflow controller for URL requests.

The role of the ecommerce analyst is to determine the viability of setting up a Web server environment. There is an important protocol component, however, that must

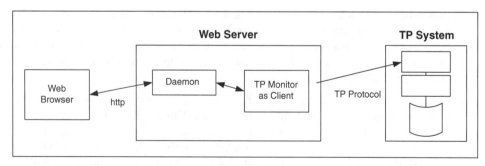

Figure 7.15   Using Web browsers to run transactions.

exist between the Web server and the TP system. The communication protocols vary based on hardware platform. Thus, the ecommerce analyst needs to review the existing or planned network topology to determine if and how a Web server configuration will be adopted in the application infrastructure.

Transaction Processing Communications

TP object programs communicate with each other, especially when they execute in a distributed ecommerce environment. Ecommerce analysts need to provide the requirements for the communications, which typically occur through various parameters passed from one application program to another. These parameters or messages can be communicated from one program to another using one of three methods:

Remote procedure call (RPC). This involves the "calling" of one program by another. This means that the called program gets loaded and executed. After the called program performs its function, it transfers control back to the calling program. Called programs, sometimes known as subprograms or subroutines, often return parameters or data back to the calling program. For example, a subprogram that calculates the square root of a number would send the number via a parameter (from the calling program), and the square-root program would calculate the value and send it back as a parameter to the calling application (see Figure 7.16).

When using RPC as the communication link among TP objects, the analyst must address the security exposure. Security becomes an issue in RPC in relation to the authentication of object access. Indeed, not all objects applications should be able to call any other subprogram. So the purpose of RPC security is to allow both client and server objects to authenticate the message and require it to hold infor-

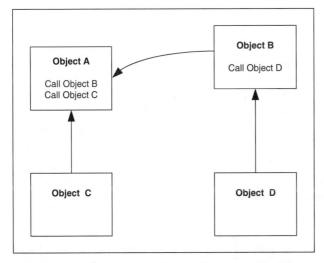

Figure 7.16   Remote procedure call between TP objects.

REMOTE PROCEDURE CALL SPECIFICATION

Date:	Requesting Application:	TP System ID:

Called Object	Access Security	Send Parameters	Return Parameters

Parameter Formats

Send:

Element Name:				
Value				

Return:

Element Name				
Value				

Comments:

Figure 7.17   RPC technical specification.

mation about what process has invoked the message and the response it requires. Once authentication is accomplished, there is yet another level of security—the security of the nature of the service itself. For example, a process may have authorization or security to access a record, but not to update that record. Therefore, all RPC specifications must provide a section where RPC calls are appropriately defined. Figure 7.17 is a sample RPC technical specification.

Peer-to-peer. This type of application communication is simply a formatted message sent from one program to another. There is no subcomponent as described in RPC. In object technology, this type of communication is called *collaboration* (see Figure 7.18).

Messages via queues. The message is formatted and placed in a queue. A queue is a data structure that is designed as an array (or single-dimensional table) and holds the message until another program reads it from the queue. The importance of a queue is that the calling program does not need to be executing in memory in

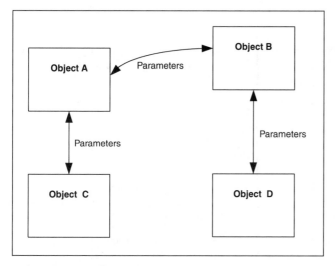

Figure 7.18 Peer-to-peer TP communication.

order to leave a parameter of data for another application. The benefit of this is twofold. First, the original program does not need to be executing; its removal from RAM provides efficient memory management. This means that RAM is freed for use by another program. In distributed ecommerce environments, analysts should always assume that there are more programs waiting to execute in RAM, so freeing programs from memory greatly increases the performance of the entire network. Second, there are no time limits on when the called program can pick up the message. This means that the data may need to be stored in the queue for a significant timeframe. Thus, whenever the application is loaded or requires that data, it can find it in the queue (see Figure 7.19).

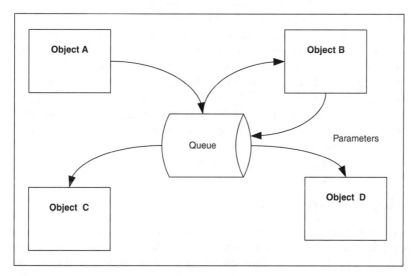

Figure 7.19 Parameter passing using queues.

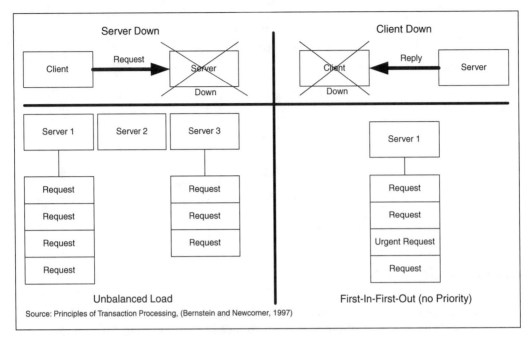

Figure 7.20   Queuing and direct TP messaging.

Another important reason for using queues is load balancing. *Load balancing* refers to a situation where there are more requests for a server or a client than the server or client can handle at one time. Unfortunately, if this should occur, the transaction will fail because the target is unable to respond. Queues represent a solution to this problem because they provide a strong facility to hold requests until the target is available. This is what is meant by "queuing transactions." Figure 7.20 shows how queuing can resolve direct TP messaging.

In terms of structure, a queue is designed to operate under the auspices of the first-in, first-out (FIFO) algorithm, which stipulates that requests are processed sequentially as they are received. However, more advanced queue facilities can handle priority-based scheduling where each request can be tagged with a different priority setting. This allows a transaction to be processed before another transaction, based on its priority setting. The mechanisms available in queuing are subject to the features and functions of the operating system environment. For example, the Unix operating system supports queues called *pipes*. Analysts must understand the network operating system in order to designate what communications protocol they want used in the development of the ecommerce system.

Database Replication

Replication is the technique of using multiple copies of the same data as a means of improving performance as well as improved availability. Each copy of a server database is called a replica. In this chapter we have previously covered examples of program

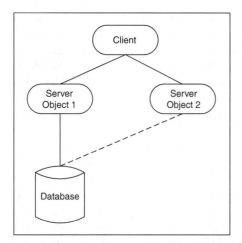

Figure 7.21   Replication of object services.

replication using object instances and the responsibilities associated with tracking the states of multiple instances of the same object. This concept is shown in Figure 7.21.

This section focuses on *data* replication: the challenges of having multiple copies of the same data, and the integrity challenges associated with keeping multiple copies of this data. The concept behind a data replication infrastructure is to provide another layer of improved access and performance. Thus, there is a time when multiple instances of objects can no longer provide appreciable performance improvements. Analysts must therefore consider data replication as another means of performance enhancements. Figure 7.22 represents the architecture of data and process replication.

Another reason data replication may be preferred relates to the nature of the application. There are essentially two types of application behavior: memory and input/out-

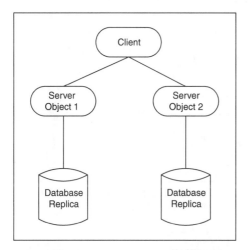

Figure 7.22   Data replication architecture.

put (I/O). Memory-oriented programs need RAM to perform their functions. This often is the case in products such as spreadsheets that need to store vast amounts of data within RAM to complete its functions. I/O applications, on the other hand, are those that must continually perform data access. These programs read data, change it, delete it, and update it. Therefore, I/O programs are constantly accessing the server databases, which, in turn, creates data access contention. Data replication will have its greatest impact on I/O systems because it relieves this contention by allowing different applications to be served by a copy of the same database.

The challenge of successfully implementing data replication is another story. A copy of any data immediately raises the issue of how to keep such data or replicas synchronized. *Synchronized data* means that replicas are identical at all times. This requires that all replicas be updated simultaneously. While architecturally feasible, this goal is often unrealistic. There are two major obstacles to data replication. The first obstacle relates to performance. Multiple update processes for each I/O against the database will create major performance barriers. Indeed, updating one record in a database could result in repeating the update for many replicas. The second obstacle is hardware and process failure. Earlier in this chapter we examined the intricacies of ensuring that transactions complete their tasks. The two-phase commit was the vehicle to ensure that all resources were capable of completing the transaction before allowing the process to actually occur. Database replication establishes another tier of potential problems in that the replication could fail because one of the replicas has not completed—perhaps because of a hardware malfunction. Furthermore, one of the replicas could be engaged in a process that is tied up and its database cannot respond in time to handle the request. Each of these dilemmas suggests that synchronization will fail at some point in time. The question then becomes How will the databases be resynchronized? The answer to this question is "with great pain"! Providing synchronized data replications forces ecommerce analysts to provide backup processes that will need to reindex themselves regularly to ensure that data is reliable. This means that a failed database replica might have to be reindexed during production time. This could result in system delays because one server failed. Another practice is to have backup replicas—replicas that are synchronized, but offline. When a server fails, the backup replica is brought online. Another term for this process is "database fail-over." The use of fail-over systems, including their advantages and disadvantages, will be discussed further in Chapter 8. Figure 7.23 shows how synchronized replication occurs.

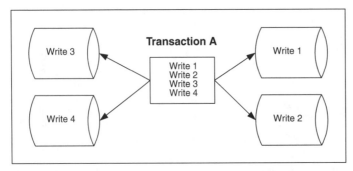

Figure 7.23 Synchronous replication.

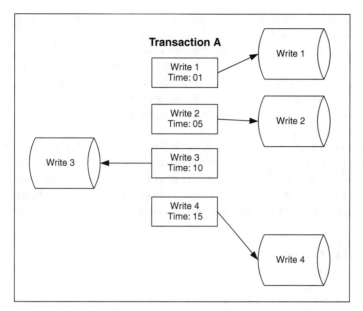

Figure 7.24 Asynchronous replication design.

The other type of data replication is asynchronous. *Asynchronous replication* means that data replicas are updated independently. Asynchronous data replications therefore are not real-time, leading to a timing difference between copies of the data. The problem is obvious: Asynchronous data replication cannot be used for production purposes because the data may not be the same across replicas. However, asynchronous replication is very useful for data warehousing. Data warehousing was conceived as a means of providing read-only replications of data for purposes of decision support (also known as decision support systems, or DSS). DSS flattens out the data (that is, creates fewer tables because there is no need for data integrity) strictly for analysis of information and reporting. This is useful in situations where a timing difference is not a problem because the user is looking at historical data. The design of data warehouses will be covered in further detail in Chapter 9. Figure 7.24 depicts asynchronous replication design.

Primary and Secondary Data Replicas

Another popular approach for analysts to consider is primary and secondary replication algorithms. This design creates a primary copy of the data that is used to capture all transactions against the original database. All updates are made from the results or accumulation of the transactions. Therefore, the exact updates are applied from the primary and are transferred and reapplied to replicas, called *secondaries*. Thus, each secondary converges toward the same state as the primary database.

The stream of the data coming into a secondary can be quite large, so there is a purification built into the process, meaning that transactions that have no effect on the data and aborted transactions can be purged from the update file. The stream can be generated from the database log file by providing triggers that update from the primary database, or, alternatively, the update can be implemented via a process in the TP system. Primary and secondary replica is another form of asynchronous replication and is very useful because analysts and designers can control and alternate the update process among different replicas of the same data. The importance of having this ability is that ecommerce designers can determine the sensitivity of data synchronization by application and design the TP monitor system accordingly, that is, by limiting copies of secondary databases to only certain applications.

While data replication is a challenging proposition, analysts must consider it during the design of the TP system. In any event analysts must understand that replication affects how the data is designed, how transaction programs will behave, what data needs to be communicated among processes, and what types of databases need to be constructed. The following is a list of ecommerce analysis tasks as they relate to data replication.

SYNCHRONOUS REPLICATION

Database name

Number of real-time copies needed

Restore time requirements

Operating systems

Number of fail-over systems

ASYNCHRONOUS REPLICATION (FOR EACH REPLICATION)

Database name

Replication type

Time sequence

Operating system

Data warehouse schema

Trigger event

Summary

The use of TP systems is being fueled by the advent of ecommerce systems that use the Web as their primary vehicle of communications with the user communities. TP systems are also becoming popular because of "commoditization," or the declining costs of server systems and the growing popularity of packaged applications. The proliferation of access needs fueled by the Web continues to drive the high volumes that TP systems serve so well.

In order to be effective and keep the costs of TP systems low, their application components must be reusable under the auspices of the object paradigm and object-oriented programming philosophy. The use of reusable components within the workflow control of TP systems must operate with database technologies. There will continue to be choices about whether to implement application procedures at the TP monitor level or at the database server tier, which uses stored procedures in SQL. Furthermore, there are mechanisms such as Web servers that must be part of the ecommerce architecture to make TP systems available over the Internet and to serve as a gateway for communicating with multiple TP systems.

Performance of TP systems is critical, and the analysis of how to employ replication concepts to both the application and database levels will be major architectural decisions that both analysts and network designers need to deal with. Ecommerce analysts will need to provide the necessary specifications that consider all of the advantages and disadvantages of how TP systems can be built in accordance with database design and client/server technologies. This will not be an easy task.

Integrating Intranet and Internet Web Applications Across Multiple Networks

The purpose of this chapter is to define the role of the ecommerce analyst in deciding how applications will operate over multiple networks—including, of course, the Internet. This role is critically important, as most application development systems will be expanded to include Intranet/Internet and Web processing. Ecommerce analysis and design therefore become an integral part of establishing how application programs will operate over a wide variety of network topologies. Indeed, application distribution across an ecommerce system will affect the network design of the entire system. Thus, the purpose of this chapter is to determine the specific processes that must occur during ecommerce systems design and to explore how ecommerce design ties in with the overall requirements analysis procedure. Analysts have an enormous contribution to make to the design of the network topology itself. Indeed, the architecture of the network is based on both hardware and software relationships. In most cases, the decisions that dictate how and where software will reside on the network will be based on access and performance measurements. It is, therefore, very important that analysts understand the relationships among network components and how each of these components affects application access and system performance. Perhaps the most important piece of the network challenge is to understand the client/server paradigm.

Client/Server Network Topology

Client/server provides the basis of distributed processing across the ecommerce system. The concept of client/server has always been based on distributed processing, where data and programs are installed in the most efficient places on the system. Furthermore, the need of a program to be on a client, server, or client/server will determine the hardware configurations needed. Client/server applications have three components: a client, a server, and a network. Before we consider the role of the network, let us first define what clients and servers do in an ecommerce environment.

A *server* is something that provides information to a requestor. Typically, a server responds to a request rather than being the initiator, although certain server activities do initiate processes. Many network configurations have permanent servers that do nothing else but provide requested information to a client. An example of this type of server is a *back-end* database, which waits for requests and then responds to them, typically by supplying the record to the requesting process. A *client*, on the other hand, is the requestor or the source of the request. In many network infrastructures the client is the workstation PC. These types of clients are known as the *front-end*. Front-end clients are dedicated clients, that is, they do nothing but request data from servers. Often, clients and servers are not dedicated: They can behave as either clients or servers, depending on the application that is executing and the configuration they have with the rest of the network. Such components are simply known as *client/servers* because of their dual capabilities. A typical client/server is used in a three-tier architecture, in which the middle tier acts as both a client and a server. It acts as a server by providing responses to the dedicated workstations or clients. It behaves as a client when it requests data from a particular database on the network. Figure 8.1 depicts a client/server network topology.

Network Servers

Network servers are those computers that contain data and/or applications that are made available to a number of workstations. A number of different combinations of software and data can reside on a particular server. In a three-tier architecture, there is a database server that provides data to many application servers. In this context, ecommerce analysts need to provide information to network engineers that identifies:

- The size of the databases
- Users' data access requirements
- Users' required response time objectives
- Users' downtime limitations

Size of the Database

The size of the database relates to the number of data elements within each entity. The expected number of records in each entity ultimately allows an analyst to predict the actual size of the data using the following formula by entity:

(Expected number of records * length of each record)

For example, if an Employee Master file has 100 employees, and each row or record is a total of 205 bytes (a byte of data is one storage unit or character of information), then the appropriate physical database size is:

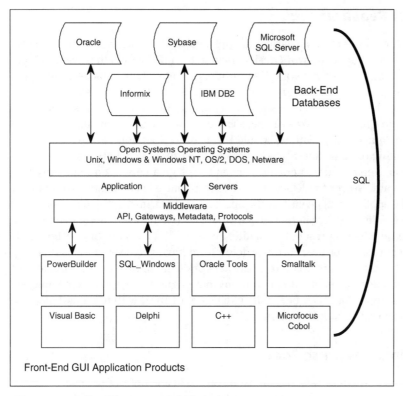

Figure 8.1   Client/server network topology. (Langer, 167)

$$100 * 205 = 20{,}500 \text{ bytes}$$

The entity of the database could then be defined as shown in Figure 8.2.

Understanding the data requirements allows analysts to provide valuable information to network designers regarding the amount of data storage needed, or disk size.

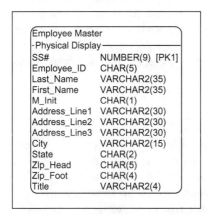

Figure 8.2   Employee Master record layout.

Data Access Requirements

Access requirements refers to the variety of applications that users are allowed to use. Access requirements supply network designers with the information they need to "configure" a user's profile on the network. User profiles dictate which databases and applications users have access to. In addition, access rights may be restricted to read-only, insert/update, or delete. This relates specifically to the design of the TP systems that were discussed in Chapter 7. However, access requirements also come into play when deciding where data and applications should reside on the network. For instance, suppose an accounting organization needs access to most of its accounting software in a specific location. Network designers might need to design a network architecture that provides a dedicated server to the accounting department. This dedicated server might contain only the applications needed by the accounting department. The purpose of this infrastructure would be to create better performance for the accounting department, which in this case might represent the significant users of the accounting system. This does not suggest that other users are restricted from having access to the accounting system, but rather that the architecture of the network can improve the performance of certain application departments. It is important to recognize that ecommerce analysts must provide the input for this process since they are involved with users and have the skills to gather the required information.

User Required Response Times

User required response time objectives must be obtained and defined to ensure that the network meets user response time requirements. Indeed, response time is the most crucial component of the user's view. Response times that exceed 6 seconds are often seen as unacceptable to users; however, this can vary based on application and the industry being supported. For example, there are many stock market activities that require strict response time performance. Thus, during the interview process, ecommerce analysts need to be aware of the importance of examining response time limitations. In fact, all screen designs should contain an area that addresses response time requirements. It should be recognized that response time performance is not limited to the network. The design of the application and the way it is organized by the programmers are equally critical. Unfortunately, many GUI-based applications cannot overcome performance response time problems solely through their design. Response time design must be augmented by careful client/server design of the network; therefore the ecommerce analyst, programmer, and network engineer must jointly participate in the design of the hardware infrastructure.

Downtime Limitations

User downtime limitations relate to the period of time in which the system can be inoperable before there are serious consequences to the organization. This problem is addressed in two areas: (1) hardware architecture, and (2) software design.

The hardware solution to downtime problems is known as "no single point of failure." This means that all critical parts of the network hardware are examined, and replication of hardware is implemented wherever downtime issues become critical (see

Chapter 7, relating to replication of databases). Imagine "no single point of failure" as a train track system, in which a train can be put on an alternate track if there is a block or backup on its normal track. Advanced long-distance telephone systems have used this concept for decades, and current Web-based network communications systems usually employ a third-party frame-relay system, which provides similar multiple-path protection schemes. Thus, "no single point of failure" is a type of insurance policy against disaster. The amount of network redundancy needed is directly related to the critical nature of the application. Because of the critical nature of ecommerce systems, multiple path architecture is required, both for the internal Intranet, and for the external Internet linkages.

Software design can also provide protection against downtime problems. Redundant databases, or replicas, as defined in Chapter 7, can provide protection against lost data and can quicken data restoration. An example of complex data restoration is Microsoft's Exchange server. Many systems today have integrated email with telephony. Thus Exchange becomes a vital component in keeping both email and telephones working, with the latter being the most critical component. The restoration of email and telephone data from tape backup could take many hours and in some cases more than a day. The way to address this problem is to have the Exchange server broken down into multiple servers so that no single server can bring down the entire system. The Exchange database has the ability to operate among multiple servers, so that the actual number of servers could be determined by the user's defined downtime limitation and the time required for tape restoration. To ensure that certain key users always have email, duplicate or alias accounts can be put on each subset Exchange server. The restoration requirements of data can dramatically change the network infrastructure, as in this case from one Exchange email server to multiple servers working together. In terms of application redundancy, multiple application servers can be installed under the auspices of the client/server middle tier. Application redundancy is probably the easiest of the redundancies to implement, although the costs for hardware and communication may be high.

Network Workstations

Network workstations represent the desktop of the user community. Today, most desktop workstations are comprised of a microcomputer using the Microsoft Windows environment. While this is the most common desktop operating system, it is not the only possible workstation configuration. Apple workstations are still common in businesses that use desktop publishing and video software. Apple Macintosh workstations may indeed expand with the proliferation of Web-based applications that require video and high performance graphics as discussed in Chapter 6. Furthermore, Unix- and Linux-based systems are very popular and require what is called a "dumb" terminal interface. Thus, there are three potential hardware "clients": Windows PC, Apple Macintosh, and "dumb" terminal interfaces. Ecommerce systems need to support all three.

More important than the type of hardware client is the configuration of the workstation itself and whether multiple types of interfaces are required. In some cases, a workstation may need to be configured to interface with a number of different host computers. Each interface may require unique software. For example, a Unix interface might require a non-GUI dumb terminal interface as opposed to a GUI Windows-based application.

The most far-reaching issue in workstation ecommerce analysis is deciding what software should reside on the "client" itself. To make this decision, ecommerce analysts need to determine what software needs to reside on a particular server, client workstation, or TP system. The analyst must work cooperatively with network engineers to determine how software will be configured. The ultimate question is Which component—hardware or software—influences the design first? Specifically, should the decision about the size and configuration of a network workstation be made before applications are designed? The decision about what software resides on a workstation should emanate from the ecommerce software requirements. Execution expectations, reusability needs, and ease of maintenance all play a major role in network design. This suggests, then, that workstation configuration should not be finalized without input from analysts who have performed application requirements analysis.

Another important aspect of workstation software analysis is the interfaces with "office" software products. "Office" software typically includes off-the-shelf products such as Microsoft's Word, Excel, and PowerPoint. Users often require software that makes use of these products and thus requires direct product interfaces. Another popular implementation is the connectivity between electronic mail (email) and applications. The usual bridge relates to the contact management features of Microsoft's Outlook Exchange database and its integration with application products. For example, Exchange has a built-in customer database feature that integrates with email. Users can create lists of contacts with relevant information such as phone number, address, etc., in Exchange. The information can also be seamlessly integrated with email, providing users with a useful interface. Furthermore, many application products such as accounts payable and accounts receivable keep lists of contacts. The Exchange database can be integrated with the application to form one central database among all the products. Today, this type of ecommerce interfacing among applications is known as Contact Resource Management, or "CRM." CRM not only centralizes contact information but also reduces data entry time and eliminates redundancy. The effects of this integration are dramatic for users, particularly those that are supporting a client base via the Web. There are essentially three major issues to focus on in order to implement application integration with office products. First, there is the complexity of integrating the data. The format of the Exchange database may need to be modified or enhanced to meet the needs of the application. Furthermore, not all components of the Exchange database are in 3rd Normal Form (see Chapter 4). Second is the determination of what portion of the application can and should be integrated with Exchange. In this situation, analysts must be able to understand the Exchange database configuration and to apply good database design to integrate its entities with the other databases that exist. Third, the analyst needs to work with network engineers on where the applications should reside—on the workstation or the server—and what impact they will have on the overall network topology.

The Middle Tier

The middle tier of the client/server three-tier architecture is usually reserved for application software and the TP system. The middle tier is called the *application server level* because it contains what is often referred to as the "production software." *Production software* is defined as the software that is used to complete the production

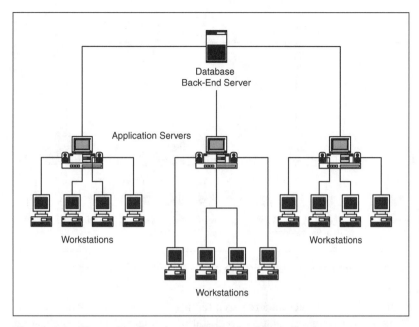

Figure 8.3 Three-tier client/server network with application servers.

cycle. The middle tier is considered the best level to install applications because it is scalable, that is, performance can be maintained or improved by simply adding more application servers to the middle tier. Scalability is attained because increasing the number of application servers reduces the number of workstations per server, thus decreasing or maintaining the ratio of workstations to servers. For example, Figure 8.3 depicts an existing three-tier architecture that contains one database back-end server, three application servers, and 12 workstations. The application servers are each handling four workstations.

Figure 8.4 depicts the same network with an additional application server that reduces the number of workstations per application server by one. Thus, the additional application server improves performance because it reduces the ratio of server to workstation by one, or a 25 percent reduction in hardware load. This example is limited; it reflects a network design that has consistent symmetry between each workstation group. This means that the number of workstations to servers is equivalent. In reality, this is often not the case. Whether each workstation is symmetrically aligned with servers depends on other variables, such as location and user work habits. This example also assumes that every server contains the same application software configuration, which in many situations may not be the case.

There is ongoing debate about the extent to which application products should reside on the workstation versus on the middle tier. Generally, there are advantages and disadvantages on both sides. Keeping the office software on the workstation increases performance but creates a "fatter" and more expensive client. Keeping application products on the middle tier, on the other hand, makes them easier to administer, and creates "thinner" and cheaper clients, but can cause network traffic conflicts. These decisions should be made jointly, since neither the analyst nor the network engineer should make

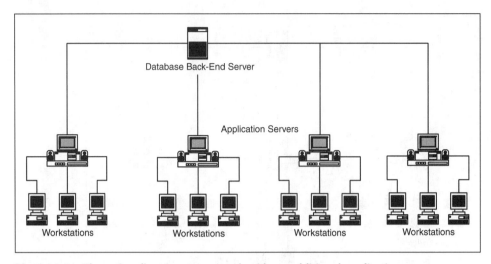

Figure 8.4   Three-tier client/server network with an additional application server.

the decision alone. However, the ecommerce architecture, because of its assumed interface with the Web, needs to support multiple workstation configurations. As such, good analysis will often support schemas that reduce the amount of software at the client level. This is known as a "thin client." The advantages of the thin client include portability and maintainability. Portability is maximized because the application is downloaded directly to the user's workstation, where it can dynamically determine its hardware environment and execute properly. Maintainability is increased because only one version of the application is needed. Furthermore, changes to the application can be made without worrying about copies that exist on multiple workstations. The thin-client paradigm ensures that only the current copy of the application is used for each new instance or execution. The problem with thin clients is performance. The time required to dynamically transfer application programs across the Web and local area networks is relatively long and subject to network traffic delays. Thus, ecommerce analysts need to compromise between portability and performance. Furthermore, ecommerce analysts cannot ignore cost constraints. Hardware, although cheaper than in the past, can still be very expensive. The constraints of cost must be understood before determining what might be the "best" solution. That is, "best" includes cost considerations and constraints.

Client/Server Application Design

Client/server systems must adhere to the object paradigm. Based on an object-oriented (OO) implementation, client/server essentially requires another step: the determination of what components of a class should become part of client-only operations, server-only operations, or both. I have previously defined client/server topology in this chapter. Client/server with respect to OO design operates essentially the same, that is, a class can be designed to be server-only, client-only, or both. This determination must affect

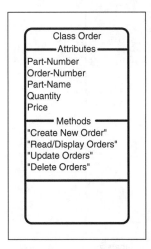

Figure 8.5   Class Order.

functional decomposition of the class. Therefore, upon extending the definition of client/server to applications, we look at the behavior of an object or class and categorize it as a client (requesting service), server (providing services), or both (providing and requesting services).

The difficulty in client/server application design is in the further separation of attributes and methods for purposes of performance across an ecommerce network. This means that methods and attributes of a class that represent server-only activities might need to be separated from those that are client-only specific. For example, in Chapter 3, I discussed the concept of program reuse and how to determine which methods were to become part of which classes. I stated that the best approach was to find methods that established CRUD (Create, Read, Update, and Delete). The sample class contained four methods: "Create New Order," "Read/Display New Order," "Update New Order," and "Delete Order" as shown in Figure 8.5.

Suppose, however, that certain of these methods were used by a specific part of the network or at a particular tier for performance purposes. For example, if new orders were placed only by a certain department and that department had its own local area network connected to the entire system, it would be possible to have the "New Orders" methods installed on their application server only. Furthermore, suppose updates and deletions to orders were handled by another department that also had its own internal network. All users, on the other hand, could display existing orders. The Class Order could be decomposed into three classes as shown in Figure 8.6.

First, it is important to understand the relationship between these classes. Classes (in this case, objects) have the ability to inherit attributes and methods from other objects when they are placed within the same class diagram as they have been in Figure 8.6. The line that connects two classes creates what is known as a parent-child relationship. The parent is the server, and the child is the client. In Figure 8.6, Class Order is the parent (server) and Classes Update/Delete and Read/Display Orders are the children (clients). Thus, Class Order can provide its attributes and methods to both of its children. This capability is called Object Inheritance and means that all children objects effectively

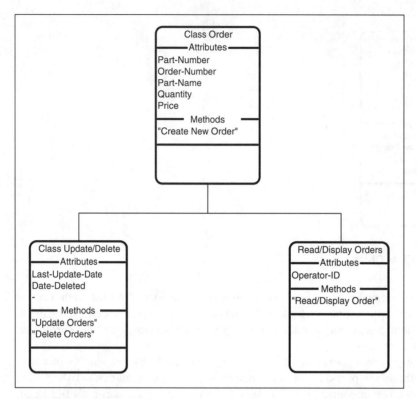

Figure 8.6 Decomposed class order.

contain all of the capabilities of their parents. Inheritance is implemented as a tree structure. [A *tree structure* is a data structure containing zero or more nodes that are linked together in a hierarchical fashion. The topmost node is called the *root* or *parent*. The root can contain zero to many children nodes, connected by links. Each child node can in turn have zero or more children of its own (*Computer Dictionary*, 2nd ed., Microsoft Press, p. 397).] However, instead of information flowing upward (as in most tree data structures), the data flows downward to the lowest-level children. For this reason, object inheritance is said to behave as an inverted tree. Object inheritance is the structure that allows objects to be decomposed and distributed across the network. Therefore, an object can be installed on one machine but inherit attributes and methods from its parents that are installed on another computer across the network. It is this capability that allows objects to be decomposed and installed on a client/server network as shown in Figure 8.7.

Web Platform Choices

One of the most challenging aspects of ecommerce systems is the selection of the operating systems and hardware platforms to host the data and execute the applications. The selection of hardware goes hand in hand with operating system and application

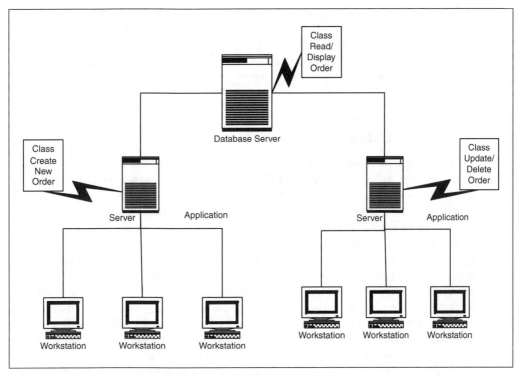

Figure 8.7 Client/server distribution of Class Order methods.

server software choices. Because of the impact of the platform, ecommerce analysts must be aware of or participate in its selection. Indeed, many decisions about client/server design depend on the hardware platform. Furthermore, the decision of platform and ultimately software architecture will have a significant impact on the performance of the network. Platforms generally fall into three categories: mainframe, mid-range, and workstation or PC. While there are no formal rules about what each platform does best, the following sections provide guidelines on their typical uses in complex networks.

Mainframe Computers

Mainframe computers belong to a family of large machines purchased to handle voluminous amounts of data and processing. Many of these machines were originally purchased during the 1960s and 1970s and contain legacy applications written in third-generation programming languages. Most mainframes have what is called "proprietary operating systems," meaning that the operating system supports only that platform. This results in software that cannot be easily ported to or from the hardware environment. The most popular mainframe is the IBM line of machines, which originally emanated from the 360/370 family of computers and are now called the OS/390 series. These machines have tremendous input/output power, but are very expensive to maintain and support. Applications that exist on these machines are usually "homegrown" enterprise systems that support production operations such as enterprise resource planning operations (ERP). Furthermore, mainframes store huge databases that are often fed by these proprietary applications. IBM's DB2 is the most prevalent relational database resident on the OS/390 systems, with Oracle a distant second. Thus, mainframe systems are rarely purchased as part of a new client/server ecommerce system, but rather "inherited" as part of the important legacy operations of the organization.

Midrange Computers

The midrange computers are used in the middle tier and the back end. These computers were originally called *minicomputers* because they were cheaper but did not have the speed and storage of a mainframe computer. However, the ability of these computers to be scaled upward has made them the most versatile machines. Scaling is accomplished not only by increasing hardware components but also by containing operating systems that can handle the software responsibilities of larger systems. The first such operating system to handle scalability across networked computers was Unix. Indeed, Unix remains one of the most powerful portable operating systems available for ecommerce solutions. Windows NT and 2000 operating systems have also supported scalable network needs. In most instances, Unix and Windows work together to provide the most portable, reliable, and scalable network solutions in the industry. The growth of ecommerce application servers has also established an important "server" role for midrange machines. As previously defined, application servers do the work for authenticating users, generating transactions (TP systems), and retrieving data that may be stored on back-end servers. Furthermore, most new hardware configurations also use midrange computers to host databases, rather than large and expensive mainframes. The Unix and Windows platforms are supported by most of the major database vendors including Oracle, Sybase, Informix, and DB2. Microsoft SQL Server supports only the Windows operating systems. Ecommerce analysts will need to be involved with the decision about which operating system to use with which hardware. For example, if Microsoft SQL Server were selected, then only Windows-based servers could be used in the network. Decisions about whether to use SQL Server over Oracle are complex. While SQL Server might be cheaper to use, it is not as scalable as Oracle.

Workstation Computers

Ecommerce workstations are dominated by Windows-based operating systems (Windows 95, 98, NT, and 2000). This is particularly true for Intranet personnel, and for many businesses and consumers. Workstations typically store the browser product that will be used to launch any Web applications. However, as stated previously, workstations could also be Macintosh or dumb terminal. Should this be the case, as it is in most ecommerce Web systems, the critical issue facing ecommerce analysts relates to Java versus ASP. Java is an open-system middleware tool that allows applications to be dynamically downloaded to the workstation. The advantage of using Java is that it has an interpretive run time that allows it to adapt to the hardware environment. Therefore, Java can be used to execute software on a variety of platforms, including Windows, Macintosh, and certain dumb terminals. The problem is that Java, while portable, is slow. On the other hand, Active Server Page (ASP) is a competing product created by Microsoft. ASP supports only Windows-based hardware. Because of its limited support, ASP is less interpretive, and thus runs faster. When analysts need to consider the design of TP systems, middleware selection of Java and/or ASP is critical for the compatibility and design of workstation support. As is expected, ecommerce applications may need to support multiple workstations. In these situations, Java is the only alternative to providing the necessary portability across workstations.

Fail-Over Technology

Fail-over is defined as the process of taking a group of resources offline on one cluster node and bringing them online on another cluster node (Clarke, 2001). The overall benefit of fail-over systems is to minimize or eliminate the high cost of network downtime, particularly as it relates to database operations. Ecommerce analysts, as the initial designers of the database, need to be the drivers for architecting database infrastructures that allow for fail-over. Indeed, the prevention of ecommerce downtime can often pay for the entire deployment costs of ebusiness operations. A fail-over can be unplanned or planned. *Unplanned fail-over* is a response to an unexpected problem, such as a resource or system failure. *Planned fail-over* is a preplanned event such as a hardware or software upgrade. A *cluster* is any physical or logical group of processes. Clusters are, in effect, groups of independent computers that operate as a single virtual system. Clusters thus become the component that can eliminate single points of failures in the network. Ecommerce analysts must participate in determining what groups of client/server network components will be combined to form a cluster. Furthermore, analysts need to design the type of fail-over system to be employed. These decisions can affect the overall support and dependability of the network. In terms of physically creating clusters, all major hardware vendors produce cluster configurations.

Before proceeding with the different types of fail-over systems that can be used, it is important to understand some of the key concepts surrounding fail-over technology.

Cluster resource. Any physical or logical component (computer or software) that is configured and managed within the cluster and provides a service to a requesting client.

Group. A logical container that can hold zero or more cluster resources. A group is the minimum unit of fail-over. Each cluster resource must be a member of exactly one group.

Virtual server. A logical server available to clients at a fixed Internet Protocol (IP) address and configured to operate on any one of a set of physical computer servers. This means that a physical computer server can contain many virtual or logical servers within one physical unit. From a system perspective, it appears as multiple servers even though it is on one physical machine. Therefore, a client cannot determine which physical server and physical cluster is hosting the virtual server.

Virtual address. A fixed location that is independent of the physical network address from which clients can access resources in a group regardless of where

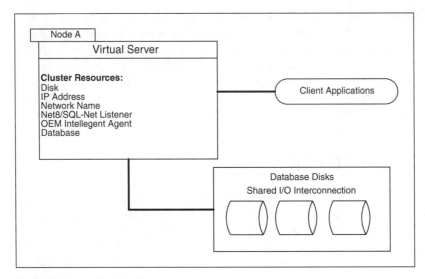

Figure 8.8   Network cluster.

the specific hardware is located. By utilizing virtual addressing, physical hardware locations can be changed (which is required in fail-over) without affecting the logical coding in software applications. That is, the software programs that access the information need not be changed if the physical location of the information is moved to another computer.

Figure 8.8 reflects the components of a network cluster.

Fail-Over Process

The essential goal in fail-over technology is to provide a transparent reconnection of a system that restores a new cluster that appeared as the original did prior to the failure. This essentially means that there is a mirror system that exists in another part of the system that will substitute for the failed member. Thus it prevents a single point of failure from shutting down a complex ecommerce system.

From the client request perspective, a fail-over appears as a server reboot. Typically the client needs to reconnect to the new virtual server, and all uncommitted work in progress is probably lost. Reconnection, particularly in Web applications, could be as simple as rebooting the workstation or refreshing a browser. Figure 8.9 provides a graphic depiction of the process of client connection before and after fail-over occurs.

Figure 8.9 illustrates how a two-node cluster changes after a fail-over occurs. In this example, the client is originally configured to access the database on virtual server C. The virtual server C is resident on physical server Node A. When Node A fails, the system automatically fails-over to a different physical machine, which is virtually coded as Node B. The reconnection to the new server is invisible in that the user never knows that the data is on another machine.

When selecting the software components on a cluster, analysts can select from a number of different deployment architectures. Three options are available:

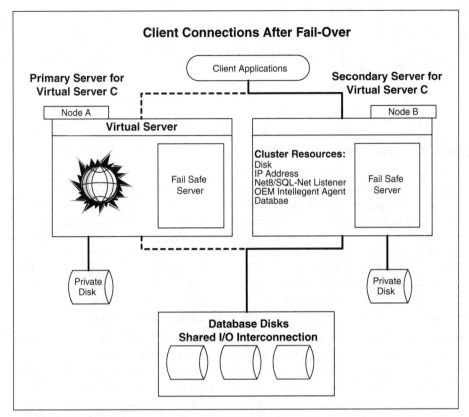

Figure 8.9   Client connection changes before and after fail-over.

Active/Passive. This is a cluster configuration where one node is idle in anticipation of a fail-over. It is an idle backup. This configuration is usually used if there is a single virtual server or with multiple servers and users that need the fastest possible fail-over time. This option can be costly, since a mirror hardware system must be provided to anticipate a full load of operation at any given time. Figure 8.10 depicts an Active/Passive cluster deployment.

Active/Active. This cluster deployment is configured so that all nodes perform work simultaneously. If one of the nodes fails, its workload is distributed to the surviv-

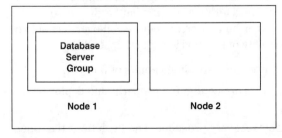

Figure 8.10   Active/Passive cluster deployment.

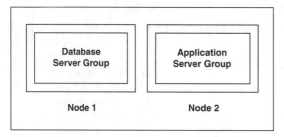

Figure 8.11 Active/Active cluster deployment.

ing node, which continues to handle its original responsibilities. Therefore, this type of configuration must ensure that all nodes have excess capacity so that they can handle unexpected spikes in memory and disk space. This configuration is used when there is more than one virtual server and engineers want to leverage backups across multiple machines. This method then is more about economy of scale in that there is no longer a one-to-one relationship between nodes and fail-over nodes. The penalty is in performance. Active/Active configurations are much slower to fail-over and require that each node have additional space that may never be required. Figure 8.11 shows an Active/Active configuration.

Multitiered. This deployment method is a hybrid in that it allows multiple layers of different cluster configurations. This is a common configuration when there is a need to separate cluster configurations between application and database nodes. It allows scalable needs to vary based on the needs of the business. Multitiered configurations offer flexibility and diverse deployment capability within the same node, which is often required for ecommerce solutions. Figure 8.12 shows a Multitiered configuration.

Best Practices in Fail-Over Analysis

While ecommerce analysts need not be the actual implementers of the fail-over system, I believe they should be responsible for the procedure that determines which process best supports the software architecture and user needs. This is a complex process. Therefore, a set of best practices needs to be followed to ensure that the solution provides the remedy that best fits the business. In order to properly accomplish this, ecommerce analysts need to examine the risks associated with all components and to identify potential points of failure. I suggest that analysts do this because network engineers alone are not positioned to make such a decision. Indeed, the determination of what hardware, software, external power, network connections, and human error require fail-over technology must include the user community. Reliability of systems in general depends on:

- Identifying and eliminating what users feel are single points of failure.

- Ensuring that software and hardware are configured properly, and deployed and maintained in a consistent way.

- Providing the appropriate disaster recovery procedures and solutions that operate within the constraints of the designed fail-over configuration.

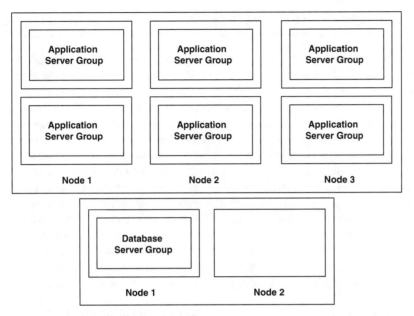

Figure 8.12 Multitiered cluster deployment.

- Defining the cycle of hardware and software verification. This means that there are procedures to ensure that maintenance checks are done periodically to avoid system failure.

Because of the variation and complex nature of network topology and software installation alternatives, best practices to meet the above guidelines must be specifically tailored for each system. However, the list below provides some general guidelines about issues that every ecommerce analyst should consider before finalizing fail-over requirements.

- Ensure that all cluster hardware is compatible throughout the network components.

- Configure the disk and file system to handle growth and fail-over system requirements.

- Use redundant array of inexpensive disks (RAID) to eliminate the need for mirrored copies of data. RAID is a disk storage technique that improves performance and fault tolerance. Therefore, most database storage devices are placed on RAID to provide mirrored copies of the data on multiple smaller disks. Virtually, these disks are divided into logical segments, and the system contains algorithms that provide copies of the data.

- Use separate logical disks for each defined workload of data and/or applications. By using separate logical disks, each independent workload unit can be hosted by a separate virtual server and fail-over system.

- Assign the same administrative user name and password on each cluster node to simplify maintenance.

Network Connectivity Analysis

Because the Internet is a set of interconnected networks, Internet access can be accomplished only via another LAN, an Intranet, or a telephone connection. Because of the number of alternative ways that a user may want to access the ecommerce system, it is important for analysts to ensure that systems can support the minimum bandwidth available to users. This means that application design must take into consideration network topology communications. Another way of looking at this challenge is to realize that application architecture cannot be completed without consideration of the communication capabilities of the users. There are actually three ways of dealing with network connectivity. First, network access and application architecture can be mandated based on a pre-set configuration. This requires users to have a specific configuration if they wish to connect to the ecommerce system. Second, network design must include support for all communication capabilities that exist in the user base. The third alternative is to take into consideration both the first and second alternatives! That is, support most configurations but not all of them. Another way of describing this approach is to determine the minimum configuration that can be supported without diminishing the features and functions of the applications.

There are seven external or Internet connection choices, as shown in Table 8.1.

The most common way to connect to an ecommerce system is through the telephone provider, or Plain Old Telephone Service (POTS). These lines are analog connections that are made possible through the use of a modem connection. A modem translates analog signals to digital, and vice versa. The maximum bandwidth that is supported is 56 Kbps (56,000 bits per second). Some telephone companies have been offering a higher grade of service called Digital Subscriber Loop (DSL) protocol, which uses Integrated Services Digital Network (ISDN) connectivity. ISDN increases speed to 128 bites per second. Still another technology, which uses the DSL protocol, is Asymmetric Digital Subscriber Line (ADSL). This device provides access speeds of up to 640 Kbps during upstream connections and 9 million bits per second (Mbps) during downstream operations. Ecommerce analysts need to understand the impact of providing software to any of these access

Table 8.1   Internet Connection Choices

DEVICE	UPSTREAM SPEED (KBPS)	DOWNSTREAM SPEED (KBPS)	STARTUP FEES, $	MONTHLY CHARGES, $
Modem	56	56	$20	$20
ISDN	128	128	400	80
Cable modem	500	1,500	200	50
T1 leased line	1,544	1,544	3,000	1,100
ASDL	640	9,000	3,000	1,000
T3 leased line	44,700	44,700	7,500	8,000
ATM	622,000	622,000		

devices. In the consumer market, dial-up 56 Kbps is still dominant, whereas the growth of DSL-related services seems to be diminishing. The importance of determining this support directly correlates to the type of software used and the intensity of complex graphics as discussed in Chapters 6 and 7.

Cable modems, on the other hand, utilize the same coaxial cable that drives communication for cable television. Cable modems provide both low-cost and relatively high bandwidth connection to an Internet Service Provider (ISP), which in this case would actually be the cable company. Cable connections offer upstream bandwidths of 300 to 500 Kbps and downstream bandwidths of up to 1.5 Mbps. Unlike DSL, however, cable modems are subject to competing traffic because cable operates over shared data lines. This means simply that service can be significantly decreased in areas where there is congestion. In any event, users, particularly consumers, are likely to migrate to either cable or DSL type hookups, which means that Web products can begin to support more intensive graphics and media.

Most professional firms provide high network traffic support using telephone connections called T1 and T3 (Terrestrial 1 and 3, respectively). T lines offer substantially higher speeds at a much higher cost, but this level of service can be assumed to exist in most large organizations. Furthermore, many companies can share the use of T1 and T3 lines through the use of shared network environments, the most common being frame relay. Asynchronous Transfer Mode (ATM) represents yet another high-speed connection that can support bandwidths up to 622 gigabytes (a gigabyte is 1 billion bits). Obviously, those environments that support high-speed lines can provide the most advanced Web application interfaces. Such environments will likely exist for Intranet and consumer-based ecommerce systems.

Because ecommerce Web applications use client/server architecture and often serve a wide range of users, there is typically a need to support many of the communication connections reflected in Figure 8.13. The high-end powerful communications devices are easier for the analyst/designer because they can support more robust applications that can utilize some of today's more advanced graphics and multimedia. Unfortunately, 56 Kbps will be around for some time and therefore will require that ecommerce systems support them. In Chapter 5 the complexities of offering multiple Web sites were discussed, particularly with respect to user design preferences. However, communications can also create the need for separate Web sites because of the different communications devices they can support. Furthermore, hand-held devices use wireless communication, which poses major Web site compatibility problems for ecommerce designers. Wireless technology is subject to different communications delays, and many of the hand-held devices do not contain enough memory to support many existing Web sites. Yet the user requirement to support such devices is significant, and increases in bandwidth seem to be lagging behind user connectivity requirements. I believe that ecommerce sites of the future will need to deliver multiple screen design versions to support the many different communications devices that will proliferate in the marketplace and require special protocol considerations.

Client/Server Database Architecture

Database design for ecommerce systems is particularly challenging because of the need to make different parts of the data available to different users. This means that the system might allow certain data information to be available to consumers (or the general public) whereas other data elements are accessible only by internal users. Data made available to consumers and customers through the Internet is said to reside outside the firewall. A *firewall* is a hardware server that protects organizations from illegal access by unauthorized users who could corrupt or steal data. The design and use of firewalls will be discussed further in Chapter 11. Ecommerce analysts are, therefore, challenged to design database systems that have data outside the firewall and available to all, and data inside and secured for only those that have correct access security. This challenge creates a comprehensive synchronization database design issue. Unlike the synchronization discussed in Chapter 7, this issue relates to only portions of the data that may be common among database copies. This means that many database copies that reside outside the firewall are really subsets of the original database. Data that resides outside the firewall may need to be refreshed from time to time with data from the internal system. Unlike normal replication, however, there must also be a way of obtaining new data or updates from the data residing outside the firewall. Finally, and most important, is the reality that two or more databases may indeed need to coexist. Multiple databases that contain some of the same data elements create redundancy and integrity problems as discussed in Chapter 7. Thus, ecommerce analysts need to go beyond just database replication to a more comprehensive database design structure. Further complications are the challenges of maintaining the performance of internal production data and the impact of potentially massive amounts of access from the general public. While there is no single right answer, there are a few ways to address these issues.

Maintain one database. This is certainly not easy, but it provides the best control over redundancies and integrity issues. As described in Chapter 7, there are many methods of creating replicated copies and keeping them current. The ecommerce analyst has little to do with respect to design, but a lot to address as to which data may be accessed by external users such as customers and consumers. This means that data access outside the firewall must be completely controlled by an application program that filters requests to the main database server. Outside requests must be guarded by special screen programs that operate over the Internet and control which elements are available to these external users. Furthermore, data elements that are added or updated outside the firewall must be received by the database system and handled under the auspices of the product's database manager, as shown in Figure 8.13.

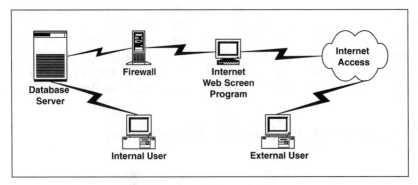

Figure 8.13   Ecommerce central database architecture.

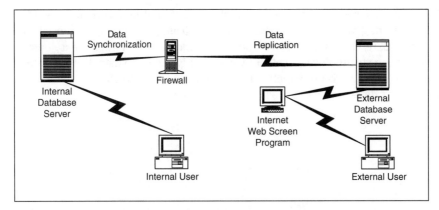

Figure 8.14   Ecommerce synchronized replication database architecture.

Database replication and synchronization. This provides more security over the internal data by allowing the specific database product to use its replication capabilities to generate a mirror database. Thus, all the database changes outside the firewall would need to be synchronized back to the internal copy. The external database would still allow access only to certain data elements, deemed accessible to external users as shown in Figure 8.14.

Separate databases. This design concept creates two separate databases. The synchronization between the databases is delayed and occurs through an application that ensures that the elements are updated in a batch mode. This means that the production database, which resides behind the firewall, goes through a number of replications and updates a subset database for the general Internet user (see Figure 8.15). The second database contains only the elements that are deemed accessible to external users. The separate database method establishes two separate systems. The second, or external, database serves the external portion of the ecommerce system and is never in synchronization with the master database. This approach requires that the external data be used for query and reporting purposes

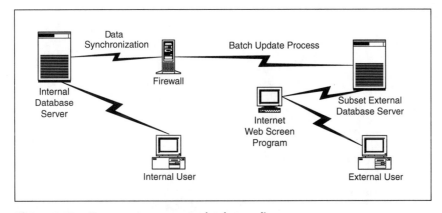

Figure 8.15   Ecommerce separate databases diagram.

only because changes to the external database could not be returned to the production system. Thus, synchronization goes only from production to external, not vice versa. External databases that use this design are often implemented using data warehouse technology, which allows read-only access to data. Unfortunately, this design technique is not effective for systems that need to allow outside users to create new data—often required by ecommerce systems.

CHAPTER 9

Legacy Systems and Integration

Legacy systems are existing application systems in operation. While this is an accurate definition, there is a perception that legacy systems are old and antiquated applications operating on mainframe computers. Indeed, Brodie and Stonebraker (1995) state that, "a legacy information system is any information system that significantly resists modification and evolution" (p. 3). They define typical legacy systems as follows:

- They are large applications with millions of lines of code.

- Typical legacy systems are usually more than 10 years old.

- They are written in legacy languages such as COBOL.

- They are built around a legacy database service (such as IBM's IMS), and some do not use a database management system. Instead they use older flat-file systems such as ISAM and VSAM.

- The applications are very autonomous. Legacy applications tend to operate independently from other applications, which means that there is very limited interface among application programs. When interfaces among applications are available, they are usually based on export and import models of data and these interfaces lack data consistency.

While many legacy systems do fit these scenarios, many do not. However, those that do not fit these scenarios can still be considered legacies under my original definition— that is, any application in operation. What this means is that there are what I call "generations" of legacy systems that can exist in any organization. Thus, the definitions of what constitutes a legacy system are much broader than Brodie and Stonebraker's descriptions. The more important issue to address is the relationship of legacy systems with ecommerce systems. In Chapter 1, I defined an ecommerce system as one that encompassed both internal and external applications. Thus, existing internal production systems, including third-party outsourced products, must be part of any ecommerce strategy. Furthermore, there are many legacy systems that perform external functions as well, albeit not in an Internet interface.

This chapter defines the type of legacy systems that exist and provides guidelines on how to approach their integration with ecommerce applications. The ecommerce analyst must determine whether a legacy system should be replaced, enhanced, or remain as is. This chapter also provides the procedures for dealing with each of these three choices and its effect on the overall architecture of the ecommerce system.

Types of Legacy Systems

The types of legacy systems tend to mirror the life cycle of software development. Software development is usually defined within a framework called *generations*. Most professionals agree that there are five generations of programming languages:

First-generation. The first generation was known as machine language. Machine language is considered a low-level language because it uses binary symbols to communicate instructions to the hardware. These binary symbols form a one-to-one relationship between a machine language command and a machine activity, that is, one machine language command performs one machine instruction. It is rare that any legacy systems have first-generation software.

Second-generation. This generation was comprised of assembler programming languages. Assembler languages are proprietary software that translates a higher-level coding scheme into more than one machine language instruction. Therefore, it was necessary to design an assembler, which would translate the symbolic codes into machine instructions. Mainframe shops may still have a considerable amount of existing assembly code, particularly with applications that perform intricate algorithms and calculations.

Third-generation. These languages continued the growth of high-level symbolic languages that had translators into machine code. Examples of third-generation languages are COBOL, FORTRAN, BASIC, RPG, and C. These languages use more English-like commands and have a higher ratio of machine language produced from one instruction. Third-generation languages tend to be more specialized. For example, FORTRAN is better suited for mathematical and scientific calculations. Therefore, many insurance companies have FORTRAN because of the high concentration on actuarial mathematic calculations. COBOL, on the other hand, was designed as the business language and has special features to allow it to manipulate file and database information. More COBOL applications exist than any other programming language. Most mainframe legacy systems still have COBOL applications. RPG is yet another specialized language that was designed for use on

IBM's mid-range machines, including the System 36, System 38, and AS/400 computers.

Fourth-generation (4GL). These programming languages are less procedural than third-generation languages. In addition, the symbols are more English-like and emphasize more about desired output results than how the programming statements need to be written. As a result of this feature, many less technical programmers have learned how to program using 4GLs. The most powerful features of 4GLs include query of databases, code-generation, and graphic screen generation abilities. Such languages include Visual Basic, C++, Visual Basic, Powerbuilder, Delphi, and many others. Furthermore, 4GL languages also include what is known as *query languages* because they contain English-like questions that are used to produce results by directly accessing relational databases. The most popular 4GL query language is Structured Query Language (SQL).

Fifth-generation. These programming languages combine what is known as rule-based code generation, component management, and visual programming techniques. The rule-based code generation became popular in the late 1980s with the creation of artificial intelligence software. This software uses an approach called *knowledge-based programming*, which means that the developer does not tell the computer how to solve problems, but rather just states the problem (Stair and Reynolds, 1999). The program figures out how to solve the problem. While knowledge-based programming has become popular in specialized applications, such as in the medical industry, it has not been as popular in business.

Most legacy applications will either be third- or fourth-generation language systems; therefore, ecommerce analysts need to have a process and methodology to determine how to integrate ecommerce technology with these applications.

Third-Generation Language Legacy System Integration

As previously discussed, most third-generation language legacy systems were developed using COBOL. COBOL was developed to provide a method of forcing programmers to self-document their code so that other programmers could maintain it. Unfortunately, COBOL requires what is known as a *File Description* table (FD). The FD defines the record layout for every file used by the COBOL program. In other words, every file is described within the program and must match the format of the actual physical data file. This means that any change to a file structure must be synchronized with every COBOL program that uses that data file. Thus, COBOL is somewhat eclectic: There is no real separation of the data description and the program logic. In COBOL programs then, a change in data format could necessitate a change in the program code. That is why COBOL programs suffer from large degrees of coupling of code. Coupling is defined as the reliance of one piece of code on another.

COBOL programs may or may not use a relational database as its source of data. I earlier defined two other common formats called ISAM and VSAM, which are flat-file formats, meaning that all data elements are contained in one record as opposed to mul-

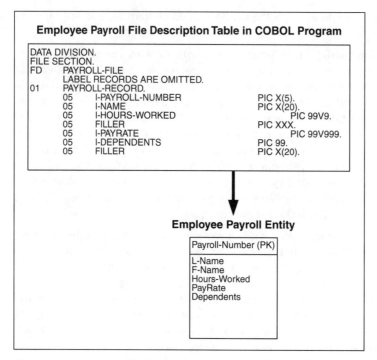

Figure 9.1 COBOL File Description interface with database manager.

tiple files as is the case in the relational database model. However, many COBOL legacy systems have been converted to work with relational databases such as IBM's DB2. In this situation, the FD tables interface with the database's file manager so that the two entities can communicate with each other. Figure 9.1 depicts the interface between program and database.

Notwithstanding whether the COBOL legacy is using a database interface or flat-files, the ecommerce analyst needs to determine whether to replace the application, enhance it, or leave it as is.

Replacing Third-Generation Legacy Systems

When replacing third-generation legacies, ecommerce analysts must focus on both the data and processes. Because of the age of these systems, it is likely that there will be little documentation available, and the amount available will most likely be outdated. Indeed, the lack of proper documentation is the major reason why legacy systems are slow to be replaced: Rewriting code without documentation can be an overwhelming and time-consuming task. Unfortunately, all things must eventually be replaced. Delaying replacement leads to legacy systems that keep businesses from remaining competitive. The following sections provide a step-by-step approach to COBOL-based legacies.

```
FD      REPORT-FILE
        LABEL RECORDS ARE OMITTED.
01      REPORT-RECORD.
        05      O-PAYROLL-NUMBER              PIC X(5).
        05      FILLER                        PIC XX.
        05      O-NAME                        PIC X(20).
        05      FILLER                        PIC XX.
        05      O-HOURS-WORKED                PIC 99.9.
        05      FILLER                        PIC XX.
        05      O-PAYRATE                     PIC 99.999.
        05      FILLER                        PIC XX.
        05      O-DEPENDENTS                  PIC 99.
        05      FILLER                        PIC XX.
        05      O-GROSS-PAY                   PIC 999.99.
        05      FILLER                        PIC XX.
        05      O-TAX                         PIC 999.99.
        05      FILLER                        PIC XX.
        05      O-NET-PAY                     PIC 999.99.
```

Figure 9.2   COBOL File Description tables.

Approaches to Logic Reconstruction

The best way to reconstruct the logic in COBOL applications is to separate the data from the processes. This can be accomplished by creating data flow diagrams (DFD) for each program. Having a DFD will result in defining all of the inputs and outputs of the application. This can be accomplished by the following tasks:

1. Print the source code (actual COBOL-written code) from each application. Each application will contain an "FD" section that defines all of the inputs and outputs of the program. These will represent the data stores of the data flow diagrams (see Figure 9.2).

2. DFDs should be decomposed so that they are at the functional primitive level (one-in and one-out, preferred). This provides functional decomposition for the old application and sets the framing for how it will be decomposed into an object-oriented solution.

3. By reviewing the code, write the process specifications for each functional primitive.

4. Follow the steps as outlined in Chapter 7 to determine which functional primitive DFDs become methods of a particular class.

5. Capture all of the data elements or attributes required by each functional primitive DFD. These attributes are added to the data dictionary (DD).

6. Take each major data store and create an entity. Do Normalization and Logic Data Modeling in accordance with the procedures in Chapter 4, combining these elements with the ecommerce system as appropriate.

7. Data stores that represent reports should be compared against sample outputs. These reports will need to be redeveloped using a report writer such as Crystal's report writer or a data warehouse product (see Chapter 12).

8. Examine all existing data files and/or databases in the legacy system. Compare these elements against those discovered during the logic reconstruction. In third-generation products there will be many data elements or fields that are redundant or used as logic "flags." *Logic flags* consist of fields used to store a value that depicts a certain state of the data. For example, suppose a particular program has updated a record. One method of knowing that this occurred is to have the application program set a certain field with a code that identifies that it has been updated. This method would not be necessary in a relational database product because file managers automatically keep logs on the last time a record has been updated. This example illustrates how different third-generation legacy technology differs from more contemporary technologies.

There is no question that replacing third-generation legacies is time-consuming. However, the procedures outlined above will prove to be accurate and effective. In many situations, users will decide that it makes sense to reexamine their legacy processes, especially when the decision has been made to rewrite the program and integrate it with an ecommerce system. We call this *business process reengineering*. Business process reengineering is therefore synonymous with enhancing the legacy system.

Enhancing Third-Generation Legacy Systems

Business process reengineering (BPR) is one of the more popular methodologies used to enhance third-generation applications. A more formal definition of BPR is "a requirement to study fundamental business processes, independent of organization units and information systems support, to determine if the underlying business processes can be significantly streamlined and improved." BPR is not just rebuilding the existing applications for the sake of applying new technology to older systems, but it is also an event that allows for the application of new procedures designed around the OO ecommerce paradigm. In this scenario, however, BPR is used to enhance existing applications without rewriting them in another generation language. Instead, the ecommerce analyst needs to make changes to the system that will make it function more like an object component even though it is written in a third-generation language. In order to accomplish this task, it is necessary for the analyst to create the essential components of the legacy operation. Essential components represent the core business requirements of a unit. Another way of defining core business requirements is to view essential components as the reasons why the unit exists— what does it do—and for what reasons. For example, Figure 9.3 depicts the essential components of a bank.

Once the essential components have been created, then the legacy applications need to be placed in the appropriate component so that it can be linked with its related ecommerce applications.

The first step to applying successful BPR is to develop an approach to defining the existing system and extracting its data elements and applications. Once again, this is similar to the process described above when replacing third-generation legacy applications in that the data needs to be captured into the data repository and the appli-

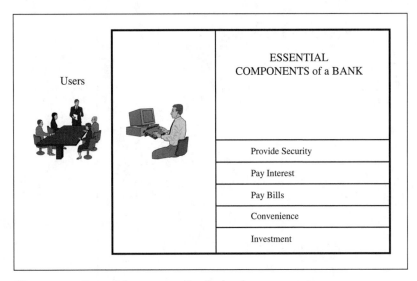

Figure 9.3   Essential components of a bank.

cations need to be defined and compared to a new model based on essential components.

Data Element Enhancements

The ecommerce analyst will need to design conversion programs that will access the data files that are not in relational database format and place them in a data repository. The ultimate focus is to replace all of the existing data files in the legacy with relational databases that can be linked with ecommerce databases. This methodology differs from replacing legacies. In replacement engineering, data files are integrated directly into ecommerce systems. This means that the legacy data will often be used to enhance the ecommerce databases. However, the process of enhancing legacy systems means that the legacy data will remain separate but converted into the relational model. For legacies that already have relational databases, there is no restructuring required beyond setting up links with the ecommerce database. Figure 9.4 reflects the difference between replacing legacy data and enhancing it.

Another interesting difference between the two approaches is that enhanced legacies will likely have intentional data redundancy. This means that the same element may indeed exist in multiple databases—a violation of third-normal form. However, the redundancy must exist for the sake of maintaining separate identities of the systems. Duplicate elements may take on different formats. The most obvious is where a data element has aliases, meaning that an element has many different names, but the same attributes. Another type is the same element name, but with different attributes. The third type, and the most challenging, is the duplicate elements that have different names and different attributes. While duplicate data elements may exist in enhanced legacy applications that are integrated with ecommerce, it is still important to identify dupli-

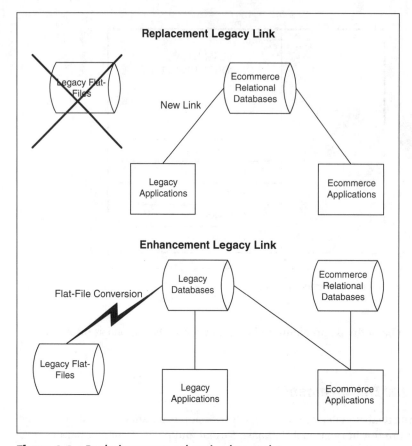

Figure 9.4   Replacing versus enhancing legacy data.

cate data relationships. This can be accomplished by documenting data relationships in a CASE tool and in the database's physical data dictionary where aliases can exist.

Application Enhancements

BPR typically involves a methodology called Business Area Analysis (BAA). The purpose of BAA is to:

- Establish the various legacy business areas that will be linked with the ecommerce system
- Reengineer the new and old requirements of each business area
- Develop requirements that provide an OO perspective of each legacy business area, meaning that there is no need to map its requirements to the existing physical organization structure
- Define the links that create relationships among all the legacy business areas and the ecommerce business areas

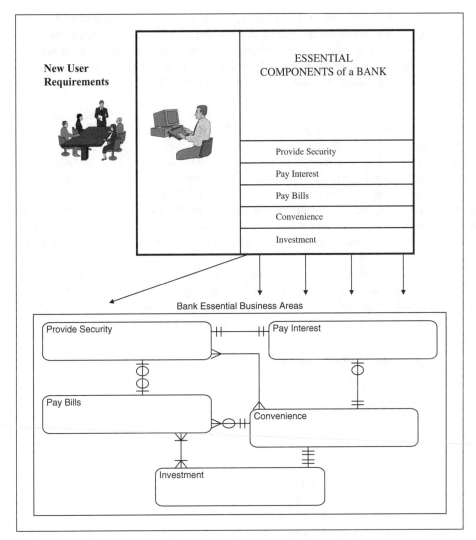

Figure 9.5   BPR legacy modeling using essential components.

This is accomplished by mapping business areas to specific essential components. Applications designed for the ecommerce system must also be mapped to an essential component. Once this has occurred, the legacy applications and ecommerce applications must be designed to share common processes and databases as shown in Figure 9.5.

Once the legacy and ecommerce applications have been placed in their appropriate essential component, they will need to be linked, that is, communicate with each other to complete the integration of the internal and external systems. Linking occurs in two ways: parameter messaging and database. Parameter messaging requires that the legacy programs be modified to receive data in the form of parameters. This allows the ecommerce system to deliver information directly to the legacy program. Conversely, the legacy program may need to return information back to the ecommerce system. Therefore, legacy applications need to be enhanced so they can actually format and send a data message to the ecommerce system. A database interface is essentially the same concept except that it occurs differently. Instead of the ecommerce application sending the data directly to another program, it forwards it as a record in a database file. The legacy program that returns the data also needs to be modified to forward messages to a database.

There are advantages and disadvantages of using either method. First, parameters use little overhead and are easy to program. They do not provide reusable data. In other words, once a message has been received it is no longer available to another program. Parameters are also limited in size. Databases, on the other hand, allow programs to send the information to multiple destinations because it can be read many times. Unfortunately, it is difficult to control what applications or queries can access the data, which does raise questions about how secure the data is. Furthermore, applications must remember to delete a record in the database if it is no longer required. Figure 9.6 reflects the two methods of transferring data between legacy systems and ecommerce applications.

Once the legacy and the new ecommerce applications have all been mapped to the essential components, analysts can use a CRUD diagram to assist them in reconciling whether all of the data and processes have been found. The use of CRUD in the object

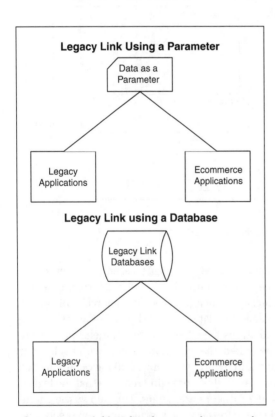

Figure 9.6   Linking data between legacy and ecommerce systems.

Processes or Business Function / Data Subject or Entity	Process Orders	Validate Products	Shipping	Commission
Customers	R		R,U	
Orders	C, U		U	R
Items	R	C,U,D	R	R
Inventory	R,U	C,U	U	
Expense Section				
Market Person	R			U

Figure 9.7 Sample CRUD diagram.

paradigm was discussed in Chapter 8. The importance of the CRUD diagram is that it ensures that:

- An essential component has complete control over its data.
- All of the entities are accessible by at least one process.
- Processes are accessing data.

The CRUD matrix in Figure 9.7 tells us a lot about the status and activities of our business area data and processes:

1. Only the Items entity has enough component processes to control its objects data; that is, by spelling CRUD its processes have the minimum capabilities to control the cycle of any data element. Although this does not guarantee that all processes are present, it is a good indicator that the analysis has covered the life cycle of an entity.

2. The Expense category is not accessed by any process. This means that we have a file that the system is not using. This is an excellent indicator that processes are missing.

3. The Customer, Expense category, and Salesperson data are created and deleted by some other processes or business area. This could be a situation where the physical location of a business function is not where it logically should be processing. The analyst should look for the missing processes to complete the spelling of CRUD before finalizing both the processes and data of any business area.

While CRUD is not 100 percent accurate, it certainly uncovers potential problems as shown above. Even if BPR is not used, the CRUD diagram is an excellent tool to determine the processes and data needed for an essential component or an object. Once the CRUD diagram is finalized, the objects and classes would then be created as shown in Figure 9.8. Some of these objects are still in the form of a third-generation COBOL program while others are in a Java-based ecommerce format.

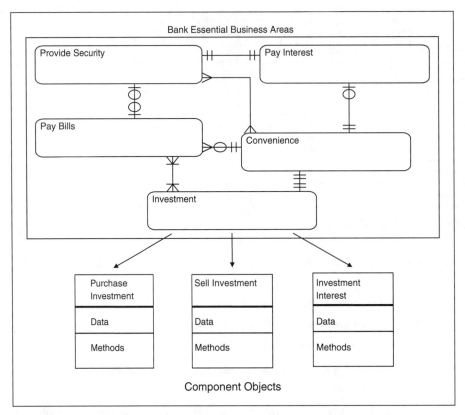

Figure 9.8   Essential Component component Object object diagrams.

"Leaving As Is" Third-Generation Legacy Systems

Moving to an ecommerce object-oriented and client/server paradigm from a third-generation product such as COBOL may not be feasible. The language design of third-generation procedural programs may result in conceptual gaps between procedural and object-oriented philosophies. For example, distributed object-oriented programs require more detailed technical infrastructure knowledge and graphics manipulation than was required in older legacy systems. Native object-oriented features such as inheritance, polymorphism, and encapsulation do not apply in traditional third-generation procedural design. It is difficult, if not impossible, to introduce new object concepts and philosophies during a direct COBOL to Java migration. If the translation is attempted without significant restructuring (as discussed earlier in this chapter), then the resulting product will likely contain slower code that is more difficult to maintain.

A cultural divide can also occur. Veteran COBOL programmers and newer Java developers do not understand each others' technologies. This scenario will often create bias during any conversion effort. Furthermore, COBOL programmers learning new technology can present them with self-specified threats to their cultural status. Furthermore, COBOL and RPG applications have benefited from the more lengthy testing,

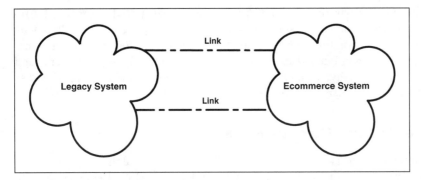

Figure 9.9   "As-is" legacy links.

debugging, and overall refinement than newer programming generations. While Java is more dynamic, it is less stable, and the procedure for debugging and fixing problems is very different than for COBOL or RPG. Therefore, the ecommerce analyst will leave the legacy "as is," and create only ecommerce links for passing information that is required between the two systems. While this is similar to the "linking" proposed for enhancing legacy systems, it is different because legacy programs are not enhanced, except for the external links needed to pass information. This is graphically shown in Figure 9.9.

Using parameters or databases to link connecting information is still relevant, but analysts must be cognizant that legacy data formats will not be changed. This means that the legacy applications will continue to use their original file formats. Another concept used to describe "links" is called *bridges*. The word suggests that the link serves to connect a gap between the ecommerce system and the legacy applications. Bridging can also imply a temporary link. Very often "as is" can be seen as a temporary condition because legacy conversions cannot occur all at once, so they are typically planned in phases. However, while parts of the system are being converted, some portions may need temporary bridges until it is time to actually enhance them. An example of this would be a temporary "road block" or detour that occurs when there is highway construction.

Fourth-Generation Language Legacy System Integration

Integrating fourth-generation legacy systems with ecommerce technology is much easier than third-generation languages. The reasons are twofold. First, most fourth-generation implementations are already using a relational database, so conversion of data to ecommerce is less complex. Second, fourth-generation language applications typically use SQL-based code, so conversion to an object-oriented system is also less involved.

Replacing Fourth-Generation Legacy Systems

As stated above, replacement of fourth-generation language systems is less complex than third-generation languages with respect to ecommerce conversion. As with any system replacement, separating data and process is the suggested approach. Fortunately, in fourth-generation language systems, process and data are likely to already be separate, because of the nature of its architecture. Specifically, fourth-generation languages typically use relational databases, which architecturally separate data and process. Therefore, replacing the legacy is more about examining the existing processes and determining where the applications need to be reengineered.

Approaches to Logic Reconstruction

The best approach to logic analysis is to print out the source code of the programs. If the source is written in SQL, then the analyst should search for all SELECT statements. SQL SELECT FROM statements define the databases that the program is using as shown here:

```
Select    IdNo, Last-Name, First-Name
from      employee
where     IDNo = "054475643"
```

As in third-generation language logic reconstruction, the ecommerce analyst should produce a DFD for every program as follows:

1. SELECT statements define all inputs and outputs that a program uses. Each SELECT statement file will be represented by a DFD data store. Reviewing the logic of the application program will reveal whether the data is being created, read, updated, or deleted (CRUD).

2. DFDs should be decomposed to the functional primitive level so that the framework to an object-oriented system is established.

3. For each DFD, copy the relevant SQL code, making modifications where necessary to provide more object-oriented functionality to the program. This means that the decomposition of the code will likely require that some new logic be added to transform it to a method. This is shown in Figure 9.10.

4. Examine existing ecommerce objects and determine if functional primitive DFDs belong to an existing class as a new method, or whether it truly represents a new object in the ecommerce system.

5. Capture all of the data elements required by the new methods and add them to their respective object. Ensure that the ecommerce DD is updated appropriately.

6. Determine whether any new objects need to become a reusable component in the TP monitor (middleware), a reusable component in the client application, or as a stored procedure at the database level.

7. Examine the legacy databases and do logic data modeling to place the entities in third-normal form (3NF).

8. Combine and integrate data elements with ecommerce databases, ensuring that each data field from the legacy system is properly matched with ecommerce data elements. New elements must be added to the appropriate entity or require that new entities be created for them.

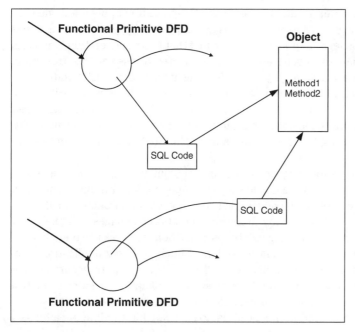

Figure 9.10   SQL code transition to object method.

9. Link new entities with existing models using third-normal form referential integrity rules.

10. Determine which data elements are redundant, such as calculations. These data elements will be removed; however, logic to their calculations may need to be added as a method as shown in Figure 9.11.

Enhancing Fourth-Generation Legacy Systems

Enhancing fourth-generation language legacy systems is really the process of converting it to an object-oriented client/server system. Business Process Reengineering (BPR) is also used on fourth-generation language legacy systems to accomplish this transition. The process, as one might expect, is much easier than for third-generation languages; however, the process of determining essential components is the same in both types of

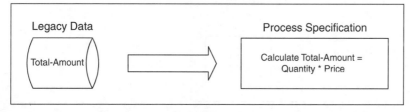

Figure 9.11   Transition of redundant data elements to process specifications.

systems. Once essential components are established, the existing applications need to be decomposed and realigned as needed. This is accomplished by using BAA, as it was used for third-generation legacy applications. The fact that fourth-generation languages are less procedural than third-generation languages greatly assists this transition. Fourth-generation language systems, by simply looking at the SQL SELECT statements, can identify which data files are used by the application. Using logic modularity rules, as discussed in Chapter 7, an ecommerce analyst can establish cohesive classes based on applications that use the same data. This can be accomplished without using DFDs, although reengineering using DFDs is always a more thorough method for analysts to follow.

Linkage of fourth-generation language legacy and ecommerce applications needs to be accomplished after application reengineering is completed. As with third-generation language systems, this can either be accomplished using a data parameter or the creation of a special database. However, with fourth-generation languages it is likely that application integration will occur using databases, since both systems use them in their native architectures. An ecommerce analyst will most likely find that application communication with fourth-generation languages will not always require separate databases to be designed solely for the purpose of system linkage. The more attractive solution to integration is to identify the data elements that are common between the two systems so it can be shared in a central database available to all applications as shown in Figure 9.12.

The use of CRUD in fourth-generation languages is used less, but is certainly applicable and should be implemented by the ecommerce analyst if he or she feels that the code is too procedural. In other words, the code architecture resembles third-generation as opposed to fourth-generation.

"Leaving As Is" Fourth-Generation Legacy Systems

The process of limiting integration to just the sharing of data is similar to the design architecture that I used for third-generation language systems. Indeed, the architecture

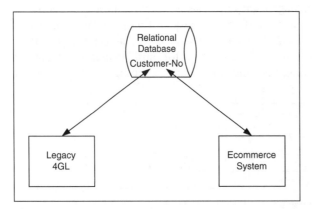

Figure 9.12 Fourth-generation language legacy shared database architecture.

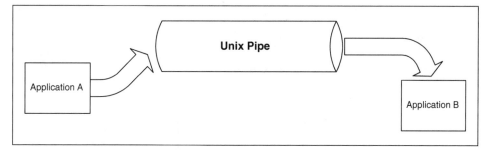

Figure 9.13 Intra-application communication using a Unix pipe.

of linking separate and distinct software systems can only be accomplished by sharing common data. Once again this data can be shared either using a data parameter or data file.

Because many fourth-generation language systems utilize the same architecture as an ecommerce system (three-tier client/server using Windows NT/2000 or Unix/Linux), it is sometimes advantageous to make use of certain operating system level communication facilities. For example, Unix allows applications to pass data using an operating system facility called a "pipe." A *pipe* resembles a parameter, in that it allows an application to pass a message or data to another application without creating an actual new data structure, like a database. Furthermore, a pipe uses an access method called "FIFO" (first-in, first-out), which is the same access criteria used by parameters. FIFO also requires that once the data is read, it cannot be read again. The major advantage of using a pipe is that the message and/or data can be stored long after the application that created the message has terminated in memory. Thus linkage of information among ecommerce and fourth-generation language applications can be accomplished in RAM at execution time, which is called *intra-application communication*. This capability reduces overhead as well as the need to design separate modules that would just handle data communication as shown in Figure 9.13.

Hybrid Methods: The Gateway Approach

Thus far in this chapter I have focused on the interface between a specific type of legacy and an ecommerce system. Each type was defined with respect to its "generation" type. In reality, however, legacy systems are not that self-defined. Many large organizations have "legacy layers," meaning that multiple generations exist throughout the enterprise. In this case, attempting to integrate each generation with a central ecommerce system is difficult and time-consuming. Indeed, migrating and integrating legacy systems are difficult enough. In these complex models, another method used for migration of legacy applications is a "hybrid" approach called *gateway*. The gateway approach means that there will be a software module that mediates requests between the ecommerce system and the legacy applications. In many ways, a gateway performs tasks similar to a TP system. Thus, the gateway acts as a broker between applications. Specifically, gateways:

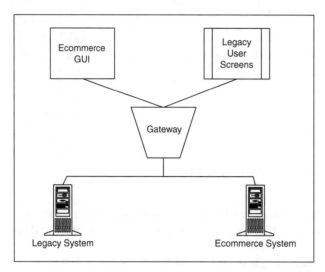

Figure 9.14 Gateway architecture for legacy integration.

- Separate yet integrate components from different generation languages. Gateways allow for the linkages among multiple-generation language systems.

- Translate requests and data between multiple components.

- Coordinate between multiple components to ensure update consistency. This means that the gateway will ensure that redundant data elements are synchronized.

Typical gateway architectures would be designed as shown in Figure 9.14.

The most beneficial role of the gateway is that it allows for the phasing of legacy components. The infrastructure provides for an incremental approach to conversion by establishing a consistent update process for both data and applications.

Incremental Application Integration

A gateway establishes a transparency for graphical user interfaces (GUI), character-based interfaces, and automated interfaces (batch updates) to appear the same to the ecommerce system. Hence, the gateway insulates the legacy system so that its interface with the ecommerce systems seems seamless. This is accomplished through an interface that translates requests for process functions and routes them to their appropriate application, regardless of the generation of the software and its particular phase in the ecommerce migration. Figure 9.15 depicts the process functions of the gateway system.

The most salient benefit of the gateway approach is its consistency with the object-oriented paradigm and the concept of application reusability. Specifically, it allows any module to behave "like" a reusable component notwithstanding its technical design. Under this architectural philosophy, a particular program, let's say, a third-generation language system, may eventually be replaced and placed into the gateway, with temporary bridges built until the overall migration is completed. This procedure also sup-

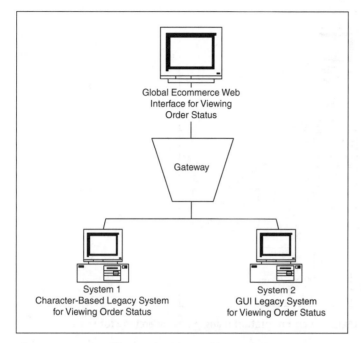

Figure 9.15 Application functions of legacy gateways.

ports a more "global" view of the enterprise as opposed to just focusing on a particular subsystem. Figure 9.16 depicts the concept of process integration using the gateway architecture.

Incremental Data Integration

Incremental data integration focuses on the challenge of keeping multiple sets of data coordinated throughout the ecommerce system. While this objective seems straightforward, it has all of the complexities that were discussed in Chapter 8 relating to database replication architecture.

The two primary issues relating to data integration focus on queries and updates. Queries involve the access of complete information about a data set (collection of related data elements) across multiple systems. Much of the query challenges can be addressed by using a data warehouse or data mining architecture. This will be discussed in detail in Chapter 12. The gateway would serve as the infrastructure that would determine how many copies of the data exist and their locations.

The more difficult and more important concept of data integration is the ability of the gateway to coordinate multiple updates across databases and flat-file systems. This means that the changing of a data element in one component would "trigger" an automatic update to the other components. There are four scenarios that could exist regarding the different definitions of data elements:

1. **The data elements in each system have the same name.** This at least allows analysts to identify how many copies of the element exist in the system.

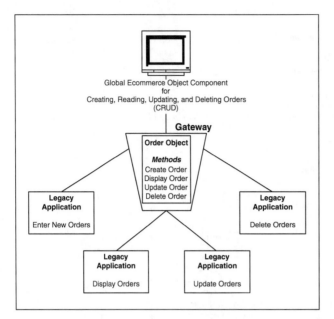

Figure 9.16 Process integration and migration using gateway architecture.

2. **The data elements do not match up by name.** This requires that the analyst design a "mapping" algorithm that tracks the corresponding name of each alias.

3. **Data elements match by name but not by attribute.** In this case the analyst must propagate updates to the data element by tracking the different attribute definitions it has across systems. These differences can vary dramatically. The most obvious is element length. If the length of the data element is shorter than the one that has been updated then there is the problem of field truncation. This means that either the beginning or ending value of the string will be lost when the value is propagated to the system with the shorter length definition. On the other hand, if the target is longer, then the process must populate either the beginning or end of the string so that the element has a complete value. This is graphically depicted in Figure 9.17.

   Furthermore, the same data element might have different data types, meaning that one is alphanumeric and the other numeric. In this case, ecommerce analysts need to know that certain values (e.g., a leading zero) will not be stored in the same way, depending on its data type classification.

4. **There is not a one-to-one relationship among data elements.** This suggests that a data element in one system may be based on the results of a calculation (a derived data element). This would require a more in-depth analysis and mapping often solved by creating a stored procedure that replicates the business rule to calculate the data element's value. So in this case there might be simple copies of the element moved from one system to another, as well as one data element value that needs to first be calculated and then propagated across multiple systems. For example, if the data element "Total-Amount" is entered in

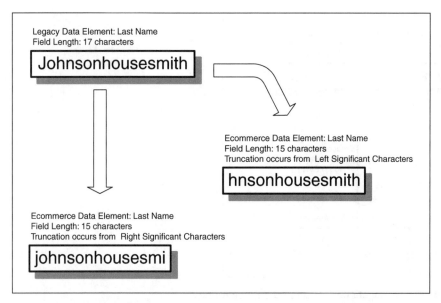

Legacy Data Element: Last Name
Field Length: 17 characters

Johnsonhousesmith

Ecommerce Data Element: Last Name
Field Length: 15 characters
Truncation occurs from Left Significant Characters

hnsonhousesmith

Ecommerce Data Element: Last Name
Field Length: 15 characters
Truncation occurs from Right Significant Characters

johnsonhousesmi

Figure 9.17   Propagating data elements with different field lengths.

one system but calculated as Quantity times Price in another, the propagation of the values is very complex. First, the analyst must know whether the calculated value is performed before the resultant value; in this case, Total-Amount is reentered in another system. If this is true, then the propagation is much easier; once the calculation is made, then the result is copied to the "entered" element. The converse is much more complex. If the Total-Amount was entered, but the values of Quantity and Price were not, then it would be very difficult to propagate until both Quantity and Price were entered. The example is further complicated if adjustments are made to the Quantity, Price, or Total-Amount. For any change, the systems would need to automatically be "triggered" to recalculate the values to ensure they are in synchronization. Figure 9.18 graphically shows this process.

Converting Legacy Character-Based Screens

It would be naïve to assume that most legacy systems do not have character-based screens. Character-based screens are those that do not make use of the GUI. While most character-based screens in existence emanate from third-generation language mainframe implementations, there are also many early fourth-generation language systems that preceded the GUI paradigm. Unfortunately, character-based screens often do not map easily to its GUI counterparts. The analyst must be especially careful not to attempt to simply duplicate the screens in the legacy software. Figure 9.19 shows a typical character-based legacy screen. Note that there can be up to four Contract/POs as shown in the upper right-hand corner. The user is required to enter each Contract/PO on a separate screen.

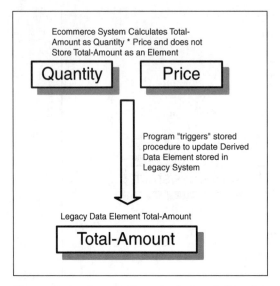

Figure 9.18 Propagation of calculated data elements.

On the other hand, the replacement GUI screen in Figure 9.20 takes advantage of the view bar that allows for scrolling in a window. Therefore, the GUI version requires only one physical screen, as opposed to four.

	Bill of Lading Container		Screen 1 of 4

B/L:____ SCAC: _____	VESSEL: _____	Total: _____	
	VOYAGE: _____	CTN: _____	

PO Information

Contract/PO: _____	Tot Unit: _____
Item: _____	GWT: _____
Style: _____	CBM: _____
Stat: _____	O/F Chrg: _____
Orig Country: _____	Con Rate: _____

Activities

Activity	Descr	Date	Location

Figure 9.19 Character-based user screen.

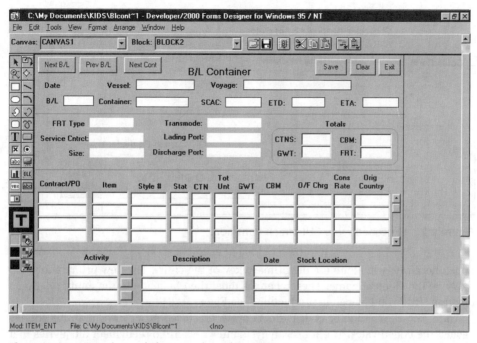

Figure 9.20   Transformed character-based to GUI screen.

The Challenge with Encoded Legacy Screen Values

In most legacy character-based screens, a common practice was used to create codes that represented another, more meaningful data value. For example, numeric codes (1, 2, 3, 4, etc.) might be used to represent product colors such as blue, green, dark red, etc. Legacy applications used codes because they reduced the number of characters needed to type in the value on a screen. The technology to implement common GUI features such as drop-down menus and pop-up windows were not available. Indeed, many people used codes just from habit, or had to use them in order to implement computer systems. When transitioning to a GUI system, especially on the Web, it is wise to phase out any data elements that are in an encoded form unless the codes are user-defined and are meaningful within the industry or business area. This essentially means that certain codes, such as state abbreviations (NY, CT, CA, etc.), are industry standards that are required by the business, as opposed to those created to aid in the implementation of software—like color codes. In the latter case, the color name itself is unique and would be stored in an entity with just its descriptive name, as opposed to a code, which then identifies the actual description. Figure 9.21 shows the character-based and GUI screen transition.

Changing character-based screens that contain encoded values has a trickle-down effect on the data dictionary and then on logic data modeling. First, the elimination of a coded value inevitably deletes a data element from the data dictionary. Second, codes are often key attributes, which become primary keys of entities. The elimination of the

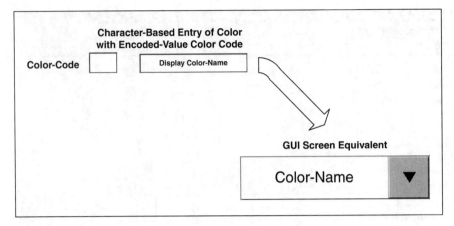

Figure 9.21 Encoded value GUI screen transition.

code, therefore, will eliminate the primary key of the entity. The new primary key will likely be the element name. These changes must then be made to the entity relational diagram (ERD) and placed in production (see Figure 9.22).

Third, the elimination of codes affects previous stored procedures that use queries against the coded vales. Therefore, analysts must be sure to reengineer all queries that use the codes. This transition will add tremendous value since encoded elements typi-

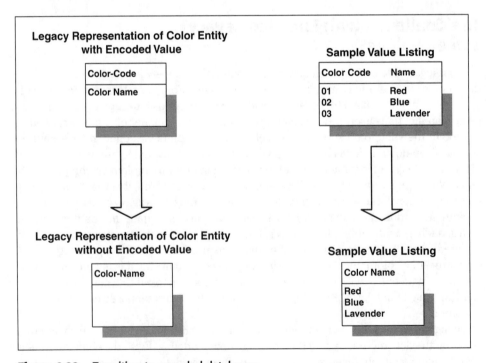

Figure 9.22 Transition to encoded databases.

cally add unnecessary overhead and time delays to queries. Finally, the elimination of encoded values will free up considerable space and index overhead. This will result in an increase in performance of the legacy system.

Legacy Migration Methodology

As stated earlier, all legacy systems inevitably must reach the end of their original life cycle. Therefore, notwithstanding whether certain components will remain "as is" or enhanced, eventually IT management must plan for migration to another system. The issue that this section addresses is how to establish a migration life cycle that takes into consideration an incremental approach to replacement of various legacy components within an enterprise computer system. The previous sections provided a framework of what can be done with legacy systems and their integration with ecommerce systems. This section provides a step-by-step template of procedures to follow that can assist ecommerce analysts on the schedule of legacy migration, including temporary and permanent integration. This approach is an incremental one, so analysts can use it as a checklist of the progression they have made in the legacy migration life cycle. In all, there are 12 steps:

1. Analyze the existing legacy systems.

2. Decompose legacy systems to determine schedules of migration and linkage strategies.

3. Design "as-is" links.

4. Design legacy enhancements.

5. Design legacy replacements.

6. Design and integrate new databases.

7. Determine new infrastructure and environment, including gateways.

8. Implement enhancements.

9. Implement links.

10. Migrate legacy databases.

11. Migrate replacement legacy applications.

12. Incrementally cut over to new systems.

The above steps are graphically depicted in Figure 9.23.

Note that there are two streams of steps, that is, steps 3 to 5 and 8 to 10 that can occur in parallel. These steps encompass the three types of legacy migration choices that can be made: replacement, enhancement, and "as is." While this life cycle seems simple, in reality it is a significant challenge for most migrations to plan, manage, and modify these steps and their interactions. Indeed, creating a migration plan and adequately coordinating the incremental and parallel steps is a difficult project. Subsequent sections in this chapter will provide more details for each of these 12 steps.

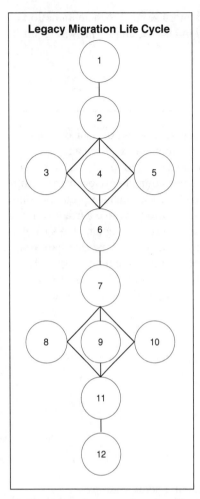

Figure 9.23   Legacy migration life cycle.

Step 1: Analyze the Existing Legacy Systems

It is obviously important that ecommerce analysts fully understand all of the existing legacy components that exist in the system. The objective is to provide the requirements of each system and how it relates to the ecommerce system. Analysts must remember that little to no documentation will be available to fully represent the architecture of the legacy system. However, ecommerce analysts should compile as much available information as possible, including but not limited to:

- User and programming documentation
- Existing users, software developers, and managers
- Required inputs and outputs and known services of the legacy system
- Any historical perspective on the history of the system itself

Regardless of what existing information and documentation is available, certain aspects of reverse engineering must be used. Various Computer Aided Software Engineering (CASE) tools should be used that allow analysts to create a repository of data and certain levels of code analysis, particularly for third-generation language migrations. Products that exist on the market are ADW's Knowledgeware Legacy Workbench, Bachman's Information Systems' Analyst, and Popkin's System Architect. The analyst should create DFDs and PFDs for process analysis, and logic data modeling (LDM) and entity relational diagramming (ERD) for representation of the data. The ecommerce analyst should also determine which legacy components are decomposable and nondecomposable. Inevitably, regardless of whether the decision is to replace immediately, enhance, or leave "as is," relatively little of the existing code will survive the ultimate migration of a legacy system (Brodie and Stonebraker, 1995).

Step 2: Decompose Legacy Systems to Determine Schedules of Migration and Linkage Strategies

The gradual migration of legacy systems is more easily accomplished when analysts utilize decomposition engineering. Previous chapters have outlined the process of functional decomposition, which is based on the breaking down of a system into its functional components. Decomposition, which results in components, also allows for reusability of code. Since the fundamental premises of ecommerce systems are reusability, the process of decomposition is a mandatory part of the life cycle of any legacy migration. Thus, ecommerce analysts should decompose all DFDs to functional primitives. Process analysis continues with the writing of process specifications for each functional primitive. These functional primitives will either be rewritten from the existing code or documentation or recreated from analyzing the functionality of the program. Analysts need to remove all dependency logic that links modules from the legacy code because it represents coupling among the programs. Module dependencies can typically be identified by finding *procedure calls* from within the legacy code. Ultimately, each of these process specifications will become methods. Eventually, all methods will be mapped to classes and identify the attributes that each class needs. While this sounds simple, there will be a number of processes for which decomposition will be problematic. This will typically occur for legacy code that is too eclectic and simply needs to be reengineered. In these cases, ecommerce analysts may want to interview users to understand the functionality that is required, as opposed to relying solely on the written legacy code.

From a data perspective, entity relational diagrams (ERD) need to undergo Normalization. Remember that the DD and ERD produced in Step 1 are a mirror of the existing system, which most likely will not be in third-normal form. Thus this step will result in the propagation of new entities and even new data elements. Furthermore, data redundancies will be discovered as well as derived elements that should be removed from the logic model. However, while these steps are taking place, ecommerce analysts need to be cognizant that the process of Normalization represents the total new blueprint of how the data should have been originally engineered. The actual removal of elements or reconstruction of the physical database needs to be a phased plan in accordance with the overall legacy migration effort. Thus Step 2 provides the decomposed framework, but not the schedule of implementation.

Finally ecommerce analysts must always be aware of the challenges of decomposition, particularly overdecomposition, meaning that too many classes have been formed that will ultimately hurt system performance. There needs to be a mix of decomposed levels, which will serve as the basis of the new migration architecture.

Step 3: Design "As-Is" Links

This step involves determining and designing which components will remain untouched except for linkages that are necessary with other ecommerce components. These modules are determined not to be part of the initial migration plans; however, they need to function *within* the ecommerce infrastructure and are therefore part of its architecture. Part of the decision needs to include how data will be migrated into the ecommerce framework. In most cases, "as-is" components continue to use their legacy data sources. Consideration must be given to how legacy data will be communicated to other components in the ecommerce system. Ecommerce analysts need to consider either a parameter-based communication system, or a centrally shared database repository as outlined earlier.

Step 4: Design Legacy Enhancements

This step determines which modules will be enhanced. Business process reengineering (BPR) will be used to design new features and functions in each business area. Analysts should identify essential components and determine what changes need to be employed to make the existing system behave more like an object-oriented system. Common processes and databases also need to be mapped so that shared resources can be designed between legacy and ecommerce systems. New linkages will also be needed, and the ecommerce analyst must determine whether to use parameters, databases, or both, to implement the communication among application systems.

User screens may also need to be updated as necessary, especially to remove encoded values or moving certain character-based screens to GUI. Many of the enhancements to a legacy application are implemented based on the analysis performed in Step 1. Any modifications will need to eventually operate on newer platforms once the total migration of legacy systems is completed. Analysts need to be cognizant that additional requirements mean increasing risk, which should be avoided when possible. However, during enhancement consideration, it is almost impossible to ignore new requirements. Therefore, ecommerce analysts need to focus on risk assessment as part of the life cycle of legacy migration.

Step 5: Design Legacy Replacements

Ecommerce analysts must focus on how to reconstruct logic in a later generation of software architecture. Therefore, it is important to understand the differences in generation language design. This chapter provided two types of legacy software systems:

third- and fourth-generation languages. Third-generation languages were depicted as being more procedural and more difficult to convert.

Ecommerce analysts must design the target applications so they will operate in accordance with the business rules and processes that will be supported in the new ecommerce environment. Because of this integration, most replacement legacy migrations require significant reengineering activities. These activities necessitate the inclusion of new business rules that may have evolved since the legacy system was placed in production. Furthermore, new business rules can be created simply by the requirement of being an ecommerce system.

Another important component of legacy migration is screen design. When replacing legacy systems, analysts must view the migration as assimilation, that is, the old system is becoming part of the new one. As a result, all existing ecommerce screens need to be reviewed so that designers can determine whether they need to be modified to adopt some of the legacy functionality. This is not to suggest that all of the legacy systems screens will be absorbed into the existing ecommerce system. Rather, there will be a combination of new and absorbed functionality added to the target environment.

Step 6: Design and Integrate New Databases

From an enterprise perspective, ecommerce analysts must gather all of the permutations of legacy systems that exist and seek to provide a plan on how to integrate the data into one source. For "as-is" solutions, legacy data files will most likely remain separate from the ecommerce system until the complete legacy is migrated. However, the process of enhancing and replacing legacy data should have the objective of creating one central database source that will serve the entire ecommerce enterprise. Indeed, a central data source reduces data redundancy and significantly increases data integrity.

The process of data integration can only be accomplished by "combining user views," which is the process of matching up the multiple data element definitions that overlap and identifying data redundancies and alternative definitions. This can only be completed by creating a repository of data elements and by representing the data graphically using an ERD. Once each system is represented in this fashion, then the ecommerce analyst must perform logic data modeling as prescribed in Chapter 4. The result will be the creation of one central database system cluster that can provide the type of integration necessary for successful ecommerce implementations.

While this is the goal for all ecommerce analysts, the road to successful implementation is challenging. First, the process of Normalization will require that some data elements be deleted (e.g., encoded values) whereas others will need to be added. Second, full data integration cannot be attained until all replacement screens are complete. Third, applications must be redesigned so that the centrality of the data source is assumed to exist. Since this process may be very time-consuming, it may not be feasible to attempt a full database migration at one time. Therefore, the legacy data may need to be logically partitioned to facilitate incremental database migration. Thus, there will be legacy data subsets that are created to remain independent of the central database until some later migration phase is deemed feasible. Of course this strategy requires the design of temporary "bridges" that allows the entire ecommerce system to appear cohesive to users.

Another important factor in planning data migration is to determine how much is really known about the legacy data itself. The less knowledge available, the longer the period where legacy data and ecommerce data need to run separately and in parallel.

Step 7: Determine New Infrastructure and Environment, Including Gateways

Prior to the migration of any system, the necessary hardware and software infrastructure must be planned and installed. A common error in legacy migration is not factoring in the time and effort to provide this infrastructure. Furthermore, this process, which may create a new network environment, needs to determine the placement of software in a three-tier client/server platform. This means that further decomposition may be required of all processes, especially object classes. You may recall in Chapter 8 that classes may undergo further decomposition, depending on the need to distribute application across the network.

Another important factor is performance. In many instances it is difficult for network engineers to predict performance in large ecommerce environments. It may be necessary to plan for several benchmarks in performance early in the design phase. Benchmarking is the process of setting up an environment that replicates a production network so that modifications can be made, if necessary, to the design of the system to increase performance.

Another decision that must be made at this juncture is whether a gateway infrastructure will be created to mediate legacy layers. This decision, of course, is highly dependent on the migration life cycle; the more legacy layers that will be phased in over time, the higher the chances that a gateway processor for data and applications will be necessary. The decision to go with a gateway is significant, not only from the perspective of software design, but network infrastructure as well. Constructing a gateway can be very costly. It involves writing the system from scratch or tailoring a commercial product to meet the migration requirements. It is also costly because of the amount of additional hardware necessary to optimize the performance of the gateway servers. However, the benefits of a gateway are real, as it could provide a dependable structure to slowly migrate all components in an ecommerce environment.

Step 8: Implement Enhancements

This step requires a schedule of when legacy enhancements will be implemented and become part of the production system. Many analysts suggest that the simplest modules go into production first so that any unexpected problems can be dealt with quickly and efficiently. Furthermore, simple modules tend to have small consequences should there be a problem in processing or performance. There are some other aspects of coordination, however. For example, enhancements that feed off of the same data or use the same subsystems should obviously be implemented at the same time.

Another factor in the decision of which enhanced components go first relates to the effects each component has on other subsystems. This means that the priority may indeed be influenced by what other systems need or are dependent on from other systems. Another issue could be the nature of the legacy links. Should a link be very complex or dependent on other subsystem enhancements, its schedule could be affected. Finally, the nature of the enhancements has much to do with the decision as opposed to just the application's complexity. There may be simple enhancements that are crucial for the ecommerce system and vice versa.

Step 9: Implement Links

As I alluded to in Step 8, the determination of legacy links greatly affects the scheduling of the migration cycle. Once the determination is made in Step 8, the related legacy links must be put in place. This could also mean that the gateway, if designed, must also be in operation since many links might be filtered through the gateway infrastructure. So, the implementation of legacy links relates to both hardware and software. Notwithstanding whether a gateway is in place, database links often require separate servers. In many cases, because these servers interface with the Internet, there is a need to install firewalls to ensure security protection.

From a software perspective, legacy links can almost be treated like conversion programs. There needs to be substantial testing done to ensure they work properly. Once legacy links are in production, as with data conversions, they tend to keep working. It is also important to ensure that legacy links are documented. Indeed, any link will eventually be changed based on the incremental migration schedule. Remember that most legacy links are accomplished by building temporary "bridges." The concept of *temporary* can be dangerous, in that many of these links, over time, tend to be more permanent. That is, their temporary life can sometimes extend beyond the predicted life of a permanent component. The message here should be that legacy links, while they are a temporary solution, should be designed with the same intensity and adherence to quality as any other software development component.

Step 10: Migrate Legacy Databases

The migration of data is so complex that it should be handled as a separate and distinct step in the migration life cycle. Data affects everything in the system, and often if it is not migrated properly it can cause immense problems. First, the analyst must decide on the phasing of data based on the schedule of application migration. Hopefully, the process of data migration should be done in parallel with Steps 8 and 9.

The most challenging aspect of data migration is the physical steps in the process. Migrating new entities and schema changes are complex. For example, changes to databases require that the tables be "dropped," meaning that they are taken offline. Data dictionaries need to be updated, and changes to stored procedures and triggers are extremely time-consuming. Most problematic is the process of quality assurance. While some testing can be done in a controlled environment, most of the final testing must be done once the system is actually in production. Therefore the coordination with users to test the system early is critical. Furthermore, there must be back-up procedures in case the database migration does not work properly. This means that there must be an alternative fail-safe plan to reinstall the old system should major problems arise. Finally, a programming team should be ready to deal with any problems that arise that do not warrant reinstalling the old version. This might include the discovery of application "bugs" that can be fixed within a reasonable period and are not deemed critical to operations (which means there is usually a "work-around" for the problem). Ecommerce analysts must understand that this process must be followed each time a new database migration takes place!

Database migration is even more complex when there is a gateway. The reason is that the gateway, from an incremental perspective, contains more and more database responsibilities each time there is a migration. Therefore, for every migration, the amount of data that can potentially be affected grows larger. In addition, the number of data that becomes integrated usually grows exponentially, so the planning and conversion process becomes a critical path to successful migration life cycles. Since the migration of legacy databases becomes so much more difficult as the project progresses, the end of the life cycle becomes even more challenging to reach. That is why many migrations have never been completed!

Step 11: Migrate Replacement Legacy Applications

Once the database migration is completed, then the remainder of the legacy applications can be migrated to the new system. These applications are usually the replacement components, which have been reengineered in the object-oriented paradigm. These programs, then, have been designed to operate against the target databases with the new functionality required for the ecommerce system. Since replacement applications usually do not create links, there is typically little effect on gateway operations. What is more challenging is the quality assurance process. Users need to be aware that the code is relatively new and will contain problems regardless of the amount of pre-production testing that has been performed. In any event, programmers, database administrators, and quality assurance personnel should be on call for weeks after system cutover.

Step 12: Incrementally Cutover to New Systems

As discussed above, testing and application turnover are two areas that frequently are overlooked. Because projects typically run over budget and miss the scheduled deadline, the final procedures like testing and verification are usually shortened. The results of this decision can be devastating to successful legacy migrations. Because of the size and complexity of many ecommerce systems, to go "cold turkey" is unrealistic and irresponsible. Therefore, an ecommerce analyst should consider providing test scenarios that provide more confidence that the system is ready to be cutover. This approach is called "acceptance testing" and requires that users be involved in the determination of what tests must be performed before the system is ready to go live. Thus, acceptance test plans can be defined as the set of tests that, if passed, will establish that the software can be used in production. Acceptance tests need to be established early in the product life cycle and should begin during the analysis phase. It is only logical then that

Quality Assurance
Acceptance Test Plan

Product: Contact - Using Enter Key	Number:

Test Plan #: 1G	Vendor:	
	QA Technician:	Date:

Test No.	Condition Being Tested	Expected Results	Actual Results	Comply Y/N	Comments
1	Enter LAST NAME for a new contact, press enter key. Repeat and enter FIRST NAME, press enter key	Should accept and prompt for COMPANY SITE			
2	Select COMPANY Site from picklist	Should accept and prompt for next field			
3	Enter LAST NAMEand FIRST NAME for a CONTACT that is already in the System.	Should accept and prompt for COMPANY SITE			

Figure 9.24 Acceptance test plan.

the development of acceptance test plans should involve ecommerce analysts. As with requirements development, the analyst must participate with the user community. Only users can make the final decision about the content and scope of the test plans. The design and development of acceptance test plans should not be confused with the testing phase of the software development life cycle.

Another perspective on acceptance testing is that it becomes a formal checklist that defines the minimal criteria for incrementally migrating systems. However, one must work with the understanding that no new product will ever be fault-free. The permutations of testing everything would make the timetable for completion unacceptable and cost-prohibitive. Therefore, the acceptance test plan is a strategy to get the most important components tested completely enough for production. Figure 9.24 represents a sample acceptance test plan.

CHAPTER

10

XML and Component Middleware: Integrating Data and Processes

The Extensible Markup Language (XML) is a significant development that adds flexibility and richness to the exchange of data on the Net. Specifically, XML and its related standards improve Web data exchange by providing a method for structured data transfer. This structured data transfer allows different systems to exchange data through standard or agreed-upon formats. Furthermore, XML supports an object model that allows for the sorting, selecting, and manipulating of data in documents, regardless of whether the data resides on the server or on the client computer.

The purpose of XML is to allow for data exchange across multiple tiers of Web applications. Like HTML, XML is a subset of Structured Generalized Markup Language (SGML), optimized for delivery over the Web. HTML, however, restricts developers to a finite set of tags designed to describe Web pages for presentation, as opposed to exchange of reusable information or data. Unlike HTML, which tags only elements in Web pages for presentation by a browser, XML tags elements and stores them as data. This means that XML can be used to identify text or numeric elements within a Web page, allowing text to be passed into the page as data. This is accomplished by a coding system that makes use of data tags that precede the value. For this reason, XML can be defined as a *metalanguage*—a language used to define new markup languages. With XML, developers can create languages or documents specifically for an application.

The ecommerce applications that have the most to gain from using XML are obviously those that cannot accomplish what they need to with HTML. The types of applications that can maximize their benefit from XML fall into one of four categories:

1. Applications that require a Web client to utilize data between two or more related databases.

2. Applications that have more processing on the client tier than on the server tier.

3. Applications that require Web pages to be presented differently, depending on the user and device accessing the ecommerce system.

4. Applications that allow intelligent Web agents to dynamically tailor the information provided to users, depending on the environment or Web client that the information must reside on.

In practice, then, XML is suitable for storing and exchanging data that can be plausibly coded as text (Harold and Means, 2001). On the other hand, it is unsuitable for multimedia data, such as photographs, sound, and video.

XML Structure

As stated earlier, XML can be considered a metalanguage. It is essentially text that can represent an element, tag, or character data. An element defines the existence of a data field, the tag delimits its beginning and ending, and the character data represents the element's actual data. Sometimes the data is an actual value; other times it is a text string. This depends, of course, on the definition of the element's attributes. An example of an XML text structure is shown in Figure 10.1.

Because XML can have multiple types of definitions, it is said to contain mixed content. The mixed content can be represented in the form of a tree structure as shown in Figure 10.2.

In Figure 10.2, the contents of the first_name and last_name are character data, whereas name and profession are elements that have tags to delimit the definition values.

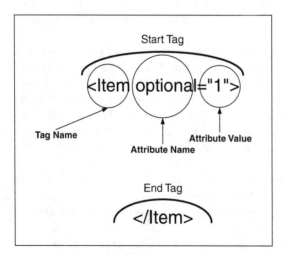

Figure 10.1   XML text format.

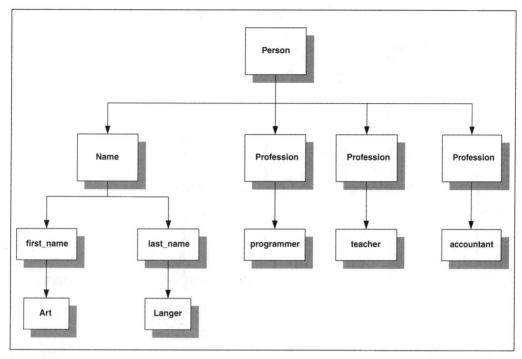

Figure 10.2   An XML tree diagram.

XML Parsing

From a process perspective, there are a number of related components or tools that provide XML with the ability to connect to various applications. The first component is called the XML Parser. In many ways a *parser* is similar to a compiler in that it is charged with the responsibility to translate source data into an object or target machine form. The XML parser is responsible for editing an XML document and breaking it down to its elements for transfer to various application programs. These programs could be Web browsers, word processing editors, database systems for storage of the source, spreadsheet, JAVA, or C++ programs, or miscellaneous third-party products. The transferring process is known as "parsing out" the data. From an edit perspective, the XML parser is responsible for validating the input data to ensure that there are no errors. This is accomplished by interfacing with a document type definition (DTD) file. The DTD contains the master list of data rules and document constraints. The data rules include the list of fields that can be used in an XML document. If the DTD does not contain a definition, an error will be generated. Error messages can have varying levels of significance, similar to the way compilers issue warning and fatal errors when editing source code.

Once an XML document has completed the parser, it can be generated to a number of different applications as shown in Figure 10.3.

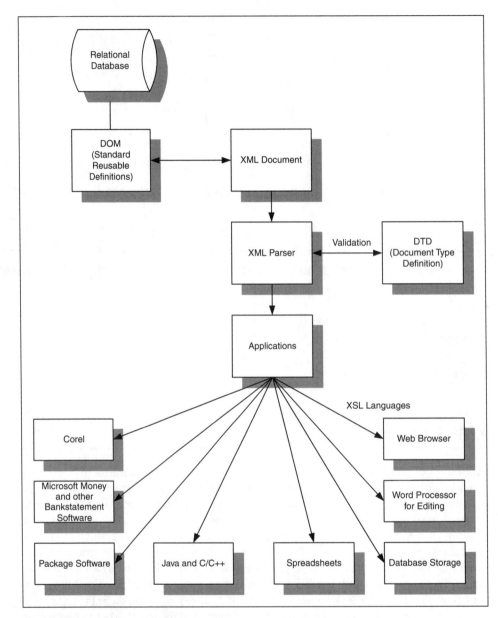

Figure 10.3 XML application generation.

What XML Does Not Do

XML is just a markup language, meaning that it is limited to the manipulation and presentation of data as text. Therefore, XML is not truly a programming language per se. Furthermore, XML is not a network protocol and therefore cannot be used to send data across a network without the assistance of other network protocols like HTTP and File Transfer Protocol (FTP). Finally, it is important to recognize that XML is not a database and cannot replace the functionalities of databases. XML can be stored within a database and provides a reuse function by providing an XML format to many different types of applications on many hardware platforms. The format is stored as data only.

Other XML Interfaces

There are other application interfaces that are used when the target is a Web browser. The functionality of these applications is to provide better formatting features that allow XML to better integrate with a Web browser screen or what is called a *stylesheet*. The Extensible Stylesheet Language (XSL) is an XML application that transforms XML documents into Web browser form. This application has been decomposed into two more specific programs: XSL Transformations (XSLT) and XSL Formatting Object (XSL-FO). XSLT is general-purpose in that it allows one XML document to be displayed in a Web browser, whereas the XSL-FO feature describes the layout of the text data. Another enhancement is that the Extensible Linking Language (XLL) is a more powerful linking construct that has greater capabilities than HTML's A tag. XLL is comprised of two separate standards: Xlink, which describes the connections between XML documents, and Xpointer, which addresses the individual components within an XML document.

Another application that can be used to format Web browser pages is Cascading Style Sheets (CSS). CSS is usually utilized as a lower-level formatter for HTML. CSS does allow styles to be reused within documents without the need to redefine them. In addition, CSS allows for the definition to be changed anywhere in the document file.

XML and Ecommerce Applications

Ecommerce systems are all about the interfacing of systems across the Web to conduct business transactions. A number of years ago, a communication standard called Electronic Data Interface (EDI) was developed. EDI is essentially a standard file format that allowed companies to provide a consistent way for vendors to interface with their systems. For example, the publications industry has a standard file format for vendors who submit invoices to them. The EDI standard became part of most internal systems in the publications industry because it saved costly custom modifications for each system for both the company and its vendors. XML provides a great deal more functionality than EDI; however, it works on the same principle of allowing standard interfacing and exchange of data. What makes XML so exciting is that the data, unlike in EDI, can also be used as text to populate applications, as well as passing over the Web so that businesses can exchange information without standard network protocols. Thus, an EDI-like data interchange can be accomplished by combining data requirements and applications; the Web page combines application interface and data interface in one package. By using XSL capabilities, an XML file can be translated into HTML and be propagated into an operational Web application in a Web browser as shown in Figure 10.4.

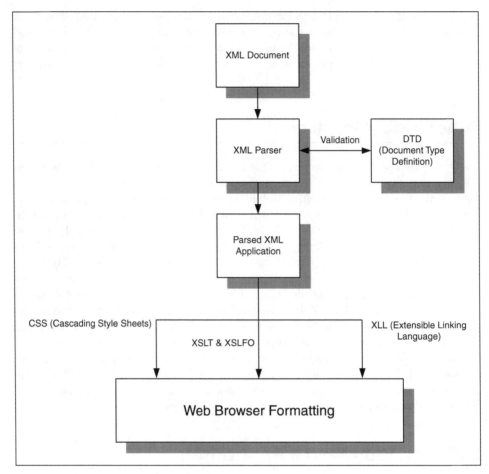

Figure 10.4 XSL Web page generation.

Document Object Model

The Document Object Model (DOM) represents the most important component application for the ecommerce analysis and design function. Indeed, ecommerce analysts must decide which portions of the system will utilize XML applications, and, more important, how these XML documents should be defined. The DOM is a powerful tool that allows XML documents (as well as other documents) to be manipulated as objects. This means that the DOM can access an XML document, reformat it, and preview it visually as an object tree structure. Given that XML is structured hierarchically, any XML document can be displayed in a tree structure as depicted in Figure 10.5.

Figure 10.5 depicts a typical university and represents each school and program logically as a tree of document tags. This structure makes it easier to understand—and to update—any XML design. The tree structure is also consistent with a class diagram structure, so the model is well suited for interface with object-oriented systems. Thus, the DOM allows developers to make modifications to the structure, which will then be automatically translated back to the XML document as shown in Figure 10.6.

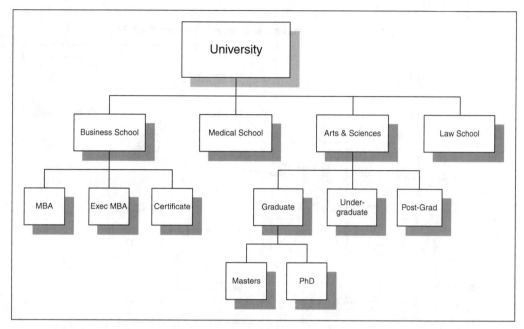

Figure 10.5 XML tree structure construct.

Furthermore, the DOM can be used to create XML documents from scratch, so it is truly full-duplex in its relationship with XML documents. So, with the DOM, XML documents can be manipulated as objects, instead of only as streams of text. Having a visual representation of an XML document makes it easier to edit the information. Furthermore, the DOM is compatible with the Interface Definition Language used in Common Object Request Broker Architecture (CORBA), often used to implement object middleware applications.

The DOM also plays a pivotal role in the interface of XML with relational databases. This is accomplished by thinking of the relational database as a set of DOM objects. If an ecommerce analyst wants to design a document that represents a particular schema

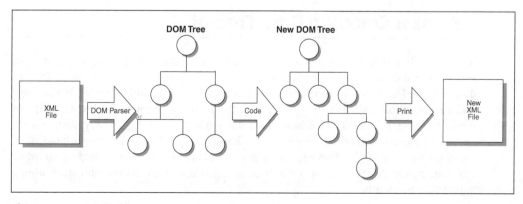

Figure 10.6 DOM document transformation system.

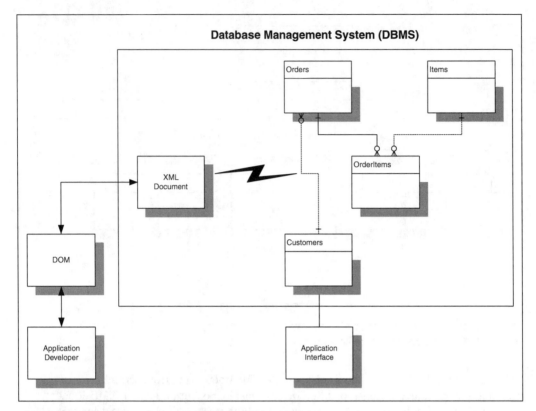

Figure 10.7   DOM interface with a relational database.

of data, it can be described by the DOM and then translated into an XML document. The XML document can then be formatted using XSL into an HTML Web application. SQL can be used and mapped via XML to the back-end relationally modeled data. Thus, database schemas can be brought together in a rather robust way using the DOM as shown in Figure 10.7.

XML as a Common Data Format

In Chapter 9, I discussed the different methods of linking legacy applications with ecommerce systems. Two methods, "Leave As Is" and "Enhance," required some form of data linkage. The format alternatives were parameter passing and database. While these options had value, XML provides yet another interesting alternative, especially in cases where the legacy link does not have a database interface. XML, as previously stated, provides linkages without concern for the hardware platform. While relational databases provide for application and platform independence, there is a huge amount of overhead associated with using a database as a method of intercommunication among application programs.

With the rapid proliferation of ecommerce interfaces, free XML tools can represent another method of providing platform-independent and database-independent program communications. The unique strengths of using XML as a software data communication method include:

Simple syntax. XML is easy to generate using the DOM, and easy to parse using XSL.

Support for nesting. The tree format allows for programs to represent data structures with nested elements—required by many program formats.

Easy to debug. XML is easy to format, especially with the DOM.

Language and platform independent. An XML data file is completely transportable across different architectures and database products.

Thus XML is becoming a popular format for enterprise data sharing, especially when there are mixed platform environments. For example, suppose a typical organization needs to take information from an IBM mainframe and display it on a Web site. Using XML, the mainframe schema of data can be accessed by the DOM, which in turn would format the output as an XML document. Using XSL, the Web server could then transform the XML into HTML, which could then be loaded into a Web browser template (see Figure 10.8). It is important to note that I am not suggesting that XML replace relational database technologies. Indeed, XML is too slow to handle high-volume transactions.

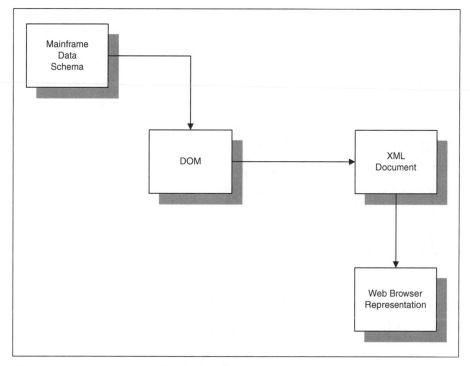

Figure 10.8   Using XML to link legacy applications.

Source: Oracle XML Applications, Muench, 2000

However, XML can be used to work with database subsets, called sub-schemas, in which a small picture of the needed data can be downloaded and formatted in a class structure for use by an ecommerce object application.

XML Applications with Database Systems

A significant issue addressed by XML is the ability to create consistent representation of data. While normalized databases were supposed to provide this consistency, most do not because they violate certain normal form rules. These violations ultimately create problems with the transportability of the data. Furthermore, stored procedures tend to be proprietary at the vendor database level, and therefore further complicate the task of providing seamless portability among databases. XML, on the other hand, creates a portable structure that allows ecommerce systems to connect multiple databases across different hardware platforms. Indeed, in some situations, an XML-based representation of data and the http protocol might be the only method of connecting legacy systems with ecommerce technology. Figure 10.9 illustrates a sample ecommerce system that uses XML to provide application integration. This integration is provided via the linking of various databases using an XML interface.

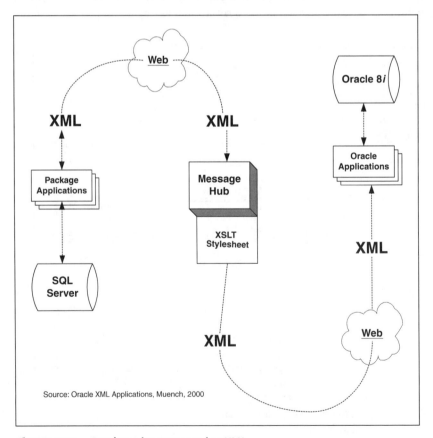

Source: Oracle XML Applications, Muench, 2000

Figure 10.9   Database integrator using XML.

Figure 10.9 reflects that XML, over the Web, provides the data integration between the Oracle and SQL Server systems. If XML were not used, the application developer would need to use separate SQL-based languages (SQL-7 for SQL Server and PLSQL for Oracle) to provide data access to each program. XML provides a means of using a central repository that can generate its own SQL necessary to access its data. This means that each database vendor supplies an SQL-XML interface that can generate (output) and access (read) XML formats. Thus, just knowing and using XML allows for access to multiple proprietary SQL coding.

The key to integrating XML and SQL is making the information in the query results easy to transform, transport, and transcribe. Figure 10.10 shows the architecture of integrating XML and SQL to produce multiple applications. Note that XSLT is used to transform the parsed XML data pages to multiple applications such as Web pages, Wireless Markup Language (WML) for cell phones, and handheld devices.

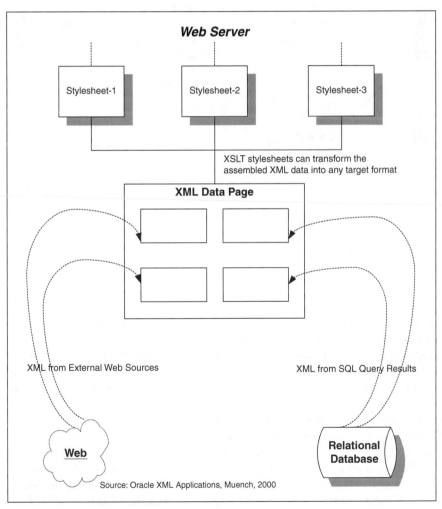

Figure 10.10   XML and SQL integrated architecture.

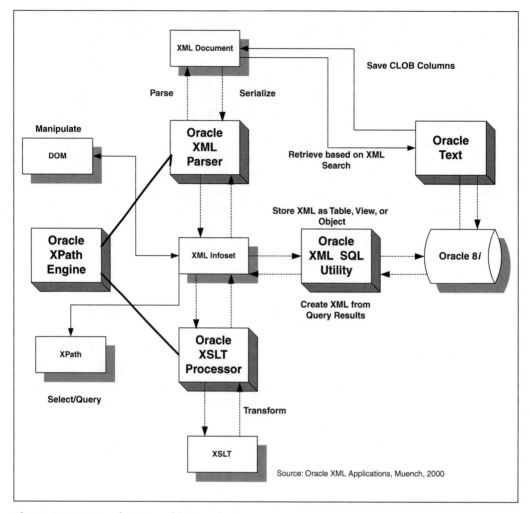

Figure 10.11   Oracle XML architecture.

Therefore, publishing XML diagrams from relational databases allows for proven portability, scalability, manageability, and performance.

Using the Oracle product as an example, we can see a more detailed view of how a relational database and XML are integrated to provide portability between XML and SQL technologies. Figure 10.11 shows how Oracle has implemented XML in its $8i$ product.

Using the Oracle XML parser, XML documents can be manipulated and modified with the DTD, which Oracle calls the information set or Infoset. The Oracle XSLT processor transforms XML into HTML or other structures. While these components are somewhat standard XML applications, Oracle adds an XPath engine that enables the querying of XML documents. The Oracle XML SQL utility then automates the tasks of producing XML from SQL query results and vice versa (that is, storing XML documents into tables in the database). The Oracle Text application provides a method of creating indexes of

Table 10.1   Oracle XML Infrastructure Component Definitions

ORACLE FEATURE/FUNCTION	DESCRIPTION
XML Parser	Edits and validates XML documents
XPath Engine	Searches for XML documents
XSLT Processor	Transforms XML documents to other output forms
XML SQL Utility	Produces XML from SQL and inserts XML into tables
XSQL Pages	Assembles XML data for use by XSLT
Oracle Text	Indexes and searches XML documents using native structure
Object Views	XML-enabled view of relational data
Oracle JVM	Java implementation on the database
JDeveloper	Java development for XML, XSLT, and XSQL
Advanced Queuing	Queues XML messages

the XML structure to support SQL queries. Table 10.1 provides a summary of the Oracle XML infrastructure.

Analysis and Design of XML Documents

The ecommerce analyst must provide XML specifications as part of the overall engineering architecture. To do so, the analyst must determine the XML components that will be used for data interface and what portions will be used for ecommerce application reuse. Therefore, the first step in designing an XML interface is to decide what will constitute an XML document. The second step is to determine what elements, text, or code will comprise the XML document. The third step is to determine the reuse and propagation of the XML document data into the various ecommerce applications.

Step 1: Determining XML Documents

The process of determining what will be an XML document relates to two factors mentioned above: (1) what data will be used as an EDI application; and (2) what will be used to populate Web applications. Regardless of which factor is used, an ecommerce analyst must determine the actual data structure for the XML tree. This data structure can be defined as a vocabulary of XML elements and attributes. The elements and attributes are the text in the vocabulary that enables communication of information.

An example of choosing the right reuse is the function provided by a search engine. A search engine is typically used for general search requirements to locate specific

Figure 10.12   Amazon search engine options.

information in the database. An XML document can be created that identifies the database elements that are required for the search application. This is then coded in the DOM, and outputted as an XML document. The XML design allows a user to search for a particular type of product, similar to the way Amazon.com allows a user to search for a particular product like a book or a DVD (see Figure 10.12). Thus the root of the XML document tree is the "type-identifier" of the product. The DOM would then structure the XML tree as shown in Figure 10.13.

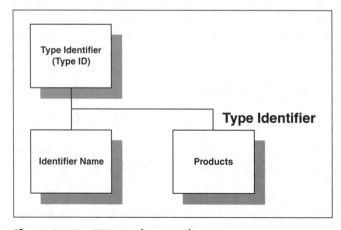

Figure 10.13   XML product search tree.

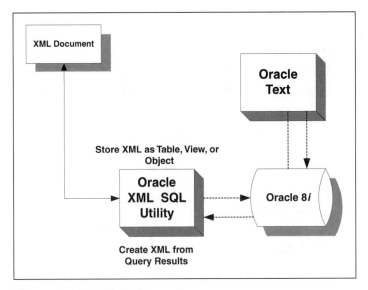

Figure 10.14 XML/SQL execution.

Thus, the "Type Identifier" element identifies a type of product that is needed to display the results of the search. The data can then be transformed into various HTML Web browser applications. The data interface can be accomplished via an SQL interface engine. So when a user wants to query the product database, he or she will use the search engine XML document. This document interfaces with the Oracle Text application, which created indexes on the related database elements that were defined in the XML document. When the query is created by the application driving the ecommerce activity, the stylesheet created from the XML document will issue an SQL call to the XML SQL interface (Oracle), which will retrieve the necessary data and convert it back to the XML format as shown in Figure 10.14.

XML as an EDI

Earlier in this chapter it was mentioned that XML is an effective application to replace the EDI traditionally used to handle standard file interfaces between clients and vendors. EDI in legacy applications was typically implemented by designing a standard file format that would be required for any entity to interface with an ecommerce system. This file format was usually delivered in a comma-delimited record (CSV file) that matched with a standard database format required by the accepting system. A special application was then programmed that was designed to read the standard CSV file and convert it into the target database format. The program operated in a batch mode and included an edit program that reported errors as appropriate and determined the validity of the input transactions.

XML can be used to create a much more robust and portable EDI. The data structure required would be converted as an object-tree structure using the DOM (or coded directly as an XML document). The DOM would then generate the XML document, which would be parsed against the DTD. An XSLT application would then create a Web browser program that would accept the required input data.

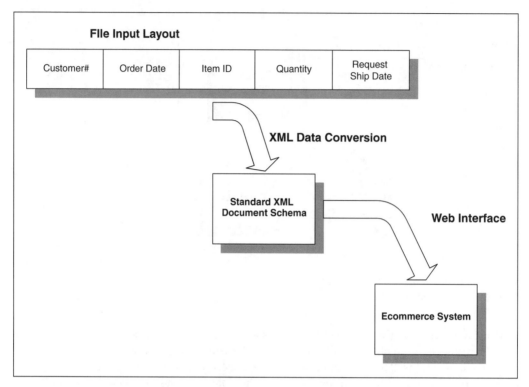

Figure 10.15 EDI XML configuration interface.

The XML solution could also be adapted to accept a file input, instead of an input screen over the Web. In this situation, the vendor would be provided with the XML schema and asked to create their data using the same XML document. Should an EDI standard exist in a particular industry group, then all parties would incorporate the XML format into their respective systems. Of course this requires all parties to agree about what that format should be. Figure 10.15 depicts the EDI XML configuration interface.

In a nutshell, the ecommerce analyst must know whether an industry standard exists, or whether the organization must create a standard for its own use and hope others will adhere to it. Typically the latter is the case, and the EDI standard format will evolve over time.

XML and Populating Web Applications

While XML can be used as a method of data interchange among applications, it is also useful to provide data that is part of a Web application. Thus, the ecommerce analyst needs to provide information about what portions of a particular application can receive data that can be used to populate its content. For example, suppose there is a particular phrase or logo that is used on multiple screens in an application. The ecommerce analyst needs to determine if this phrase or logo should be stored in a database and then formatted as an XML document. This process greatly reduces duplication of static coding on a Web page. More important, the concept of storing literals as data allows for better maintenance of text that can change over the life of a Web application. Indeed, the content in ecommerce systems is much more dynamic. Thus, XML can provide the standard format to propagate content for Web applications. In Chapter 13, we will see how XML, along with content management products, provides significant maintenance capabilities by storing content as data and incorporating it into template systems.

In addition, XML can be used to provide data that is stored inside program applications. This data could be in the form of an internal array, or multidimensional tables that are used by an application to complete an algorithm, or as a component of some conditional selection logic. Internal data structures are very common, particularly in object component programming. Once again, XML can be used to provide the data structure and allow programmers to use it in many different applications. This allows for the creation of standard data structures that can be dynamically loaded into an application. The capability to dynamically load data structures can have a profound impact on program maintenance. Not only can the data structure be stored, its values associated with the structure can also be included in the XML document. Remember, XML can store both element definitions and values. Suppose, then, that an XML document contained a table that calculated discounts for book purchases. Such a calculation could have many tiers of logic, and could be dependent on how many books have been purchased and where. The XML document could store the table of questions, as well as the questions themselves. Furthermore, the "discount codes" could be stored as values. Thus, when the XML document is propagated into the application program, it not only has the algorithm structure, but also the actual codes that it needs to formulate the final discount amount. Should any of the questions or codes change, which normally will occur, the developer need only update the XML document, changing its data structure or values, as necessary. These changes would then be reloaded into the application upon its next instance (or next execution of the program in the Web application). Figure 10.16 depicts the XML data structure for the discount algorithm.

Embracing XML goes beyond just agreeing to use it; it also means engineering applications that assume a component will change. This greatly affects the architecture of the applications. Thus, the ecommerce analyst must work closely with developers to ensure that specifications clearly establish information on what components will be stored as XML documents. Ecommerce analysts must also be aware of how text (or content) will be stored in the relational database. This topic will be discussed further in Chapter 13. As previously mentioned, the reuse aspect of XML is consistent with object technologies. These aspects are discussed in greater detail in Step 3 of this section.

Step 2: XML Data Schemas

A schema is defined as a way of describing the characteristics of data. The DTD, in many ways, constitutes the basis of the XML schema. Unfortunately, the DTD falls short in relation to some required processing needs. An XML schema must provide

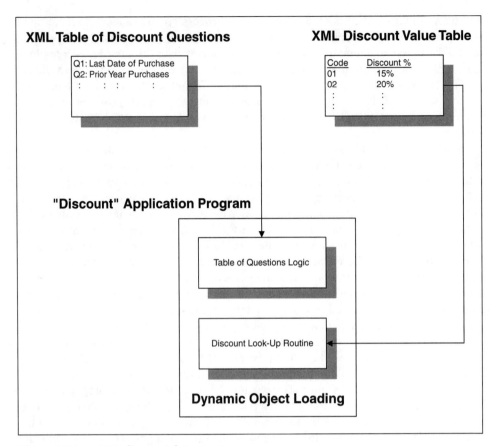

Figure 10.16 XML discount data structure.

three important benefits: (1) functionality and power, (2) ease of use, and (3) compatibility.

Functionality

The DTD alone provides limited semantic checking of XML. This means that there can be errors in the syntax of the code that will not be caught by the DTD. So it is possible to produce an XML document that will be authorized by the DTD, yet have some problems with syntax. Incorrect syntax can affect a statement's semantics or meaning.

Ease of Use

Unfortunately, good DTDs are difficult to write because of the limited infrastructure support provided by their design. Furthermore, DTDs are not easy to read and edit. The result is that it can be difficult to produce XML that correctly matches the DTD. DTDs also lack extensibility and have poor version control mechanisms. Finally, there are syntactical differences between XML and DTD, which make it even more difficult to match the two scripts.

Compatibility

The DTD is part of the first version of XML. There are many later versions of XML that have difficulty communicating with earlier versions. Ultimately this means that the relationship between XML documents and DTDs is very version-sensitive, and system personnel must ensure that versions are kept consistent. While this requirement sounds straightforward, it is difficult to enforce after the initial installations of ecommerce systems. Indeed, version control becomes progressively more challenging as the system is updated.

The weaknesses of DTD can be summarized below (Spencer, 1999):

- Poor support for semantic checking
- No data typing
- No relational support
- No support for objects features such as inheritance
- Cannot use parts of other DTDs
- Difficult to write
- No extensibility
- No version control mechanism
- Unique syntax

The schema method is obviously designed to address the DTD weaknesses summarized above. There are a number of product schemas designed to complement the DTD. A document content description (DCD) mechanism has been implemented as a schema in a number of products such as Internet Explorer 5. Internet Explorer 5 implements a schema that contains a more extensible and robust method for providing constraints on the structure and contents of XML documents. The importance of an enhanced DCD is that it can provide more advanced metadata, or data about data. The ecommerce analyst needs to be aware of whether specific DCDs are available, since this information can affect how XML documents are designed. Specifically, the more DCD capability, the more advanced the XML applications can be used in the overall engineering of the ecommerce system. More important is that the DCD has a significant influence on what data elements and structures can be included in the XML document. If the DTD edit abilities are limited, then certain data structures may be deemed too risky (from a quality perspective) for inclusion in an XML document.

No matter how ambitious the XML structure is designed, the ecommerce analyst must provide a specification that defines the data elements and specific data types to be included in the XML tree structure. While the data elements should correspond to the definitions stored in the relational database, their syntax can be different from an SQL data type and type qualifier. Table 10.2 represents the list of data types supported by XML.

Table 10.2 XML Data Types

NAME	DESCRIPTION	STORAGE TYPE	EXAMPLE
string	Alphanumeric data	string	Art Langer
number	A number that has no limits on digits	string	18, 54.596, .01
char	string	1 Unicode character (16 bits)	A, Z
int	Whole number, optional sign value	32-bit signed binary	7, 45302, -87
float	A number that has no limits on digits	64-bit IEEE 488	.3258798554E+3
Fixed 14.4	A number with a limit of up to 14 digits to the left of the decimal point, and no more than 4 decimal places to the right	64-bit signed binary	188.0458
boolean	"1" or "0"	bit	0, 1 (0="false")
dateTime.iso8601	A date in ISO 8601 format with optional time and no optional zone	Structure that contains year, month, hour, minute, second, nanosecond	20011204T09:25:01501
dateTime.iso8601tz	A date in ISO 8601 format with optional time and optional zone	Structure that contains year, month, hour, minute, second, nanosecond, zone	20011204T09:25:01501 +02
date.iso8601	A date in ISO 8601 format only	Structure that contains year, month, day	20011225
time.iso8601	A time in ISO 8601 format only	Structure that contains day, hour, minute	251548
time.iso8601.tz	A time in ISO 8601 with no date but optional time zone	Structure that contains day, hour, minute, zonehours, zoneminutes	09:25-05:00

Thus, an XML specification must list the actual names and XML definitions. One method of accomplishing this is for the ecommerce analyst to establish the corresponding XML name and attributes when building the data dictionary. Thus, an XML definition should be included for every data element that is a candidate for an XML solution. Another approach is to provide an XML definition for all data dictionary data elements. The advantage of the latter approach is that it prepares all data elements for possible inclusion in an XML document.

Step 3: XML Reuse

XML documents can be designed to provide reusable components that can be part of different Web applications. In order to design such components, ecommerce analysts must track the number of operations that are reused in applications, similar to the example of the Search Engine. An example of application reuse can be described with a function that adds a new customer. Let's say that this function is used when a caller wants to sign up as a customer to order a product. An XML document could be designed that would be comprised of the data elements necessary for inserting a new customer. The XML document would then be used through XSLT to generate an HTML screen. There is another operation that allows for entering new orders. This application requires the entry of the customer who has placed the order. Sometimes a new order is placed by a caller who has not yet signed up as a customer and is therefore not in the Customer database. Users would like the order entry screen to allow the customer to be added while the new order entry screen is operating. This is accomplished by allowing a pop-up window to be invoked when a new customer needs to be inserted during the order entry process. Instead of writing a new screen, the application can use the same XML document that was used to generate the new customer application. Thus, the XML document serves to provide a reusable application that is generated into more than one application screen. Ecommerce analysts should seek to design XML documents that link up with object classes. The purpose of this approach is to provide matching data for classes that are designed by nature to be reusable. This means that the need for reusable XML documents for applications can be mapped to classes designed to become reusable object components. Of course, this approach assumes that the host system is based on object development. In legacy systems, or even those that contain hybrid combinations (a high probability in ecommerce systems), the likelihood of using this approach to identify all reusable components is slim. XML and its relation to object components are shown in Figure 10.17.

Another area that can assist in determining the need for XML reuse application is in a TP system. You might recall that the TP system was designed as a middleware application repository. The TP monitor component was designed to provide consistent operation and data integrity among many "linked" programs from different systems. Thus, the TP monitor was the center of traffic among different system components and reduced the need to program the same logic in different program languages and for different file systems. XML can become the data vehicle to operate within the TP system. Instead of requiring the TP system to format and update data in different file systems, XML can be used to send a standard format of the data needed to multiple applications across the network. Each system would have the ability to read the data and reformat it as necessary into their respective applications and file schemas. Figure 10.18 reflects the use of XML in a TP system.

Storing XML Documents in a Database

External XML document files can be loaded into a database system so that it can be better integrated with the SQL-based relational system. Notwithstanding the fact that there is a difference in file format, most of the physical data will remain stored in the

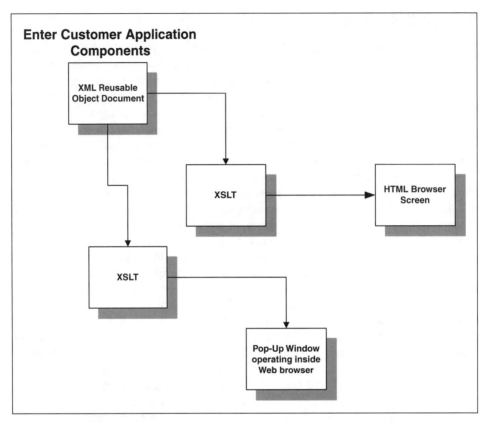

Figure 10.17   XML matching to object components.

database. The significant issue to remember is that the relational model is built under third-normal form and referential integrity rules. This, of course, focuses on a production-oriented database management component that contains a high volume of transactional processing as opposed to a data warehouse implementation (see Chapter 12). However, it is possible in a database system such as Oracle to actually store an XML document in the database without its being part of the traditional normalized schema. This means that the XML document may contain data elements unique to the document itself, thus not propagated into a particular entity. A database system like Oracle provides an XML parsing utility, which allows the XML document to be accessible via normal SQL queries and stored procedures. Thus the XML document retains its own format while being assimilated into the database infrastructure. Accessing a data element within the XML document or in the relational database can be transparent to the user community. Figure 10.19 reflects the concept of XML and relational database schema integration.

The question arises from a design perspective of whether an XML document should contain data elements that have not originated from the relational part of the database. This certainly is a question that must be answered by the ecommerce analyst. The most logical support for this occurrence is when a data element in an XML document is

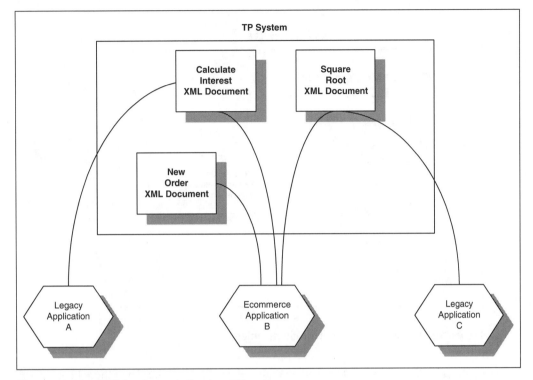

Figure 10.18 XML implementation in a TP system.

unique to a particular application. Therefore, the XML document has been designed for use in a one-on-one relationship with a specific Web program or application. To propagate the data element into the relational database under these circumstances would create unnecessary overhead and the ongoing need for data synchronization. On the other hand, leaving the data elements in XML structure eliminates the need for dual storage and allows access from multiple sources, including traditional SQL-based applications.

From a specification perspective, an ecommerce analyst needs to understand how to design the XML-relational model. This task is easier if the analyst knows the physical database features and functions that are designed to support the product's architecture. For example, Oracle supports the creation of an element known as a CLOB. "CLOB" stands for *Character Large Object*. In Oracle, a CLOB can hold character-based data such as XML documents as large as 4 gigabytes (4GB). A CLOB column is stored in the database and is fully readable and writable. Using Oracle Text, CLOB files can be indexed for fast XML document searching across millions of rows. Obviously, Oracle needed to establish an XML/SQL Application Program Interface (API) to allow for the parsing and integration of both models within the database. Essentially it allows for the coexistence of the two.

Should the physical database vendor, like Oracle, support XML document storage within their database, ecommerce analysts must still be aware of the following challenges:

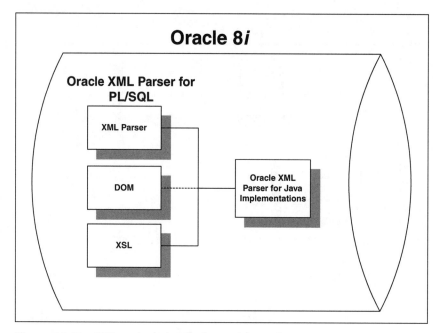

Figure 10.19 XML and relational schema integration.

1. If an XML document is used by multiple database vendors, will there be compatibility in the XML/SQL integration, or should the XML document be stripped out from one of the databases so that it is resident in only one file?

2. There cannot be any "external" references within the XML document that allow for insertion of data elements that exist, let's say, in a URL. This would be problematic since there is no existing infrastructure in Oracle that allows for the external linking outside the confines of the database infrastructure.

3. There needs to be documentation and control among the different versions of XML and DTD used in all systems. Different versions between XML and DTD could cause serious problems in the quality of the parsing process as well as the validity of the applications generated through the XSLT.

XML-Based File Types in Oracle *i*FS

Oracle provides an Internet file system (*i*FS) that supports the infrastructure for defining XML documents. The file system essentially assigns descriptors that specify the XML structure and store the schema in the database. As stated above, the CLOB allows an entire XML file to mix structured data and text markup in the same document. For example, an "Order" file type may map to an OrderHeader and OrderLines table, while a "BenefitsClaim" file type can mix methods of data and text by actually structuring text markup for a Summary Report and combining it with a Payments Report. In this case the data is stored in the traditional database, whereas the text is stored as a CLOB. Figure 10.20 shows the contents of a sample BenefitsClaim file.

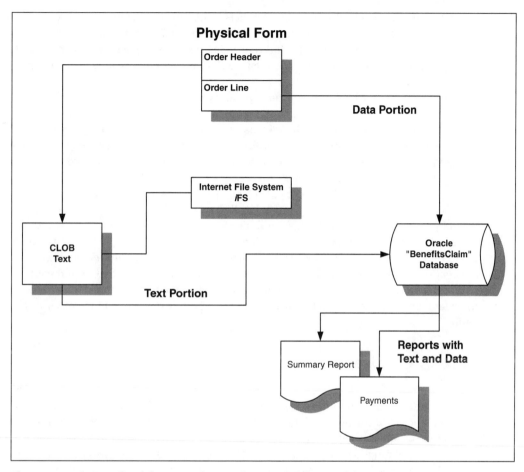

Figure 10.20   BenefitsClaim as a mixture of structured data and text.

XML as a Centralized Data Search Engine

Another application of XML is as a central search engine. A *central search engine* is one that can be used to collect information over several different systems and provide summary information on the collective meaning of the information. This can be a difficult task in large organizations that have a proliferation of legacy applications running across different hardware platforms. While Chapter 9 provided guidance on ways of integrating legacy applications, it did so with approaches that have high overhead and require significant time to install. With XML, on the other hand, the goal of centralizing information quickly and cheaply is attainable. This can be accomplished by allowing each proprietary application to generate a standard XML document that holds the needed data and text. Each XML output could then be merged in a database CLOB or integrated in a table relational format for querying of data. Furthermore, the searching could be accomplished via the Web, using the index utilities provided by the database vendor. While this "central" repository of data is similar in concept to data warehousing, it involves far less complexity in overhead, coding, and maintainability. Most important is that it can be accessed over the Internet using portable application programming. Thus, the ecommerce analyst should consider XML for all multi-data analysis requirements.

The importance of having a central repository for searching has further benefits. Common ecommerce initiatives involve accessing text documents on the Web for research, analysis, and business. Indeed, users would love to be able to query text in a document and pull out all relevant information and citations that they need, as opposed to being forced to print the entire document and find the information they need manually. We say then that such data needs to be stored as metadata. For example, suppose a user needed to access a Web site to review information about a particular subject. If the document were created in XML, it could be searched for matches on the subject, which would be looking at multiple XML documents from many systems. If a match is found, instead of just printing or copying the text, a portion of the data could be extracted from the document in order to populate another application. This application could be a spreadsheet program, or database system, that would capture the data or text and categorize it as appropriate. Thus, the text document has become metadata, and the user can select what portions of the text are useful for other applications.

XML Query Usage

Database products such as Oracle and Microsoft's SQL Server must provide a set of query functions that support the manipulation of data as provided by SQL on the relational model. Obviously, with a hybrid model of XML integrated with the database, not all typical SQL queries can be supported. Ecommerce analysts need to understand the extent of query functionality available in XML documents and the types of documents that can be queried before making final design decisions relating to what will be stored as XML and what will be stored as a traditional data element. The World Wide Web Consortium (W3C) has issued "query usage scenarios" that provide guidelines on the query usage for XML documents as follows:

Human-readable documents. Perform queries on structured documents and collections of documents, such as technical manuals, to retrieve individual documents, to generate tables of contents, to search for information in structures found within a document, or to generate new documents as the result of a query.

Data-oriented documents. Perform queries on the XML representation of database data, object data, or other traditional data sources to extract data from these sources, to transform data into new XML representations, or to integrate data from multiple heterogeneous data sources. The XML representation of data sources may be either physical or virtual; that is, data may be physically encoded in XML, or an XML representation of the data may be produced.

Mixed-model documents. Perform both document-oriented and data-oriented queries on documents with embedded data, such as catalogs, patient health records, employment records, or business analysis documents.

Administrative data. Perform queries on configuration files, user profiles, or administrative logs represented in XML.

Filtering streams. Perform queries on streams of XML data to process the data in a manner analogous to Unix filters. This might be used to process logs of email messages, network packets, stock market data, newswire feeds, EDI, or weather data to filter and route messages represented in XML, to extract data from XML streams, or to transform data in XML streams.

Document object model (DOM). Perform queries on DOM structures to return sets of nodes that meet the specified criteria.

Native XML repositories and Web servers. Perform queries on collections of documents managed by native XML repositories or Web servers.

Catalog search. Perform queries to search catalogs that describe document servers, document types, XML schemas, or documents. Such catalogs may be combined to support search among multiple servers. A document-retrieval system could use queries to allow the user to select server catalogs, represented in XML, by the information provided by the servers, by access cost, or by authorization. Once a server is selected, a retrieval system could query the kinds of documents found on the server and allow the user to query those documents.

Multiple syntactic environments. Queries may be used in many environments. For example, a query might be embedded in a URL, an XML page, or a JSP or ASP page; represented by a string in a program written in a general-purpose programming language; or provided as an argument on the command-line or standard input.

XML versus the Database

XML appears to provide many storage and content benefits. However, I did not mean to suggest that the relational database model is no longer necessary and should be scrapped for total XML-based storage. The reality is that XML deals much better with content than storage. During complex searches on large databases, XML searches for data elements will be considerably slower than through the relational model. Furthermore, relational databases provide better facilities for security and the maintainability of the data itself.

However, databases have their downsides also. Their content cannot easily be shared, and the standardization of their design is questionable; therefore, exchanging data between two different database systems can be very difficult. Furthermore, field value among multiple systems may not map well, and, as a result, there can be significant incompatibilities when passing data among applications. XML addresses this shortfall by providing a neutral data format that supports easy data exchange.

The results of this chapter's discussion on XML is that, like so many other system components, XML is best integrated within a framework, in this case in the traditional relational database. Indeed, XML works best when it is integrated with the relational model, where each component can be used to the fullest extent of its design advantages.

Thus, it is not XML versus the database; it is XML *and* the relational database as a new hybrid storage model.

XML and SVG

SVG or Scalable Vector Graphics is a language for describing two-dimensional graphics in XML. SVG allows for three types of graphic objects: vector graphic shapes (images consisting of straight lines and curves), images, and text. Graphical objects can be grouped, styled, transformed, and composited into previously completed objects, meaning that they can be exported to XML and then imported back as an XML version of the original graphic. Text can be included as part of the XML SVG, which enhances the document's searchability and the accessibility of the SVG graphics within the document. Therefore, SVG enables the creation of resolution- and media-independent graphics in a text-based format that permits integration with XHTML, XSL and XSLT, XLink, DOM and other W3 specifications, including support for CSS, scripting, and animation.

SVG drawings can be dynamic and interactive. The Document Object Model (DOM) for SVG, which includes the full XML DOM, supports vector graphics animation through scripting languages. The power of this model is that it allows for scripting to be used for both XML text and XML SVG drawings within the same document simultaneously. This means that one search will examine both text and graphic images within the domain of the search. Furthermore, SVG files are not proprietary binary data files as are many other graphic formats. Because SVG files use XML, their syntax is readable as text files. This means that developers can easily create scripts that dynamically modify content as well as exchange designs between tools. XML also describes information in terms of a structured data format, thus allowing applications to process the same SVG image differently.

SVG is currently a W3C candidate for recommendation, meaning that it has not yet been authorized as a W3C standard. However, soon SVG is expected to undergo widespread testing and eventual acceptance as a standard. The ability of XML to be extended beyond just text-based documents allows for much greater use within Web applications. In Chapter 6, I described the complex and extensive features of animation and interactivity being used in today's Web applications. The inclusion of XML into graphics establishes much greater capabilities to combine database operations with interactive objects using XML as the standard delivery medium.

SVG Formats

Defining objects, such as text and shapes, in an SVG image is relatively straightforward. While a software developer can code most SVG formats directly, there are a number of third-party products such as Adobe and Illustrator 9.0 that allow designers to generate complex images easily by simply exporting the files as SVG. However, an ecommerce analyst must have a general understanding of how SVG objects are defined, and what the various coordinates and elements refer to in the syntax when considering animation and interactivity in any Web design project. Listed below is some important information about the types of graphics supported by SVG and the most common data type formats.

This information may need to be identified in the DOM and possibly the database system. Most important, it needs to be described in the repository of data, meaning that graphic images and their formats need to be organized in a central place so that they can be reused in the same manner as data and applications.

SVG supports three fundamental types of graphics elements that can be rendered onto the canvas:

1. *Shapes*—representing combinations of straight lines and curves
2. *Text*—representing combinations of characters
3. *Raster images*—representing an array of values that specify the paint color at a series of points on a rectangular grid

The common data types for SVG properties and attributes fall into the following categories:

<integer>   A whole number.

<number>   A real number value.

<length>   A length is a distance measurement.

<coordinate>   Represents a length in the user coordinate system that is the given distance from the origin of the user coordinate system along the relevant axis (the x axis for X coordinates, the y axis for Y coordinates).

<angle>   An angle value is a number optionally followed immediately with an angle unit identifier. Angle unit identifiers are deg, degrees grad, grads rad, and radians.

<color>   The basic color type.

<paint>   Specifications of the type of paint to use when filling or stroking a given graphics element.

<percentage>   The format of a percentage value is a number immediately followed by a "%." Percentage values are always relative to another value, for example, a length.

<uri>   Uniform Resource Identifiers [URI] references. A URI is the address of a resource on the Web.

<frequency>   A frequency value is a number immediately followed by a frequency unit identifier. Frequency unit identifiers are: Hz, Hertz, kHz, and kilo Hertz.

<time>   A time value is a number immediately followed by a time unit identifier. Time unit identifiers are ms for milliseconds and s for seconds.

Summary of SVG Features

SVG has many advantages over other image formats, and particularly over JPEG and GIF, the most common graphic formats used on the Web today. Listed below is a summary of SVG features that the ecommerce analyst should keep in mind when considering the integration of animation and graphics as an XML extension.

Plain text format. SVG files can be accessed by a number of software tools and are usually smaller and more compressible than JPEG or GIF images.

Scalable. Unlike bitmapped GIF and JPEG formats, SVG is a vector format, which means that SVG images can be printed with high quality at any resolution.

Zoomable. Images can be zoomed in on any portion of an SVG image without any visible degradation.

Searchable and selectable text. Unlike bitmapped images, text in SVG text is selectable and searchable. For example, you can search for specific text strings, like city names in a map.

Scripting and animation. Enables dynamic and interactive graphics far more sophisticated than bitmapped or Flash images.

Works with Java technology. SVG complements Java technologies' high-end graphics engine.

Open standard. SVG is an open recommendation developed by a cross-industry consortium. Unlike some other graphics formats, SVG is not proprietary.

True XML. As an XML grammar, SVG offers all the advantages of XML.

CHAPTER

11

Securing an Ecommerce Site

The ecommerce analyst must be involved with the security of the network system. Security responsibility covers a number of areas. The primary involvement is in application security, which includes access security, data security, and functional screen security. *Access security* regulates who is authorized to use an application. *Data security* covers transaction data and stored data across the ecommerce system, and how to validate and secure it. *Functional screen security* involves determining what features and functions are made available to which users *within* an application. In addition, the ecommerce analyst must also participate in network design decisions and decisions about what hardware and operating system conventions should be implemented to help protect the systems from vulnerabilities in browsers, servers, protocols, and firewalls.

Obviously, ecommerce systems need to provide security architectures similar to those of any network system. But ecommerce services are designed somewhat differently from those of regular Internet networks. Specifically, ecommerce systems require verification of who is ordering goods and who is paying for them and these systems have an overall need to maintain confidentiality. Finally, the issue of availability and accountability of ecommerce systems to generate revenues and services to customers and consumers goes well beyond the general information services offered by traditional public Internet systems.

By the end of 2001, the number of users surfing the Internet is expected to exceed 700 million. Figure 11.1 reflects the dramatic growth in Internet usage from its core beginnings in the early 1990s. The result of this increase is that users will be downloading and

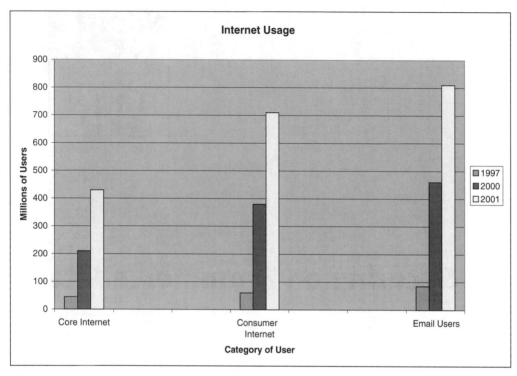

Figure 11.1 Internet Usage 1990–2001.

executing programs from within their own Web browser applications. In many cases, users will not even be aware that they are receiving programs from another Web server.

Since the frequency of downloading software has increased, ecommerce analysts need to ensure that applications operating over the Internet are secure and not vulnerable to problems associated with automatic installation of active content programs. Furthermore, ecommerce analysts need to participate in deciding whether the ecommerce system will provide active content to its users. This means that user systems, especially external ones, may have safeguards against downloading active contents on their respective network system. Thus, ecommerce applications that rely on downloaded animation and other configuration software may not be compatible across all user environments, which could certainly be a problem for consumer-based ecommerce systems.

Examples of Ecommerce Security Needs

This section presents some examples to demonstrate the crucial importance of verification, confidentiality, accountability, and availability in application security. Suppose a company is engaged in the process of selling goods. In this scenario, a consumer will come to the Web site and examine the goods being offered, eventually deciding to purchase a product offering. The consumer will order the product by submitting a credit card number. Below are the security requirements for the applications.

Confidentiality. The application must ensure that the credit card number is kept confidential.

Verification and accountability. The system will need to ensure that the correct goods and process are charged to the consumer. Furthermore, the ecommerce system must validate that the correct goods are shipped within the timeframe requested on the order (if one is provided).

A second example of ecommerce security entails a company providing information on books and periodicals. The information is shared with customers who subscribe to the service.

Confidentiality. In this example there is no credit card, but customer information must be kept confidential because customers need to sign on to the system.

Verification and accountability. The system needs to ensure that the correct information is returned to the customer based on the query for data. The system must also provide authentication and identification of the customer who is attempting to use the system.

Availability

Availability is at the heart of security issues for ecommerce systems. Put simply: If the site is not available, there is no business. Ecommerce systems that are not available begin to affect consumer and customer confidence, which eventually hurts business performance. While a failure in the other components of security mentioned above could certainly affect user confidence, none has greater impact than a Web site that is not working. Indeed, there have been a number of books and studies that suggest that user loyalty does not last long in the cyber community, especially when Web sites are not available (Reid-Smith, 2000). Therefore, availability of the ecommerce system is deemed a component of security responsibility. The first step in ensuring availability is to understand exactly what expectations the user community has for the site's availability. Recall that the user community consists of three types of users: internal users, customers, and consumers.

There are two issues of availability that must be addressed with consumers, generally the user over whom we have the least control and of whom we have the least knowledge.

1. Service: Ecommerce analysts need to know how often consumers expect the service to be available. It is easy to assume "all the time," but this may not be practical for many sites. For example, banks often have certain hours during which online banking is not available because the file systems are being updated. In such a case, it is the users' expectations that should receive the analyst's attention. It matters little what the organization feels is a fair downtime in service; ecommerce analysts must respond to the requirements of the user base. Just having the Web site available is only one part of the system. Ecommerce analysts must be aware that all of the other components will also need to be available to assist in the complete processing of the order.

2. The issue of availability is linked to order fulfillment, at least in the minds of customers. Failure to have product available can quickly erode consumer and client confidence. For example, the industry has already seen the demise of some online companies that failed to fulfill orders at various times, especially at Christmas. Once a company earns a reputation for not fulfilling orders, that reputation can be difficult to change.

The second type of user is the customer. The model for customers or business-to-business (B2B) is somewhat different than consumers. As previously stated, customers are more controlled users than consumers, in that they typically have a preexisting relationship with the business. Because of this relationship, issues of availability might be more stringent, but are also more clearly defined. In this kind of situation, the marketing group or support organization of the ecommerce company is likely to know the customer's requirements rather than having to derive them from marketing trends. An example of special B2B customer needs occurs when a customer needs to order goods at different times throughout the day, as opposed to ordering them at fixed intervals. This type of on-demand ordering is known as "just-in-time," which is a standard inventory model for the manufacturing industry. Should this type of availability be required, it is crucial that the Web site not fail at any time during operation because of the unpredictability of order requests.

The third type are internal users. Internal users are yet another group that depends on the ecommerce system. The importance of this group, because they are internal and in a somewhat controlled environment, can sometimes be overlooked. However, internal users are an important constituency. Remember that internal users are those that process or "fulfill" the orders. Today, more than ever, internal users need remote access to provide the 24-hour operation that most external users demand. The access required by internal users, then, must mirror the access needed by the firm's customers and consumers. Such access is usually provided through corporate Intranets that are accessible via the Web. In this case, protecting against outside interference is critical, especially since Intranet users have access to more sensitive data and programs than typical external users.

In the end, ecommerce systems must satisfy the user's comfort zone—a zone that becomes more demanding as competition over the Internet continues to stiffen. Furthermore, ecommerce systems are governed by the concept of global time, meaning that the system is never out of operation and it must take into account the multiple time zones in which it operates. This concern can be especially important with respect to peak-time processing planning. Peak-time processing is required during the time in which most activity occurs in a business or in a market. So, for example, if most manufacturers process their orders at 4 p.m., ecommerce systems need to be available at 4 P.M. all over the world!

All of these issues demonstrate the significance of ecommerce availability. Given that I define availability as a component of security, it makes sense that the ecommerce analyst needs to integrate its requirements during the engineering process. It is important to recognize the severity and cost of downtime. Maiwald (2001) measures the cost of ecommerce downtime by taking the average number of transactions over a period of time and comparing it against the revenue generated by the average transaction. However, this method may not identify the total cost because there may be customers that do not even get on the Web site as a result of bad publicity from other users. Whatever the exact cost of the ecommerce downtime, most professionals agree that it is a very high-risk problem for the future of the business.

Ecommerce Application Security

If ecommerce systems are to be secure, the analyst must start by establishing a method of creating application security. Because ecommerce systems are built under the auspices of object-oriented development, software applications are often referred to as software components. These software components can reside in a number of different places on the network and provide different services as follows:

- Web client software
- Data transactions
- Web server software

Each of these major components and their associated security responsibilities will be discussed in greater detail in this chapter with the ultimate intent to provide ecommerce analysts with an approach to generating effective security architecture requirements.

Web Client Software Security

Communications security for ecommerce applications covers the security of information that is sent between the user's computer (client) and the ecommerce server. This information might include sensitive data such as credit card data or confidential data that is sent in a file format. Most important, however, is the authentication of what is being sent and the ability of the applications to protect against malicious data that can hurt the system.

The advent of executable content applications that are embedded in Web pages has created many security risks. These executable components allow programs to be dynamically loaded and run on a local workstation or client computer. Executable content, which is sometimes called *active content*, can exist in many forms. ActiveX by Microsoft and Java applets are examples of object component programs that can be downloaded from the Internet and executed from within a Web browser. There are also scripting languages such as JavaScript and VBScript, which are run-time programs that are often sent from other Web sites that allow for certain functionalities to be dynamically added during a Web browser session. Finally, many files that are traditionally considered data, such as images, can also be classified as an executable component because they are used as plug-ins. Plug-ins can easily be integrated with a Web browser to give it more functionality. Figure 11.2 reflects the components of client-side security.

Web applications today also make use of "push" and "pull" technologies. *Push technology* is a way of minimizing user efforts to obtain data and applications by automatically sending it to a client from a server operation. *Pull technology* is somewhat opposite in that it allows users to surf the Web from their client machine and to retrieve the data application that they want to use.

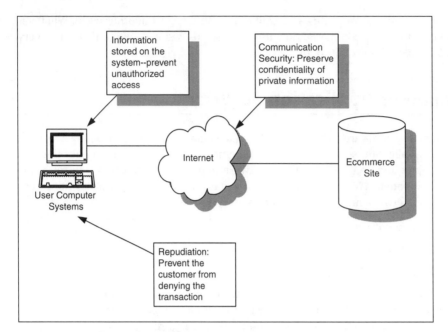

Figure 11.2   Client-side security components.

The fact that the Web is open to interaction with the Internet provides both benefits and problems. The security problems with downloaded software fall into two areas: (1) authenticity of content and (2) virus security risks. Specifically, users of push and pull technology are authorizing these applications to be downloaded and written to a client local computer. Providing this function allows content that may not have been authenticated (in terms of data credibility) and opens the door for violations of security and privacy.

Because Web sessions do not by themselves retain information on prior executions, they need to contain an *agent* that holds information from past interactions. This agent is called a *cookie*. Cookies are stored on the client computer and typically collect Web site usage information. This includes information about whether the user has visited a site before as well as what activities they performed while they were on the site. Unfortunately, cookies pose privacy and security problems for users. First, the collection of personal information might constitute a breach of personal privacy. Second, the residence of a cookie on the local drive can allow files to be read and written to it beyond its intended purpose. This opens the door for virus propagation.

Authentication: A Way to Establish Trust in Software Components

Authentication provides a means of dealing with illegal intrusion or untrustworthy software. When dealing with authentication, the ecommerce analyst must focus on the type of middleware component architecture being used. For example, Microsoft uses a technology called *Authenticode*, which is designed to help thwart malicious code from executing inside a Windows application. This is accomplished by assigning a code that is verified by the sending application and the receiving application. This code is sometimes called a *digital signature* and represents an endorsement of the code for valid use. Thus, authentication is gained by validating the data's validity. Authenticode can provide two methods of checking ActiveX controls:

1. Verification of who signs the code
2. Verification of whether the code has been altered since it was signed

These verifications are necessary because ActiveX controls have the ability to run on a workstation like any other program. Thus a malicious ActiveX control could forge email, monitor Web page usage, and write damaging data or programs to the user's local machine. Authenticode essentially deals with ensuring that both sides of the transaction are in sync. Before a code can be assigned, each participant in the transaction (the downloading of the ActiveX control from the sender to the receiver) must apply for and receive a Software Publisher Certificate (SPC) from a particular Central Authority (CA) such as VeriSign, who issues valid digital signatures. Essentially, the role of the CA is to bridge the trust gap between the end user and the software publisher.

Once the software publisher has created a valid signature, the end user can verify the identity of the publisher and the integrity of the component when it is downloaded. This is accomplished by the browser, which detaches the signature code from the software and performs the necessary checks using Microsoft's Authenticode product. In order to accomplish this, the browser goes through a two-step process. First, it verifies that the SPC has been signed by a valid CA. Second, it uses the public keys provided with the original authentication to verify that the message was signed by the software publisher, thus verifying that it was sent from them. Figure 11.3 shows a sample SPC.

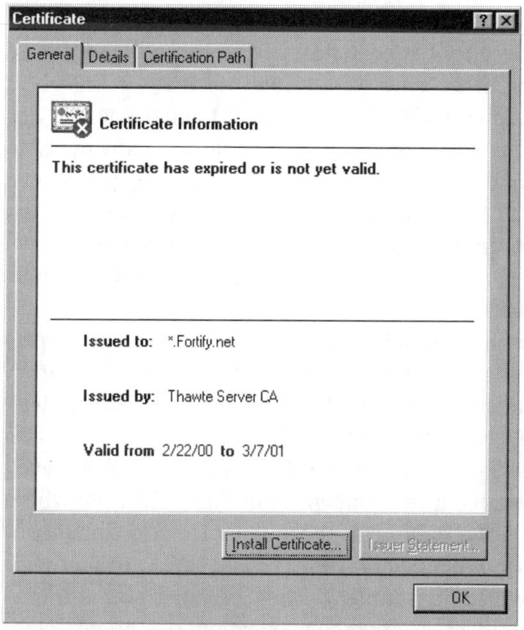

Figure 11.3 Software publisher certificate.

Authenticode also determines whether the active content was altered in any way during transit so that it also offers protection against any tinkering during the transport of the data from sender to receiver.

However, as with most software applications, ecommerce analysts need to be aware of Authenticode's shortcomings. For example, Authenticode does not ensure that simply because an ActiveX control is signed it has not been maliciously tampered with. In other words, the process of security is based on a "trust" model. Therefore, the user who checks signatures may get a false sense of security that the code is secure. Furthermore, since ActiveX controls can communicate across distributed ecommerce systems, they can be manipulated during transit, without an effective method of verifying the changes; the result can be trust in something that indeed is malicious. All of these situations, of course, do occur. One way of ensuring that a component is truly safe is by limiting its ability to compromise the user's privacy or violate any client security settings. So, an ecommerce analyst can limit what an ActiveX component can or cannot do based on settings within the infrastructure. The important message here is that the ecommerce analyst, not just the networking organization, should be very much involved with the decision.

Another default scenario is using the security options available in Windows. If the active content is enabled, a dialog box will be displayed each time an ActiveX control is downloaded. The user will have the ability to choose whether or not to enable or authorize an ActiveX control to be stored. Some developers call this option "making security decisions on the fly." Unfortunately, this is a rather haphazard way of protecting client-side security. Users are a dangerous group to allow this type of decision-making power, and, in many ways, it is an unfair way of making the user responsible instead of the system.

Another important issue that the ecommerce analyst must be aware of is incompatibilities between Microsoft's ActiveX and Java, particularly as they relate to authentication handling. The essential security difference between the two is that ActiveX is based wholly on the trust of the code signer, whereas a Java applet security is based on restricting the actual behavior of the applet itself. This difference further complicates the process of establishing a consistent security policy. For this reason, many analysts prefer to use Java because of its true multiplatform compatibility; it is simply easier to create standard security policies for this reason (remember that ActiveX is supported only on Windows-based systems). Furthermore, from a programmer's perspective, Java offers true object-oriented programming, rather than those that have object extensions to a third-generation procedural language.

The security model used with Java applets is called Java sandbox. The sandbox prevents "untrusted" Java applets from accessing sensitive system resources. It is important to note that the sandbox applies only to Web-based Java programs or Java applets, as opposed to Java applications, which have access to unrestricted program resources. Another way of separating Java versions is to focus only on Java applets for Web development. The Java "sandbox" name came from the concept of defining the area where the Java applet is allowed to "play" but not escape. This means that the functionality of the Java applet can be restricted to certain behaviors such as just reading or just writing information within a specific network environment. The Java sandbox is implemented or enforced by three technologies: the bytecode verifier, the applet class loader, and the security manager (McGraw & Felton, 1996). The three technologies must work together to restrict the privileges of any Java applet. Unfortunately, the design of the sandbox must be complete—any breaks in coding will cause the entire sandbox to malfunction. Therefore, the ecommerce analyst must be careful in the design and testing of the sandbox functions. Ultimately, the selection of Java and the standards created to support its implementation are a prime directive of the ecommerce analyst.

Risks Associated with Push Technology and Active Channels

This section focuses on active content that can be embedded in applications without the awareness of users. Such applications include the use of JavaScript, a run-time version of Java that downloads itself onto a client computer. This section also discusses the challenges of working with plug-ins, viewing graphic files, and executing email attachments. The objective is not only to have secure ecommerce systems protected from outside scrutiny but also to determine what types of active content should be offered to users, both internal and external, as part of the features and functions designed into the Web application and overall architecture of the system. Remember that security issues go both ways: one from the perspective of the ecommerce system and the other from the user's view. Ecommerce analysts must always be aware of what other systems will do to check against the active contents that the ecommerce system may wish to use.

JavaScript

JavaScript is a scripting language that can be distributed over the Web using the client/server paradigm. If JavaScript is embedded in the browser, as it is in Microsoft's Internet Explorer, the user's browser will automatically download and execute the JavaScript unless the user specifically turns the option off. JavaScript is typically used to enhance the appearance of the browser interface and Web page. JavaScript is also used to check data validity, especially data that is submitted through Web browser forms. What makes JavaScript so dangerous is that a hardware firewall cannot help once the file is downloaded for execution. Therefore, once the script is loaded, it can do damage both inside the ecommerce system as well as to the client workstation. Obviously, the safest form of action is to disable JavaScript from executing on the browser, but that stops its use completely. Thus, ecommerce analysts need to know that using JavaScript to deliver applications to their clients may be problematic because the client's machine may not accept it.

Plug-Ins and Graphic Files

Plug-ins are special applications that are integrated into a specific Web browser. The purpose of the plug-in is to allow the browser to support a certain type of program that will be downloaded to the client workstation. Typically, plug-ins are first downloaded and then executed so the application can embed itself into the Web browser. This usually means that once the plug-in is installed, it does not need to be reinstalled each time the browser is executed. An example of a plug-in is RealPlayer, which is a tool that supports streaming video over the Internet (see Figure 11.4). Very often if a user wants to view a streaming video file over the Web, the application will automatically scan the

Figure 11.4   RealPlayer plug-in application.

workstation to determine whether the plug-in software exists. If it does not, the user will be given the option to download it during the session so that a streaming file can be viewed. Regardless of whether the plug-in is preinstalled or dynamically provided, the user opens the door to potential viruses that can be embedded in the code.

One of the better-known plug-in vulnerabilities is a program called Shockwave, which is a program that allows for the downloading of movies played over the Internet. There is a flaw that allows a Shockwave file to get into the Netscape Mailer and thus invade email accounts. There are no known ways of preventing this, other than, of course, fixing it once it occurs. The prevention of downloaded files that could contain malicious programs within a plug-in depends highly on what type of plug-in is being used. The situation with Shockwave involves greater risk because the data is coming through a more open environment where hackers can modify files or create phony ones. On the other hand, Shockwave could be used to show a film about the company and could be well protected from an intruder, depending on how the server is secured (for example, a firewall). As with most security issues, the idea is to make illegal break-in so difficult that it appears to be impossible.

Attachments

There are a number of cases where ecommerce systems allow attachments to be forwarded and received from users. These are often email attachments because they are the easiest and cheapest way to transmit messages and files. Loading email attachments becomes more dangerous to users when there are Web pages attached rather than just a file attachment. The risk then is not with the delivery, but rather with those who send attachments into the ecommerce system. The degree of risk exposure can be correlated to the relationship with the user (this, of course, assumes that the user is intentionally sending a malicious email attachment). If the user is known, for example, an internal user or customer, then the degree of exposure in allowing upload attachments is less than if it is a consumer. While users are allowed to send responses, it is probably not wise to allow them to upload anything beyond that. Furthermore, ecommerce analysts can build in scanning of uploaded software that can detect a virus; however, as we have seen, embedded programs cannot be easily detected. Although dealing with attachments does not seem as serious as the other components that have been examined in this section, analysts attempting to design elaborate email interfaces should be aware of the potential exposure to malicious acts.

This section covered security of the client part of the ecommerce system. The security issues relate to both the author of the system (which entailed protecting the ecommerce system from receiving malicious software from a client and the spreading of problem software to users), and to the more relevant problems associated with ecommerce systems. In summary, the most important issues for the ecommerce analyst to understand are:

- How internal users might obtain malicious software within the network domain

- How users through the ecommerce software might return something inadvertently

- The challenge of what application technologies have to offer to users that might not be accepted through their standard configurations (like turning off JavaScript)

- What dangers there are to providing active content because the system might become infected and thus be a carrier of viruses and other damaging software to its most valued entity—its external users

Securing Data Transactions

This section focuses on security issues related to protecting the data transaction. The data transaction is perhaps the most important component of the ecommerce system. Data transaction protection is implemented using various protocols such as encryption and authentication. Furthermore, there are protocols that operate only on certain types of transactions, such as payments. The issue of securing data transactions is complex, and this section will provide the types of protocols available and how ecommerce analysts can choose the most appropriate data security protocol to fit the needs of the application they are designing.

Much of the data transaction concern in ecommerce systems is focused on the need to secure payment transactions. There are two basic types of data transaction systems used for ecommerce technology: stored account and stored value. Stored account systems are designed in the same way that electronic payment systems handle debit and credit card transactions. Stored account payment systems designed for ecommerce really represent a new way of accessing banks to move funds electronically over the Internet. On the other hand, stored value systems use what is known as bearer certificates, which emulate hard cash transactions. These systems use smart cards for transferring cash between parties. Stored value systems replace cash with an electronic equivalent called *e-cash*. This involves transferring a unit of money between two parties without authorization from a bank. While both systems offer the ability to facilitate ecommerce, the decision about which one to use is often based on the cheapest (cost

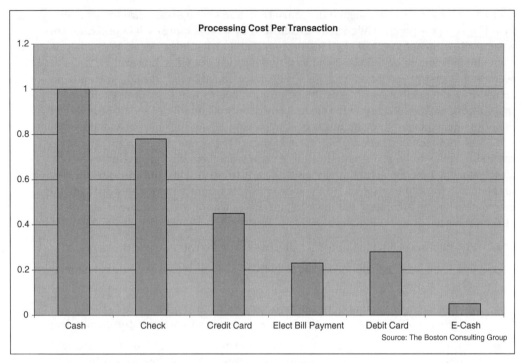

Figure 11.5 Comparison of electronic costs per transaction.

per transaction) method. Figure 11.5 shows a comparison of transaction costs for electronic systems.

However, it is clear that stored value systems are much riskier because an intermediate bank is not involved in securing the transaction. Stored value systems, as a result of this lack of security, are usually used for smaller-valued transactions, such as purchasing candy from a vending machine.

Before designing payment transaction systems, the ecommerce analyst must recognize which protocols can be used to secure Web-based transactions. The most popular protocol is Secure Sockets Layer (SSL). SSL does not actually handle the payment but rather provides confidentiality during the Web session and authentication to both Web servers and clients. Secure HTTP is another less widely used protocol that wraps the transaction in a secure digital envelope. Both protocols use cryptology to provide confidentiality, data integrity, and nonrepudiation (no denial) of the transactions. Because the Internet is inherently an insecure channel, the processing of important data transactions that require protection should be sent via secured channels. A secured channel is one that is not open to others while a message of data is traveling from the originator or source to the destination or what is often called in computer engineering a "sink." Unfortunately, the Internet was not designed to provide this level of security. Data is sent across the Internet using a transferring protocol called TCP/IP. TCP stands for Transport Control Protocol, which runs on top of the Internet Protocol (IP). SSL is used to provide security to a TCP/IP transaction by providing end-to-end encryption of the data that is sent between the client and the server. Encryption is the process of scram-

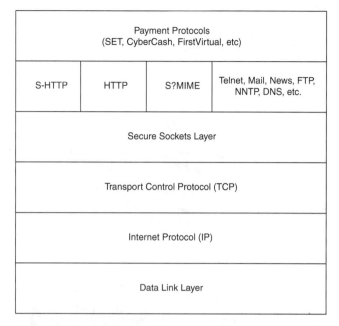

Payment Protocols (SET, CyberCash, FirstVirtual, etc)			
S-HTTP	HTTP	S?MIME	Telnet, Mail, News, FTP, NNTP, DNS, etc.
Secure Sockets Layer			
Transport Control Protocol (TCP)			
Internet Protocol (IP)			
Data Link Layer			

Figure 11.6   Protocol stack for secured Internet connection.

bling the data using a sophisticated algorithm so that the data cannot be interpreted even if it is copied during a transmission. The originator of the message encrypts it, and the receiver decrypts the message using the same algorithm. Thus SSL is added to the protocol stack with TCP/IP to secure messages against theft while the transaction is in transit. The protocol stack with TCP/IP and SSL is shown in Figure 11.6.

Stored Account Payment Systems

The ecommerce analyst needs to be aware that some form of transaction security needs to be implemented as part of ecommerce systems design. Unlike many other system components, security software for data transaction systems is usually provided through third-party software vendors. Currently, there are three major vendors that supply transaction systems: FirstVirtual, CyberCash's Secure Internet Payment System, and Secure Electronic Transaction (SET).

FirstVirtual is based on an exchange of email messages and the honesty of the customer. There is no cryptography used by the firm. Essentially, a consumer must first get an account with FirstVirtual, usually secured by a credit card. The handling of the transaction is thus bartered through FirstVirtual as an outsourced third party doing a service for the ecommerce system. The most attractive feature of using a service like this is its simplicity, and there is no special software that needs to be purchased by the user. FirstVirtual has some built-in software to monitor any abuses of the system.

CyberCash's Secure Internet Payment system does use cryptography to protect the transaction data. CyberCash provides a protocol similar to SSL to secure purchases over the Web. The system contains a back-end credit card architecture that protects

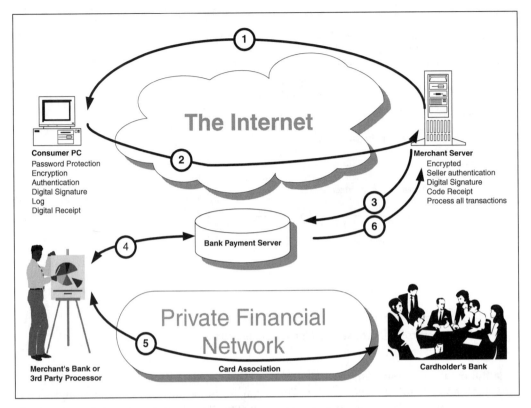

Figure 11.7   Secure Internet payment process.

confidentiality and authenticity of the user, who in many cases is a merchant. Figure 11.7 outlines the six steps in securing an Internet payment.

The steps for this type of transaction security are described below:

1. A consumer selects a product and an invoice is sent from the merchant to the consumer.

2. The consumer accepts the invoice and the browser sends the payment information encrypted with a protection key from the third-party vendor.

3. The merchant processes the transaction and forwards it to the vendor for decryption.

4. The vendor (such as CyberCash) decrypts the payment and verifies the information through authentication procedures. The vendor brokers the payment with the bank.

5. The bank requests authorization from the credit card company.

6. Payment IDs are forwarded to the merchant.

It is important to note that the processing of transactions made between the bank and credit card company uses private secured networks, which also strengthens the protection of the payment. In summary, this method provides an excellent way to

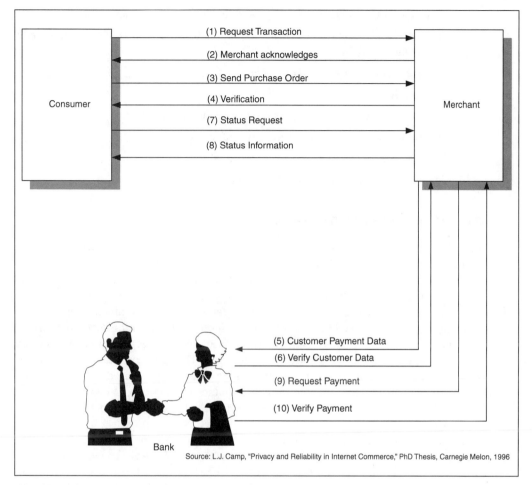

Figure 11.8   SET security process.

Source: L. J. Camp, "Privacy and Reliability in Internet Commerce," Ph.D. Thesis, Carnegie Mellon, 1996.

secure purchases of goods through ecommerce transactions that rely on multiple parties (merchants, banks, and credit cards). It does this by ensuring that all parties get paid and that confidentiality is maintained.

Secure Electronic Transaction, or SET, is an open standard that has received support from many industry credit card associations like VISA and MasterCard. SET was also developed in cooperation with GTE, IBM, Microsoft, Netscape, and VeriSign. SET is not as complex as the CyberCash model; it can be implemented over the Web or via email. SET does not attempt to secure the order information, only the payment information. Payment security is handled using cryptography algorithms. Figure 11.8 specifies the 10 steps in a SET process.

The 10 steps are described below:

1. Consumer sends the request for transaction to merchant.

2. Merchant acknowledges the request.

3. Consumer digitally signs a message and the credit card is encrypted.

4. The merchant sends the purchase amount to be approved along with the credit card number.

5. The transaction is approved or rejected.

6. The merchant confirms the purchase with the consumer.

7. The consumer may send a status request to the merchant.

8. The merchant responds with the status information.

9. The merchant requests payment to the bank.

10. The bank sends confirmation of payment.

Stored Value Payment Systems

Stored value systems replace currency with the digital equivalent and thus have the ability to preserve the privacy of traditional cash-based transactions while taking advantage of the power of electronic systems. The major downside of the stored value model is that it requires identification of the buyer and seller, which in some instances is not what both parties want. By contrast, e-cash systems are stored in an electronic device called a *hardware token*. The token is used to hold a predetermined and authorized amount of money. The related bank account of the consumer is automatically debited and the token is incremented with the same value. This process allows the payment transaction to occur more in a real-time mode than in the stored account model. Although the stored value method supports online transactions, it can also be used offline if the consumer prefers. Offline transactions are more secure because they are less traceable.

The stored value model is not as secure as the stored account system. The main reason is that there is less of an audit trail of the transaction. This is expected since there are fewer checks and balances in the process. Furthermore, the transactions themselves are less secure because a token can be tampered with, thus changing its value in the system. Electronic cash can be represented in a hardware device or in a coin that is encrypted. In a hardware device, the prepaid amount is resident and is decreased every time there is an authorized payment. Hardware tokens are usually valid for a limited time period because they are more difficult to update. Yet another method is called *smart cards*. These are similar to hardware tokens in that they contain a prepaid amount of money on a physical device—in this case a card. Figure 11.9 provides an example of an e-cash transaction using the stored value method.

Summary

Securing data transactions, especially those used for payment systems, is typically handled through third-party vendor software and systems. Ecommerce systems, therefore, will need to interface with them, unless the ecommerce analyst deems that it is more advantageous to design and support an internal proprietary system. Overall, it seems easier to integrate an ecommerce system with a third-party payment security system than to create a proprietary system. If the stored value method is used, then ecommerce

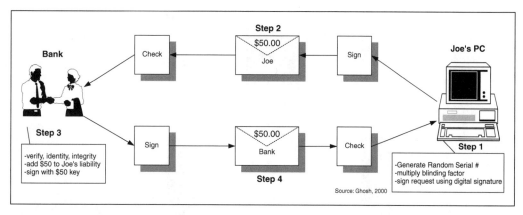

Figure 11.9   Stored value secure transaction process.

analysts must consider how these hardware devices, cards, and software tokens will be issued and updated. These requirements will need to be part of the technical specifications that are provided to the development team. Obviously, securing data transactions may also require that vendors be interviewed to determine which of their products and services best fit the needs of the ecommerce system being built.

Securing the Ecommerce Server

The security issues governing the ecommerce server are multifaceted. The security components include the Web server software, the databases, and the applications that reside on them. It also includes a middle layer that provides communication between the tiered servers.

Web Server

The Web server software can include applications, mail, File Transfer Protocol (FTP), news, and remote login, as well as the operating system itself. Since most ecommerce systems are server centric, meaning that most of the application software is resident on the server and downloaded to the workstation per execution, the security of the server side is integral to the ongoing dependability of the system. As can be expected, the complexity of both the server software and its configurations can be a huge area of vulnerability.

The Web server can be decomposed into three components: front-end server, back-end server, and middleware interface software. In many ways the Web server architecture has its own client/server infrastructure where there are higher-end servers that provide information to lower-end servers. The middle tier acts as a communication buffer between the back-end and front-end servers similar to the structure in a three-tier architecture. Figure 11.10 represents a more decomposed architecture of the three-tier client/server design.

From a security perspective, any one of these components that receive malicious events could result in problems with integrity and confidentiality. The best way to deal

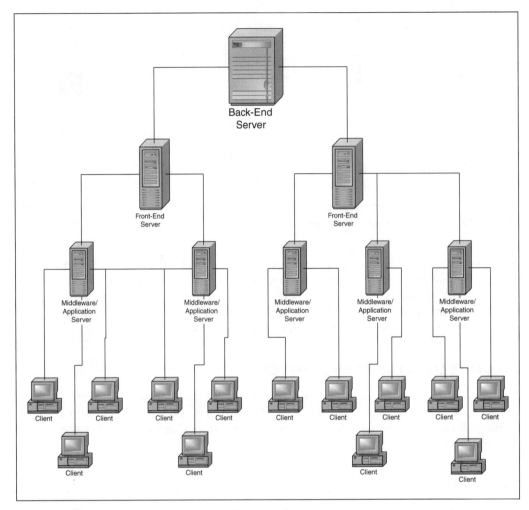

Figure 11.10 Decomposed three-tier client/server architecture.

with security problems is first to understand where the system is most vulnerable. That is, once you know where the exposure is, then an antiexposure solution can be designed. This section examines each decomposed component and establishes the type of security needed to maximize its dependability and confidentiality. The ecommerce analyst must be involved as a driver of the process because of the amount of application and data integrity software that must be integrated into the design of the overall system. Figure 11.11 depicts the decomposed server components.

Database Server

Database security involves protection against unauthorized access to sensitive data. This data could be confidential client data, such as account information and payment history. Database security usually correlates to hardware security because most break-

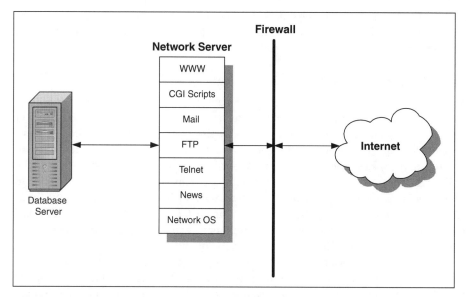

Figure 11.11   Ecommerce server components.

ins occur through hardware server penetration. However, because SQL provides the method of accessing databases from external applications, there must be security against its use. The problem with SQL is that once you can access the data it is difficult to stop the spread of any malicious acts. This means that it is more difficult to limit access once it has been granted. While it is easy to limit access to data through custom applications that require sign-on, it is much more difficult to implement against direct SQL query. It is unattractive to take away the use of direct query altogether, since this is such a powerful tool for analyzing data without the need for senior programmers. Furthermore, databases provide an unauthorized user with the ability to access data without the use of the underlying operating system. Therefore, to secure databases properly, the operating system logs and database logs should be regularly examined. For the ecommerce analyst to determine how to maximize database server security, he or she must know the following information:

- The location of the database server
- How the database server communicates with the Web server
- How the database server is protected from internal users

Location of the Database Server

The physical location of the system can provide some added protection against illegal access of the data. The best location for the database server is in the organization's central network system. Since the database should never be accessed directly by external users, there is no reason that the database server should be connected directly to the Internet. It is important to clarify this point. I am not saying that the database should be accessible from the Internet; rather I am merely saying that external access should be obtainable only through authorized application programs. Thus, direct SQL query should not be allowed. In some instances, because of the level of sensitivity of the data, the server is actually placed in an even more secure location, and protected further with an internal firewall.

Communication with the Ecommerce Server

Inevitably, the database server must communicate with the application server so that transactions can be processed. In most well-secured environments, the database server will initiate the connection, but in reality it cannot always operate in this sequence. Thus, eventually the application server will need to initiate connection to the database server using SQL. In these situations, it will be necessary for the application server to store the User ID and password to gain access to the database. This ID and password will need to be embedded in a program or file on the system, which will need to be determined during the design of the system by the ecommerce analyst. Unfortunately, an unauthorized intruder can discover anything stored in a computer system, especially intruders who are aware of the architecture of the system. A solution of sorts is to limit every password to only one part of the transaction: for example, requiring one password for access and another for retrieval. At least this solution would make it harder to obtain a complete sequence of codes. Furthermore, the distribution of codes could also be kept in separate data files and matched using a special algorithm that would calculate the matched key sequences to complete a database transaction. While this approach sounds convincing, there are some drawbacks. First, the distribution of security levels would create the need for many IDs and passwords in the system. Users may find it difficult to remember multiple IDs and passwords. Second, the distribution of codes will inevitably begin to affect performance. Third, matching files always have the risk that indexed data will become out of sync, causing major reindexing to occur, possibly during a peak production cycle.

Another approach to reducing database exposure is to divide the functionalities between the database server and the application server. This can be accomplished by simply reducing the roles of each component, yet requiring all of them to exist for the successful completion of a database operation. This is shown in Figure 11.12.

Internal User Protection

While many systems focus on preventing illegal access by external users, they fall short of providing similar securities against internal users. The solution to this problem is rather simple, in that the same procedures should be followed for both internal and external users. Sometimes there are databases that are available only to internal employees, such as those that contain human resource benefit information. These databases should be separated from the central network, and separate IDs and passwords should be required. Furthermore, as is practiced by many IT managers, passwords need to be changed periodically. Finally, the organization must have procedures to ensure that new users are signed up properly and that terminated employees are removed from access authorization.

Application Server

The application server provides the entrance for most users to the system. Indeed, the applications provide not only the functionality of the system but also the access to its

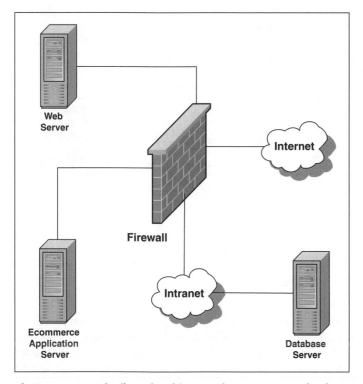

Figure 11.12   Distributed architecture for ecommerce database operations.

data. The first component of application security is user authentication. User authentication is a way to validate users and to determine the extent of functionality that they are authorized to use in the system. Furthermore, sophisticated authentication systems can determine within an application what CRUD activities (*C*reate transactions, *R*ead-only existing data, *U*pdate existing data transactions, and *D*elete transactions) a user is authorized to perform. Further security can actually be attained within an application Web page, in which only certain functions are available, depending on the ID and password entered by the user.

Most companies use the following mechanisms to restrict access to Web applications:

- Client hostname and IP address security
- User and password authentication
- Digital certificates

Client Hostname and IP Address Security

This is one of the most basic forms of Web page security. It is accomplished by having the Web server restrict access to certain or all Web pages based on a specific client hostname or range of IP addresses. This process is usually straightforward because a Web request to a document residing on a host server must include the hostname of the client and its IP address. Thus, the server can use this information to verify that the request

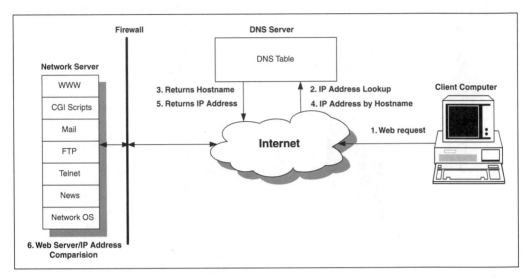

Figure 11.13   Hostname and IP address authentication.

has come from an authorized requesting site. This type of security simply establishes a way of blocking access to a specific or group of Web pages. The Web server can also use the Domain Name Service (DNS) to check to see if the hostname that was sent actually agrees with the IP address sent. Figure 11.13 shows the process of hostname and IP address authentication.

User and Password Authentication

User authentication is essentially a process whereby an application verifies the validity or identification of the requestor. This is accomplished using some user identification and a password—so it is a two-tiered security authentication. To set up an ID and password system, the ecommerce analyst must first design a database to hold the names, ID, and passwords of its valid users. Furthermore, there needs to be additional fields that will store information about the level of the user ID. This means that a coding system must be designed so that the lookup tables can store codes that identify the specific capabilities of the requestor. The ecommerce analyst must also design an application program that allows for the maintenance of all user security databases so that IDs can be added, deleted, or changed. In most database servers, the authentication file is designed using a flat-file architecture. Figure 11.14 provides the architecture flow of user authentication.

It is important to note that ecommerce analysts can provide "nested" authentication tables within an ecommerce system. This means that there are multiple tables, or ones that are multidimensional, that list all of the security levels that the user is able to perform. In Unix, this type of security is implemented with a "user profile" table that holds all of the information in one file. This file is usually formatted as a matrix, or two-dimensional table. Each column refers to a specific enabling (or restricting) access capability. The user authentication design is geared toward providing easier maintenance of the user's security levels. It also assumes that the security settings will be maintained by

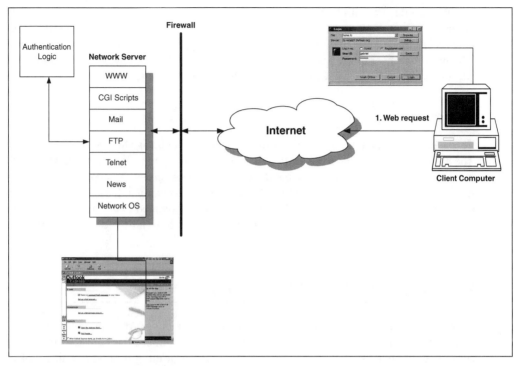

Figure 11.14   User authentication flow.

one unit rather than by many different units. For example, if a password is needed for a specific operation, it is handled by a central security operation as opposed to each department having a separate authentication individual and system. Table 11.1 shows a typical user profile security system.

Digital Certificates

Most of the security measures surrounding applications have been based on access control. Using access control to secure application security has a major flaw: The data holding the ID and password can be seen over the Internet—meaning that during transition, they can be illegally copied. A higher level of security can be attained by using a digital

Table 11.1   User Profile Format

USER ID	SECURITY LEVEL	APPLICATION A	B	C
A143	0	7	4	3
B783	1	6	3	8
R815	3	4	7	6
C777	0	1	4	4

certificate, which requires that both parties are involved with authenticating the transaction. This was discussed earlier in the section on SSL. Essentially, digital certificates contain the necessary ID and password in an encrypted state, so it does not matter whether the transaction is seen or copied during transit. The receiver of the digital certificate has the decrypt software to unravel the coded message.

Summary

This section provided an overview of the methods of securing the ecommerce server. The model is complex because each component has its own security issues, while still needing to operate together to strengthen effectiveness across the ecommerce operation. This section also identified the different types of security software available, and suggested where the ecommerce analyst needed to be involved in the process of determining what third-party products were necessary and how authentication should be implemented.

Ecommerce Network Security

Most of this chapter has focused on the application side of security and how the ecommerce analyst needed to participate and design an ecommerce system that could be reliable, could perform, and could have a high degree of integrity and confidentiality. This part of the chapter discusses the network architecture in terms of its impact on security issues. This section will outline the role the ecommerce analyst and designer should play to ensure that the infrastructure is maximized to support the application design. Indeed, the ecommerce network should not be completed without the participation of software engineers.

The DMZ

The DMZ or the "demilitarized zone" is commonly understood to be a portion of the network that is not completely trusted. The job of ecommerce analysts should be to reduce the number of DMZs that exist in the system. DMZs often appear between network components and firewalls. DMZs are constructed to place certain systems that are accessed by external users away from those that are for internal users. Thus, the strategy is to partition the ecommerce network to focus on security issues inside the DMZ, which is always used for external users. Internal users are behind the firewall in a much more controlled environment. This concept is consistent with the way I described user groups in Chapter 2. Figure 11.15 depicts the layout of the DMZ with the rest of the ecommerce network.

Common network components that should be in the DMZ and receive different security attention are as follows:

Mail. There should be both an internal and external mail server. The external mail server is used to receive inbound mail and to forward outbound mail. Both inbound mail and outbound mail are eventually handled by the internal mail

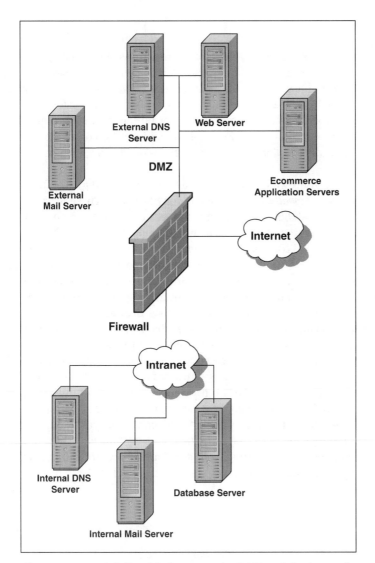

Figure 11.15 Relationship between the DMZ and the internal network.

server, which actually processes the mail. The external mail server then really acts as a testing repository against emails that might damage the central system.

Web. The DMZ has publicly accessible Web sites. Many public Web servers offer places where external users can add content without the fear of hurting the central ecommerce system. These types of servers can allow certain interactive chat room activities to transpire.

Control systems. These include external DNS servers, which must be accessible to queries from external users. Most DNS servers are replicated inside the firewall in the central network.

Firewalls

A *firewall* is a device that restricts access and validates transactions before they physically reach the central components of the ecommerce system. Maiwald (2001) defines a firewall as "a network access control device that is designed to deny all traffic except that which is explicitly allowed" (p. 152). A firewall then is really a buffer system. For example, all database servers should contain a firewall that buffers them from unauthorized access and potential malicious acts. Firewalls should not be confused with routers, which are network devices that simply route traffic as quickly as possible to a predefined destination.

There are two general types of firewalls: application layer firewalls and packet filtering firewalls. *Application layer firewalls* are also called proxy firewalls. These firewalls are software packages that are installed on top of the resident operating system (Windows NT, 2000, Unix) and act to protect the servers from problem transactions. They do so by examining all transactions and comparing them against their internal policy rules. Policy rules are enforced by proxies, which are individual rules governing each protocol rule. One protocol has one proxy. In an application firewall design, all connections must terminate at the firewall, meaning that there are no direct connections to any back-end architecture. Figure 11.16 shows the application layer firewall connections.

Packet filtering firewalls can also be software packages that run on top of operating systems. Unlike application layer firewalls, this type can connect to many interfaces or networks. This means that many packets of data are arriving from different sources. Like the application layer, the packet system also uses proxies to validate the incoming transactions. The major difference between the two firewalls is that packet firewalls do not terminate at the firewall as they do in the application layer design. Instead, transaction packets travel directly to the destination system. As the packet arrives at the firewall, it is examined and either rejected or passed through. It is something like a customs line, where those entering the country go through a line and are either stopped or sent through into the country of arrival. Figure 11.17 reflects the packet filter firewall method.

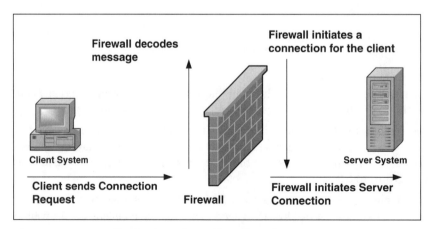

Figure 11.16 Application layer firewall configuration.

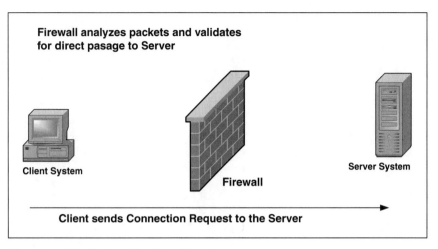

Figure 11.17   Packet filter firewall system.

Summary

While network hardware security is somewhat outside the responsibilities of the ecommerce analyst, the knowledge of how the DMZ and firewall systems operate provides important information that the ecommerce analyst must be aware of. Knowing what is inside and outside the firewall is crucial for both network designers and software architects. Indeed, knowing where to place the software and how best to secure it in a complex network environment are integrated decisions that require input from both parties.

CHAPTER

12

Database Query, Report, and Transaction Processing

This chapter focuses on how to extract information from the ecommerce system. This information will be used for decision support purposes (DSS) and typically be presented to the user in an online display format or in a report. The concept behind DSS is that it deals with data "after the fact," meaning that the data is no longer in a production mode, but rather in a storage mode where it can be used for different forms of analytical processing. The major benefit of operating on processed data is that it cannot be changed and therefore can be accessed without concern for data integrity. Another salient issue is that because the data is not subject to change, it can be copied multiple times, allowing for some interesting performance improvements and "flattening" of the data stored in the relational database. The referential integrity that was attained in a production database does not maximize performance for the query of data for reporting purposes.

In order to maximize the efficiency of accessing and analyzing data, it is necessary to separate it from the production system. This is accomplished by creating copies of the data solely for decision support analysis. There are a number of different ways to do this separation. One way is *data warehousing*, where data is reformatted from one or more data sources and placed in a special repository for analytical processing. Another approach is to create data marts. While similar to a data warehouse, *data marts* are defined as more strategic in nature and more specifically organized to support the gathering of departmental data. Data warehouses can be composed of many data marts. Still another method is called *data mining*, in which multiple definitions of data from different systems are collected and analyzed for similarities. Data mining provides more artificial intelligence features and can perform advanced analysis against multiple data warehouses and data marts, especially when the data comes from multiple computer systems. All of these alternatives and their relationship to the analysis and design of ecommerce systems will be examined in this chapter. In order to provide effective data warehouses, data marts, and data mining, it is necessary to understand how to obtain the data that is needed to populate these data structures.

A major component of creating effective repositories of data for DSS is how to extract the information through database query. In order to accomplish this effectively, it is important to understand the transaction processing system, since some transactions might need to be captured when they occur as opposed to after they have updated database files. Furthermore, the process of creating reports and screen displays needs to be included as part of the ecommerce analyst's specification. Some reports are pre-coded, while others are generated through user-initiated query applications.

Data Warehousing Concepts

Operational databases are those that are designed to track business events in real time. In operational databases, processing data usually correlates to cost while the completion of the data's process relates to revenue. In Chapter 4, we saw that the data in operational databases are accessed at the detailed level where individual records are created, read, updated, or deleted (CRUD). Entities in the relational model are constantly updated to ensure that the integrity of the data is preserved and that no historical information on the entity's previous status is stored.

Data warehouses, on the other hand, can capture both completed events *and* their original transactions. This gives data warehouse implementations the ability to characterize more about how the data was produced at a much more detailed and granular level than is usually available in operational databases. However, it is also important to remember that data warehouses are static snapshots of historical events. As a result, they are often not in sync with an operational database, which always reflects the current aggregate picture of the data. This has both advantages and disadvantages. From an advantage point of view, a data warehouse can contain multiple copies of the same data. Each set could represent the same data at a different moment in time, or could represent different views of the same data, or any combination of all of these. Figure 12.1 depicts the relationship between a data warehouse and the operational databases in an ecommerce system.

The issue of data synchronization between the operational databases and the data warehouses are significant. The ultimate consideration, when designing a data warehouse system, relates to the age of the data in the warehouse and how often this data needs to be refreshed. For example, if an accounting department needs to produce a report by the 15th of every month on the previous month's activity, then the data refresh would need to occur sometime after the end of the previous month and before the 15th of the new month. On the other hand, if a daily report were needed on the previous day's activities, then an evening refresh would be required. Data refreshment requires that the data from the operational database be copied to the warehouse. Unfortunately, this may not be the end of the data refresh procedure, since the format of the data in the warehouse may be very different from that of the operational system. Thus, there is typically

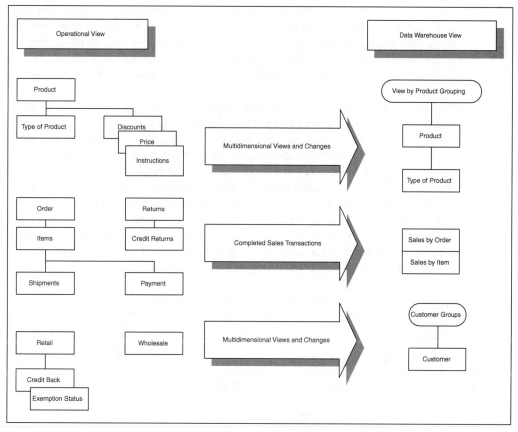

Figure 12.1 Operational and data warehouse databases.

a need for the data to be reformatted so it can be fed into the warehouse structure directly. Because a data warehouse might be an aggregation of the operational data, it can be necessary to perform mathematical computations on the ported data to produce derived data information. You might recall that derived data is a violation of Normalization and not allowed in the operational database. Therefore, data warehouses are denormalized models of the operational systems and will typically contain data elements that were removed through third-normal form implementation.

Performance Benefits of Data Warehouses

The advantages of developing a warehouse are many. First, it allows users to analyze data without interfering with the operational systems. This is a significant benefit because of the inherent problems associated with SQL. When queries are produced against an operational database to produce reports, they often require what are known as *database joins*. These joins create intermediate databases until the final report is produced. Furthermore, the final database of these joins is in the format of the report being requested. This means that a report from an SQL query is really a sub-schema picture of the original database. Issuing complex queries that require multiple joins can easily tie up an operational database, thus creating serious confrontations between production personnel and support organizations. Therefore, the process of performing DSS requires SQL, which in turn hinders the performance of the production system. Figure 12.2 shows an example of the quantity of dynamic tables that can be produced as a result of a simple SQL join statement.

The example in Figure 12.2 shows how an SQL PROJECT statement creates a subset schema of columns of the parent entity. Thus, the sub-schema contains the same number of records, but fewer columns or attributes. The SELECT statement also creates another entity, which reduces the number of rows, but contains the same number of attributes as the parent database. Finally, the join combines the results of the two sub-schemas to produce a third entity, which is in the format of the report requested by the query. This sample shows how much overhead is involved with the production of a simple report. When voluminous data is involved, the time to complete the query is even more significant. Indeed, some queries have been known to run over 24 hours! Therefore, data warehouse solutions should be the preferred method for analyzing data rather than using standard SQL directly against production databases.

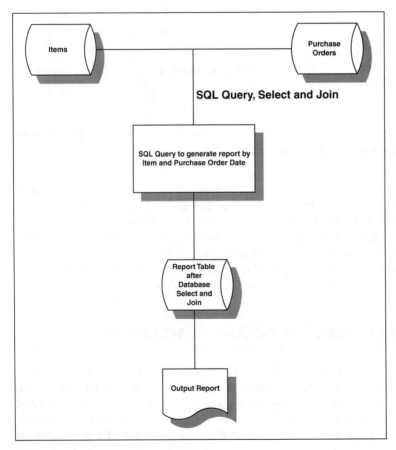

Figure 12.2 Dynamic SQL table joins.

Item	Market	Period	Quatity
Books	New York	Q1	1200
Books	New York	Q4	300
Books	St. Louis	Q2	568
Books	St. Louis	Q3	985
Books	Los Angeles	Q2	3500
DVDs	Los Angeles	Q1	5440
DVDs	Austin	Q4	1500

Figure 12.3 Relational table and multidimensional cubes with three aggregations.

Concept of Multiple Dimensions

Data warehousing has often been referred to as a three-dimensional way of representing data. The three dimensions are seen as a cube of data. Each cell is viewed as a box within an array. This cube represents one data warehouse aggregation (combination) and provides a number of ways to view the data. Figure 12.3 shows a data warehouse aggregation of three viewable dimensions of information. The relational table is two-dimensional; it contains rows and columns, which are synonymous with records and attributes. The corresponding multidimensional cube reflects a three-attribute dimensional view of the data. The two-dimensional part is Orders and Items; the third dimension is Markets. Figure 12.4 reflects another third dimension—the addition of the price attribute to the array. From a reporting perspective, a user could query for Orders and Items, which would use only two of the three dimensions, or ask for Orders by Item within Market. To use all the dimensions available, the user could search on Orders, by Item within Market by Price.

These examples picture the data warehouse from a logical perspective; that is, the cube does not exist physically, just conceptually. From a physical perspective, data warehouses use a standard data structure called the *star schema*. The star schema contains the main table in the center of the star, and each node represents another dimension of the data as shown in Figure 12.5.

The star schema in Figure 12.5 allows for queries to be performed based on an Order. In many ways it resembles an ERD in an operational database. However, most star schemas start with a multidimensioned center (concatenated primary key), so that query time is enormously reduced because there are less joins. Figures 12.6 through 12.8 show how the number of tables is dramatically reduced as the number of primary

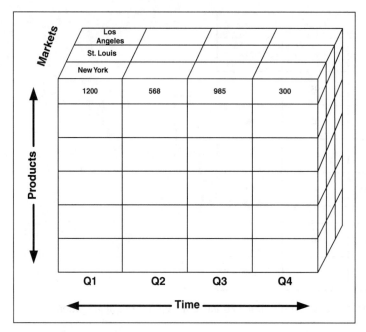

Figure 12.4 Relational table and multidimensional cubes with four aggregations.

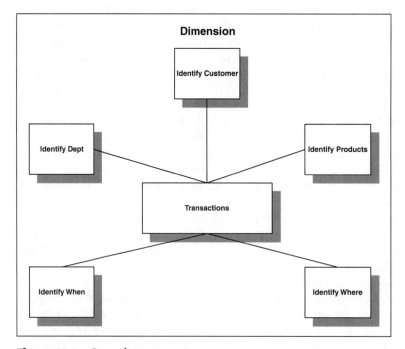

Figure 12.5 Star schema.

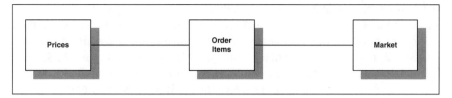

Figure 12.6   Alternative star schema architecture.

Figure 12.7   Alternative star schema architecture.

Figure 12.8   Alternative star schema architecture.

key concatenations in the center table increases. It is important to recognize that more key concatenations in the center table greatly reduce the types of searches that can be performed on the data; that is, the flatter the schema the fewer dimensions are available to view the data. For example, in Figure 12.8, there are no nodes in the star schema because there are no dimensions. Therefore, a user can only query the data warehouse to view Items within Orders, by Market and Price. It is also important to recognize that Figure 12.8 contains no validation or look-up tables, which are normally used to validate the data of certain data elements. Data validation is not required in a warehouse architecture because the data is read-only; that is, records cannot be inserted, updated, or deleted. This is significant because this structure greatly improves data access performance. The removal of validation tables eliminates index pointers and the need for multiple joins of tables, which simply reduces overhead and increases the performance of report queries. Figures 12.6 through 12.8 also depict the number of dynamic searches that are needed to produce one report. It is also feasible to design ecommerce data warehouses that contain all four types of star schemas. This could occur if there were four departments that had three different fixed views of how they wanted the data to be represented to them.

Because there can be multiple copies of data in a data warehouse environment, there is an advantage to creating additional schemas that represent the data as needed for a specific report or analysis, as opposed to designing one elaborate star schema that allows for multiple views of the data. The reason for this position is simple: Why design a data warehouse that resembles an operation database? Another way of looking at this model is to conceptualize that every data warehouse is nothing more than a view of data for a specific user view. The more alternative searches you offer the user, the less attractive the model is from a performance perspective. However, multiple warehouses require multiple conversions from the operational systems. So, the ecommerce analyst must balance the design, taking into consideration both performance and overhead issues.

Data Warehouse Architecture

The first step in creating an ecommerce decision support system is designing the data warehouse structure. This structure, or architecture, provides a framework for identifying how data will be utilized within the ecommerce system. A basic data warehouse architecture is shown in Figure 12.9

The fundamental characteristics of the basic data warehouse architecture are:

- Data is extracted from operational databases, flat-files, and other data sources.

- The data from all of the source systems is first integrated and transformed into another format before being loaded into the actual data warehouse.

- The data warehouse can only be used for read-only activities for DSS.

- Users obtain access to the data warehouse through a front-end application tool, usually supplied by the warehouse vendor.

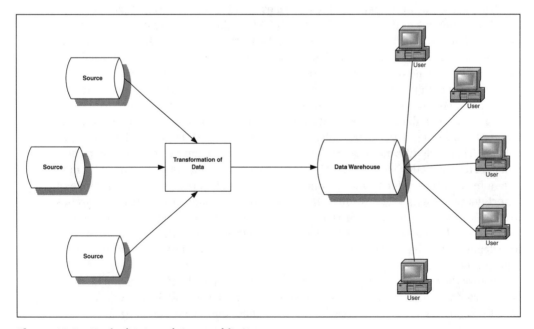

Figure 12.9 Basic data warehouse architecture.

Extracting Data from the Source

The data warehouse process starts with identifying the source of the data needed for the DSS. These will typically come from two places: (1) the operational databases that exist in the new ecommerce system; and (2) the data files that exist in legacy systems. The most difficult part of the process is to identify the meaning of the data elements in each system so they can be transformed properly into the data warehouse. This can only be accomplished by first creating a central repository of the data—typically by using a CASE (Computer-Aided Software Engineering) tool. Porting data into a central repository is easier when working with relational databases because they are better documented and can be reverse-engineered into a CASE tool. However, legacy data is more challenging because of its lack of documentation and its less conventional data formats. Notwithstanding the format of the source data, the process to define the operational data is time-consuming but, for the project to be successful, it is extremely valuable. Many data warehouse products like Sagent, provide their own metadata dictionaries that can be used instead of a CASE tool. These metadata libraries store the relationships that exist among the different, yet related, databases in the production systems. Ecommerce analysts also need to extract data from third-party products that are part of the operational system, for example, a weekly stock price file that is integrated into the production system. In any event, most data warehouse systems can extract data from multiple databases from multiple systems.

Many operational systems can be categorized as "transaction-processing" based. This means that they are heavily geared toward capturing transactions that occur throughout the day. Typically, transaction-processing systems are those that take orders, ship them, and then record financial information. Transaction-processing systems have the following characteristics:

- High transaction rate
- Constantly changing
- No data redundancy to ensure integrity
- Optimized indexes to ensure SQL query efficiency
- Two-phase commit architecture to ensure recoverability

DSSs using data warehouses provide tremendous advantages for transaction-processing systems because they can reformat data into dimensions so that users can better understand the meaning and results of the transactions.

Staging the Extracted Data

As previously stated, a significant component of the data warehouse product is a load server that compiles the data and establishes the links among duplicate data elements. Furthermore, the load server allows for the definition of elements, especially for those attributes that have complex meanings. These attributes are called *intelligent keys* where portions of the attribute have special meanings. This is shown in Figure 12.10 for a Part Number data element.

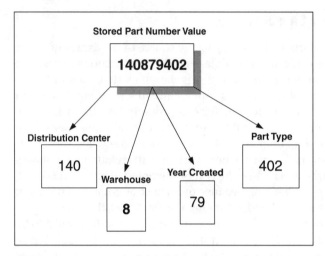

Figure 12.10 Encoded data elements.

The load server has the ability to store information about the Part Number so the warehouse can easily identify the data element's components during a query. Overall, the load server prepares the raw data, and creates a new repository of information in the format required by the data warehouse schema.

Read-Only Activities

As previously stated, the data warehouse is a read-only copy of operational data. The philosophy is that operational data and DSS data are inherently different. Specifically, DSS provides easy-to-understand formats of data so that analytical information can be created to support better tactical and strategic business decisions within the company. These analytical processes require that historical data be kept in different views, unlike the single normalized view required in operational databases. Indeed, one database format alone cannot efficiently provide for both types of functional need. Thus, at the core of all warehouse products is a read-only database that represents the primary component of information analysis.

Front-End Tools

In most data warehouse systems, the data access infrastructure makes up the next most important component of the DSS architecture. This data access is composed of front-end query tools and application programs that provide useful and accessible decision support information from the data warehouse. Thus, ecommerce analysts need to design the warehouse schemas, query logic, and applications to create a useful data warehouse environment that operates under the auspices of the production systems. The important components of application and query support are the third-party applications that are provided with the purchase of the data warehouse. Most warehouse products, like SAS, Sagent, and Oracle all come with sophisticated developer tool kits that allow for the generation of advanced query and application development. These add-on application products do not, however, provide the proper analysis and design process to determine what they need to do.

Types of Data Warehouse Architecture

Thus far we have only looked at what can be called a "generic" data warehouse architecture. However, there are more sophisticated design considerations when formulating an ecommerce enterprise warehouse system. Figure 12.11 depicts a slightly more complex data warehouse that loads data into what is known as business areas. A *business area* represents a defined segment of the organization and is based on perceived business similarities. These similarities could be based on where income is derived, type of clients, etc. Therefore, each business has its own view and use for a warehouse. All of these multiple warehouses are derived from one enterprise warehouse that has been ported from the integration of multiple data sources.

In Figure 12.11, data is extracted from various source systems and integrated and transformed before being loaded into an enterprise data warehouse. This data is then restructured, redesigned, and moved into separate business area warehouses, which are then used for DSS. The major benefits of using a business area architecture are to:

- Ensure that all business areas are deriving data from a central warehouse system.

- Create subwarehouses that can better facilitate the needs of smaller departments.

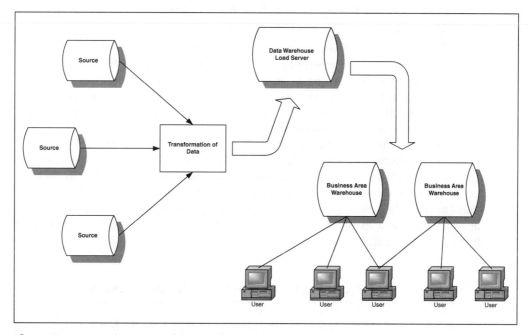

Figure 12.11 Business area data warehouses.

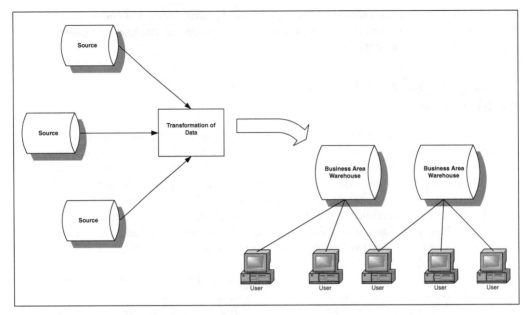

Figure 12.12   Direct business area data warehouse.

- Provide access to different user communities. Internal users, consumers, and customers all have different business area needs and access authorization criteria.

- Ensure that the timing of the data is consistent across all warehouses. In this way comparisons of data across the enterprise are consistent.

Another hybrid version of the business area model is to create separate area warehouses directly from the load server as shown in Figure 12.12. While this architecture does not contain a central enterprise data warehouse, it has all of the constructs that represent a true data warehouse. Obviously, the advantage is the time and space saving of creating an intermediate enterprise data warehouse. This model is advantageous when there is little need for a centralized warehouse and when there are multiple updates of the warehouse from multiple source files.

Still another intricate architecture is shown in Figure 12.13. This model creates an integrated relational database in third-normal form. The data that comes from source operational systems remains read-only; however, new data can be added to the integrated database directly from users. The purpose of these updates is to provide additional data that facilitates expanded decision support activities. Sometimes this process also helps to "clean up" bad data. Once the new data has been entered, it is transformed into a data warehouse.

The Ecommerce Decision Support Life Cycle

The System Development Life Cycle (SDLC) for ecommerce DSS focuses on data, as opposed to processing and functionality. As a result of the elimination of many process-

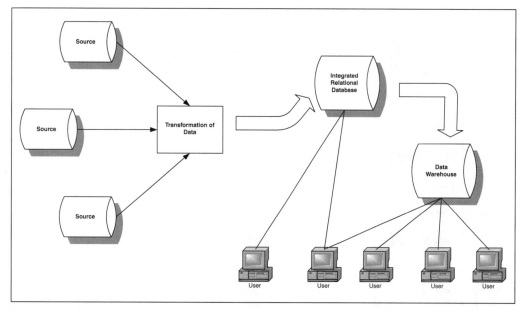

Figure 12.13 Integrated relational data warehouse.

oriented steps, the DSS life cycle is much faster and less complex than its traditional counterpart. The main activity for the ecommerce analysts is to take data from various sources and platforms and provide multiple strategic views of the data in another infrastructure.

The 10 phases of the ecommerce DSS are as follows:

1. Planning
2. Gathering data requirements and modeling
3. Physical database design and development
4. Data mapping and transformation
5. Data extraction and load
6. Automating the data management process
7. Application development and reporting
8. Data validation and testing
9. Training
10. Rollout

Phase 1: Planning

The planning phase in ecommerce DSS is very similar to the project life cycle and entails the creation of a project plan and realistic time estimates. Planning, like that for any project, includes defining the project scope, plan, resources, tasks, timeliness, and deliverables. Figure 12.14 depicts the project planning components.

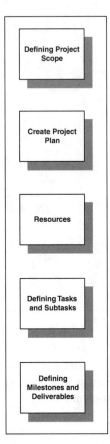

Figure 12.14   DSS project planning components.

Furthermore, the DSS will require changes to the network infrastructure. Therefore, there will be technical infrastructure design that needs to be implemented while formulating the proper DSS environment. The technical components include capacity planning, archival strategies, data refresh and/or update strategies, and operations and job scheduling.

Phase 2: Gathering Data Requirements and Modeling

During this phase the ecommerce analyst must understand the business needs and data requirements of the users of the system. Because ecommerce systems are comprised of internal users, customers, and consumers, the data modeling requirements for data warehouses will vary depending on the different user views. Essentially, data requirements will involve the process of identifying what elements are needed for DSS by each group of users. The assumption should be that normalized databases exist, legacy links have been made, and intermediate transaction processing systems are in place. If a central repository of all data elements is in a CASE product, then identifying the components of the warehouse will be much easier and productive. Unlike regular data gathering, ecommerce analysts should be looking at what users need to see in the form of screen displays and printed reports. Thus, it is the output that identifies what is needed for the data warehouse. Therefore, the ecommerce analyst does not need to use process models like DFDs to model the data warehouse; rather the specification will consist of query screens for data access, sample reports, and screen display views. The reports and screen displays need to be in prototype form so that users can validate that the information and format are correct. Another interesting aspect of data warehouse design is to determine what users might want to see in addition to what they have already identified. Basically most users will want to see the reports and screen displays that they recognize from their existing system. However, data warehousing allows so much more that the ecommerce analysts need to consider what users might want to see, given the robust power of the data warehouse query software. While this activity might seem counter to my previous position that analysts should never create requirements, I do believe that the ecommerce analyst must at least inform each user constituency, usually through demonstrations, about the power of the data warehouse. Obviously, this process may not be practical for consumers, except where the marketing department is involved with focus groups. Ecommerce analysts must remember to inform users that data warehouses do not contain current data. Although it is possible to design real-time data warehouses, it is rarely done and difficult to implement.

What is most important, however, is not the reports and displays, but the strategy of designing the data warehouse (or data mart) architecture. Reports can usually be modified without great pain, but schema design is more complicated. This process requires that the ecommerce analyst determine which type of warehouse designs to use. Remember that there can be multiple data warehouses produced from multiple sources, so the options for design are many-to-many, as shown in Figure 12.15.

Notwithstanding the relationships between data sources and data warehouses, it is important to focus on the schema design. What is the design of the star schema? There are essentially three approaches. The first approach suggests that the data warehouse contain a star schema that resembles the report or screen display. This design was discussed earlier in this chapter. The advantage of this approach is that data is already placed in the format required so there is little need for data manipulation. As a result, the production of the reports and displays is very efficient. Furthermore, there is little that the user needs to do other than just selecting the option to produce the report. The bad news is that the warehouse is very limited because all it can do is produce the report. The economies of scale for creating the report in a data warehouse form may seem like overkill, unless the process of obtaining the data in one central repository has significant time-saving for the user. Figure 12.16 shows a data warehouse report schema.

The second approach is to create sophisticated star schemas that support a grouping of needs. Each schema would contain a central table that provides a data repository required by a group of users. Each node would provide the supplemental data that might be needed, depending on the user group and the report subject. The benefit of this model is somewhat obvious in that it allows warehouses to serve multiple needs and provides for more DSS analysis of the data. The downsides are also obvious; users need

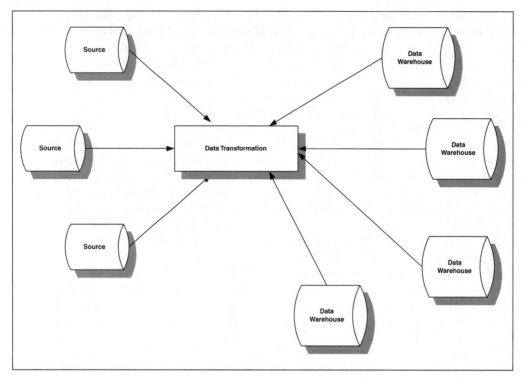

Figure 12.15 Data source and data warehouse relationships.

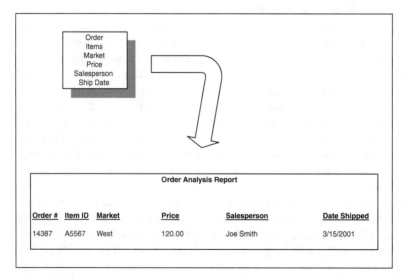

Figure 12.16 Data warehouse report schema.

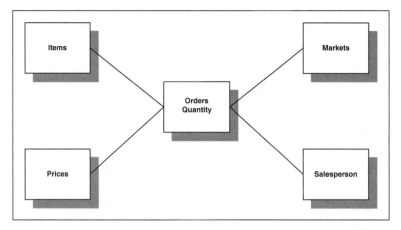

Figure 12.17   User group star schema.

more knowledge on how to query the data and therefore need training and an understanding of what data is available for analysis. In addition, the performance of the reports and displays will vary, depending on the level of sophistication of the queries that are afforded to the end users. Figure 12.17 depicts a star schema for group user query.

The third approach comes back to the earlier example of the enterprise-level data warehouse. Rather than have multiple warehouses serving many users, one central complex star schema can be designed to afford the needs of an entire organization, group, or department. These types of data warehouses will contain the most nodes on the schema, and look very much like a third-normal form database. The advantage is that data is copied once per cycle to one data warehouse, thus ensuring that the data all represents the same time period. The downside is that the warehouse becomes voluminous and requires significant data query manipulation in order to extract the needed information.

Another challenge in the movement of data from operations sources to data warehouses is derived elements. I previously discussed the handling of derived data as being a violation of third-normal form and a database redundancy. As a result, all derived data elements were removed from the production database. However, because data warehouses are read-only, there is no need to eliminate derived data. In fact, warehouses that contain derivations will be much more efficient for query and report production. The question to answer is how to populate derived data back into the database. If a CASE tool was used to produce the normalized operational database, then there is a good chance that derived elements might exist in the data dictionary. You might recall from Chapter 4 that many derived elements are first placed in the data dictionary and defined in a process specification. Thus, the identity of these derived data elements and their calculations can be extracted from the data dictionary. Unfortunately, such is not the case when dealing with legacy databases and flat-file systems. In these situations, the ecommerce analyst must reconcile each report and screen display against the existing data dictionary to determine where derived elements exist. Furthermore, just identifying them is not enough—ecommerce analysts must work with users to understand

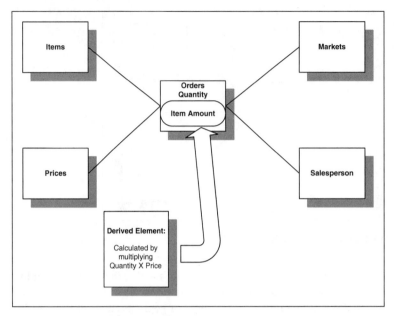

Figure 12.18   Adding derived data elements to the data warehouse.

how they are derived. Once all derived elements have been discovered and defined, they need to be added to the metadata dictionary usually provided with a data warehouse product. The use of *metadata* (data that defines data) will be discussed later in this chapter; however, its use is important when integrating derived data elements in the data warehouse. The metadata repository will allow ecommerce analysts to store the calculation formula. When the data warehouse is produced (or refreshed), a triggering operation will examine the data and calculate the derived values as set forth in the metadata repository. The process of calculating derived data elements is shown in Figure 12.18.

There may also be derived data elements that cannot be directly calculated from the supplied data sources. This means that the derived elements must be calculated outside the data warehouse domain and then imported directly into the data warehouse. This is shown in Figure 12.19.

In summary, the data gathering and modeling phase must address the following key questions:

- What will be the number and design of the data warehouses?
- How will data be reflected in the data warehouse model, particularly the derived data, which does not exist in the production database?
- Is there a CASE tool that will allow for the transformation of derived data elements from a data dictionary to the data warehouse?
- How often does data need to be refreshed?

Figure 12.20 reflects the major steps that ecommerce analysts must complete in this phase.

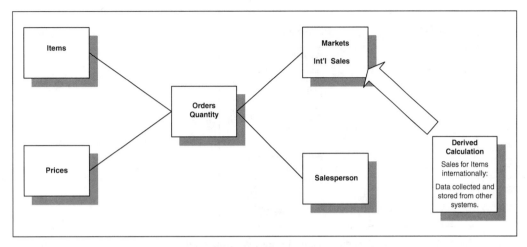

Figure 12.19   Porting derived data elements directly into a data warehouse.

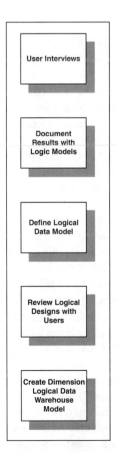

Figure 12.20   DSS gathering data requirements and data modeling components.

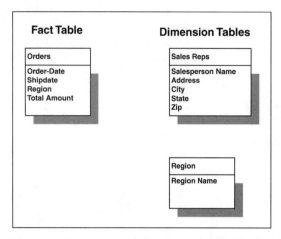

Figure 12.21 Fact and dimensional data warehouse tables.

Phase 3: Physical Database Design and Development

The physical database design entails a number of steps that enable the database to operate efficiently. There are three main components involved in the physical design process: fact tables, dimension tables, and look-up tables.

Fact tables, which are sometimes known as major tables, contain the quantitative or factual data about a business. It is, in effect, the information for which users are doing the query (Poe, 1996). Fact table information is often numerical measurements of data that contain many attributes and sometimes millions of occurrences. For example, a marketing database can contain data on various sales for the company. *Dimension tables*, or minor tables, on the other hand, are smaller than fact tables and hold descriptive data that reflects various dimensions of the facts—like month, year, region, etc. In the previous example, dimensions of sales could be product, markets, etc. Figure 12.21 reflects the marketing data warehouse with dimension tables.

Thus, the combination of fact tables and dimension tables provides for the basis of the initial star schema. This star schema can then allow users to scan the data, and with the appropriate database constraints provide interesting analysis of the information. *Look-up tables* are another type of dimension table. They provide fill-in information used to describe possible values that certain fact data needs. They represent entities that are similar to third-normal form validation tables. An example of a look-up table is the available colors of a particular model of car. Figure 12.22 shows a combined star schema physical database that combines facts, dimensions, and look-up tables.

In many ways, many of the physical database design concepts discussed in this section could be considered part of the logic data modeling phase (Phase 2). While much of this design could be done during Phase 2, there are some related decisions that require more knowledge about the physical environment, that is, the actual data warehouse environment. Furthermore, the process of de-normalization is often accom-

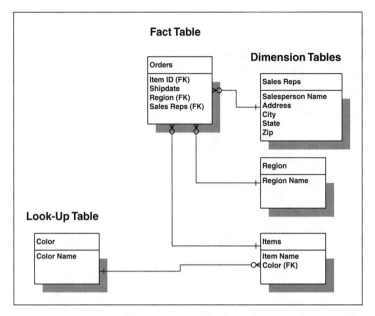

Figure 12.22   Fact, dimensions, and look-up data warehouse tables.

plished during physical, as opposed to logical, database design. Beyond just database design, the ecommerce analyst also needs to:

1. **Identify the actual primary and secondary key structures.** Sometimes this could involve de-normalized data elements.

2. **Develop aggregation strategies.** Aggregation is the process of accumulating fact data from other transactions. This means that a derived data element transaction could be generated that depicts the results of many detailed transactions.

3. **Create indexing strategies.** Indexes are separate tables that are internally created to improve look-up performance. An index is an indirect address that points to where specific information exists in the database, without having to search every record. Figure 12.23 depicts an index look-up table. Any field can be indexed so that query speed to access that information can be dramatically increased.

4. **Develop partition tables.** *Partitioning* is the process of breaking up physical databases into many different storage areas. Logically, these multiple partitions are treated as one database, but physically are distributed on many different areas of a disk, or across multiple physical hard disks. The benefit of partitioning is purely performance. Partitioning of data maximizes performance of the data warehouse when specific users need particular parts of the data. So, in theory, two users can be using the same logical data warehouse, yet be accessing two separate physical partitions of the same database.

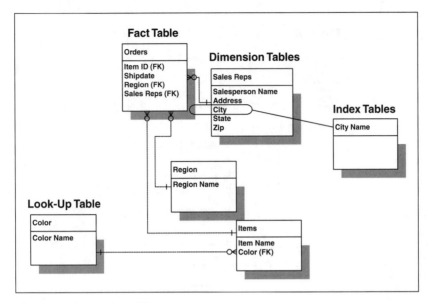

Figure 12.23 Index tables.

5. **Perform capacity planning.** Ecommerce analysts must determine the amount of storage space and processor speed that they will need in order to provide an efficient data warehouse environment. Ecommerce analysts should not do this configuration alone; network architects must be involved to assist in the determination as to what processor types might best handle the load and perceived growth of the data warehouse. The key input needed from the ecommerce analyst is the number of records that will be estimated in each data warehouse. There are two components that are needed to determine space requirements. The first, which was covered in an earlier chapter, calculates the size of each data warehouse record by multiplying the total number of maximum characters in each attribute within a record. By "maximum" I mean the largest size for all VAR-CHAR2 (variable length) data elements. The result of this calculation will establish each record size. The analyst needs to then calculate the database size by multiplying this total record size by the estimated number of records in the data warehouse (see Figure 12.24).

This last step might not be very easy, but sometimes estimating maximum data warehouse sizes (that is, the largest it could be) is the safest calculation. Furthermore, ecommerce analysts must take into consideration the needs for temporary storage that are required during SQL JOINS, PROJECTS, and SELECTS of data from tables. Remember that SQL-based queries generate dynamic database tables for reporting. Thus, ecommerce analysts need to consider doubling or even tripling the storage requirements of the host data warehouse. This is why partitioning can be so effective; it allows network architects to scale storage by attaching more physical hard disks. The issues of how many processors to have, the memory size, and disk access speeds need to be determined by the proper network professionals, but are heavily based on the input supplied by the ecommerce analyst as well.

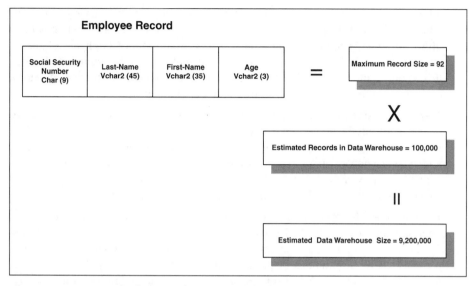

Figure 12.24   Sample data warehouse size calculation.

Phase 4: Data Mapping and Transformation

The data mapping and transformation phase is one where the ecommerce analyst must locate the source of the data in the operational systems, do analysis to understand the types of data migrations and transformations that need to occur, and map the source data to target data warehouses. This phase ultimately determines what the source data will be, how it will be converted, and where the data will be ported. The specific steps within this phase are as follows:

1. **Define the data sources.** Much of this activity can be accelerated if the ecommerce analyst has loaded the data elements of each system into a central CASE tool repository. Other factors are the extent of legacy data that exists in the system, and the nature of how the data is stored. Furthermore, the amount of data redundancy and derived data elements is a factor in the time requirements to ascertain where the data is and how it is defined.

2. **Determine file layouts.** Once data sources have been defined, the ecommerce analyst must clearly understand the file layouts of these systems and how the files interrelate with each other within a particular source repository. For example, a file that contains fact data may be linked to another table in the same system that provides validation information. Thus, the ecommerce analyst needs to understand the schema of each source system. If the source is a relational database, then the best approach is to generate (if unavailable) an entity relational diagram (ERD). The ERD will expose the referential integrity that exists at the database level and expose those relationships that have been implemented at the application level. It might also expose data redundancies. If the system is a flat-file legacy application, then the ecommerce analyst should print out the file description

tables (particularly if the system is written in COBOL). The file description tables will identify all of the data elements in each file. By creating a simple template or utility program, ecommerce analysts can determine where duplicate elements exist among these flat-files. This will allow the analyst to understand how the files link to one another, where there are redundancies, and how to schematically look at the system from a dimensional and relational perspective.

3. **Map source data to target data.** Once the source systems and schematic have been identified, the ecommerce analyst needs to map or identify the source data to the data warehouse star schemas. This can be accomplished by creating a matrix that shows source elements and their attributes as well as their corresponding data warehouse data elements. Figure 12.25 shows a sample matching source-to-target matrix developed using a spreadsheet program.

4. **Develop transformation specifications.** The above matrix is only one component of what is called the *Transformation Specification*. Another name for transformation specifications is conversion document. A *Conversion Document* provides the requirements for a programmer to develop a utility program that prepares, moves, and transforms source data to a data-staging file. The *data-staging file* is an intermediate data store that is created for actual transport to the data warehouse.

5. **Review the update cycle.** This process establishes the refresh cycle required for each data warehouse. Refresh cycles define when a cycle begins, when it ends, and how long it runs. It is also important for the ecommerce analyst to have some idea about how long a refresh cycle might take. This can best be determined by running tests on sample source files and then forecasting the total update time based on the results of the test. The determination of conversion time could be critical since the update cycle needs to complete prior to the user wanting to see the data results. Therefore, if an update cycle runs every 24 hours, then the update cycle needs to complete by the beginning of the next morning. While this might sound like plenty of time, many large-scale update cycles can take substantial time to complete. The time to complete also depends heavily on the amount of data manipulation that occurs during the conversion of data from source to target.

Source Data Element	Attribute	Source Table	Data Warehouse Data Element	Attribute	Target Table
Company	Char(3)	Items	Company-Name	Vchar2(15)	Company
Designator	Char(15)	Items	Vendor-Style	Char(18)	PO-Item
Group-ID	Char(10)	Items	Dept-No	Char(2)	Purchase-Order
Frt-Term	Char(3)	PO	Freight-Terms	Char(1)	PO-Header
Final-Dest	Vchar2(30)	PO	Import-Whse-No	Char(4)	PO-Header
Purchase-Term	Char(4)	Contract	FOB-Terms	Char(1)	PO-Detail
Discharge-Point	Char(30)	Contract			
Arrive-By-Date	Date	Contract	Cancel-Date	Date	PO-Detail
Sup-Approval	Char(30)	Import	Whse-Message	Char(60)	Header-Mess
Coord-Item	Vchar(80)	Merchandise	Item-Message	Char(80)	PO-Detail

Figure 12.25 Source-to-target data element mapping matrix.

6. **Develop strategies for archival.** This step entails the decision of what portions of warehouse data can be archived or deleted from the DSS. Typically this becomes more of an issue when looking at transaction-based information. The decision is to determine when dated transactions, which are used to formulate results of the data, are no longer providing enough value to keep them actively stored in the live data warehouse. The reason for purging a certain transaction is because of the performance degradation that it causes during warehouse queries. Sooner or later, historical transaction data needs to be removed from the active warehouse. Ecommerce analysts have two options. Option one is to generate a summary transaction record that might represent a group of detailed transactions. This means that the summary transaction would provide a view of the meanings of the detailed transactions. Figure 12.25 provides an example of representing detailed transaction in a summary record. If this option is selected then the detailed transactions can be deleted or archived. The creation of summary records may also require that specific program changes be made to query applications so that a summary record can be appropriately identified from a detailed transaction. The second option is to just create a separate file of purged transactions that can be accessed using a different set of query applications. This purged file would typically be resident on a separate processor so that it would not conflict with normal data warehouse activities. Regardless of which option is used, the ecommerce analyst needs to create specifications that identify the conditions for purging data and where the data is to be stored. Both options also require the development of specific query applications that can access purged data when needed.

7. **Review security requirements.** Once the data warehouse is in place, the ecommerce analyst must integrate security requirements into the specification. Unlike many security issues, because data warehouses are read-only, there are no concerns about the creation of illegal or dangerous records. However, data warehouse information is still proprietary and could provide valuable information for those with malicious or illegal intentions. Thus, securing data warehouses from unauthorized use is a key component of data warehouse design. This is especially important because most access to data warehouses in ecommerce systems will occur via the Web, either from an Intranet or an Internet. So who has access to what features in a Web-based data warehouse query becomes very important in the design of the warehouse system. Many of the design issues covered in Chapter 11 are relevant in data warehouse development as well. Therefore, ecommerce analysts should review the security requirements of the data warehouse using the same approach as in any other system.

8. **Review capacity plan.** Once the data mapping and conversion methodologies have been completed, the ecommerce analyst will have a much better perspective on the specific capacity requirements. This step simply suggests that the capacity planning and space determination are an iterative process in which the ecommerce analyst and network architects will fine-tune the capacity needs as each phase in the life cycle is completed.

Phase 5: Populating the Data Warehouse

This phase involves the actual extraction, conversion, and population of the target data warehouses. This is typically accomplished with a combination of conversion and update software supplied with the data warehouse vendor's product, and with the development of specific conversion programs designed by the ecommerce analyst. The steps involved with completing the population of data warehouse data are as follows:

1. **Loading and staging the data.** This step may involve an intermediate program that begins the process of building a repository of data from which the data warehouse software will extract the information. While many data warehouse products will allow for the loading of data directly from an operational database or file system, this is often not recommended. Accessing operational data is usually not a best practice for data architects.

2. **Converting and integrating data.** This step entails the execution of the actual conversion programs and the integration of multiple data sources. The process involves the confirmation that multiple data source migrations have been completed and the execution of one or more conversion programs (that migrate the data as per the specification) has occurred. This step should result in the formation of a warehouse load server that is ready for testing before being moved to the live data warehouse. Figure 12.26 shows the process.

3. **Testing and loading.** The test and load phase is the final step to creating the data warehouse. The test part of this step is to provide various reconciliation results that provide assurance that data has been converted to specifications. For the most part, the testing should be consistent with audit-trail philosophies, including the verification that the number of records read, written, and transferred is correct. If records are rejected for whatever reason, these should also be reported. The load portion of this step involves the actual porting of the data into the warehouse for use by users. There should also be an audit trail report specifying that the process of final load has been successful.

4. **Capacity review.** Once again, the ecommerce analyst should review the capacity needs of the system after the final data warehouses have been created, since the storage at the time of completion will represent the actual storage prior to query operations on the data.

Phase 6: Automating Data Management Procedures

While much of the work has been performed to generate the data warehouse, there is a need to create automated processes that refresh the information periodically. The periods may vary, depending on the type and number of data warehouses that have been designed. Thus, once the first data extraction is completed and data warehouses are created, the ecommerce analyst needs to design automated utilities that migrate new data to a preexisting data warehouse. These utilities must be automatically activated based on time and/or conditions. They must also activate the application operations

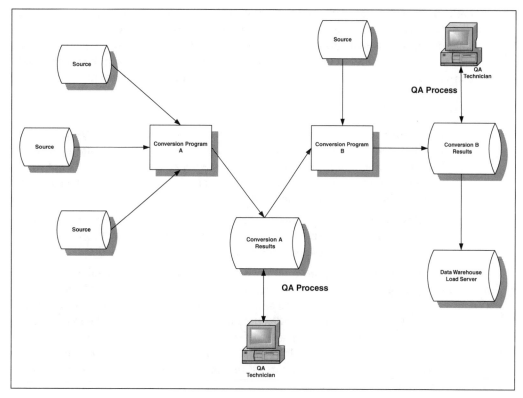

Figure 12.26   Source conversion to data warehouse load server.

that are part of the life cycle of refreshing data, namely Data Mapping, Conversion, Extraction, and Load. When subsequent or ongoing refresh is in place, data will be replaced in the load server and ultimately in the data warehouse. The procedures for verifying that this process has occurred properly also involve the creation of utility applications that report on the outcomes of each automated step, each time the refresh occurs.

There also needs to be an automatic backup and restore process should data become corrupt or damaged because of a hardware failure. There is typically a backup and/or restore feature available in data warehouse products, as well as from third-party vendors. Restoration procedures must be designed and tested in order to ensure that data warehouse information can be restored correctly and within the time constraints set forth by the user communities. Of course, all automated processes need to be tested; therefore, the ecommerce analyst needs to design test case scenarios that will assist in the verification that data can be backed up and restored correctly.

Phase 7: Application Development and Reporting

This phase focuses on the delivery of output from the data warehouse. DSS application development is usually accomplished by using special data access tools to design and prebuild reports. Indeed, the tools selected to generate reports are critical to the success of any data warehouse. Ecommerce analysts need to determine the environment to support data access and information analysis rather than just selecting a front-end software package. There are several steps that are required to understand the complexities of providing a reporting environment for users in an ecommerce environment. The first issue to address is the ways in which users can receive information from the data warehouse. There are four types of reporting as follows:

1. **Parameter-based ad hoc.** This allows users to enter particular information that will act as a parameter into the report application. Parameters often consist of date information, or domain constraints like department or group. Users, while changing parameters, are not creating new reports, but rather modifying existing reports within a predefined range of choices.

2. **Display access.** This involves the display of reports on the Web or some other central place on the system. The important concept here is that reports are generated as needed but assumed to be effective in a view-only mode.

3. **Complete ad hoc.** The user interacts directly with the data warehouse, using the query tools that support the warehouse product. Thus, users will need to be trained on how to issue queries, and how to manipulate the data in the warehouse. While this option provides the most versatility, it is also the most difficult report to use successfully. The problem is whether users can really master the query tool, be knowledgeable on how the data is stored, and can appropriately test their results. Indeed, the largest risk for users is generating reports that are not accurate.

4. **Hard copy.** These are predefined and developed by the ecommerce analyst. They typically have a fixed format and are printed and forwarded to the appropriate requester.

There are also a number of ways that users need to navigate through an ecommerce DSS. This is based on user needs, similar to my earlier definition of user categories. The three primary methods are:

1. **Executive.** Allows executives to get predefined reports quickly and on a regular basis.

2. **Structured decision support.** Contains predefined and ad hoc reports and outputs. Thus, structured decision support provides another level of analysis offered to the user community. This hybrid approach is usually required by middle-tier users such as line managers and supervisors, where there is a clear need to generate what-if analysis in a dynamic day-to-day environment.

3. **Unstructured decision support.** These users have access to all types of reports, but prefer to design ad hoc reports from scratch and use them when they are needed for a particular analysis. These users are more activity-based on the information they need.

The levels and categories of users vary in how they use reports. What reports are needed by users also depends heavily on whether they are internal users, customers, or consumers. Typically, internal users can be trained to use unstructured techniques to

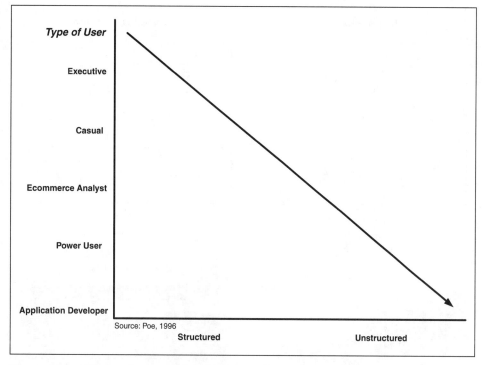

Figure 12.27 Types of users and their report access preferences.

access data warehouse information. Figure 12.27 represents another view of how certain types of users use report options.

Report Access and Analysis

A data warehouse is not an automated method of getting the information you want without working to find it. Users should not be disillusioned about what a data warehouse product will allow them to do. Understanding the commitment that data warehouses require, both from designers and users, is a critical factor for success (Poe, 1996). The following are the sequential steps that users should follow when using DSS and when analyzing their data:

1. Understand and visualize the data warehouse
2. Understand how to formulate a request
3. Understand how the request is processed
4. Learn how to present results
5. Understand how to perform advanced analysis
6. Formulate how to communicate results and findings

The viewing of the reports is another important component of analysis of DSS. Users may want to specify what format they want to view the data. Thus, ecommerce analysts

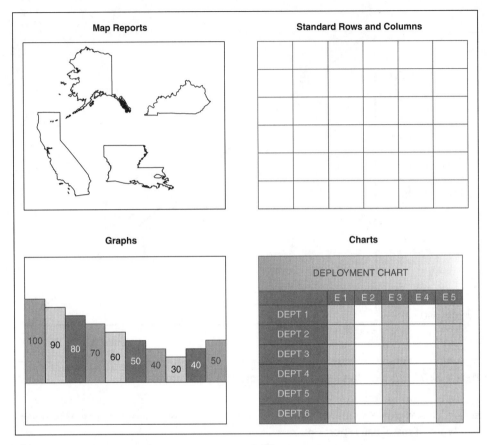

Figure 12.28   Data warehouse report presentations.

need to provide options for users where they can select from a fixed menu of display options. While tabular and cross-tabular reports are most common, graphical output is also a common way of analyzing what reports are telling users about their data. Figure 12.28 shows various types of data warehouse report presentations.

Listed below are the most common report functions that DSS should provide to users:

- Changing the axis, which allows users to swap rows and columns
- Changing sort order
- Adding and deleting subtotals and other information breaks
- Creating color reports with highlighting of certain variables
- Format options for fonts, styles, sizes, and colors
- Graphical display of information to support line graphs, dimensional and stacked bars, pie, scatter, bubble, tape, and area
- Ability to change graph axis labels, colors, and titles

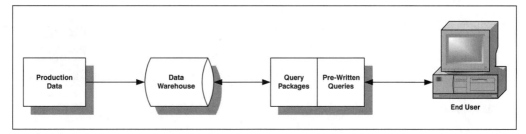

Figure 12.29 Report Writer DSS.

Types of Query Tools

There are a number of types of queries that allow for the production and viewing of the information that has been defined in this book. There are four types of query tools:

Report Writers. These are third-party products that access the data warehouse directly and produce reports based on SQL type queries. Examples of third-party report writers are Crystal Reports and Cognos (see Figure 12.29).

Multidimensional Database Management Systems (MDBMS). These tools create a subset database that can be populated by both operational systems and data warehouses. These databases are usually multidimensional and are often defined as Online Analytical Processing systems (OLAP). They allow for specialized reporting of data in an aggregate form that can support advanced data mining activities (see Figure 12.30).

Advanced DSS Tools. Advanced tools are very similar to report writers except they support more advanced query capabilities and dimensional analysis. They specifically support access to multiple data warehouses from one query.

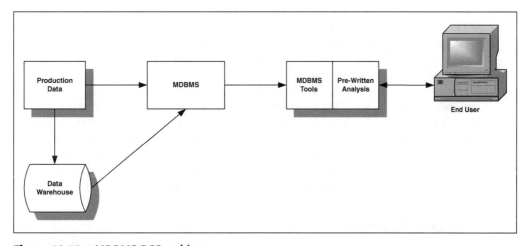

Figure 12.30 MDBMS DSS architecture.

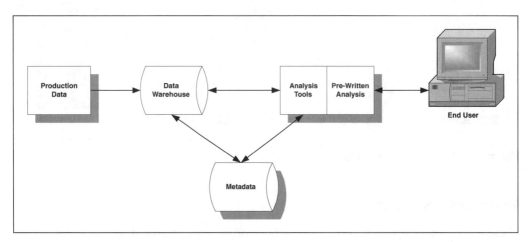

Figure 12.31 EIS DSS architecture.

> **Executive Information Systems (EIS).** EIS represents a higher level of DSS. These systems contain advanced metadata facilities that can create sophisticated and predefined analysis of data. EIS also supports Artificial Intelligence activities, which are fundamental infrastructures to the support of trend analysis and decision-making alternatives (see Figure 12.31).

Phase 8: Data Validation and Testing

Even though I have mentioned that testing must occur throughout the data warehouse implementation, there is a need to have a central test plan strategy. Although each phase has a quality assurance process, the entire data warehouse life cycle requires integrated test scripts. These scripts establish what the expected results should be from each previous life-cycle step. Sometimes this is best accomplished by having reports that provide reconciliation of what the warehouse contains. However, ecommerce analysts should also suggest that users review the output reports. Users should be encouraged to hand check certain reports until they are satisfied that the system is calculating and collecting information based on their requirements. All too often we see users who just accept what the output of a report tells them!

Furthermore, ecommerce analysts should plan for change—because change is inevitable with DSS ecommerce systems. Not only are there changes to reporting modifications but the addition or changing of the data needs to be supplied to the data warehouse and its forms. In addition, new systems are added and need to be integrated into the overall data warehouse schema. With this in mind, ecommerce analysts need to design and maintain sophisticated testing systems that can be reused each time a change is made to the warehouse infrastructure or transformation process.

Phase 9: Training

While this might not be the actual responsibility of the ecommerce analyst, it is important to plan for the training of users with the objective of teaching them how to work

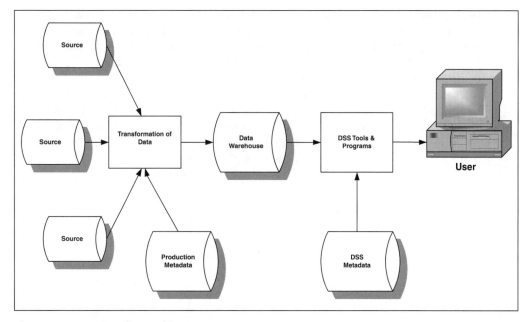

Figure 12.32 Metadata architecture.

with the data warehouse. Notwithstanding that predesigned reports do not require much data warehouse knowledge from the users, most systems will always have "super users" who want to do advanced analysis on the DSS. The training phase of the DSS life cycle includes the following considerations:

- Understanding the scope of information in the data warehouse
- Training on the front-end tools and how to write queries
- Understanding of how to use existing reports and how to modify them
- Train-the-trainer concepts so users can eventually own the responsibility of training new employees or other users

Phase 10: Rollout

This phase essentially involves the process of going live. It requires the actual deployment of the data warehouse into the production network environment, creating user support infrastructures. This deployment includes adding new users, creating the physical procedures for users to request new reports and options, providing the procedures for backup and restore, and creating a team to troubleshoot problems that inevitably occur early in the DSS rollout.

Understanding Metadata

Metadata is data about data. Metadata is the fundamental component that allows data warehouse systems to provide the complex information that users require. There are two primary forms of metadata: operational and DSS. Operational metadata contains the information about where the data is in the production systems and/or in the staged database system prior to conversion. The DSS metadata establishes a catalog of the data in the data warehouse and maps this data to the query applications. Figure 12.32 depicts the metadata architecture.

Therefore, the metadata infrastructure provides the front-end users with the ability to manipulate the data without working directly with the data. That is, the user works directly with the metadata, which, in turn, operates on the data warehouse attributes. Thus, the metadata provides a higher level of abstraction about the data. This abstraction allows for the ease of use of operating with the database.

Best Practices for Site Architecture

This chapter focuses on how to manage the ongoing development and maintenance of ecommerce systems. In particular, this chapter targets the problem of ecommerce systems that have dynamic content changes on a regular basis. Indeed, businesses have become more dynamic and reactive in their thinking because of the Web. Web sites that contain old images are considered slow to react to market needs. Users expect to see up-to-date information immediately. Take the *New York Times* Web site, for example. It generates new content dynamically as stories become available (see Figure 13.1).

The problem facing many organizations is how to provide a development infrastructure that can allow users to change content without the assistance of developers, and how these systems can provide easier development for programmers and database administrators. Furthermore, there are many organizations that need to receive ecommerce content from multiple users at different locations without having to submit them to programmers for retrofitting into the existing Web screens. Indeed, static Web sites are expensive to maintain, difficult to update, and do not support the flexibility that is needed to provide competitive ecommerce on the Internet. With the average business Web site having over 8,000 pages of HTML and graphical components, content management systems provide an attractive new way to build Web sites while reducing costs.

The answer to the problem is to implement what is called *Content Management Systems*. Content management systems provide an infrastructure that allows nontechnical users to control their Web site commerce and communications using standardized browser interfaces, reusable template objects, and a central administrative engine that

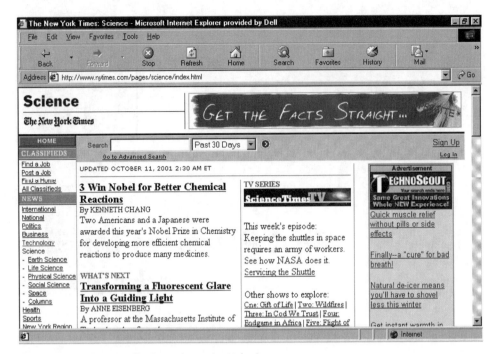

Figure 13.1   *New York Times* dynamic Web site.

allows automated methods to update and secure an existing ecommerce Web system. Content management systems also support site administration, which allows Web administrators to control access, set design standards, edit new materials for submission to the site, and determine the procedures for information delivery.

In today's ecommerce environment, it is better to generate content dynamically than to create and store static pages (Dalgleish, 2000). Dynamic content infrastructures are faster, more efficient, and easier to maintain than static architectures. Most content management systems utilize object-oriented design principles to implement ecommerce sites, which enhance reuse of Web components. Essentially, Web content management systems, which utilize object management, allow organizations to:

- Implement standards and styles through the use of template components
- Combine components from different sources into one or more central template frames
- Have control of content by a central resource
- Have a workflow process that allows for changes to be made to content with approval controls
- Contain a scheduling environment that allows certain content to become available automatically on a certain date and for a specific period of time
- Have multiple types of approval processes that ensure that no content is available on the Web until all requisite approvals have been met
- Contain multiple versions of content for Web site reuse

- Provide detailed audit trails and reporting that gives authors a clear understanding of how long it takes to update content, and who is working on the system

- Implement different levels of privileges, meaning that users have different levels of security access

- Have users (e.g., content writers, editors, content managers, Webmasters, and content approvers) make significant content changes and modifications to the Web site without programmer interface

Dynamic Web Pages

Dynamic Web pages provide the key to creating maintainable, user-driven Web sites for ecommerce systems. The content itself may be reusable (e.g., the company logo) and can be stored in a template or in the database so that it can be reused when needed across many Web pages in the ecommerce system. While the logo itself can be stored as a file in static-based systems, any changes to the logo would require a developer to reload each occurrence of the logo in the ecommerce system. With a dynamic content management product, ecommerce analysts can utilize an infrastructure that automatically loads the new content into every Web page that uses it. Thus, the content management engine resembles the reusable object component strategy. Just as object systems use a central brokering architecture such as Common Object Request Broker Architecture (CORBA) and Microsoft's Component Object Model (COM), the content management system provides the engine for component content for complex Web systems like ecommerce.

Dynamic Web pages in ecommerce systems do not exist until the client browser issues a request for a particular Web URL. Dynamic architecture through the content management infrastructure will build the Web page using stored components, thus always ensuring that the current content is being used (or whatever content has been identified in the content management system). Many content management systems are database-centered, as opposed to folder-centric. *Folder-centric* means that content is stored on a hard disk server and accessed through intelligent Windows folder systems. *Database-centered content*, on the other hand, stores the content in a relational and/or object database like Oracle 8 or Microsoft SQL Server 7. These database products identify and store the content as an image, and present the content to any Web page requesting it (with the appropriate authorization, of course). Many of the content management products are now using XML as a key vehicle to link stored database content with Web pages. You might recall that XML provides a versatile method of storing documents in the database and integrates its functionality with the power of the relational model. Dynamic Web pages in accordance with database-centric support can also provide powerful metadata support. This allows the data that describes an image or content group to be utilized as part of the selection criteria for relevant information. This means that the tagging of what the content represents can be extremely effective for ecommerce systems that provide various search functionalities. Suppose, for example, that a particular ecommerce Web site allowed for the searching of certain animals. The dynamic content management system, using metadata tags, could identify animals that match or closely match the searching criteria.

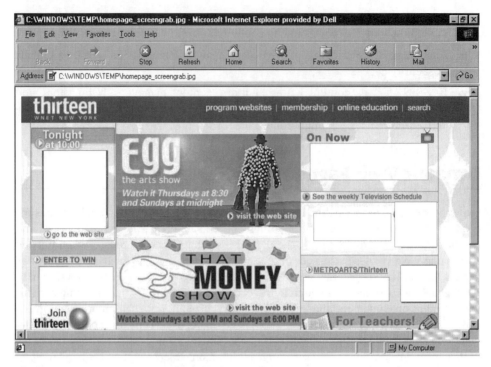

Figure 13.2 Content management Web page frame.

Content Management as a Web Site Builder

More advanced content management systems provide architectural infrastructures that allow Web pages to be generated using a template-based design system. This entails a structured approach to building a Web site for ecommerce. First, starter or "base" templates are created in the content management system so that all Web pages have a similar "look and feel" that is consistent with the firm's branding and identity. These starter templates represent a "frame" for every Web page in the system. Thus, when a new Web page is required, the first component to load is one of the base frame templates. Typically, there are a few different starter templates: one for the main Web page and multiple starter frames for the various subpages. In many ways the process of designing templates is similar to creating a consistent navigation style for the entire ecommerce system. Figure 13.2 shows a standard base frame for a Web page.

After the main frame is generated, developers, rather than generating HTML code from scratch, begin to load various templates that contain specific features and functions. In reality, the Web site builder resembles an object-based approach to building programs. Rather than rewriting code over and over, the site builder architecture allows for a component approach to Web development. While a developer is loading a template, he or she can decide on the specific content to place into the template frame. A template frame's content can be defined as "dynamic," meaning that its content can be changed dynamically. Dynamic changes can be scheduled using the content management system, or changed when deemed necessary. Therefore, every template component on every page can be "addressable," meaning that its content can be changed without directly modifying the Web page. Furthermore, the template can be changed in various ways. For example, a template might appear in multiple locations. The content manager can change just one occurrence or can change all of them. Thus, the content management system contains an infrastructure that can update the content and set rules on who can update it (security). Content management systems also support calendaring, which allows content to be updated automatically based on a specific time schedule. In summary, the content management site builder represents a new development environment that allows ecommerce analysts to specify programming requirements using template architecture. This architecture allows programmers to build Web pages from a reservoir of standard templates. In addition, it allows authorized business personnel to update content without requiring programming assistance. Content management systems are also multitasking environments. While designers are creating HTML screens, users can be updating content. Furthermore, site builder products allow for the creation of multiple versions of a site, so ecommerce systems can actually reuse screens, or contain different screens for a specific user base. Figure 13.3 shows the component Web page templates.

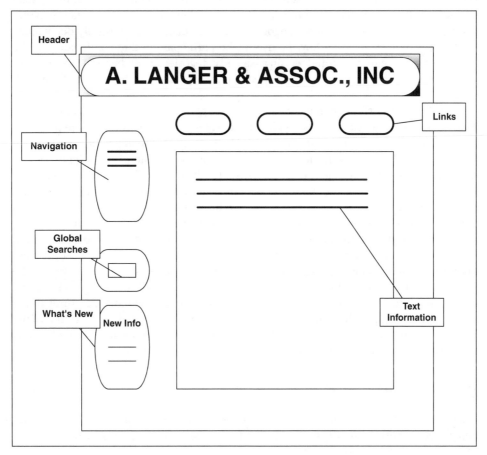

Figure 13.3 Web page component templates.

Thus, a content management infrastructure must support a site layout system that enables ecommerce analysts and designers to create an overall navigation structure for a Web site. Because of the ease of use of the site builder, business users without knowledge of HTML can change content. These systems also uphold the business branding strategy and identity requirements. Furthermore, the site builder architecture provides security so access is controlled for only those that have been authorized to work on the Web site.

What is so unique about implementing content management is that it supports the integration of nontechnical developers, that is, super users who will use the system to modify and update content without the need for a technical interface. This part of content management strategy provides a new concept in how software is developed by allowing nontechnical people to update the site frequently, keeping it fresh and appealing to users.

Creating Objects

Another important component of content management is its ability to search and find relevant content when building Web sites. In other words, a complex indexing system exists that allows for content to be placed in an intelligent repository. This repository can be indexed within assigned categories. These categories are typically determined by the development team and by the users who participate in the maintenance of the Web site. Once content is stored within assigned categories, it can be used to search for particular images, graphics, or text that can be incorporated in the design of any Web site.

Part of the strategy for ecommerce systems is to generate common content for reuse. This is similar to the way object-oriented systems are developed for reusable programming. That is why it is so important to know whether a content management system will be used. Once this has been determined, the design of prebuilt object types can be designed and used by developers to construct the Web sites. Even with this process, modifications or custom programming may be required when using content management software. Indeed, developers still need to provide specific coding to handle complex ecommerce functions. However, content management does offer a structured approach to start the foundation. Content management philosophy can be compared to building homes using a prefabricated model. Prefabricated homes are those that are built off-site in a standard specification. Once built, these homes are delivered to the site, and then completed by the builder. The builder may need to add specialized features that are not included in the standard specification from the manufacturer of the home. In this example, the content template represents the prefabricated portion of the Web site and the developer is the builder who may need to add the specialized features required for that particular version of the prefabricated template.

Content Delivery

Creating content is only one part of the content management infrastructure. Another component is how content is delivered to an ecommerce system. This requires the use of various tools that allow developers to:

- Preselect which content is to be published on the Web site
- Assign publishing schedules to specific content items
- Predefine rules that automate what content gets used for particular users
- Determine when content should be removed and replaced with updated graphics or text
- Determine how content is to be displayed, depending on the type of browser used on the requesting client

For example, a retail operation could display special products on sale for a period of time. The content to be displayed could be scheduled to appear at 9 a.m. and then be replaced or removed two days later. The developer or content manager could establish certain criteria in the content management system that would change the display content, depending on where the user came from in the system (such as the clicks used to get to the content), the user's profile that might be stored, and the type of browser being used.

Workflow and Process Automation

Another important part of best practices for Web site design is the integration of workflow and process automation. Workflow and process automation simply provide a foundation of how content makes its way onto a Web site. Each step in the design and development of Web content needs to be mapped to its related business process. Whether this involves enforcing a production process, setting up authorization steps that are required in the development of content, or creating a method of handling incoming orders, workflow and process automation help an organization to understand how to migrate their current processes to ecommerce in an efficient and consistent manner.

In order to implement a workflow process, the ecommerce analyst needs to interact with business managers to define the different processes and tasks needed for their Web businesses. This could include needs for articles, pictures, videos, etc. Furthermore, business users most likely will have ecommerce needs that could include new product promotions, handling incoming user service requests, and generating special broadcast types of announcements to an entire population or group of users. The ecommerce analysts will provide the framework for what each component needs to do, and Web developers will program it using a content management product like Allaire, SOHOnet, Interwoven, or Vinette to build the necessary templates that allow business users to modify the contents as needed. These templates are commonly referred to as *workflow templates*. Once the process is in place, business users can invoke the content workflow product to prepare new content for their Web site. A workflow process is designed to assign a task to a particular user, group of users, or department. Under the auspices of the security component of the content management system, users can access their workflow templates and submit new content, or change existing content. For example, suppose there is a new article that a company wants to add to the Web site, which could promote its bicycle business. The article has a photograph of the new

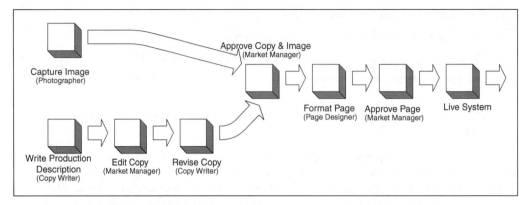

Figure 13.4   Ecommerce workflow process.

model bicycle and an accompanying story about how a particular consumer has used the bicycle. A photographer takes a group of pictures and submits them to the marketing manager who is responsible for approving the Web content story. Simultaneously, a copywriter works on the text of the story. After the copywriter has completed the first draft of the article, it is sent to a marketing manager who edits it and sends the revised copy back to the copywriter. This process is iterative until the text is ready for submission to the marketing manager responsible for approving the copy and image. After the marketing manager has approved both the photograph and the text, it is forwarded to a page designer who is responsible for formatting the photo and text in a sample frame, which replicates how it will appear on the actual site. The frame is approved by the marketing manager and then deployed to the actual Web site. Figure 13.4 depicts this workflow process.

The workflow example in Figure 13.4 shows how new content is submitted, edited, approved, and deployed onto the Web site. An automated workflow component in a content management system provides the infrastructure that allows each individual in the process to sign on, review, approve, and forward the content to the next individual in the life cycle. This is just a typical example; the ecommerce analyst must work with the organization to determine what the appropriate workflow process should be. Furthermore, there may be multiple workflows, depending on the nature of the department or its particular business process.

Ecommerce Order Processing

Advanced content management products support workflow processes that involve online ordering, registration, and other real-time–based transaction systems. Such systems represent the heart of what ecommerce products are designed to do. The workflow cycle for processing ecommerce transactions is similar to the internal development cycle, yet the cycle has some unique steps, which include designing the procedures for registration, submitting requests, and purchasing a product using an online store.

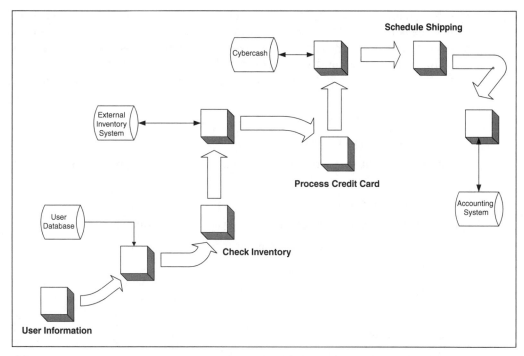

Figure 13.5 Workflow process for an ecommerce order.

Let's use an example of purchasing a product in an online store. A consumer would select a product or group of products for purchase. The first step validates whether the user has an account. If it is a new user, the workflow product will initiate the execution of the new registration module. Once the user has an account, the order is taken, using one-click ordering. The next step in the workflow is to check inventory, process the credit card, and determine the method of shipping. Once all information has been verified, including additional payment information, the consumer receives an email notification confirming the order and the shipping information. Another internal workflow process may be initiated to manage the processing of the order until it is shipped. This process would service the internal users who are responsible for ensuring that the product is shipped. Figure 13.5 shows the workflow process for an ecommerce order.

An ecommerce workflow component should also provide a toolbox for managing error conditions and product exceptions. These utility products allow developers to specialize the code so that the error messages and processing alternatives can be customized to fit the business model of the enterprise. The error handling of the work process software must be sophisticated enough to handle user Web browser crashes, whereby the product would recognize an account the next time it signs onto the system that did not complete its order.

The ecommerce analyst must be the main driver to design the internal and external workflow processes. The content management software is only as good as the process that defines what it needs to do. Furthermore, the workflow processes should be defined before any selections are made on which content management product to use, since the requirements of the workflow will define what the content management product needs to offer. The workflow process is invoked using the same business process reengineering (BPR) strategy discussed in Chapter 2. Essentially this form of BPR is focused on defining the e-service workflows and rules for processing orders and services over the Internet. The main processes that need to be considered are as follows:

- Making service requests
- Ordering a product or service
- Providing input to online requests, such as surveys and product development input
- Registration for service(s)
- Updating personal information that is required by the company
- Request or receive emails and other push content
- Evaluation of products and services
- Provide feedback after completing a transaction
- Getting help online
- Contacting support
- Participating in an online forum or chat room

Each of the above ebusiness activities must be designed in a workflow and mapped to the features and functions offered by a sophisticated content product. Figure 13.6 depicts a typical workflow diagram for processing an order. Workflow diagrams are very similar to process flow diagrams (PDFs).

With respect to the entire order processing activity, common issues that need to be resolved by the ecommerce analyst include:

- What minimum information needs to be provided by a user to order product?
- What are the specific rules that govern how each product can be ordered? This includes what constitutes an acceptable payment method, available service levels, shipping alternatives, etc.
- What format should the user's request be provided in to facilitate processing in the workflow and content management system?
- What product options can be identified as part of the order process and what processes require manual intervention?
- What product selections by customers affect pricing changes in their total order; that is, what are the complexities of purchase discounts?
- Can orders to affiliated parties be automated so that there is no requirement for manual retransmission of the user's order?

The ecommerce analyst must also cover the following general areas not typically covered during process analysis. These central themes are critical for the successful integration of content and workflow products.

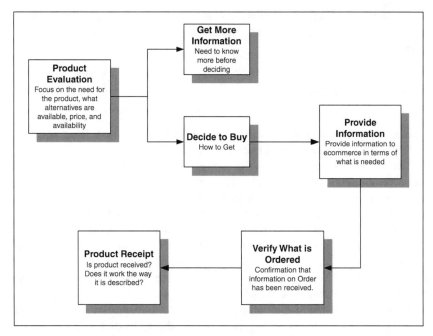

Figure 13.6 Workflow diagram for processing an order.

Product development strategy. Internal users need to define how new product will evolve on the ecommerce system. The concept of using templates to generate new content and applications can be a whole new culture to convey to management. Template generation is only one component of this complex commitment; it also includes service issues, transaction processing, reporting requirements, and methods to evaluate the effectiveness of the ecommerce system on an ongoing basis.

Product promotion. The firm will want to use the ecommerce system to promote itself. Typically, this will require the use of media and other animated content. The marketing department will need to provide a perspective on how they envision promotional content to be integrated into the system. Promotional content is also temporary and needs to be integrated with the content system's calendaring component. There also needs to be advanced features that ensure that the promotions are displayed to the appropriate external users.

Customer and consumer management. Management must determine the extent that they want external users to be able to personalize their ecommerce experience. Personalization, which will be discussed later in this chapter, involves the storage of user profiles and rule-based analysis. It also affects the overall design of the Web site.

Service improvement. The information obtained from the use of the ecommerce system may need to be compared against other service indicators, both inside the company and across the industry. This means that the content system must have the appropriate reporting infrastructure to produce the information required. There also needs to be an understanding of how that information will be compared to other systems. The ecommerce analyst does not want to implement the content system without first knowing what information is required by management on service responses.

Automated Security

Content management and workflow products should contain a sophisticated security system that automates the assignment of security levels based on the construction of the workflow roles and responsibilities. The primary security roles include system administrators, developers, analysts, business users and managers, ecommerce site members, and ecommerce site affiliates. Within each of these categories, security is based on user authentication integrated with the operating system directory (such as Windows NT/2000), and user activities that govern policies, particularly those that can control product access. As previously discussed, the most common security feature for the Internet is user authentication. Notwithstanding whether the security is focused on the Intranet or Internet, authentication is needed to identify users and map those users to their profiles and security policies.

Content management systems also support activity-based security control. This type of security provides business managers with the ability to define the types of activities that can be performed on a template or object. This means that when an object is produced, the developer can define whether it can be changed or deleted and how it can be displayed. Certain activity-based controls allow internal users, like a business manager, to define a set of policies for controlling how a product can be used. For example, a policy might dictate whether another user can access the image without approval from the business manager. In effect, activity-based controls can be used to store confidential information that is available only to authorized users. Furthermore, the mapping of users to activities is a very important capability of any content management product. This feature not only controls the content, but limits access to any Web page that contains that content. Thus, this feature integrates content and application security.

Database integration is yet another important component of security. Content management software should allow outside databases that contain security directories to be integrated with the activity-based control system. Having this level of integration allows companies with other application control systems to reuse them with other systems. This is typically accomplished by mapping the external database fields with the fields in the content management engine.

Personalization

Personalization is the process of keeping user profile information in the ecommerce system. User profiling allows ecommerce sites to store and track simple and complex values associated with a given user or group of users. These values can then be used to generate dynamic content when the user signs onto the system. Figure 13.7 shows the Amazon.com personalization format.

Figure 13.7   Amazon.com dynamic personalization.

Typical user profile systems capture the name, country, email address, and certain user-defined preferences, which can be used to greet the user as shown in Figure 13.7. It can also be used to display content in different languages without requiring the user to select the language they want each time they access the system. More advanced profiling can capture information over time and determine related user preferences and track past activities such as multiple shipping addresses. Content management systems provide precoded objects that can provide this type of functionality. Many of these products, such as Allaire, provide the end user with links to favorite content or parts of a site, thus allowing them to personalize the entire Web site configuration. This software effectively builds a special Web page for that specific user. A more advanced method is called rules-based personalization, where information is created based on a more sophisticated set of stored rules for each individual or type of user. Rules can be dynamically added because the data is stored in a separate file. So, for example, if a new personalization screen was developed for buyers who spend over $500, a rule could be added to the rules file, which then would be enforced by the content system. Any user meeting this profile would automatically trigger the rule and thus see the special offering information during the browser session.

While dynamic personalization offers tremendous capabilities, it also presents challenges. Content can only be as dynamic as the organization that supports it. The ecommerce analyst must convey to management the overhead that is associated with supporting this type of ecommerce system. That is why having the ecommerce analyst simultaneously create the corresponding workflows is so important to the setup of any content management product.

Syndication

Another important component that content systems provide for ecommerce systems is syndication services. *Syndication* is the function of integrating site affiliates with the ecommerce system. This means that business partners who exchange information or are part of product fulfillment can utilize all or parts of the ecommerce system. These affiliates are treated as limited Intranet users. Thus, the syndication architecture allows for site-to-site relationships to help drive the business. In today's complex business relationships, ecommerce partnerships are not unusual and integration of site features is a significant advantage. Most content systems treat site affiliates as just another group of users. However, syndication features provide a mechanism where site affiliates can link to the ecommerce system using remote site automation functions that allow the affiliate to actually use certain features of the ecommerce system. Thus, syndication allows Web systems to share and integrate specific functions as well as their corresponding databases. To attempt to automate such a system from scratch would be a very difficult challenge for developers. That is why content systems can be so attractive for the automation of these types of ecommerce activities.

Remote site automation must support multiple Application Program Interfaces (APIs) in order to provide true portability. This portability is important should other sites have different architectures. Truly open content architecture must support the following platforms and APIs:

- Windows/Java client

- JavaScript browser

- Coldfusion server

- Microsoft ASP server

- XML

Figure 13.8 shows the architecture for a syndication ecommerce system.

Automated Reporting

Content systems typically contain an administrative reporting function that can provide valuable information about who is accessing the ecommerce system, what Web pages users are visiting, how long users spend on the site, etc. These reports allow managers to assess the effectiveness of the ecommerce system. The infrastructure that provides this information is often implemented using a logging architecture that captures all user events, including detailed information about what screens and paths the user takes when on the system. Sophisticated content systems allow managers to specify what information they want to track, what level of reports they need, and how often they need the information. Furthermore, content systems usually have a DSS infrastructure that allows managers to access the log database and query for information that might not be available in one of the standard reports supplied with the package.

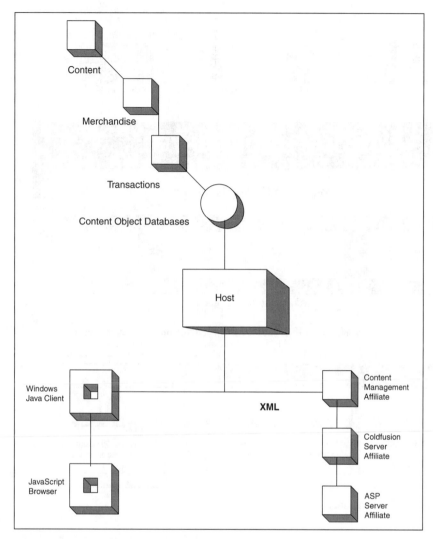

Figure 13.8   Ecommerce syndication architecture.

These query options support SQL-based logic and allow for export to other databases or applications.

Server Engine Technologies

There are two types of server engines that most content systems use: Macromedia's Coldfusion and Microsoft's Active Server Page (ASP). These technologies provide the internal server engines that drive the architecture for these products. The controversy over which engine best serves the needs of ecommerce systems is not clear. One significant difference between the two products, however, is that ASP can only operate on a

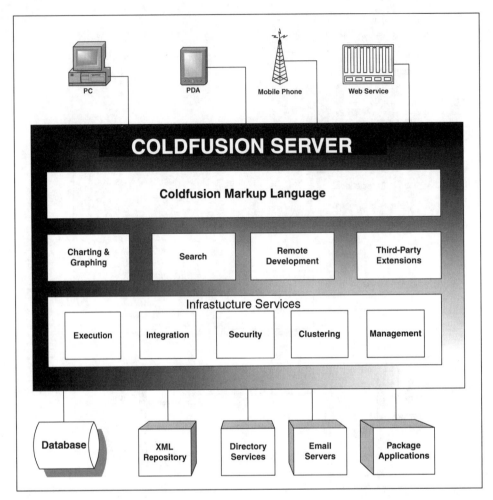

Figure 13.9 Coldfusion server architecture.

Microsoft Windows server platform. This does not suggest that ASP cannot interface with other hardware platforms, but rather just limits the operation of the software on a Windows NT or 2000 server. Essentially these server engines have built-in software that supports much of the functionality that has been discussed thus far in this chapter, including recording of ecommerce Web activities, integration, personalization, database interface, directory services, and email interface. These products also support various client configurations, including mobile phones, Web services, hand-held devices, and, of course, PCs. Figure 13.9 shows the Coldfusion architecture.

The use of content products that either use Coldfusion or ASP does create a certain level of proprietary activity in the architecture of the content system. There are differences in data manipulation, database connectivity, and syntax. Most of these proprietary features are invisible to developers and users. Table 13.1 compares Coldfusion and ASP features.

Table 13.1 Coldfusion and ASP Compared

FEATURE	ASP	COLDFUSION	COMMENTS
Syntax	Script-based, developer-friendly, supports Visual Basic syntax	Tag-based, HTML author-friendly, supports JavaScript style scripting	ASP supports multiple, extensible scripting languages. Coldfusion tag syntax is simpler and easier to use.
Database connectivity	Connectivity through ADO COM object-ODBC (Open Database Connectivity)	Connectivity through tags-ODBC, has native drivers, OLE DB, ADO COM objects	Coldfusion tags are easier to use.
Data manipulation	Direct, through ADO objects	Implicit, through tag usage	ASP's recordset objects instead of tags are more flexible and powerful.
Architecture	ISAPI filter	ISAPI, WSAPI, NSAPI filters, and Apache	Coldfusion runs on more servers.
Extendibility	Server components can be created in any tool that produces COM objects	C++, API, or any COM objects, CORBA support	Coldfusion can use all ASP components.
Application framework	Dynamic, using server-side objects and event programming	Dynamic or static	ASP is event-based; Coldfusion is include-based.
Debugging	Error messages sent to browser upon runtime	Configurable debugging	Coldfusion has better debugging.
Web server support	IIS only	Any CGI-compliant Web server	Coldfusion has an edge.

XML Support

Most content systems have or will offer support for XML by providing conversion utilities that will automatically transfer text and graphics into the XML format. This feature allows content that has been created outside the content system to be easily imported into the content repository by simply converting it first into an XML document. This feature also allows for content objects that reside in the content system to be exported into a relational database so they can be incorporated into the entire back-end repository of data. This further supports the use of a content system as a central repository to transfer text and graphics among databases, legacy systems, and Web sites. It also allows for a better ecommerce system because information can be integrated with legacy information without replacing them.

Email and Push Technologies

Content systems have built-in engines that allow for messaging among users of the ecommerce system. This can be used to market new products and services, and obtain valuable feedback from customers and consumers. The push technology is quite sophisticated in that it allows users to be grouped into various categories. These categories can be nested, meaning that the number of subcategories is somewhat unlimited. Ultimately, this means that the ecommerce analyst must consider this interface when designing the user profile information that is captured to support Web personalization.

Another component of email and push technology is the support of chat rooms. Many content products have built-in chat room software that can allow users to share information. This may or may not be something that a business wants to do, but there are certainly operations that can benefit from users that can share information. The importance of having a chat room that is part of a content system should be obvious. The value of being able to capture certain parts of activity (this does not suggest violating any confidential conversations that might be allowed), and the sharing of this information among users could be a very powerful ecommerce feature.

Content Scheduling

I previously mentioned that most content systems provide the ability for content to be "calendarized," meaning that it can be automatically scheduled for loading and removal from the ecommerce system. While this feature is available, the ecommerce analyst may need to develop a content schedule that assists business users in managing the status of their content. The content schedule is a detailed spreadsheet in which a business can monitor the progress of content development and activity across the system. In essence it represents an inventory of what content exists. The exact format of the content schedule will vary, depending on the type of ecommerce system and the type of content being used. Figure 13.10 depicts a sample content schedule. Note that it contains active content, inactive content, and content in process.

Summary

The purpose of this chapter was to provide best practices for site architecture. The major emphasis was to implement a central content and/or workflow product that

ID	Content Type	Content Owner	Source	Due Date	Status	File Name	Ecommerce Activity	Template
1.1	Text with Links	Marketing	Current Web site	9/15	In process	Xyz.doc	Marketing Sales	Main Page
1.2	Text	Production	Previous Web site		Inactive	WProd	Warehouse	
1.3	Text with Links	Shipping	Ship Request	Completed	Active	Ship.doc	Fulfillment	Orders

Figure 13.10   Sample content schedule.

could help centralize many utility type functions required for all ecommerce systems. As I have emphasized, the architecture is heavily dependent on how content is created, maintained, and stored. The following are some of the problems that ecommerce analysts need to overcome to ensure that content systems are designed properly.

- It is critical that management appreciates the value of spending money and time on investing in a content management facility. Management does not always understand why content management systems are necessary or what they ultimately do for the firm. Good content management products can cost over $200,000.

- Template design needs to occur early in the life cycle. If the ecommerce analyst does not include template design in the interviews it may be too late to effectively implement them later. The message here is not to develop the content management templates without first understanding what the users need.

- Content priority should be based on what the company feels is most critical, not always what customers and consumers want. This means that the ecommerce analyst must be careful when gathering specifications from focus groups. Ultimately, the company must decide what they want to provide in an ecommerce system.

- There needs to be an internal user organization to support the ownership of the content. It is important for users to understand that IT does not own the content responsibility, only the programming of it. Implementing a workflow process means establishing ownership positions for copywriting, editing, and approvals. This may require that some firms invest in skilled Web writers and a dedicated content manager to support the organization.

- Content that needs to emanate from other departments or from third parties needs to be clarified and become part of the workflow process. The ecommerce analyst may need to become the central person to coordinate where there are holes in the flow of content in the organization.

- The design of search criteria on the Web must be accomplished in parallel to the design of content. Attempting to design search criteria after content has been finalized can be difficult if not impossible. This is particularly true with respect to XML documents that need to contain the proper tags so they can be categorized properly, especially when being stored in a relational database (see Chapter 12).

- The development of the ecommerce system and the content management system requires that content be defined first. Therefore, a content system should not be designed until all content analysis is completed. This means that the ecommerce analyst needs to produce another document, which defines the content necessary for each Web page. Furthermore, he or she must be cognizant at all times that content can be treated as objects for reuse. The content management system becomes the equivalent repository for content object administration. The content system can store content either in a folder system or in a relational database.

- It is important that the marketing department or the marketing effort be completed before using any content. Marketing efforts tend to be dynamic and can change up until the last moment. Changing rules on how content is treated could be a setback in the development project.

- The entire issue of content consistency is critical. This particularly addresses inconsistencies in writing and presentation. This issue further supports the need to have a centralized position that manages the writing of text and the presentation of photos and other graphics material. The consistency of Web content becomes more difficult if the company is less centralized.

- The legality of content must be addressed. This means that certain content needs to be reviewed and approved by a legal source. This approval should be clearly defined in the content life cycle and discussed with management so that the return of content occurs on a timely basis. Another productive approach is to get as much input from legal counsel as possible. I have found that many legal issues can be worked out with users ahead of time so that most of the content sent to legal has a high rate of approval. Issuing legal guidelines can be very effective.

- It is important that the content for use by customers and consumers is user-friendly to them, not just to the writers. Content writers and designers are not usually in touch with customers and consumers. Therefore, they do not understand how customers and consumers think or how they make choices. Content effectiveness can be dramatically improved if writers participated in some of the JAD sessions and focus groups.

- The turnaround of content changes is slow and not in accordance with the Web site schedules. Content writers are usually divorced from the rest of the organization, particularly the IT staff. Content writer schedules must be planned and managed as part of the Web schedule.

- There needs to be a sophisticated system that assigns numbers or values to content. Content managers should not rely on the content management software to identify what the content means to the business. Failure to do this will result in a system where all content can be found, but few content managers know what it represents. This is particularly important when tracking multiple versions of the same content.

- Web content needs to be reviewed after it is populated on the Web site and before it is published. This means that the ecommerce analyst should have a system that allows content to be viewed on a staged system prior to being rolled in a live environment. This can get complicated when using an automated update scheduling system, since the updates go directly to the production system. There are two solutions to this dilemma. First, the updates could be initially rolled to a staged system, reviewed, and then moved to the production server. While this adds another step, it is a safe way to go. It also requires that there is always someone available to approve the content. Second, the updates can be done directly to the production system, but must be reviewed immediately. This requires that updates are made in the morning or at night, and that there are support personnel available at those times.

- Prototypes must be shown to users with their content included. To demonstrate a prototype without content has no real value.

- There is a need for audit trail of how customer and consumer requests get resolved and recorded in the ecommerce system. I have seen too many designs that do not make it through the process of user resolution and the result is unhappy external users who have unresolved issues.

- All departmental interfaces must be clarified as they relate to fulfilling a user request. If this is not done, orders that require manual intervention will get lost.

- The process of Web branding and identity must be simplified. Web sites typically cannot get finalized unless the image of the business is clear and simple.

- There needs to be constant communication between marketing activities and Web design activities. Too often market personnel are working on campaigns that have not been discussed with ecommerce support staff. New marketing content tends to get thrown at Webmasters without enough prior notice and planning.

- Product rules must be clear, especially in terms of how they are purchased, their price, and shipping criteria.

CHAPTER

14

Project Management for Ecommerce Systems

This chapter provides guidance on the alternative Web development life-cycle methodologies and best practices for project management of ecommerce systems. Project organization, including roles and responsibilities, are covered. There are many aspects of ecommerce management that are generic; however, there are certainly unique aspects when managing ecommerce systems. Thus, this chapter provides an understanding of where these unique challenges occur in the life cycle of ecommerce projects. It also focuses on the ongoing support issues that must be addressed to attain best practices.

A project manager who comes from a traditional software development background and understands the phases of software development will probably do fine in overseeing the progress of ecommerce projects. Indeed, traditional project managers will focus on budget, the schedule, the resources, and the project plan. Unfortunately, ecommerce systems, because of their widespread involvement with many parts of the business, need to go beyond just watching and managing the software development process. That is, the project management of ecommerce systems requires much more integration with the internal and external user communities. It must combine traditional development with artistic creation, and, because of content management, it also delves into the internal organization's structure and requires the participation of everyone in every phase of the development and implementation cycle. Listed below are some of the unique components of ecommerce development projects.

Project managers as complex managers. Ecommerce projects require multiple interfaces that are outside the traditional user community. They can include interfacing with writers, editors, marketing personnel, customers, and consumers—all who might be stakeholders in the success of the system.

Shorter and dynamic development schedules. Because of the dynamic nature of ecommerce systems, the development is less linear. Because there is less experience and more stakeholders, there is a tendency to underestimate the time and cost to complete.

New untested technologies. There is so much new technology offered to Web developers that there is a practice of using new versions of development software that has not matured. The method of obtaining new software is easily distributed over the Web, so it is relatively easy to try new versions as soon as they become available.

Degree of scope changes. Ecommerce systems, because of their dynamic nature, tend to be much more prone to scope creep. Project managers need to work closely with internal users, customers, and consumers to advise them of the impact of changes on the schedule and the cost of the project. Unfortunately, scope changes that are influenced by changes in market trends may be unavoidable. Thus, part of a good strategy is to manage scope changes rather than attempt to avoid them—which might be unrealistic.

Costing ecommerce systems are difficult. The software industry has always had difficulties in knowing how to cost a project. Ecommerce systems are even more difficult because of the number of variables, unknowns, and use of new technologies and procedures.

Lack of standards. The software industry continues to be a profession that does not have a governing body. Thus it is impossible to have real enforced standards that other professions enjoy. While there are suggestions and best practices, many of them are unproven and are not kept current with new developments. Because of the lack of successful ecommerce projects, there are few success stories to create new and better best practices.

Fewer specialized roles and responsibilities. The software development team tends to have staff members that have varying responsibilities. Unlike traditional software projects, separation of roles and responsibilities is more difficult when operating in a Web environment. Defining the exact role of a Web developer can be very tricky; for example, are Web developers programmers, database developers, or content designers? The reality is that all of these roles can be part of a developer's responsibility.

Who bears the cost? There is general uncertainty as to who should bear the cost of the ecommerce system. This refers to the internal organization of stakeholders who need to agree on the funding. This becomes even more complex when there are delays and cost overruns, because the constituents cannot easily agree on who is at fault and therefore who should bear the burden of the additional costs.

Project management responsibilities are very broad. Ecommerce project management responsibilities need to go beyond those of the traditional IT project manager. Ecommerce project managers are required to provide management services outside the traditional software staff. They need to interact more with internal and

Table 14.1   Ecommerce and Traditional Projects Compared

ECOMMERCE PROJECTS	TRADITIONAL PROJECTS
Project managers are not always trained client managers.	Different
Development project schedules tend to be short.	Similar
New and untested third-party software is often implemented.	Usually never
Changes in scope occur during implementation.	Similar
Pricing model does not really exist.	Different
Standards for Web production do not exist.	Similar
Team roles are less specialized.	Different
Clients have difficulty bearing the costs of Web development, especially during planning.	Different
Project manager responsibilities are broad.	Different

Source: Burdman, 1999

external users as well as with nontraditional members of the development team, such as content managers. Therefore, there are many more obstacles that can cause project managers to fail at their jobs.

Ecommerce never ends. The nature of how ecommerce systems are built and deployed suggests that they are living systems. This means that they have a long life cycle made up of ongoing maintenance and enhancements. So the traditional "begin-and-end" type of project does not apply to an ecommerce project that inherently must be developed in ongoing phases.

Table 14.1 summarizes these differences between traditional and ecommerce projects.

The questions that need to be answered are not limited to what the process and responsibilities should be, but also who should handle them. It is my position that the ecommerce analyst should take the responsibility of managing the process from inception to completion. The duties and responsibilities of senior ecommerce analysts are excellent prerequisites for understanding the intricacies of project management. Their roles as analysts require them to have relationships with the organization and an understanding of the politics and culture that drive the business. I am not suggesting that every ecommerce analyst should become a project manager, but rather that one of the ecommerce analysts should also be the project manager. In order to determine the right fit, it is important to define the skill sets that are required for successful project management. These are summarized below:

- Software experience
- Understanding of budgeting, scheduling, and resource allocation
- Excellent written and verbal communication skills

- Ability to hold and lead meeting discussions
- Detail-oriented yet globally motivated (can see the difference between the forest and the trees)
- Pragmatic
- A sense of humor that comes across as a natural personal trait as opposed to an acted one
- Ability to be calm and level-headed during a crisis
- Experience with Web technologies, multimedia, and software engineering

Unfortunately, it is difficult to find a project manager who has all of these traits. In many cases it is wise to promote from within and develop the expertise internally. This is especially effective because an internal individual is a known quantity, and most likely already fits into the culture of the organization. Most important is that the individual is accepted in the culture. On the downside, it takes time to develop internal talent, and sometimes this trained talent leaves the company once he or she has received the training. There is benefit to bringing in someone from the outside because this person will have a fresh view of the project, and offer more objective input on what needs to be done to get the project finished on time.

Defining the Ecommerce Project

The first step for the ecommerce manager is to develop a mission statement for the project. A mission statement helps managers and users to focus on three core tasks:

1. Identify the project's objectives
2. Identify the users
3. Determine the scope of the project

Identify Objectives

Project objectives are defined as the results that must be attained during the project. According to Lewis (1995), project objectives must be specific, measurable, attainable, realistic, and time-limited. The most difficult of these objectives tends to be *measurable* and *attainable*. Ultimately, objectives state the desired outcomes and focus on how the organization will know when it is reached. The project's stakeholders typically devise objectives. These individuals are usually executives and managers that have the most to gain from the successful implementation of the ecommerce system. Unfortunately, although this sounds good, it is difficult to implement. In reality, it is difficult for executives to articulate what they are looking for. Indeed, the ecommerce paradigm has forced many executives to create Web sites simply because they think it is a competitive advantage for their companies to have one. This, in essence, means that executives might be driven by the fear that they must do something, or that something is better than nothing.

Ecommerce objectives evolve and cause many iterative events to occur, especially in the early phases of the ecommerce project. Good and effective objectives tend to be short sentences that are written down. Using this format, objectives can be used by project managers to effectively avoid scope creep. The objectives should be distributed to all stakeholders and project members so that everyone understands them.

Identify Users

Chapter 2 covered the significance of users and their importance to the success of any project. In Chapter 2, I defined three types of users: internal, customers, and consumers. It is important for ecommerce project managers to understand the value of the input from each of these users. Indeed, the users who access the Web site will ultimately determine its content. However, managers and developers often disagree on how much input is needed from users. This is further complicated when managing ecommerce projects because of the diversity of the users and the complexity of decisions that must be made. Furthermore, there is always limited time, so ecommerce project managers need to be as productive as possible with how user input is obtained, the types of interviewing that is done, and the method of measuring the value of the user's input.

Since the only way to measure a site's success is to determine whether the objectives have been met, the philosophy of who gets interviewed and how much value their input has should be mapped to the original objectives set forth by management. Thus, besides the internal users, the real obstacle for project managers is to identify which users know best what they want from the ecommerce system. Besides one-on-one interviews and JADs, the project manager can also obtain information from two other sources: market research and focus groups.

There are many firms that provide market research services. Such firms have databases of researched information relating to user preferences and behaviors. They also collect information about Web site preferences and what users expect from them. Every ecommerce system should have a budget that includes a market research firm so that they can obtain an objective and independent opinion about user preferences, particularly within a certain market segment. Conducting a focus group is a cheaper yet effective way to get objective input from users. It is particularly useful when attempting to assess consumer preferences. Focus groups involve the selection of sample consumers that the project manager feels represents the typical user. The sessions are filmed behind a mirror, and users respond to questions about their preferences when using an ecommerce system. The focus group typically needs a moderator who controls the meeting agenda and ensures that the participants answer all of the research questions. During all sessions it is important that the project manager ensure that the objectives of the ecommerce system are clearly defined to the audience. The objectives should be in writing and reviewed before the start and end of each session. In addition, the objectives should be written on a whiteboard or flip chart so participants can be reminded of the scope of the project should certain users start discussions on tangent subjects.

Determining the Scope of the Project

The scope of the project relates to the time it needs to be completed and the budget. Because there is always a limited amount of time and money to create product, the scope of the project must be negotiated against what can be done with what users want done. Thus, *scope* is the domain of functions and features that will be included in the ecommerce system based on a specific time commitment and cost outlay. The best approach to formulating a scope statement is to first create a work breakdown structure that contains the mission statement, lists the objectives, and formulates the tasks and subtasks to complete each objective. Thus, a work breakdown structure is really a form of functional decomposition of the tasks necessary to meet the objectives. Once stakeholders and the project manager agree on the objectives and what tasks will be done to attain them, then the scope of the project is complete. Figure 14.1 depicts a sample work breakdown structure.

Once tasks and subtasks have been determined, the ecommerce project manager needs to determine the time and cost of completing each component. Thus, the work breakdown structure will eventually contain the costs for each task within each objective for the entire project as proposed. Management and the project manager can then begin the process of negotiating what can be completed on time and on budget by removing subtasks or tasks as appropriate.

Another valuable approach to building ecommerce projects is phasing deliverables. Because ecommerce projects tend never to be finished, it might be advisable to deliver some portion of the system first and then add on functionality in subsequent releases of the system. Obviously this might not always be feasible. There are ecommerce systems that cannot be phased; that is, they are all or nothing at all. However, I believe that all projects can have some level of phased development, and that such development in the long run benefits the entire scope of the project. Indeed, first releases of Web sites typ-

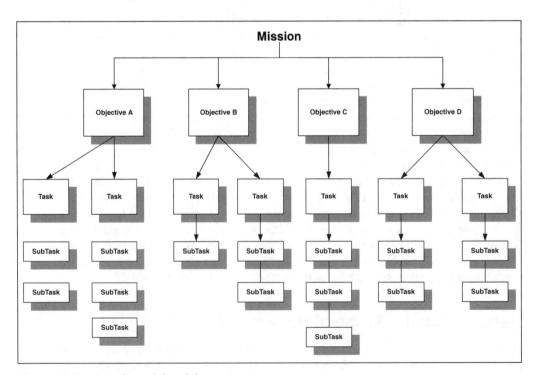

Figure 14.1   Sample work breakdown structure.

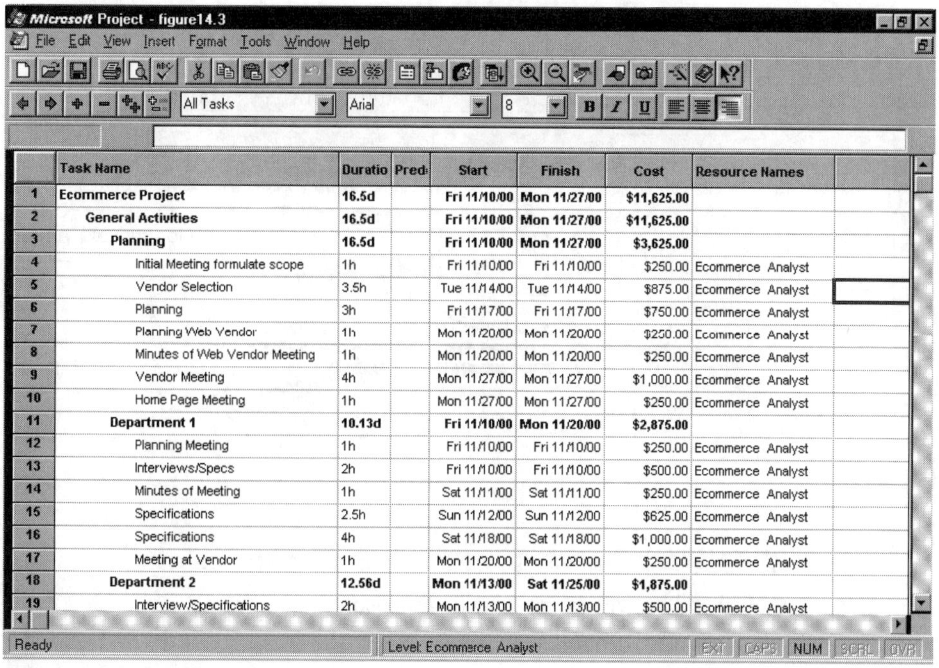

	Task Name	Duratio	Pred	Start	Finish	Cost	Resource Names
1	**Ecommerce Project**	**16.5d**		**Fri 11/10/00**	**Mon 11/27/00**	**$11,625.00**	
2	**General Activities**	**16.5d**		**Fri 11/10/00**	**Mon 11/27/00**	**$11,625.00**	
3	**Planning**	**16.5d**		**Fri 11/10/00**	**Mon 11/27/00**	**$3,625.00**	
4	Initial Meeting formulate scope	1h		Fri 11/10/00	Fri 11/10/00	$250.00	Ecommerce Analyst
5	Vendor Selection	3.5h		Tue 11/14/00	Tue 11/14/00	$875.00	Ecommerce Analyst
6	Planning	3h		Fri 11/17/00	Fri 11/17/00	$750.00	Ecommerce Analyst
7	Planning Web Vendor	1h		Mon 11/20/00	Mon 11/20/00	$250.00	Ecommerce Analyst
8	Minutes of Web Vendor Meeting	1h		Mon 11/20/00	Mon 11/20/00	$250.00	Ecommerce Analyst
9	Vendor Meeting	4h		Mon 11/27/00	Mon 11/27/00	$1,000.00	Ecommerce Analyst
10	Home Page Meeting	1h		Mon 11/27/00	Mon 11/27/00	$250.00	Ecommerce Analyst
11	**Department 1**	**10.13d**		**Fri 11/10/00**	**Mon 11/20/00**	**$2,875.00**	
12	Planning Meeting	1h		Fri 11/10/00	Fri 11/10/00	$250.00	Ecommerce Analyst
13	Interviews/Specs	2h		Fri 11/10/00	Fri 11/10/00	$500.00	Ecommerce Analyst
14	Minutes of Meeting	1h		Sat 11/11/00	Sat 11/11/00	$250.00	Ecommerce Analyst
15	Specifications	2.5h		Sun 11/12/00	Sun 11/12/00	$625.00	Ecommerce Analyst
16	Specifications	4h		Sat 11/18/00	Sat 11/18/00	$1,000.00	Ecommerce Analyst
17	Meeting at Vendor	1h		Mon 11/20/00	Mon 11/20/00	$250.00	Ecommerce Analyst
18	**Department 2**	**12.56d**		**Mon 11/13/00**	**Sat 11/25/00**	**$1,875.00**	
19	Interview/Specifications	2h		Mon 11/13/00	Mon 11/13/00	$500.00	Ecommerce Analyst

Figure 14.2 Ecommerce project plan.

ically need revision anyway, and the second phase or version might be a better time to add certain features and functions.

I stated that the final work breakdown schedule represents the scope of the project. Typically, the ecommerce project manager will finalize the scope statement by preparing a document that includes the work breakdown structure and articulates how this structure will be formulated into deliverables for the project. In many ways the scope document acts as a management report and reiterates the mission and objectives of the project along with the project plan. Figure 14.2 shows a typical project plan developed in Microsoft Project.

Managing Scope

A project plan can sometimes be referred to as a work breakdown schedule, or WBS. As shown in Figure 14.3, it depicts every step in the project and can enforce dependencies within tasks and subtasks. This is important, because changes to the plan may affect other tasks. A WBS product like Microsoft's Project provides an automated way of tracking changes and determining its effect on the entire project. A popular method of tracking changes is called *critical path analysis*. Critical path analysis involves the monitoring of tasks that can have an effect on the entire scope of the project, meaning it can change the timeframe and cost of delivery. A *critical path* is defined as a task that if delayed will cause a delay in the entire project. A task that can delay the project is then called a *critical task*. The importance of managing critical tasks is crucial for successful management of ecommerce projects. Project managers are often

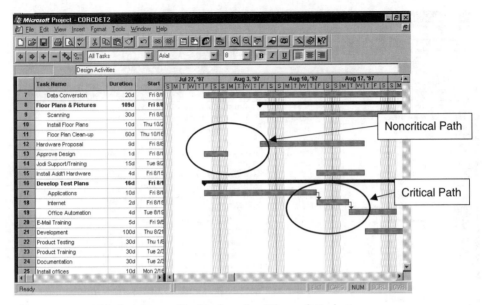

Figure 14.3 Critical and noncritical tasks using Microsoft Project.

faced with the reality that some task has slipped behind schedule. When faced with this dilemma, the project manager needs to decide whether dedicating more resources to the task might get it back on schedule. However, the first thing that the project manager needs to assess is whether the task can affect the critical path. If the answer is yes, then the project manager must attempt to use other resources to avoid a scope delay. If the task is not critical, then the delay may be acceptable without needing to change the project plan. Figure 14.3 shows a critical task and a noncritical task.

The Budget

Budgeting is one of the most important responsibilities of an ecommerce project manager. The budget effectively prices the tasks that must be delivered and rolls them up to the project cost level. It is important to recognize that all budgets are estimates. Therefore, they are never 100 percent accurate—if they were, they would not be budgets. The concept behind budgeting is that some tasks will be over budget and others will be under budget, resulting in an offset that essentially balances out to the assumptions outlined in the original plan. Budgets are typically built on expense categories. Figure 14.4 shows the common budget categories that ecommerce projects should be tracking.

As stated above, a project budget is a set of assumptions. Typical budget assumptions are:

- All content will be provided in machine-readable form.

- The content manager will approve content design within 24 hours.

Ecommerce Project Budget Sample		12/12/00		
Description		**Low**	**High**	**Comments**
Hardware				
Servers	$	150,000	200,000	
Workstations		400,000	600,000	
Modems		25,000	30,000	
Scanners		5,000	20,000	
Total Hardware		580,000	850,000	
Software				
Ecommerce Base Product Development		250,000	350,000	Cost of vendor base product software
Database		100,000	250,000	Database vendor software license
Office Automation		40,000	100,000	Forms elimination and e-mail intranet
CAD/CAM-Scanning		40,000	100,000	Scanning software
Media Production		90,000	150,000	
Software Modifications		75,000	125,000	Modification costs to vendors product to meet needs
Total Software		595,000	1,075,000	
Services				
Network and Software Design		5,000	8,500	Analysis & design of system
Consultants		240,000	285,000	Specialists that may be needed
Scanning Documents		125,000	135,000	Service to put all plans in system
Conversion of Data		120,000	130,000	
Installation		45,000	87,000	low: 300x150 high 300x250 plus servers
Training		25,000	85,000	Train the trainer all train everyone
Total Services		560,000	730,500	
Total	$	1,735,000	2,655,500	

Figure 14.4 Sample ecommerce project budget expense categories.

- The Web design team will present two alternative design schemas.
- Graphics for the Web site will be finalized and ready for integration.

It is not a bad idea for the ecommerce project manager to create a budget document that includes a list of the assumptions because it allows the manager to track whether incorrect assumptions caused delays in the scope of the project. Unfortunately, there are also hidden costs that tend not to be included in project budgets. The following is a list of common hidden costs that are missed by the project manager:

- Meetings
- Phone calls
- Research
- Development of documents and status reports
- Project administration
- Review sessions
- Presentations to management

Some project managers add a 10 to 15 percent cushion to their budgets to absorb common hidden costs. While I do not support cushions, they are acceptable if actually listed as a budget item, as opposed to a cushion on each budget line item.

The Ecommerce Project Team

The ecommerce project team is unique from other traditional project organizations. Most of the significant differences are attributable to the addition of the Web responsibilities. Original Web teams consisted of a Webmaster who did everything from HTML coding, page maintenance, and Web server support. Today, the roles and responsibilities for developing and supporting an ecommerce Web team are far more complex and specialized. The ecommerce project team has evolved because business managers understand the importance of ecommerce in transforming the way business is done. On the other hand, there are certainly traditional roles and responsibilities that have not changed and are generalizable across any software development project.

While the structure of project teams can vary depending on the type of project, the size of the system, and the time to complete, typical organizations contain the following roles and responsibilities:

Ecommerce project manager. The project manager is responsible for the scope of work, developing the project plan, scheduling, allocating resources, budgeting, managing the team, interfacing with users, and reporting to management on progress. The ecommerce project manager also deals with politics and other business issues, which include but are not limited to contract negotiations, licensing of third-party products, and staff hiring. In some instances, the project manager is responsible for handling customer and consumer needs as they relate to the design and development of the ecommerce system. Perhaps the most important responsibility of the ecommerce project manager is to know at all times what has been done and what needs to be done.

Account manager. The account manager is usually a senior manager who is responsible for a number of projects. Account managers also serve clients in a number of ways, from selling new product to providing client support. In many ways, the account manager is the representative of the client's needs to the internal development team. Account managers can be called upon to obtain information from customers about their needs and their feedback on how the ecommerce system supports their needs.

Technical manager. This individual is the senior technologist of the project. He or she is usually from the development team and is the most experienced developer. The technical manager is responsible for ensuring that the correct technology is being used and deployed properly. This individual manages the programmers, database developers, and other system integrators. The technical manager provides feedback on the development status of each task and reports to the project manager.

Programmer. An ecommerce programmer is responsible for coding applications for the project. These applications are coded to spec and can include a myriad of technologies, including but not limited to server-scripts, database applications, applets, and ActiveX controls. Development languages used on ecommerce projects vary, but the Web uses such languages as Java, JavaScript, Visual Basic, VBScript, SQL, and C/C++. The technical manager usually manages this individual; however, large projects may employ multiple levels of programmers. In certain situations, junior programmers report to senior developers, who act as mentors to them.

Creative manager. This individual is responsible for the overall design and creative look of the ecommerce system. While this person may not do the actual design, he or she acts as the art director for the project. The creative manager interacts with the technical manager, programmers, and Web designers on what is technically possible and artistically desirable. The creative manager reports directly to the project manager.

Ecommerce analyst. This individual is responsible for gathering all of the user requirements and designing the logic models and architecture of the system, which include process models, data models, transactions system design, and process specifications. Ultimately, the ecommerce analyst is responsible for site architecture, navigation, search and data retrieval, and interaction design. This role is sometimes called an information architect.

Designer. Designers create the look and feel of the Web sites. They use various tools to design template content and overall Web structure. Web designers report to the creative manager who sets the overall design philosophy.

Database administrator (DBA). The DBA is responsible for all physical database design and development. This individual must also fine-tune the database to ensure efficient operation. Other responsibilities include data partitioning, data warehouse setup, data replication, and report generation.

Network engineers. These individuals are responsible for designing network configurations that support the ecommerce system. Sometimes a network engineer is also a security specialist who is responsible for registering domain names and setting up email servers and chat rooms.

Security expert. Although this might also be the network specialist, larger ecommerce projects employ a dedicated security expert who works with encryption formulas, integrates with content systems, and focuses on securing online transactions. This individual can also advise the project manager on strategies to implement certain component applications.

Web production specialist. A Web production specialist is responsible for integrating content and graphics. These people, in essence, put the pieces together. This involves the integration of content, object programs, and XML documents. The Web production specialist is a type of programmer in that he or she can code HTML and integrate Java programs. This individual is also responsible for managing a content system and provides certain types of quality assurance to ensure that content, links, and programs are working properly.

Copywriter. This is a dedicated or part-time person who develops text content for the ecommerce sites. The copywriter usually reports to the creative manager and interacts with the design team members and the Web production specialist.

Production artist. This individual is responsible for transforming artwork that the designer has created into Web-ready art. Web-ready art involves the process of editing graphics to optimize their appearance and performance on the Web site. The production artist needs to be skilled in color-reduction and image-compression techniques.

Quality assurance specialist. This individual is responsible for creating test scripts to ensure that the ecommerce system operates within spec. The purpose of the test plans, sometimes called *acceptance test plans*, is to provide the minimal set of tests that must be passed for the site to go into production. The reporting structure for quality assurance personnel varies. Some believe that it is part of the development team and therefore should report to the technical manager while others believe that it needs to report directly to the project manager. There are still others who believe that the quality assurance staff should report to the chief information officer (CIO). The reporting structure is dependent on how highly the department values the independence of the testing function.

Tester. A tester is simply a person who carries out the test plans developed by the quality assurance staff. These people typically report to quality assurance staff; however, sometimes testers are users who are working with the account manager to assist in the testing of the product. These testers are in a sense beta test users (*beta test* means that the software is tested in a live environment).

Audio engineer. An audio engineer is responsible for designing sounds for Web sites. Sound designs range from music to miscellaneous sounds that occur when a user completes a task or initiates an activity. Audio engineers usually interact with creative managers and technical managers.

Video engineer. The video engineer develops images and delivers them in digital format to the creative manager or the Web production specialist.

This is an exhaustive list of potential positions to have on a project, but it is unlikely that every one of these positions will exist in any given ecommerce project. In reality, it is more important that the functionality of each of these positions is carried out, regardless of who takes on the responsibility. In order to provide better insight to the roles and responsibilities of each position, Table 14.2 is a matrix that compares roles with responsibilities.

Table 14.2   Ecommerce Project Team Roles and Responsibilities Matrix

TYPE OF WEB ACTIVITY	STAFF ORGANIZATION
Marketing and media	Account executive, project manager, creative manager, designer, copywriter, production artist, quality assurance specialist
Ecommerce transactions	Project manager, technical manager, ecommerce analyst, creative manager, database administrator, tester
Input/output data	Project manager, technical manager, creative manager, database administrator, ecommerce analyst, Web production specialist, quality assurance specialist
Intranet	Project manager, technical manager, creative manager, network engineer, Web production specialist, quality assurance specialist

Table 14.3   Necessary Ecommerce Project Skill Sets

SKILL SET	DESCRIPTION
Project management	Ability to communicate with staff, executives, and users; keep project on schedule
Architecture	Ability to design the user interface and interact with technical development personnel
Graphic design	Ability to transform requirements into visual solutions
Graphic production	Ability to develop efficient graphics for Web browser use
Programming	Ability to use HTML, JavaScript, etc.

Table 14.3 identifies the necessary skills of each of the critical members of the ecommerce project team.

Project Team Dynamics

It is not unusual for ecommerce development projects to operate from multiple sites with multiple interfaces. This may require much more organization and communication among the members of the team.

Set Rules and Guidelines for Communication

When project members are separated by locations or even by work schedules, it is very important that everyone know what their roles are, and what everybody else's responsibilities are to each other. Project managers should establish guidelines on communication and require each member to provide short statuses periodically on where they are in the project. While this might seem like a bother to team members, I have found that it provides immense value to the project manager because it forces each person to discipline him- or herself and report on where they are in their respective worlds. Furthermore, it forces project staff to articulate in writing what they have accomplished, what is outstanding, and what they plan to get done. Figure 14.5 shows a sample status report that tracks previous objectives with current objectives. It should not take more than 15 minutes to complete.

Extranet Review Sites

Project managers should create extranets that allow project staff to view the work of the project team. This also allows work to be approved virtually over the Web. Furthermore, status reports and general announcements can be viewed by authorized members

<table>
<tr><td colspan="3" align="center">**XYZ CORP**

Project Plan

Project Status Report</td></tr>
</table>

Date 1/31/01	Vendor: XSP	Consultant: Art Langer

Previous Objectives: Objective	Previous Target Date	Status
Send out Software Proposals	1/23/01	Done
Send out Hardware Bids and check labor rates	1/25/01	2/6/01
Get XSP to modify detail design contract to include specifics on deliverables.	1/23/01	Done, waiting approv
Speak with Ecommerce consultant and contract with him for data and layouts	1/25/01	2/3/01
Finalize Network Design Requirements Document	1/23/01	2/3/01

New Project Objectives: Objective	Target Date
Get specification on hardware certification machines from XSP	2/5/01
Get room to do JAD interviews and reviews	2/10/01
Ensure that accounting features are integrated in Ecommerce specs	2/10/01
Art to interview Joe	2/3/01
Check ability of MAS-90 to create output files for display on Web	2/6/01
Identify and meet with brokers as part of interviews	2/3/01
Get prices for Scanning of floor plans for Web browsing	2/10/01

Attendees	A. Langer & Assoc.	Art Langer	XSP	Michael

\gprojst Copyright © 1995-2001 A. Langer & Assoc., Inc

Figure 14.5 Sample ecommerce status report.

of the project team, as well as by stakeholders and users. Often extranet documents can be coupled with regular conference call sessions where project members can openly discuss reports, Web site samples, and determine new milestones as appropriate. Unfortunately, managing an extranet review site requires overhead and someone who can do the work. This simply means that someone on the project's staff or some assigned administrative person needs to take on the responsibility. There is also the challenge of dealing with staff that do not comply with procedures, or need to be reminded about delivering their status reports on a regular basis. While this is unfortunate, it is a reality. However, it also tells the project manager who needs to be watched more closely than other team members.

Working with User Resources

Users are an interesting yet challenging resource. While they are clearly needed to perform reviews and quality assurance, they are not officially assigned to the project and are therefore not under the control of the project manager. Unfortunately, this can cause problems if a user is not responsive to the needs of the project team. This can be very damaging because the staff will be dependent on receiving timely feedback from these resources. Lack of responsiveness from a user can also alienate him or her from the project team. Indeed, there is nothing more damaging than a user that shows disinterest in the project that is being designed to serve them. Therefore, the ecommerce project manager needs to be careful about what commitments are made when a user resource is made available. Obviously, the project manager would want the individual to report directly to him or her and be a full-time resource. This could also be wishful thinking. It certainly can be dangerous to turn down the help. While this may appear to be a catch-22, it can be managed. First, the ecommerce project manager should establish the need for user assistance early in the project and include it in the requirements documentation (it should be part of the assumptions section). Second, the project manager may need to limit the amount of work assigned to the user if he or she indeed is just a part-time resource.

Outsourcing

Not all ecommerce projects can be completed using internal staff. In fact, most cannot. Using outsourced resources makes sense for many projects, especially those that might need very unique and qualified personnel that are not on staff, or not deemed worthy of full-time employment. There may also be a lack of talent, which is the usual reason why consultants are hired in the first place. Sometimes, outsourced relationships are managed as strategic partnerships, which means that an outside business provides specific services for the firm on a regular basis. Ecommerce strategic partnerships can be made in many different areas or phases of the project. Outsource firms can provide video or audio engineers as needed, or network support personnel to assist in installing the ecommerce site. On the other hand, the entire project should not be outsourced because there may be a false sense of comfort that the firm's personnel need not be involved in the responsibility. In the long run, I believe this is a mistake. Remember that outsourced firms have their own destiny and growth to manage.

Planning and Process Development

In order to operationalize the project plan and to meet the budget, it is necessary to develop a phased implementation guide that helps members of the team understand where they are in the process. Unfortunately, the project task plan is much too detailed to use, so it is a good idea for the project manager to develop a higher-level document that can be used during the development project. Such a plan typically contains four phases: (1) Strategy, (2) Design, (3) Development, and (4) Testing. Figure 14.6 reflects the ecommerce major development phases and includes the activities and output of each phase.

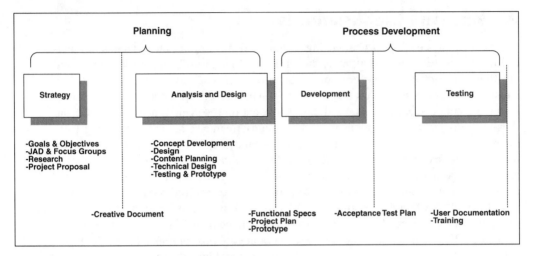

Figure 14.6   Ecommerce development phases.

Strategy. This phase requires that the stakeholders, account executives, users, and the project manager all meet to agree on the objectives, requirements, key milestones, and needs of the target audience. The activities in this phase are made up of the goals and objectives, feedback from users, research from outside sources, and the project proposal document. The culmination of these steps should be summarized in a document to be used by the project team. This document is sometimes referred to as a *creative brief*. The creative brief is really a summary of the original proposal in template form and created so that project team members can quickly refer to it and obtain the information they need. Figure 14.7 depicts a creative brief template.

Creative briefs allow the project manager to conduct effective brainstorming sessions with staff. The document acts as an agenda, and also a checkpoint to ensure that discussions are not going beyond the objectives of the project and that the products are designed in accordance with the target audience's needs.

Design. Design represents the second major phase. It is comprised of all the tasks that participate in the design of the user interface, the analysis and design of technical specifications, and the overall architecture of the ecommerce system. The results of the design phase are the functional specifications, detailed project plan timeline and budget, and Web site and report prototypes. The design phase typically requires that stakeholders and other users review and sign off on the specification document before the project can proceed. Of course, the approval process of the design document can be done in phases; that is, portions of the document can be approved so that the implementation can go forward on some limited basis. During the process of designing the ecommerce system, it is important that the project team have access to the content of all Web sites. This is especially important for large projects where there can be more than one design group creating content. As stated in the previous chapter, content development is an iterative process; therefore, the team members need to constantly

```
┌─────────────────────────────────────────────────────────────┐
│                        XYZ, INC.                             │
│                  Creative Brief Template                     │
│            Client:_____                   │
└─────────────────────────────────────────────────────────────┘
```

Dates:	Dept:	User:

Project Scope:

Objectives:

Target Audiences:

Image: (Explain the image that the ecommerce system must convey to users)

Current Brand: (Explain the current brand and image of the business to its users)

User Experience: (Explain the most important thing that users should experience from using the ecommerce system)

\gminutes Copyright © 1995-2001 A. Langer & Assoc., Inc

Figure 14.7 Sample creative brief.

have access to the current site architecture and schematic designs. That is why it is so important to have the technical specifications in a CASE tool and content system so that all members can have instant access to the current state of the project.

<table>
<tr><td colspan="5" align="center">*Quality Assurance*

Acceptance Test Plan</td></tr>
</table>

Purpose: To ensure that Contact screens operate properly when supplying new good data. **This plan entry mode with nothing on the screen.**	Product: Contact - Using Enter Key	Number:
	Vendor:	Page: 1 of 4
Test Plan #: 1G	QA Technician:	Date:

Test No.	Condition Being Tested	Expected Results	Actual Results	Comply Y/N	Comments
1	Enter LAST NAME for a new contact, press enter key. Repeat and enter FIRST NAME, press enter key	Should accept and prompt for COMPANY SITE			
2	Select COMPANY Site from picklist	Should accept and prompt for next field			
3	Enter LAST NAME and FIRST NAME for a CONTACT that is already in the System.	Should accept and prompt for COMPANY SITE			

Figure 14.8   QA test plan.

Development. This phase includes all of the activities that are involved with actually building the site. The challenge for project managers is to control changes made to the original specifications. This typically occurs after the first prototype reviews where users begin to change or enhance their original requirements. While it is not impossible to change specifications, it is certainly dangerous and can be a major cause of scope creep.

Testing. During this phase, developers and users are testing the site and reporting errors. Errors are tricky issues; they must be classified in particular areas and levels of severity. For example, some errors cause an application to abort, which would be considered a critical error. Others might be aesthetic in nature and can be scheduled for fixing but are not severe enough to hold up going live. Still other errors are not really errors, but rather deficiencies in design. This means that the program is performing to the specification but not in the way the user really expects. All of these issues need to be part of an overall test plan, which identifies what types of errors are critical and how they affect the development process. Figure 14.8 shows a typical test plan.

Technical Planning

Technical planning is the process where the project team develops a working strategy for building the features of the ecommerce system. These features include all of the components of ecommerce development including database, programming, transaction systems, multimedia, and scripting. Technical planning is simple in concept: How do all of the technology pieces come together, how do they interface, and what is the schedule of implementation? Because of the object-oriented methods that are employed by ecommerce systems, it is easy to have components developed by separate teams of programmers. However, there comes a time when all components must come together and interface with each other. When the components interface correctly, the system works. Project managers never quite know if interfaces will work until they are actually tested. The concept of "working" means many things in software development. The obvious definition is that the program performs its tasks correctly and to specification. There is another part of what *working* means. This relates to performance of the application. While an application might calculate the correct output, it may not do so efficiently. Application performance problems tend to first show up during component interface testing. Fortunately this is at a time where applications can be fine-tuned before they go into production. Unfortunately, many interface-oriented performance problems first appear in the production system because the testing environment was not a true representation of the live system. Therefore, it is important for ecommerce project managers to ensure that the test system correctly matches the live environment. Indeed, many performance problems occur because of the unexpected stress load on the system. Notwithstanding when an application performance problem is discovered, the main challenge is to fix the problem. Sometimes performance interface problems can be serious, especially if the solution requires a redesign of the application architecture or substantial changes to the network infrastructure. Any problems of this caliber could cause serious setbacks to the project schedule and its cost. Crucial steps for the project team to make include planning and decision making regarding how applications are designed, which program languages should be used, and what network platforms to choose. The project manager must attempt to surround him- or herself with the best knowledge available. This knowledge base of people might not exist in the organization. Therefore, the project manager might need to seek guidance from third-party consultants who can act as specialists during these critical decision times.

Defining Technical Development Requirements

A large part of whether systems are developed properly has to do with how well the detailed technical requirements are prepared. The technical project team needs to define the technical requirements to implement the logical specifications. Remember that logical specifications do not necessarily specify what hardware or software to use. Thus, the technical team must evaluate the logical specification and make recommendations on how the actual technical specifications are to be built. The project manager can be more effective if he or she asks some key questions:

- *Are we thinking of using technologies that we have not used before?* Using unknown technologies can be very dangerous. An unknown technology is not only a new product; it is a product that the development team has never used. Because of the extent of new developments in Web technology, dealing with unknown hardware and software needs to be addressed and risks assessed by the project manager.

- *What benefits will be derived from new technologies?* Implementing new technologies for the sake of new technologies is not a good reason to implement unknowns. This concept gets back to the old cliché: "If it's not broken, don't fix it!"

■ *What type of coding is being done?* This relates to whether program code is being developed from scratch or via modified software packages. Each has its advantages and disadvantages. Writing code from scratch takes longer, but provides the architecture that best fits the design. Package software is faster to develop, but may not fit well with the overall needs of the company. The rule of thumb is never to modify packages by more than 20 percent of their total code. When this percentage is exceeded, the benefit realized from the package is so minimal that developers might as well write their own program code.

■ *Will there be access to production-like testing environments?* This was covered earlier. Project managers must ensure that the proper testing facilities are available to mirror the production environment.

Maintenance

Ecommerce projects should never be developed without considering how to preserve maintainability. *Maintainability* is a universal concept that relates to what defines a quality product. Products that work are one thing—those that work and are maintainable is another. In ecommerce systems, product that cannot be maintained easily is problematic. I have previously discussed the power of content management systems and CASE software as vehicles to support maintenance of ecommerce systems. There are other best practices that need to be performed during the planning stage. First, the manner in which code will be developed and the standards to be upheld need to be agreed upon and put in writing. Technical managers should also define how they intend to enforce these standards. Documentation of code should also be addressed in the documents. Furthermore, there needs to be agreement on the database design as well. This involves getting the database administrators to agree on limits to de-normalization, naming standards, and the methods of coding stored procedures and database triggers.

Another important component of maintenance quality is planning for growth. The issue of growth relates more to network infrastructure than to software development. First, the project manager needs to address issues of hardware scalability. This relates to the capacity of the network before the hardware architecture needs to be changed to accommodate new applications. Second, database servers must be configured with real-time backup architecture (no single point of failure concepts), and data warehouses need to be designed to perform at peak times.

Project Management and Communication

Successful project managers communicate well, not only with their staffs, but with vendors, management, and users. Indeed, sometimes communications skills are more important than technical ones. Obviously, a complete project manager has both. However, the advent of ecommerce systems has placed even more emphasis on the importance of communication within the project team. There are many reasons why poor communications occur during project life cycles. According to Burdman (1999), there are 11 leading causes for communication problems on a project team.

1. *People come from different disciplines.* Communication is difficult enough among those who work together every day. The influx of many different disciplines on an ecommerce project creates more challenges because staffs are not as familiar with each other. Remember that relationships are very important for team interaction. Many ecommerce teams need to spend time just getting acclimated to each other's business styles.

2. *Lack of mutual understanding of the technology.* Project members do not have consistent understandings of the technology. For example, some staff might use the word *table* to define a logical database entity, while others call it a file. The best solution to this problem is to distribute a list of common technology definitions to all project participants.

3. *Personalities.* This occurs in all projects. Some people have conflicting personalities and do not naturally get along.

4. *Hidden agenda.* Team members often have political agendas. They are sometimes difficult to assess, but they definitely cause problems with communication among project staff. These individuals are set in their ways and have questionable dedication to the success of the project; that is, they have a more important political agenda.

5. *Ineffective meetings.* Meetings for the sake of meetings is no reason to meet. Sometimes too many meetings can be counterproductive to getting things done. It can sometimes be a false solution to other problems that exist in the project team. Some meetings are necessary but run too long, and participants begin to lose focus on the agenda. Project managers need to be cognizant of the time allotments they make to meetings and to respect those timeframes.

6. *Proximity.* The demographics of where project team members reside is obviously a factor in hindering communications among the team members. While this is a disadvantage, teleconferencing and video conferencing are all possible antidotes for managing communication projects at a distance. Communication can be further hindered because of long distances between staff, especially when there are time zone changes. In these situations, even conferencing is not feasible. Usually the best way of communicating is through email and extranets.

7. *Assumptions.* Team members can often make assumptions about things that can cause communication breakdowns. Usually assumptions create problems because things that are believed to be true are not written down.

8. *Poor infrastructure and support.* The severity of this problem is often overlooked. It includes the frustrations of having computer troubles, email incompatibilities, and other hardware failures that contribute to communications problems. The best approach to avoiding these frustrations is for the project manager to insist that these problems be fixed properly and on a timely basis.

9. *Being an expert.* Every project has one or two "know-it-alls" who attempt to dominate meetings and want to orchestrate their point of view to the rest of the staff. These individuals spend so much time telling others what to do that they forget what they have to do to make the project successful. Ecommerce project man-

agers should be very aggressive with these types of participants by making it clear what everyone's role is, including the project manager's, responsibilities!

10. *Fear.* Fear is a very large barrier with certain staff. Staff members can become overwhelmed with the size, complexity, and length of an ecommerce project and this can cause them to lose their perspective and creativity. Project managers need to interject and provide assistance to those members who struggle with an ecommerce system.

11. *Lack of good communications structure.* Good communications systems fit in with the culture of the organization and are realistic in what they might accomplish. Many communications problems exist simply because the infrastructure does not relate to the needs of the staff.

Summary

This chapter attempted to provide the ecommerce project manager with a perspective on the salient issues that can help them be successful. This chapter was not intended to provide a complete step-by-step approach to managing complex projects. I included this chapter because I believe that many ecommerce analysts can also serve as excellent project managers. Indeed, many of the important issues discussed in this chapter relate to many of the skills that ecommerce analysts must have to perform their responsibilities as software engineers. These include:

Communications skills. Analysts have significant experience in working with users to obtain input so they can develop system requirements properly.

Meeting management. JAD sessions are more complex meetings than typical project meetings. Analysts that have also been JAD facilitators are very well trained on how to control meetings.

Politically astute. Analysts are experienced with working with people who have hidden agendas and are driven by politics.

Technically proficient. Analysts are educated in logic modeling and are familiar with many of the technical issues that come up during the project life cycle.

Project planning. Analysts are accustomed to developing project plans and managing to deliverables; each analysis and design task can be seen as a miniproject.

Documentation. Analysts are supporters of good documentation and understand the value of having maintainable processes.

Executive presence. Analysts work with executive users and understand how to interact with them.

Quality assurance. Analysts are familiar with quality assurance test plans and testing methodologies. They are often involved with test plan development.

Bibliography

Bernstein, P. A., and Newcomer, E. (1997). *Principles of Transaction Processing.* (San Francisco, CA: Morgan Kaufmann Publishers, Inc).

Brodie, M. L., and Stonebraker, M. (1995). *Migrating Legacy Systems: Gateways, Interfaces & the Incremental Approach.* (San Francisco, CA: Morgan Kaufmann Publishers, Inc).

Burdman, J. (1999). *Collaborative Web Development.* (New York: Addison-Wesley).

Conger, S. H., and Mason, R. O. (1998). *Planning and Designing Effective Web Sites.* (Cambridge, MA: Course Technology).

Curtis, H. (2000). *Flash Web Design: The Art of Motion Graphics.* (Indianapolis, IN: New Riders Publishing).

Clark, L. "Highly Available e-business Solutions with Oracle Fail Safe," *Deploying, Managing, and Administering the Oracle Internet Platform*, 231, 2001, 1–11.

Dalgleish, J. (2000). *Customer-Effective Web Sites.* (Upper Saddle River, NJ: Prentice Hall).

Ewald, T. (2001). *Transactional COM+: Building Scalable Applications.* (New York, Addison-Wesley).

Fleming, C. C., and von Halle, B. (1989). *The Handbook of Relational database Design.* (New York: Addison-Wesley).

Fleming, J. (1998). *Web Navigation: Designing the User Experience.* (Sebastopol, CA: O'Reilly & Associates, Inc).

Ghosh, A. K. (1998). *E-Commerce Security: Weak Links, Best Defenses.* (New York: John Wiley & Sons, Inc).

Gordon, V. S., and Bieman, J. M. (1995). Rapid Prototyping: Lessons Learned, *IEEE Software*, 12(1), 85–95.

Gorton, I. (2000). *Enterprise Transaction Processing Systems.* (New York: Addison-Wesley).

Grudin, J.. "The Case Against User Interface Consistency. *Comm. ACM*, 32(10), 1992, pp.1164–1173.

Harold, E. R., and Means, W. S. (2001). *XML in a Nutshell: A Desktop Quick Reference.* (Sebastopol, CA: O'Reilly & Associates, Inc).

Kalakota, R., and Whinston, A. B. (1997). *Electronic Commerce: A Manager's Guide.* (New York: Addison-Wesley).

Langer, A.M. (2001). *Analysis and Design of Information Systems*, 2d ed. (New York: Springer-Verlag).

Larson, J. A., and Larson, C. L. (2000). Data Models and Modeling Techniques in S. Purba (Ed.), *Data Management Handbook*, 3d ed. (Boca Raton, FL: CRC Press LLC).

Lewis, J. (1995). *Fundamentals of Project Management: A Worksmart Guide.* (New York: American Management Association).

McGraw, G., and Felton, E. (1996). *Java Security: Hostile Applets, Holes, and Antidotes.* (New York: John Wiley & Sons, Inc).

Miller, H. W. (1998). *Reengineering Legacy Software Systems.* (Woburn, MA: Digital Press).

Maiwald, E. (2001). *Network Security.* (Berkeley, CA: Osborne/McGraw-Hill).

Muench, S. (2000). *Building Oracle XML Applications.* (Sebastopol, CA: O'Reilly & Associates, Inc).

Poe, V. (1996). *Building a Data Warehouse for Decision Support.* (Upper Saddle River, NJ: Prentice-Hall).

Powell, T. A. (2000). *Web Design: The Complete Reference.* (Berkeley, CA: Osborne/McGraw-Hill).

Schneider, G. P., and Perry, J. T. (2000). *Electronic Commerce.* (Cambridge, MA: Course Technology).

Shuman, J. E. (2001). *Multimedia Concepts.* (Boston: Course Technology).

Simpson, J. E. (2001). *Just XML*, 2d ed. (Upper Saddle River, NJ: Prentice-Hall).

Smith, E. R. (2000). *e-Loyalty: How to Keep Customers Coming Back to Your Website.* (New York: HarperCollins Publishers, Inc).

Sommerville, I. (2001). *Software Engineering*, 6th ed. (New York: Addison-Wesley).

Spencer, P. (1999). *XML Design and Implementation.* (Birmingham, UK: Wrox Press, Ltd.).

Stair, R. M., and Reynolds, G. W. (1999). *Principles of Information Systems*, 4th ed. (Cambridge, MA: Course Technology).

Sturm, J. (2000). *Developing XML Solutions.* (Redmond, WA: Microsoft Press).

Schwartz, R. (2001). *Web Site Construction Tips & Tricks.* (New York: OnWord Press).

Whitten, J.L., Bentley, L.D., Barlow, V.M. (1994). *Systems analysis & design methods*, (3rd ed). (Boston, MA: Irwin).

Windham, L., and Orton, K. (2000). *The Soul of the New Consumer.* (New York: Allworth Communications).

Wood, J., and Silver, D. (1995). *Joint Application Development*, 2d ed. (New York: John Wiley & Sons, Inc).

Index

population of data ware-
houses phase in, 328,
329
rollout phase in, 335
training phase in, 334, 335

T
Tags, 246
Take-away value, 119
Target marketing, 30
TCP/IP transfer protocol,
286, 287
Teams, project, *see* Project
teams
Technical development
requirements, 377–378
Technical limitations, 143
Technical manager, 368
Technical planning, 376–377
Technical specification document, 24
Technical specifications,
62–64, 145–146, 165–167
Technologies, untested, 360,
377
Telephone connections, 206,
207
Template(s):
as basis of Web site design,
340–341
Cascading Style Sheets, 134
content, 118
design, 152
frames, template, 65–66,
340
Testers, 370
Testing, data warehouse, 328
Testing phase (project management), 376
Text:
in multimedia applications,
134–136
on Web pages, 114,
116–118
and Web site background,
122
"Thin clients," 196
Third-generation legacy systems, 212–223
Third-normal form testing,
81–84
Thirteen WNET New York,
105–107, 110, 154, 157

Three-dimensional, data
warehousing as, 307,
308
Three-dimensional anima-
tion, 139–140
Three-dimensional data representation, 307
TIME, 61
Time, global, 278
TIMESTAMP, 61
T lines, 207
Top-down approach, 13
Topical multimedia sce-
nario, 146
Top navigation, 125, 126
TP, *see* Transaction processing
Training phase (decision
support), 334, 335
Transaction processing
(TP), 159–187
application design for,
167–186
class diagram creation,
170–172
communications,
179–182
data access and integrity,
174–178
database replication,
182–186
indentifying classes,
171–174
reuse component archi-
tecture, 167, 168
TP monitor system,
167–169
user request format,
169–170
Web access, 178–179
applications of, 160–161
authentication in, 165–167
components of, 161–163
and properties of transactions, 162–164
scalability in, 160
two-phase commit proto-
col in, 164–165
Transformation specifica-
tions, 326
Tree structure, 198, 257–258
Triggers, 75, 100–101
TrueDoc CSS standard, 134

Two-dimensional animation,
139
Two-phase commit protocol,
164–165
Type, definition of, 86

U
UML (Unified Modeling Language), 64
Uncertainty, 40
Unified Modeling Language
(UML), 64
Unity, Web page, 148
Unix, 200, 227
UNIX-based systems, 193
Unplanned fail-over, 201
Unstructured decision support, 330
Update cycle, 326
Usefulness, definition of,
103–104
Users, 9–37
authentication of, 295–297
computer experience of,
15–16
consumers as, 30–37
customers as, 24–30
as first tier of software
development, 7
identification of, 145, 294,
297, 298, 363
interfaces for, 25–30
internal
group interviews for,
18–19
individual interviews for,
17–18
interfaces for, 10–13
interview methods for,
16–24
interview process for,
13–16
JAD sessions for, 19–24
internal vs. external, 9
prototyping of, 47–53
respecting needs of, 39–40
User request format,
169–170
User specifications, 44–54
business specification in,
47
high-level flow diagrams
in, 45–47